RELIANCE IN THE BREAKING-OFF
OF CONTRACTUAL NEGOTIATIONS

RELIANCE IN THE BREAKING-OFF OF CONTRACTUAL NEGOTIATIONS

Trust and Expectation in a Comparative Perspective

Isabel Zuloaga

intersentia
Cambridge – Antwerp – Chicago

Intersentia Ltd
8 Wellington Mews
Wellington Street | Cambridge
CB1 1HW | United Kingdom
Tel.: +44 1223 736 170
Email: mail@intersentia.co.uk
www.intersentia.com | www.intersentia.co.uk

Distribution for the UK and Ireland:
NBN International
Airport Business Centre, 10 Thornbury Road
Plymouth, PL6 7PP
United Kingdom
Tel.: +44 1752 202 301 | Fax: +44 1752 202 331
Email: orders@nbninternational.com

Distribution for Europe and all other countries:
Intersentia Publishing nv
Groenstraat 31
2640 Mortsel
Belgium
Tel.: +32 3 680 15 50 | Fax: +32 3 658 71 21
Email: mail@intersentia.be

Distribution for the USA and Canada:
Independent Publishers Group
Order Department
814 North Franklin Street
Chicago, IL 60610
USA
Tel.: +1 800 888 4741 (toll free) | Fax: +1 312 337 5985
Email: orders@ipgbook.com

Reliance in the Breaking-Off of Contractual Negotiations. Trust and Expectation in a Comparative Perspective

Artwork on cover: Clive Watts / Alamy Stock Photo

ISBN 978-1-78068-650-9
D/2019/7849/84
NUR 822

British Library Cataloguing in Publication Data. A catalogue record for this book is available from the British Library.

FOREWORD

We are delighted to introduce this book, which has been developed from the very successful doctoral thesis which Professor Zuloaga defended at the University of Oxford in 2017. We first saw her work as a Master's student when she took our course on comparative contract law in the MJur at Oxford, and later we shared the supervision of her research for her DPhil thesis.

Professor Zuloaga has put her own stamp on the topic of precontractual liability. Indeed, before she came to Oxford, her interest had already been sparked during the studies for her law degree at the Universidad Adolfo Ibáñez in Santiago, Chile, where she wrote a dissertation on this general area, published as *Teoría de la Responsabilidad Precontractual: Aplicaciones en la Formación del Consentimiento de los Contratos* (Santiago, Legal Publishing Chile, 2008). Her work for the doctoral thesis – presented now in this book – takes her research to a broader and significantly deeper level. It offers an English-speaking audience a Latin American perspective on the topic, introducing readers to the Chilean approach to precontractual liability, as well as the more well-known approaches taken in the continental European civil law systems such as German and French law. But it also addresses head-on the difficulties which arise from comparing the approaches taken by civil law systems and common law systems to precontractual liability for breaking off negotiations.

Professor Zuloaga's theme is 'reliance' in the process of negotiations; 'reliance' is a term that has to be examined carefully, and Professor Zuloaga finds in it two distinct but related dimensions, 'trust-based' reliance and 'expectation-based' reliance. Her argument is that the other party's 'reliance' can justify the imposition of liability on the party who breaks off negotiations – but that such notions of reliance already underlie the approaches to precontractual liability taken by the civil law systems which she selects for detailed study, i.e., her 'selected jurisdictions' (Germany, France and Chile). This enables her to break away from the traditional language of the duty of 'good faith' in negotiations, and thereby to frame the arguments for the imposition of precontractual liability in terms which might be more acceptable to those in systems which traditionally take a sharply contrasting approach to precontractual liability, such as English law (the system which she uses as her 'contrasting jurisdiction').

This is not a book which sets out to teach English lawyers how they should re-think their law on precontractual liability; but it is designed to help them to understand how they might go about doing so, and to provide some tools (and to remove some traditional barriers) to facilitate reform. In her Preface, Professor Zuloaga says:

> it is not the aim of the book to argue that the paradigm case [i.e., the core case of breaking off negotiations, which is the focus of the study] should be protected by the contrasting jurisdiction, but only to show that it could be protected through reliance, a notion which is already part of the current solutions provided by this jurisdiction in other precontractual cases. Moreover, like the Common Core Project, the argument is neither in favour nor against harmonisation; but it shows a tool (in the notion of reliance) that would be useful to achieve some degree of harmonisation in this area.

This is comparative law as it should be done: helping us to understand what really underlies our systems' approaches to the law.

John Cartwright
Emeritus Professor of the Law of Contract
University of Oxford

Stefan Vogenauer
Director, Max Planck Institute for European History
Frankfurt

May 2019

ACKNOWLEDGEMENTS

This book is based on the thesis submitted to the Faculty of Law at the University of Oxford for the degree of Doctor of Philosophy (DPhil), which I successfully approved in 2017. I would like to start by thanking Ann-Christin Maak-Scherpe, publisher and general manager of Intersentia in Cambridge. If it were not for Ann-Christin's constant belief in my work, even when I was still in the process of writing my thesis and the finish line for transforming it into a book seemed to be far away, this book might not exist today. Thanks to her support and understanding, it has finally come to life. I also want to thank all the team at Intersentia who contributed to the publication of this book and, especially, my editor Ahmed Hegazi, for his diligence and dedication.

I would like to express my sincere gratitude to Professors Stefan Vogenauer and John Cartwright, who, at different stages, supervised my DPhil, for believing in my project and encouraging me to get it published. I will always be grateful to them for sharing their knowledge with me, for their willingness to meet with me (in Oxford, Hamburg and Santiago), for reading my work thoroughly and for giving me timely and constructive advice. But, above all, I wish to thank them for their kindness and understanding. Their belief in me and in my project was vital to being able to finalise it and now publish it.

I wish to express my sincere gratitude to the Max Planck Institute for Comparative and International Private Law, to its directors, researchers and staff. All of the research stays that I did in Hamburg were vital for writing my thesis and now my book. I would like to thank the *Comisión Nacional de Investigación Científica y Tecnológica* (Conicyt) for the generous financial support they provided me throughout my DPhil with the programme *Becas Chile*.

I would like to thank the authorities of the Law Faculty of the Pontificia Universidad Católica de Chile, all of my colleagues, teaching assistants, administrative assistants, and all of the staff and students who have encouraged me to write this book.

I also wish to thank all the people who, in different ways, contributed to my work (for example, by reading and assessing it, meeting with me to discuss it, providing me with research materials, giving me advice, encouraging me to develop my ideas and publish them and, generally, giving me their friendship, advice and support), both at the thesis stage and then at the book stage. I especially want to thank the following professors, lecturers, lawyers, colleagues and friends from different parts of the world: Simon Whittaker,

Jan-Peter Schmidt, Angus Johnston, Wolf-Georg Ringe, Donal Nolan, Geneviève Helleringer, Philippe Stoffel-Munck, Dimitri Houtcieff, Reinhard Zimmermann, Jan Kleinheisterkamp, Stelios Andreadakis, Jorge López Santa María, Erika Isler, Magaly Damke, José Manuel Díaz de Valdés, Gerardo Caffera, Carlos Frontaura, Marcelo Barrientos, Francisco Javier Urbina, Adolfo Wegmann, Jaime Alcalde, Juan Luis Goldenberg, Álvaro Paúl, Joel González, Roberto Ríos, Javier Infante, Cristóbal Orrego, Raúl Madrid, Gonzalo Candia, Sebastián Soto, María Paz Madrid, Felipe Martínez, Hugo Rojas, Arturo Ibáñez, Alberto Pino, Sebastián Castro, Núria González, José María Castellà, Hugo Cárdenas, Ignacio Ríos, Rodrigo Momberg, Carlos Pizarro, Ximena Marcazzolo, Paulina González, Emmanuel Bernales, Nathalie Walker, Gabriela Flores, Mar Guridi, Pedro Goic, Karen Tapia, Leslie Sánchez, Ana Neira, Gabriela Santos, Beatriz López, Constanza Richards, Javiera Farías, Kristina San Miguel, Yamila Juri, Erick Chávez, Tarek Yusari, Caroline Devaux, Ségolène Balsan, Katia Guerra, Oliviero Andreussi, Elena Vasilyeva, Angela Zweifel-Leu, Daniel Leu, Salma Zibdeh, María Manuela Andrade, Yetkin Inanoz, Anuj Berry, Francisca García-Huidobro, Magdalena Bennett, Rocío Urrutia, Cristián Riveros, Flavia Vergara, María Angélica Garrido, María Luisa Planas, Germán Lledó, Germán Vera, Ángeles Saavedra, Ana Labra, Carola Puschel, Rosario Villaseca, Andrés Biehl, Jacinta Vela, Leonardo Figueroa, Claudia Sanhueza, María Olga Rivera, Andrea Herane, Verónica Fernández, Isabel Margarita Undurraga, Denise Rosselot, Constanza Bollmann, Pía Salas, María José Colomer, Vesna Blazevic, Francisca Costaguta, Barbara Chadwick, Carolina Ruiz, Carina Sfeir, Carolina Morales, Francisca González, Alejandra del Río, Loreto Nercelles, Michel González, Carmen Nass, Judith Falikmann, and María Angélica Galli.

Last, but not least, I owe my greatest debt of gratitude to my family. Without their love and support, completing the DPhil and then transforming the thesis into this book would not have been possible. I thank my husband Matías for agreeing to embark upon this journey with me and for enduring it, always giving me love, encouragement and understanding, and I thank our son Francisco and our baby daughter María Teresa for bringing infinite love and joy into our lives. I also thank my mother María Isabel and my father Hugo, my brother Hugo Ignacio, my sister Natalia, my brother-in-law Felipe, my nephew Agustín and my niece Amparo, for their unconditional love and support, for always believing in me and encouraging me to pursue my dreams. Finally but most importantly, I thank God for His many blessings, particularly for placing all these wonderful people in my life and for taking care of the ones who have already gone, especially my grandmothers, Silvia and Marta, and my grandfathers, Manuel and Mario, who I know are smiling from above.

Santiago, Chile, June 2019

CONTENTS

LIST OF CASES

GERMANY

FRANCE

CHILE

ENGLAND AND WALES

OTHER JURISDICTIONS

AUSTRALIA

CANADA

NETHERLANDS

US

LIST OF LEGISLATION

GERMANY

FRANCE

CHILE

ENGLAND AND WALES

STATUTES

STATUTORY INSTRUMENTS

OTHER JURISDICTIONS

AUSTRALIA

ITALY

US

EUROPEAN UNION

INTERNATIONAL TREATIES

LIST OF HARMONISING INSTRUMENTS

LIST OF ABBREVIATIONS

AA	*Ars Aequi*
ACQP	Acquis Principles
AEPL	Academy of European Private Lawyers
App Cas	Appeal Cases
BAG	*Bundesarbeitsgericht* (German Federal Supreme Court for Labour Law)
BB	*Der Betriebsberater*
BGB	*Bürgerliches Gesetzbuch* (German Civil Code)
BGH	*Bundesgerichtshof* (German Federal Supreme Court)
BGHZ	*Entscheidungen des Bundesgerichtshofs in Zivilsachen*
BLR	Building Law Reports
Bull civ	*Bulletin civil de la Cour de cassation*
Bull Joly	*Bulletin Joly Sociétés*
Burr	Burrow's Reports
CA	*Cour d'appel* (France), *Corte de Apelaciones* (Chile), Court of Appeal (England)
Cass civ (1, 2, 3)	*Cour de cassation, Chambre civile* (first, second, third chamber)
Cass com	*Cour de cassation, Chambre commerciale*
CCC	*Contrats, concurrence, consommation*
Cciv	*Code civil* (French Civil Code)
CCivCh	*Código Civil Chileno* (Chilean Civil Code)
CComCh	*Código de Comercio Chileno* (Chilean Commercial Code)
Ccomm	*Code de Commerce* (French Commercial Code)
CESL	Common European Sales Law
cf.	compare
Ch/ChD	Chancery Division
cic	*culpa in contrahendo*
CISG	Convention on Contracts for the International Sale of Goods
CJ	Chief Justice
CLR	Commonwealth Law Reports (Australia)
ColumJEurL	Columbia Journal of European Law
ColumLRev	Columbia Law Review

Com Ct	Commercial Court
ConstLJ	Construction Law Journal
CS	*Corte Suprema* (Chilean Supreme Court)
D	*Recueil Dalloz* or *Dalloz Sirey*
DCFR	Draft Common Frame of Reference
DH	*Dalloz, Recueil hebdomadaire de jurisprudence*
DTZ	*Deutsch-Deutsche Rechts-Zeitschrift*
edn.	edition
EGLR	Estates Gazette Law Reports
ERPL	European Review of Private Law
EU	European Union
EWCA Civ	England and Wales Court of Appeal, Civil Division
EWHC	England and Wales High Court
ff.	and following
FS	Feasibility Study
Gaz Pal	*Gazette du Palais*
HarvLRev	Harvard Law Review
HCA	High Court of Australia
HL	House of Lords
HL Sc	House of Lords (appeal from Scotland)
HR	*Hoge Raad* (Netherlands Supreme Court)
IBLJ	International Business Law Journal
ICC	International Chamber of Commerce
ICLQ	International & Comparative Law Quarterly
IR	*informations rapides*
J	Justice
JCP	*Jurisclasseur périodique, édition générale*
JCP éd E	*Jurisclasseur périodique, édition entreprise et affaires*
JLC	*Juzgado de Letras Civil*
Jur	*Jurisprudence*
JZ	*Juristenzeitung*
KB	King's Bench Division
KCLJ	King's College Law Journal
LGDJ	*Librairie générale de droit et de jurisprudence*
LJ	Law Journal/Lord Justice
LM	*Lindenmaier-Möhring, Nachschlagewerk des Bundesgerichtshofs*
LPDC	*Ley sobre Protección de los Derechos de los Consumidores*
LR	Law Reports
M&A	Mergers and Acquisitions
MOU	Memorandum of Understanding

MR	Master of the Rolls
NJ	*Nederlandse Jurisprudentie*
NJW	*Neue Juristische Wochenschrift*
NJW-RR	*Neue Juristische Wochenschrift, Rechtsprechungs-Report Zivilrecht*
Off. Cmt.	Official Comment to PICC
PA	*Les Petites Affiches*
para./paras.	paragraph/paragraphs
PC	Privy Council
PCC	*Principes Contractuels Communs*
PECL	Principles of European Contract Law
PICC	Principles of International Commercial Contracts
PLACL	Principles of Latin American Contract Law
PLDC	*Principios Latinoamericanos de Derecho de los Contratos*
pt.	part
PUAM	*Presses Universitaires d'Aix-Marseille*
PUF	*Presses Universitaires de France*
QB	Queen's Bench Division
RDyJ	*Revista de Derecho y Jurisprudencia*
Req	*Chambre de requêtes* of the *Cour de cassation*
rev.	revised
RG	*Reichsgericht*
RGZ	*Entscheidungen des Reichsgerichts in Zivilsachen*
RTDciv	*Revue Trimestrielle de Droit Civil*
RTDcom	*Revue Trimestrielle de Droit Commercial*
SCR	Supreme Court Reports, Canada
sub-s./sub-ss.	subsection/subsections
T.	*Tomo* (volume)
tr.	translator
UCC	Uniform Commercial Code
UKHL	United Kingdom House of Lords
UN	United Nations
UNIDROIT	International Institute for the Unification of Private Law
UNSWLJ	University of New South Wales Law Journal
US	United States of America
UTCCR	Unfair Terms in Consumer Contracts Regulations
UWOLRev	University of Western Ontario Law Review
WL	Westlaw Transcripts
WM	*Wertpapiermitteilungen, Zeitschrift für Wirtschafts-und Bankrecht*

PREFACE

The aim of this book is to explore precontractual liability for breaking off negotiations and to discover its theoretical basis, offering an analysis which is detached from problematic notions, such as good faith and abuse of rights (which have traditionally been claimed as bases of this liability), and finding its basis, instead, in the notion of 'reliance'. The objective is to contribute to the comparative analysis of this area of liability, removing the hurdles that obstruct the view of the core notion that is operating at its heart. Thus, it will be argued that by shifting the analysis to the notion of reliance, jurisdictions that are currently reticent in acknowledging this liability could embrace and implement it.

I. SCOPE

The scope of this book is limited in several aspects. First, the focus is on finding the doctrinal basis of precontractual liability for breaking off negotiations. Thus, remedies are only dealt with briefly in order to show that they correspond to the reliance basis.

Secondly, the analysis is limited to the 'selected jurisdictions': Germany, France and Chile. Germany and France have been selected because they are, respectively, the leading European jurisdictions of the Germanic and Franco-Roman legal families of the civil law system,[1] and because both have contributed crucially to the development of the doctrine of precontractual liability. Chile has been selected because it is a leading jurisdiction in Latin America which has had a particularly interesting reception process of this doctrine, taking elements both from the German and the French developments.[2] Additionally, by selecting Chile, precontractual liability is taken out of its typically European dimension and placed in a more global context, in order to demonstrate the relevance of the topic. English law is analysed as a 'contrasting jurisdiction' in that, as opposed to the selected jurisdictions, it does not provide a remedy in what will be called the

1 Hein Kötz, 'Legal Families' in Jürgen Basedow and others (eds.), *The Max Planck Encyclopedia of European Private Law*, vol. II (OUP, 2012) p. 1063.

2 See Ch. 2 s. I 2 (c).

'paradigm case'.[3] Harmonisation instruments are only analysed in relation to the reliance-based remedies that they provide.[4]

A third limitation is that the focus of the book is on the 'paradigm case': where no contract (not even a preliminary one) has been entered into; no preliminary works have been done, but expenses have been incurred; there is no intention to harm; and one party has relied on an expectation of the future conclusion of the contract under negotiation, that the other party has given rise to. The paradigm case has been chosen because it is the scenario where it is most difficult to justify the imposition of liability for breaking off negotiations, even in the selected jurisdictions, as it goes beyond the 'clear-cut cases'.[5] At the same time, it is the core case which evidences the operation of reliance. Additionally, it evidences a discord between the selected jurisdictions, on the one hand, and the contrasting jurisdiction, on the other hand, because although the latter does provide relief in some specific situations of broken negotiations, it does not in the paradigm case. Cartwright gives a useful example of the paradigm case: an Englishman who ran a business which he was planning to expand globally and who was looking for international partners entered into negotiations in this regard with persons from different nationalities whom he met at an international business convention. After intense negotiations, the Englishman told each of the other persons that he was sure that he would be able to enter into a contract with them as soon as they had agreed all the final details. Consequently, each of the other negotiating parties incurred significant expenses in preparation for this new business venture. However, after some time, the Englishman notified each of them that he had found a better partner in their respective countries.[6]

Other case scenarios which can be placed under the label of 'precontractual liability' are excluded from the direct scope of this work, although they might sometimes be mentioned (particularly the specific scenarios where English law currently provides relief). For instance, 'sham negotiations', i.e. cases where there is a clear intention to harm or no intention to contract (for example, the defendant never intended to contract but gave the impression that he did, or at some stage during the negotiations lost the intention to contract but did not inform the other party and continued to give the impression that he did intend

3 Defined in next para.

4 In Ch. 6 s. IV 1 (b).

5 Ingeborg Schwenzer, Pascal Hachem and Christopher Kee, *Global Sales and Contract Law* (OUP, 2012) p. 280.

6 John Cartwright, 'The English Law of Contract: Time for Review?' (2009) 17 ERPL 155, also published as John Cartwright, *The English Law of Contract: Time for Review?* (EM Meijers Instituut, 2009). Another example is situation 3 in case 7 in John Cartwright and Martijn Hesselink (eds.), *Precontractual Liability in European Private Law* (CUP, 2008) p. 192.

to contract, or conducted parallel negotiations but pretended that he did not do so).[7] Also cases which cannot properly be classified as 'breaking off' negotiations, although negotiations might have been broken off (for instance, cases of breach of confidentiality or of breach of information duties); and cases where there is no breaking-off of 'negotiations' (for example, revocation of an offer, withdrawal of an acceptance, cases where the precontractual period is regulated by a tender procedure, cases where a valid contract was entered into, and cases of personal harm suffered during negotiations).

Thus, the book is limited to situations where one negotiating party breaks off, withdraws from or refuses to continue with negotiations for the conclusion of a contract, excluding negotiations for the conclusion of other types of agreements or instruments. The notion of 'negotiations' is not easy to define, as it corresponds to a period that takes place before a contract is entered into where flexibility is required in order to accommodate the different situations that can occur. However, throughout this work, negotiations will be understood as referring both to a period that begins when one person approaches another or when they simultaneously approach each other in order to discuss the possible conclusion of a contract, and to the discussions and relationship that forms between the negotiating parties by their exchange of information and communications, with the aim of exploring the possibilities and laying down the conditions under which they would be prepared to contract.

It is important to bear in mind two particular situations which could fit into the factual scenario of the paradigm case, but where there is usually no room for precontractual liability. First, in some cases custom or commercial practices determine who bears the risk of failed negotiations. For instance, regarding the services provided by certain professionals or tradesmen, it might be the local custom that a first estimate or a first consultation is provided free of charge or that certain precontractual work is done at the professional's expense;[8] and, regarding certain negotiations with or between businesses it might be considered that the costs are already included in the 'general expenditures of the firm'.[9] Secondly, in some cases (for example M&A transactions between companies)

---

7 John Cartwright, *Contract Law: An Introduction to the English Law of Contract for the Civil Lawyer* (3rd edn., Hart, 2016) p. 84; e.g. cases 1 and 2 in Cartwright and Hesselink (n. 6) pp. 21, 64.

8 Ewan McKendrick, 'Work Done in Anticipation of a Contract Which Does Not Materialise' in W.R. Cornish and others (eds.), *Restitution, Past, Present and Future: Essays in Honour of Gareth Jones* (Hart Publishing, 1998) p. 167; editors' comparative observations to case 4 in Cartwright and Hesselink (n. 6) p. 137.

9 This view has been particularly prominent in French law, e.g. Joanna Schmidt-Szalewski, 'France' in Ewoud H. Hondius (ed.), *Precontractual Liability: Reports to the XIIIth Congress International Academy of Comparative Law, Montreal, Canada, 18–24 August 1990* (Kluwer Law, 1991) p. 150; see Ch. 4, text to (n. 282) below.

the risk of incurring liability for broken negotiations is usually lower because the negotiating parties are advised by legal counsel and normally enter into preliminary agreements (such as MOUs or letters of intent) where they expressly regulate or exclude liability for precontractual work or expenses.[10] This is not to say that liability can never arise in such situations, but it is more difficult for the requirements of liability to be fulfilled.

There are further limitations on the scope of this book. Its focus is on private law contracts, not covering issues of public law or regulatory law (such as contracts with public authorities, public tenders and competition law scenarios). Because the paradigm case is purely precontractual, the book does not deal with preliminary agreements, precontracts or preparatory contracts. Additionally, it does not deal with consumer law because the paradigm case is based on negotiations between parties with equal bargaining power. Therefore, the cases mentioned will generally refer to situations of broken negotiations for the conclusion of contracts between businesses or contracts between individuals, i.e. the book encompasses both commercial and non-commercial contracts but excludes consumer contracts.

II. METHODOLOGY

The comparative nature of this book necessarily calls for a comparative methodology. The methodology used combines elements from Zweigert and Kötz's 'functional equivalence'[11] and from the 'common core method' of the Trento Common Core Project.[12]

The book shows that there is a functional equivalence between the selected jurisdictions in that, through different regimes of liability (contractual in the case of Germany and delictual in the case of France and Chile), they provide reliance-based protection in cases of broken negotiations and, particularly, in the paradigm case. However, it also demonstrates that there is only a limited functional equivalence between the selected jurisdictions and the contrasting jurisdiction, regarding the specific cases where English law grants relief, and no functional equivalence regarding the paradigm case because English law does not provide relief in such a case. At the same time, the book argues that, in the

10 Precontractual agreements are analysed in detail by E. Allan Farnsworth, 'Precontractual Liability and Preliminary Agreements: Fair Dealing and Failed Negotiations' (1987) 87 ColumLRev 217, pp. 249 ff. Also, Héctor Marín Narros, *Estudio de los Principales Acuerdos Precontractuales con Modelos en Inglés y en Español* (Bosch Editor, 2012).

11 Konrad Zweigert and Hein Kötz, *Introduction to Comparative Law* (Tony Weir tr., 3rd rev. edn., Clarendon Press, 1998) ch. 3.

12 Mauro Bussani and Ugo Mattei, 'The Common Core Approach to European Private Law' (1997–1998) 3 ColumJEurL 339.

selected jurisdictions, reliance is the common core that explains the rationale for imposing precontractual liability for breaking off negotiations, especially in the paradigm case, and that this notion is perfectly able to explain the reasoning behind the imposition of liability in the particular cases of broken negotiations where English law grants relief. Consequently, it shows that reliance has the potential of being the common core of precontractual liability for breaking off negotiations, also with regard to the contrasting jurisdiction, if the latter were to embrace the paradigm case on the basis of the protection of reliance.

Nevertheless, it is not the aim of the book to argue that the paradigm case should be protected by the contrasting jurisdiction, but only to show that it could be protected through reliance, a notion which is already part of the current solutions provided by this jurisdiction in other precontractual cases. Moreover, like the Common Core Project,[13] the argument is neither in favour nor against harmonisation; but it shows a tool (in the notion of reliance) that would be useful to achieve some degree of harmonisation in this area.

The book is structured in seven chapters. The first chapter provides an introduction and the second chapter deals with the fundamental principles that underlie the theory of precontractual liability for breaking off negotiations and its historical origins. Each selected jurisdiction is analysed separately in one chapter (third, fourth and fifth chapters, respectively). In each of these chapters a similar structure is followed, establishing the predominance of the reliance basis over other bases of precontractual liability for breaking off negotiations, analysing the requirements for this liability to arise and the particular situation of negotiations for the conclusion of formal contracts. In each of these chapters comparative observations are made where relevant. However, it is the sixth chapter which brings together the findings of the selected jurisdictions, undertaking a detailed comparative analysis of the reliance approach as to the basis, requirements and remedies of this liability. Finally, the seventh chapter argues that the reliance approach would allow this liability to be implemented in the contrasting jurisdiction if it desired to provide relief in the paradigm case.

III. NOTE ON TRANSLATIONS

With regard to German law, the BGB, in English, is available at <https://www.gesetze-im-internet.de/englisch_bgb/index.html>.

Regarding French law, the French text of the new articles of the *Code civil* cited throughout the book is taken from <https://www.legifrance.gouv.fr>. The English translations of these articles, other legislation, reform projects, cases and

13 Bussani and Mattei (n. 12) p. 341.

literature are acknowledged throughout the book. Any other translations from French into English that are not attributed to another author were made by the author.

The text in Spanish of the different Chilean Codes and legislation can be found in Spanish in the website of the National Congress Library (*Biblioteca del Congreso Nacional*): <https://www.leychile.cl/Consulta/homebasico>. Throughout the book, all translations from Spanish into English were made by the author.

CHAPTER 1
INTRODUCTION

This book will show that the notion of reliance is the defining element of liability for breaking off negotiations in the selected jurisdictions, particularly in the paradigm case. In this way, the legitimate reliance of the claimant on the expectation of the future conclusion of the contract, induced or encouraged by the party who then breaks off, is the common factor that explains the rationale of this liability.[1] Although the scope of this work is limited to these jurisdictions, other studies have found that this notion is used to explain precontractual liability in many other jurisdictions.[2] Some legal scholars go as far as stating that the disappointment of reliance is the common element to all doctrines relating to precontractual liability.[3]

This work will demonstrate that there is no functional equivalence between the selected jurisdictions, on the one hand, and the contrasting jurisdiction, on the other, regarding the paradigm case: the latter does not provide relief for it,[4] while the former do. Following a combined common core and functional approach, this work will argue that reliance is the 'higher concept'[5] or 'common core'[6] of liability for broken negotiations in the selected jurisdictions, and will show that reliance is present in the particular liabilities where the contrasting

---

1 Similarly, Horatia Muir-Watt, 'Les Pourparlers: De la Confiance Trompée à la Relation de Confiance' in Pauline Rémy-Corlay and Dominique Fenouillet (eds.), *Les Concepts Contractuels Français à L'heure des Principes du Droit Européen des Contrats* (Dalloz, 2003) pp. 58–59.

2 e.g. John Cartwright and Martijn Hesselink (eds.), *Precontractual Liability in European Private Law* (CUP, 2008) p. 454; Alberto Manzanares, 'La Responsabilidad Precontractual en la Hipótesis de Ruptura Injustificada de las Negociaciones Preliminares' (1984) 37 Anuario de Derecho Civil 687 (analysing Italian law in particular); Andrea Maria Garofalo, 'Il ruolo dell'affidamento nella responsabilità precontrattuale' (2018) 11 Teoria e Storia del Diritto Privato <http://www.teoriaestoriadeldirittoprivato.com/media/rivista/2018/contributi/2018_Contributi_Garofalo.pdf> accessed 31 January 2019 (analysing Italian law in particular).

3 Marcelo Barrientos Zamorano, *Daños y Deberes en las Tratativas Preliminares de un Contrato* (2nd edn., Legal Publishing, 2010) p. 55.

4 See Ch. 7 s. IV below.

5 Konrad Zweigert and Hein Kötz, *Introduction to Comparative Law* (Tony Weir tr., 3rd rev. edn., Clarendon Press, 1998) p. 44.

6 Mauro Bussani and Ugo Mattei, 'The Common Core Approach to European Private Law' (1997–1998) 3 ColumJEurL 339, p. 340.

jurisdiction provides relief in cases of broken negotiations.[7] Thus, reliance has the potential of leading to a functional equivalence or a common core between the selected jurisdictions and the contrasting jurisdiction if the latter were to embrace a reliance approach to granting relief in the paradigm case.[8]

Throughout this book, the concept of reliance is used in 'a rather looser sense'[9] in order to encompass the defining notions of the two dimensions of reliance that will be identified: trust and expectation. The distinction between the two dimensions of reliance in the field of precontractual liability for broken negotiations is very relevant because it shows how reliance interacts with good faith and how the two can be separated. It is here, in particular, that this work aims to demonstrate an innovative theoretical analysis that could have important practical consequences.

In the selected jurisdictions, it will be shown that trust-based reliance and objective good faith coincide and that expectation-based reliance emanates from them. The expectation dimension of reliance is the key element to explain precontractual liability for breaking off negotiations and, therefore, this liability can be theoretically explained on the sole basis of expectation-based reliance. However, it could be questioned why it is preferable to talk in terms of expectation-based reliance rather than, say, expectation-based good faith? Providing a convincing reason to prefer the former over the latter is difficult as they are both objective and abstract concepts that require definition in the concrete case. It is suggested that the answer is simple but significant: expectation-based reliance is more specific and accurate in truly embodying the essence of this liability. Nevertheless, in view of their species-to-genus relationship, it is possible to have reliance and good faith peacefully coexisting in the selected jurisdictions.

The distinction between good faith and reliance acquires unique significance in the contrasting jurisdiction because, on the one hand, it has difficulties with the idea of good faith operating in the precontractual stage and, on the other hand, it is much more familiar with the notion of reliance. It will be shown that reliance, in both its dimensions, is a key notion present in many of the particular solutions currently provided by English law to solve precontractual

---

7 See Ch. 7 s. III 1 below.

8 Similarly, Bénédicte Fauvarque-Cosson, 'Negotiation and Renegotiation: A French Perspective' in John Cartwright, Stefan Vogenauer and Simon Whittaker (eds.), *Reforming the French Law of Obligations, Comparative Reflections on the Avant-projet de réforme du droit des obligations et de la prescription ('the Avant-projet Catala')* (Hart Publishing, 2009) p. 41, referring to 'disappointed trust' and a 'liability based on *reliance* and on loss suffered as a result of this reasonable trust'; Bertrand de Coninck, 'Le Droit Commun de la Rupture des Négociations Précontractuelles' in Marcel Fontaine (ed.), *Le Processus de Formation du Contrat: Contributions Comparatives et Interdisciplinaires à L'Harmonisation du Droit Européen* (Bruylant LGDJ, 2002) pp. 132–133, 137, referring to the protection of *confiance légitime*.

9 Cartwright and Hesselink (n. 2) p. 454.

liability cases.[10] If the two dimensions of reliance are severed, then it is possible to dispense with good faith and focus on the protection of expectation-based reliance. This shift from good faith to reliance could be the basis of a future development of English law in this area in order to provide relief in the paradigm case.

But the question remains whether English law is prepared or willing to move forward? It is prepared as it already has the tools to do so, but it does not seem, at the moment at least, to be willing to do so.

English law's unwillingness to provide protection for cases that fall outside the scope of its piecemeal solutions might generally stem from policy considerations. In addition to the legal reasons that have been mentioned for rejecting a duty to negotiate in good faith,[11] other arguments could explain the different outcome in the selected jurisdictions, on the one hand, and in English law, on the other, regarding the protection of the paradigm case. Therefore, the 'deep-rooted difference of values, attitudes, and policies' that is said to exist between English law and continental legal systems[12] could explain why English law does not protect the paradigm case. It is traditionally thought that French contract law, for instance, takes a more moralising approach while English contract law tends to favour economic arguments. Notions of solidarity and justice supposedly govern the former, while individualism and certainty reign in the latter.[13]

The fact that London is a leading financial, commercial and maritime centre, where the predominant view is that 'business life is rough and tough',[14] would be one of the reasons for English law's approach, which requires English courts to favour predictability in the outcome of a case over absolute justice. In this way, business people know where they stand on the law and can rely on judges experienced in commercial cases to give effect to their transactions.[15]

---

10 See Ch. 7 s. III 1 below.

11 See Ch. 7, text to (nn. 208–210) below.

12 Hein Kötz, 'Towards a European Civil Code: The Duty of Good Faith' in Peter Cane and Jane Stapleton (eds.), *The Law of Obligations: Essays in Celebration of John Fleming* (Clarendon Press, 1998) p. 256.

13 e.g. Pierre Legrand, 'Pre-contractual Disclosure and Information: English and French Law Compared' (1986) 6 Oxford Journal of Legal Studies 322, p. 349; Barry Nicholas, 'The Pre-contractual Obligation to Disclose Information: English Report' in Donald Harris and Denis Tallon (eds.), *Contract Law Today: Anglo-French Comparisons* (OUP, 1989) p. 187; John Bell, Sophie Boyron and Simon Whittaker, *Principles of French Law* (2nd edn., OUP, 2008) p. 334.

14 Roy Goode, 'The Codification of Commercial Law' (1988) 14 Monash University Law Review 135, p. 149.

15 Roy Goode, *The Concept of "Good Faith" in English Law* (Centro di studi e ricerche di diritto comparato e straniero, 1992) p. 9. Similarly, Holman, Fenwick, Willan, 'Global Trends in International Trade and the Laws that Underpin Them: Identifying and Analysing the Key Trends and the Legal Issues that Need to be Resolved to Support the Further Development of International Trade' (2015) <http://www.hfw.com/HFW-Global-trends-in-international-trade-February-2015> accessed 31 January 2019, p. 17.

In contrast, French law was perceived as being less commercial, less pragmatic and more uncertain in comparison to common law systems and, consequently, as less attractive for international businesses.[16] This is one of the reasons underlying the 2016 reform considered in Chapter 4.[17] However, despite its objective of becoming more attractive for foreign legislators and commercial parties, a feature of the 2016 reform is the codification of the strong protection that was already being given by the courts to contracting parties during precontractual negotiations.[18] An explanation for this apparent contradiction is that the 2016 reform has not fundamentally changed French contract law, retaining its core values and philosophical bases; therefore, enhancing legal certainty and commercial attractiveness had to be balanced with promoting substantive fairness.[19] In this way, it is said that negotiations are subject to rules which constitute a 'code of ethics' for negotiations.[20] Whether the 2016 reform has succeeded in making French contract law more attractive is open to debate but it is undoubted that by codifying the previous case law, the reform has made French contract law more accessible and predictable.[21] While this might be surprising for a common law lawyer, it can be well understood if the different characteristics (especially volume and authority) of the case law in France is taken into account.[22]

What appears to be a stark divide between English law and French law (representing the selected jurisdictions) regarding their conception of precontractual negotiations is based on the idea of adversarial precontractual dealings taking place in a commercial setting, i.e. between commercial parties. But it is debatable whether negotiations between commercial parties are always adversarial in nature and, even if that is the case, the characterisation of such a relationship does not necessarily mean that self-interested behaviour knows no limits.[23] Indeed, English legal scholars have recognised, in their criticism of some of the reasoning in *Walford v Miles*,[24] that it is not a fundamental attribute of a negotiation that the negotiating parties should have absolute freedom to walk away for any reason or no reason at all.[25] Another difficulty

---

16 Solène Rowan, 'The New French Law of Contract' (2017) 66 ICLQ 805, p. 809.
17 See Ch. 4, text to (n. 2) below.
18 Rowan (n. 16) pp. 815, 827; see Ch. 4, text to (n. 12) below.
19 Rowan (n. 16) p. 828.
20 Daniel Mainguy, 'Contract Negotiation and Formation' (2017) 6 International Business Law Journal 563, p. 570.
21 Rowan (n. 16) pp. 825–826; Jan Smits and Caroline Calomme, 'The Reform of the French Law of Obligations' (2016) 23 Maastricht Journal 1040, p. 1049.
22 Rowan (n. 16) p. 826.
23 See Ch. 7, text to (nn. 188–190) below.
24 *Walford v Miles* [1992] 2 AC 128 (HL).
25 Jack Beatson, Andrew Burrows and John Cartwright, *Anson's Law of Contract* (30th edn., OUP, 2016) p. 69.

is what is meant by the notion of 'commercial'. It is important to bear in mind that the understanding of the term 'commercial' and, hence, of commercial parties, contracts and cases, might not be the same in different jurisdictions, especially considering that some legal systems from the civil law tradition (such as the selected jurisdictions) draw a formal distinction between 'civil law' and 'commercial law' and, consequently, between 'civil law contracts' and 'commercial contracts'.[26] This relates to the argument that civil law jurisdictions tend to be more protective of the rights of the weaker party whereas the common law *laissez-faire* approach is more receptive to commercial transactions[27] which, in any case, is not applicable in the paradigm case where negotiations take place between parties of equal bargaining power.

It might be argued that the selected jurisdictions, on the one hand, and English law, on the other, have different conceptions of what is permissible hard bargaining and, therefore, set different limits to self-interested behaviour.[28] This relates to the conduct and attitude that negotiating parties would be expected to show when negotiating a contract, which should vary depending on their legal system. It seems that the question whether there really is a difference in 'national mentality'[29] between negotiating parties in England and

26 For details, John Cartwright, '"Commercial" Contracts: Do They Exist in English Law?' in Lorena Carvajal and Ángela Toso (eds.), *Estudios de Derecho Comercial: Octavas Jornadas Chilenas de Derecho Comercial* (Thomson Reuters, 2018) pp. 25 ff; Roy Goode and Ewan McKendrick (ed.), *Goode on Commercial Law* (5th edn., Penguin Books, 2016) pp. 157–158.

27 Roy Goode, Herbert Kronke and Ewan McKendrick (eds.), *Transnational Commercial Law: Texts, Cases and Materials* (2nd edn., OUP, 2015) p. 122.

28 Alexander Loke, 'Insights from Comparing the Contract Laws of Asia on Formation and Third Party Beneficiaries' in Mindy Chen-Wishart, Alexander Loke and Stefan Vogenauer (eds.), *Formation and Third Party Beneficiaries* (OUP, 2018) p. 533.

29 H.C. Gutteridge, *Comparative Law: An Introduction to the Comparative Method of Legal Study & Research* (2nd edn., Cambridge University Press, 1949) p. 6. Differences in language might also be relevant. For instance, according to the style of communication, Spanish-speaking countries (such as Chile) are generally classified as 'high context' societies (which use indirect methods of communication that often require a deep understanding of the surrounding culture to determine the speaker's meaning, and typically favour the needs of the group over the needs of the individual and place a high value on personal relationships), whereas English-speaking nations are generally classified as 'low-context' societies (which use more direct and explicit means of communication, and tend to be more individualist in nature). This classification seems to correspond with another that, based on the perception of time, classifies English-speaking countries as 'monochronist' (they value the logical progression of events in a predictable and orderly manner, and focus more on the efficient completion of a task) and Spanish-speaking countries as 'polychronist' (they view tasks and events as happening simultaneously in a much more relaxed and organic manner, and place a high value on personal relationships). All of the above in S.I. Strong, Katia Fach Gómez and Laura Carballo Piñeiro, *Comparative Law for Spanish-English Speaking Lawyers: Legal Cultures, Legal Terms and Legal Practices* (Edward Elgar Publishing, 2016) pp. 17–18. It is clear that these are only broad generalisations that admit individual and regional variations, but it might be worth noting that a popular saying in Chile is that 'Chileans are the English of Latin America'. Whether this statement has any truth to it is open to debate.

negotiating parties elsewhere cannot be categorically answered without proper empirical research.[30] However, from the study of the case law undertaken in this work it does not appear that there are any significant differences between the mentality of the negotiating parties in English law cases and those in the selected jurisdictions. Generally, in all of them the claimants behaved in the same way: they trusted the conduct of the other party and relied on a legitimate expectation that the contract under negotiation would eventually be concluded, and then they sought the protection of their reliance on this disappointed legitimate expectation. If the mentality or perhaps even instinct of negotiating parties in England were so different from those of the selected jurisdictions, it would be difficult to explain why precontractual liability cases for broken negotiation have been litigated on the basis of English law's piecemeal solutions. A sensible person would not take the time and effort (let alone the costs) to ask English courts for protection because he would know that until there is a contract, his reliance on a precontractual expectation will not be protected. This is, of course, an oversimplification of the problem but it does not detract validity from the argument that a common law system can be responsive to the legitimate expectations of fair play of the parties and of the particular business community.[31]

English law's unwillingness to move forward in the protection of the paradigm case might also be explained by legal reasons. One reason is the continued perception that precontractual liability is inextricably linked to good faith and since the latter is not generally accepted, particularly in the negotiation stage, the former cannot be accepted in general terms. The feasibility of precontractual liability functioning independently from good faith will be shown. Yet, another reason appears to be that English law is firmly attached to the technique of applying a piecemeal approach rather than general principles and that, in their content, the particular solutions remain separate rather than forming a cohesive theory. However, it is not necessary to give up this preference for piecemeal solutions because English law already has certain boxes into which precontractual liability in the paradigm case could be inserted. And it is not a question of introducing a foreign general principle (like good faith) but of using the existing boxes in ways that have not been used before (estoppel and the

---

[30] In a recent applied study on the origin of contractual obligations, it is argued that despite the differences between the civil law tradition (where the concept of contract rests on intent) and the common law (where the concept of contract rests on exchange), the main reason for keeping a promise and entering into the realm of legally enforceable obligations is very similar. It is a self-image concern: people feel bad if their action is inconsistent with their words. For details, see Christoph Engel and André Schmelzer, 'Committing the English and the Continental Way: An Experiment' (2017) Preprints of the Max Planck Institute for Research on Collective Goods <https://ssrn.com/abstract=3024525> accessed 18 April 2019.

[31] Loke (n. 28) p. 544.

tort of negligence seem to be the best suited for such a development).[32] Is this really so radical? It is no more radical than, for instance, *Hedley Byrne*[33] was at its time.

Nevertheless, a more difficult reason remains, which is the stark English view of negotiations as a period where the risk of failure remains with each party, who appear as antagonists rather than as collaborators. Under this view, while English judges might accept that expectation-based reliance is the true basis of precontractual liability (instead of good faith), they might still consider that the paradigm case is not worthy of protection because the facts of such a case simply do not give rise to a legitimate expectation-based reliance that deserves relief. This is a real possibility which would lead to a partial functional equivalence between the selected jurisdictions and English law (regarding cases where English law currently provides relief), but not to a common core as English law would still not fall in line with the selected jurisdictions regarding the paradigm case. However, this forecast is not inevitable.

This work will show that the fear of opening the floodgates is unfounded: precontractual liability for broken negotiations has operated in the selected jurisdictions under strict requirements, providing for reliance-based remedies, and without causing a flood of litigation.[34] Additionally, a glimmer of hope of moving English law closer to the selected jurisdictions, without developing a general principle, is evidenced in *Yam Seng*.[35] This case has demonstrated that it is possible to give content to good faith in the performance of contracts. Thus, it would be odd for it to be impossible to give content to good faith in the precontractual phase. Furthermore, if the troublesome notion of good faith is left aside and the emphasis is placed on protecting the reliance placed on a legitimate expectation, then it really seems that it is only a matter of having the right case come before the Supreme Court for it to decide whether it wants to embrace a broader potential for precontractual liability in order to provide relief in the paradigm case.

It could be argued that a stumbling block for English law would be determining at which point the precontractual phase should be protected,[36] which does not mean that at this point liability will necessarily arise, but only that it might arise if certain requirements are met. It is here that the comparative analysis of the operation of reliance in the selected jurisdictions[37] might be useful for English lawyers and judges, as they could take inspiration from them, without following

32 See Ch. 7 s. IV below.

33 *Hedley Byrne & Co Ltd v Heller & Partners Ltd* [1964] AC 465 (HL).

34 See Ch. 6 ss. I and IV.

35 *Yam Seng Pte Ltd v International Trade Corp Ltd* [2013] EWHC 111 (QB), [2013] 1 All ER (Comm) 1321.

36 For a general discussion, Cartwright and Hesselink (n. 2) pp. 450–453.

37 See Ch. 6 s. II below.

their solutions to the letter. For instance, while in German law the existence of a precontractual relationship marks the beginning of the potential protection provided by *culpa in contrahendo*, in French and Chilean law it is sufficient that negotiations have begun because, outside of contract, protection is provided by the general principle of delictual liability.[38]

Another hurdle might be the issue of determining where the trigger for liability is found: in the manner of conducting the negotiations or in the manner of ending them. Again, inspiration might be taken from the selected jurisdictions, which all show that, although there may be some differences as to where the emphasis is placed, fault is found in conducting the negotiations in a manner that gives rise to a legitimate expectation of the future conclusion of the contract and in later breaking them off without a justified reason.[39]

Finally, another issue might be determining the appropriate remedy. But following the solutions of the selected jurisdictions, which correspond to those of the harmonising instruments that have been analysed,[40] it is clear that the remedy in the paradigm case should be damages to the extent of the reliance interest.

To conclude this introduction, the paradigm case is not an example of a clear-cut divide between the common law and the civil law, as other common law jurisdictions are able to provide relief for it. It is a concrete example of a situation where Zweigert and Kötz's *praesumptio similitudinis*[41] fails and English law finds itself isolated not only from civil law jurisdictions but also from other common law legal systems. Undoubtedly this raises the question whether the English law view is defensible.[42] Although this book will neither focus on nor argue for the need of harmonisation of this area of the law, which faces numerous difficulties,[43] particularly considering that the UK will (probably) be leaving the EU[44] and that, at the moment, efforts to harmonise contract law within the EU have been very much watered-down,[45] it is still worthwhile to point out

---

38 See Ch. 6 s. I 3 (a) below.

39 See Ch. 6 s. I 2 below.

40 See Ch. 6 s. IV 1 below.

41 Zweigert and Kötz (n. 5) p. 40.

42 Roger Brownsword, *Contract Law: Themes for the Twenty-First Century* (2nd edn., OUP, 2006) pp.187–188.

43 Reiner Schulze and Fryderyk Zoll, *European Contract Law* (C.H. Beck, Hart, Nomos, 2016) p. 144.

44 As a result of the 'Brexit' referendum held on 23 June 2016.

45 The Proposal for a Regulation of the European Parliament and of the Council on a Common European Sales Law COM(2011) 635 (CESL) was withdrawn on 16 December 2014 by the EU Commission, and the legislative proposals that have been put forward are of a much narrower scope than the CESL: Proposal for a Directive of the European Parliament and of the Council on certain aspects concerning contracts for the supply of digital content COM(2015) 634 final, published on 9 December 2015, and Amended Proposal for a Directive of the European Parliament and of the Council on certain aspects concerning contracts for the online and other distance sales of goods COM(2017) 637 final, published on 31 October 2017.

that it will be easier to find common ground and, hence, increase the chances of harmonisation, at least in the area of liability for broken negotiations, if the common language is that of reliance rather than that of good faith.[46] After all, '[i]n a shrinking world (...) there must be some virtue in uniformity of outcome whatever the diversity of approach in reaching that outcome'.[47]

46 Similarly, de Coninck (n. 8) pp. 133, 137.

47 *Fairchild v Glenhaven Funeral Services Ltd and Others* [2002] UKHL 22, [2003] 1 AC 32 [32] (Lord Bingham).

CHAPTER 2

FUNDAMENTAL PRINCIPLES AND HISTORICAL ORIGINS

Before analysing the details of the treatment of liability for breaking off negotiations in the selected jurisdictions and in the contrasting jurisdiction, it is important to address generally the fundamental principles that underlie the doctrine of precontractual liability (reliance and freedom) and to highlight the presence of the notion of reliance since the conception of the doctrine.

I. RELIANCE

1. NOTION AND DIMENSIONS

This book does not deal with the theory of reliance which has been put forward as the foundation of the binding force of contracts,[1] but it will show that the notion of reliance applied in the precontractual period has a similar content in that it refers to a trust that is placed on an expectation: not that a contract has been concluded, but that a contract will be concluded. The use of 'reliance' throughout the book is loose and non-technical, except where it is stated otherwise, in order to encompass these notions of trust and expectation, so that this one term (which can be translated as *Vertrauen*, *croyance/confiance* and *confianza* in the selected jurisdictions) includes all these notions.

The book argues that there are two dimensions of reliance in cases of broken negotiations, referring to them as 'trust-based reliance' and 'expectation-based reliance'. The former seeks to highlight the element of trust which exists or should exist between negotiating parties and the latter focuses on a specific expectation in the future conclusion of the contract under negotiation ('the negotiated contract'). Both dimensions, as well as their interaction, are identified

1 Generally, Hugh Beale and others, *Ius Commune Casebooks for the Common Law of Europe: Cases, Materials and Text on Contract Law* (3rd edn., Hart, 2019) pp. 103–104; for an analysis of the 'reliance model' in contrast to the 'exchange model', Hugh Collins, *The Law of Contract* (4th edn., LexisNexis, 2003) ch. 5.

in each selected jurisdiction and in the contrasting jurisdiction, and analysed in detail in the comparative chapter.

2. ON THE ORIGINS OF THE DOCTRINE OF PRECONTRACTUAL LIABILITY

A historical study of this doctrine in the selected jurisdictions is outside the scope of this book, which focuses on the current state of the law in each jurisdiction. Nevertheless, it is relevant to point out briefly that the notion of reliance has been present from the conception of the doctrine in Germany and France, and, in the case of Chile, to provide a succinct historical account of the reception of the doctrine, particularly in the case of breaking off negotiations.

(a) German Law

Von Jhering, in his article on *culpa in contrahendo* (*cic*), published in the second half of the nineteenth century,[2] developed his theory of fault in contracting, drawing inspiration from Roman law. He applied his theory in certain situations of null contracts, and in certain cases of contracts that were not finally concluded due the withdrawal or the expiry of the offer. According to his theory, with the emission of an offer an obligation of *diligentia in contrahendo* arises, an obligation which does not disappear if the contract is afterwards declared null or turns out to not have been concluded. Consequently, a party who breaches this obligation is liable in contract to the other party who has suffered losses by legitimately relying on the validity or conclusion of the contract. The measure of liability is the 'negative contractual interest' which seeks to place the claimant in the position he would have been in if he had not relied on the null contract, and includes the compensation of expenses and lost opportunities to contract with other persons.[3] It can be seen that the

---

2 Rudolf von Jhering, 'Culpa in contrahendo, oder Schadensersatz bei nichtigen oder nicht zur Perfection gelangten Verträgen' (1861) 4 Jahrbücher für die Dogmatik des heutigen römischen und deutschen Privatrechts 1; translated into French by O. de Meulenaere, 'De la culpa in contrahendo ou des dommages-intérêts dans les conventions nulles ou imparfaites' (1893) II Oeuvres choisies 1. The author has had access to a translation into Portuguese, Rudolf von Jhering, *Culpa in contrahendo ou Indemnização em Contratos Nulos ou Não Chegados à Perfeição* (Paulo Mota Pinto tr., Almedina, 2008).

3 In contrast to the 'negative contractual interest' is the 'positive contractual interest', which seeks to place the claimant in the position he would have been in if the contract had been valid. These categories must not be confused with those of *damnum emergens* and *lucrum cessans*, respectively; Catalina Salgado Ramírez, 'Breve Introducción a la Responsabilidad Precontractual en la Teoría de Rudolf von Jhering' in Emilssen González de Cancino, Édgar Cortés Moncayo and Felipe Navia Arroyo (eds.), *Estudios de Derecho Civil en Memoria de*

protection of reliance 'placed on the mere semblance of a contract'[4] is at the heart of Jhering's theory.[5] It is also important to note that his theory did not consider liability for broken negotiations.[6]

The drafters of the German Civil Code (BGB) took up Jhering's idea of compensating the reliance interest in the case of null contracts in several specific provisions,[7] but not as a general principle. However, academic writers and the courts developed and expanded Jhering's theory of *cic*[8] and, through the principle of good faith,[9] were able to provide a legal basis[10] for new cases of *cic*, such as the breaking-off of negotiations (where the protection of reliance remained a core element).[11]

(b) French Law

Saleilles, in his article on precontractual liability, published at the beginning of the twentieth century,[12] approved of Faggella's[13] novel proposition that negotiations have legal value and that breaking them off can lead to precontractual liability. He explained that Faggella rejected Jhering's theory of *cic* in that he considered that this liability did not rest on the notion of fault but on a guarantee implied by a voluntary assent.[14] Following Faggella, he argued

---

Fernando Hinestrosa, vol. I (Universidad Externado de Colombia, 2014) pp. 748–750. For details, see Ch. 6, text to (n. 176) below.

4 Reinhard Zimmermann, *Roman Law, Contemporary Law, European Law: The Civilian Tradition Today* (OUP, 2001) p. 88.

5 Reliance is referred to as *confianza* in Salgado Ramírez (n. 3), especially p. 747 fn. 85.

6 *Ius Commune* (n. 1) p. 423.

7 §§122, 179(2), 307, 309 BGB. The latter two examples disappeared with the 2001 reform of the BGB, see Ch. 3, text to (n. 9).

8 For an analysis of this evolution, Zimmermann (n. 4) pp. 88–92; Alfredo Mordechai Rabello, 'The Theory Concerning Culpa in Contrahendo Precontractual Liability: From Roman Law to the German Legal System – A Hundred Years After the Death of Jhering' in Alfredo Mordechai Rabello (ed.), *European Legal Traditions and Israel* (Harry and Michael Sacher Institute for Legislative Research and Comparative Law, Hebrew University of Jerusalem 1994) pp. 142–144; Clara Asúa González, *La Culpa in Contrahendo: Tratamiento en el Derecho Alemán y Presencia en Otros Ordenamientos* (Universidad del País Vasco, 1989) pp. 40–52.

9 Sylviane Colombo, 'The Implications of Good Faith in Culpa in Contrahendo' (JSD thesis, Yale Law School, 1990) pp. 99–100.

10 §242 BGB; see Ch. 3, text to (n. 142) below.

11 Details in Ch. 3 s. II 1.

12 Raymond Saleilles, 'De la Responsabilité Précontractuelle à propos d'une Étude Nouvelle sur la Matière' (1907) 6 RTDCiv 697.

13 Gabriele Faggella, 'Dei Periodi Precontrattuali e della loro Vera ed Esatta Costruzione Scientifica' in *Studi Giuridici in Onore di Carlo Fadda*, vol. III (1906). His work considerably influenced the French and Latin American developments of precontractual liability: Ewoud H. Hondius, 'General Report' in Ewoud H. Hondius (ed.), *Precontractual Liability: Reports to the XIIIth Congress International Academy of Comparative Law, Montreal, Canada, 18–24 August 1990* (Kluwer Law, 1991) p. 5.

14 Saleilles (n. 12) p. 725.

that 'the fact alone that one has consented to negotiate requires each of the two parties to act in accordance with commercial equity and good faith',[15] and that this consent gives rise to an expectation (*attente*) and security (*sécurité*) which an arbitrary withdrawal from negotiations destroys. Therefore, equity demands that the party who has frustrated the legitimate assurances (*assurances légitimes*) to which he has given rise, be liable for the loss caused; loss which is restricted to the expenses incurred on the basis of the previous consent to negotiate. Saleilles followed Faggella in rejecting Jhering's negative contractual interest as the measure of liability in this stage of the precontractual period.[16]

Saleilles' theory encompassed expectation-based reliance in the destruction of a legitimate expectation, and trust-based reliance in the *confiance* placed on the other party when entering a business relationship with him.[17]

(c) Chilean Law

Chilean 'civil law' (*Derecho Civil*)[18] was codified in the mid-nineteenth century in the *Código Civil* (enacted in 1855 and in force since 1857).[19] The author of the Chilean Civil Code (CCivCh), Andrés Bello, took a Roman law based approach in structuring and drafting the Code which, consequently, belongs to the Roman legal tradition.[20] He relied on different sources, amongst which the French *Code civil* (Cciv) had great influence, particularly with regard to the law of obligations, and he also drew inspiration from French legal scholars (especially Pothier).[21] Therefore, Chilean civil law is considered to belong to

---

15 Saleilles (n. 12) p. 718, as translated by Arthur von Mehren, 'The Formation of Contracts' in *International Encyclopedia of Comparative Law*, vol. VII (JCB Mohr (Paul Siebeck) and Martinus Nijhoff Publishers, 1992) ch. 9, p. 65.

16 Saleilles (n. 12) pp. 722–724, 735.

17 Saleilles (n. 12) pp. 735, 741.

18 An area of private law which covers a variety of subjects, ranging from obligations, legal acts and contracts to delictual liability, property law, succession law, family law and the person as a subject of law.

19 For a detailed account of its codification, Alejandro Guzmán Brito, *Andrés Bello Codificador: Historia de la Fijación y Codificación del Derecho Civil en Chile* vol. I (Ediciones de la Universidad de Chile, 1982). For a brief analysis, Jan Kleinheisterkamp, 'Latin America, Influence of European Private Law' in Jürgen Basedow and others (eds.), *The Max Planck Encyclopedia of European Private Law*, vol. II (OUP, 2012) p. 1033.

20 Guzmán Brito (n. 19) p. 421.

21 Guzmán Brito (n. 19) pp. 422–424. Other important sources were, e.g., the *Siete Partidas* and the *Corpus Iuris Civilis*, ibid. p. 415. A German influence is found in the real estate registration system introduced by the CCivCh: Rodrigo Barcia Lehmann, 'La Influencia del *Code Civil* y del Derecho Alemán en el Sistema Patrimonial Chileno: Sistema de Derechos Reales y Personales' in Juan Andrés Varas Braun and others (eds.), *Estudios de Derecho Civil: Jornadas Nacionales de Derecho Civil 2005–2009*, vol. I (Abeledo Perrot Legal Publishing Chile, 2011) p. 450.

the Franco-Roman legal tradition.[22] This explains why, since its codification, *la jurisprudencia*[23] and *la doctrina*[24] looked towards French law in order to interpret and develop Chilean civil law.[25] The influence of French law and other relevant European jurisdictions, such as German law, continued after the codification.

A particular example is the reception by Chilean civil law of the doctrine of precontractual liability.[26] The Chilean Civil Code was enacted before the publication in Germany of Jhering's article on *culpa in contrahendo* (in 1861) and, consequently, the doctrine of *cic* could not have been included in it. However, an article of the CCivCh that deals with defects of consent has been interpreted as establishing precontractual liability in the case of an invalid contract due to mistake regarding the person with whom one intended to contract.[27] Another article of the CCivCh (relating to the invalidity of a contract of sale of a non-existent thing) has also been interpreted as giving rise to precontractual liability.[28] The Chilean Commercial Code (CComCh)

---

22 Arturo Alessandri, Manuel Somarriva and Antonio Vodanovic, *Tratado de Derecho Civil: Partes Preliminar y General*, vol. I (7th edn., Editorial Jurídica de Chile, 2005) p. 94.

23 Case law is not a source of law, although a particular judicial decision is binding on the individual parties to the dispute (art. 3(2) CCivCh). There is no doctrine of *stare decisis* but the lower courts tend to follow the decisions of the higher courts (Courts of Appeal and Supreme Court), particularly when the judgments of the latter set a particular trend.

24 The thinking of legal scholars (Chilean and foreigners) expressed in their writings have a relevant role in the Chilean legal system because, although they are not a source of law, they are often cited in judicial filings and judgments. This will be evidenced throughout Ch. 5.

25 Mauricio Tapia Rodríguez, *Código Civil 1855–2005: Evolución y Perspectivas* (Editorial Jurídica de Chile, 2005) pp. 29–30; Ramón Domínguez Águila, 'La Influencia de la Doctrina Francesa en el Derecho Chileno' in Carlos Pizarro Wilson and Mauricio Tapia Rodríguez (eds.), *Cuadernos de Análisis Jurídicos, Colección Derecho Privado II: De la Codificación a la Descodificación* (Ediciones Universidad Diego Portales, 2005).

26 A Chilean legal scholar who, despite being critical of the import into Chilean law of foreign notions that have originated under the specific characteristics of foreign legal systems, recognises that precontractual liability is an example of the reception phenomenon is Pedro Pablo Vergara Varas, 'La Responsabilidad Precontractual: Un Necesario Desvarío para Enfrentar la Cultura del Litigio' in Hugo Fábrega Vega (ed.), *Estudios Jurídicos en Homenaje a los Profesores Fernando Fueyo Laneri, Avelino León Hurtado, Francisco Merino Scheihing, Fernando Mujica Bezanilla, Hugo Rosende Subiabre* (Ediciones Universidad del Desarrollo, 2007) p. 118.

27 art. 1455(2) ('But in this case the person with whom a contract has been entered into by mistake will have the right to be compensated for the losses it suffered in good faith due to the annulment of the contract'); in favour of this view, e.g. Luis Claro Solar, *Explicaciones de Derecho Civil Chileno y Comparado*, vol. XI De las Obligaciones II (Imprenta Nascimento, 1937) p. 180; Augusto Fuentes de la Sotta, 'La Responsabilidad por el Hecho de Otro en Materia Contractual' (Licenciado en Ciencias Jurídicas thesis, Universidad de Chile, 1938) pp. 43–45; Arturo Alessandri Rodríguez, *De los Contratos* (reprint 1993 1st edn., Editorial Jurídica de Chile, 2004) p. 156; against this view, Orlando Tapia Suárez, 'De la Responsabilidad Civil en General y de la Responsabilidad Delictual entre los Contratantes' (Licenciado en Ciencias Jurídicas thesis, Universidad de Concepción, 1941) p. 411.

28 art. 1814(3) ('A person who knowingly sold a thing that did not exist in the whole or in a considerable part will compensate the losses to the buyer in good faith'); in favour of this

(enacted in 1865 and in force since 1867) did not include the specific situations of *culpa in contrahendo* conceived by Jhering,[29] but a renowned Chilean legal scholar[30] saw in two articles of this Code (establishing liability of the offeror for revocation of his offer and liability of the offeror for failure to give prompt notice to the offeree of his late acceptance) a confirmation of the theory of *culpa in contrahendo*.[31]

A landmark in the reception of precontractual liability for breaking off negotiations was the publication in 1908 of a translation into Spanish of Saleilles' article on precontractual liability[32] in the most authoritative Chilean law journal (which regularly published translations of French articles first published in the *Revue Trimestrielle de Droit Civil*).[33] In the 1930s, two theses from the Universidad de Chile were published where this liability was analysed. In both there is a clear influence of Saleilles' doctrine of *responsabilité précontractuelle*[34] and the notion of *confianza* is used to justify the imposition of liability. One thesis argued that the sole act of entering into negotiations with another person instils in that person a *confianza* that the negotiations will continue until the preparation of a non-binding draft of the contract and that, if the other party breaks off, he is responsible for having misled such *confianza*.[35] The other thesis argued that the liability that can arise before the emission of an offer is born from commercial equity and involves the compensation of the losses caused by the *confianza* or security in the conclusion of a contract.[36]

A judgment dated 25 August 1948 seems to be the first in Chile to refer to precontractual liability,[37] defining it as:

> [A]ccording to legal scholars it is such that is born from commercial equity, that has the effect of having to indemnify the losses caused by the trust [*confianza*] in the formation

view, e.g. Fuentes (n. 27) pp. 43, 45; Alessandri Rodríguez (n. 27) p. 156; Carlos Ducci, *Derecho Civil: Parte General* (4th edn., Editorial Jurídica de Chile, 2005) p. 256; against this view, Tapia Suárez (n. 27) p. 413.

29 See this subsection letter (a) above.

30 Claro Solar (n. 27) pp. 532–533 fn. 145.

31 Respectively, art. 100(1) ('The effective revocation imposes on the offeror the obligation to compensate the expenses incurred by the person to whom the offer was directed at, and the losses that that person suffered') and art. 98(3) ('In case of late acceptance, the offeror is obliged, under liability for damages, to give prompt notice of his withdrawal').

32 Saleilles (n. 12). Earlier, a thesis from the Universidad de Chile recognised the notion of *cic* regarding invalid contracts (citing examples from the BGB) and considered it to be a type of contractual fault, Rafael Cañas O'Rian, 'De la Culpa Civil' (Licenciado en la Facultad de Leyes thesis, Universidad de Chile, 1904) pp. 8–10.

33 Raymond Saleilles, 'De la Responsabilidad Precontractual a propósito de un Estudio sobre la Materia' (1908) V Revista de Derecho y Jurisprudencia 127.

34 See this subsection letter (b) above.

35 Sara Eiler, *De la Formación del Consentimiento en los Contratos* (Editorial Nascimento, 1935) p. 72.

36 Manuel Risueño, *De las Obligaciones Precontractuales* (Soc. Imp. y Lito. Universo, 1933) p. 60.

37 CA Santiago, *Caja de Crédito Popular con Schiavetti viuda de Maino*, RDyJ, T. 46, 1949, Second Part, Second Section; see details in Ch. 5, text following (n. 266) below.

> of the contract, or by the withdrawal of the offer to conclude the proposed contract, violating the security provided that the contract was to come into effect (...)

Despite this initial recognition of liability for breaking off negotiations, some Chilean authors rejected it,[38] or only accepted that there could be liability if a delict was committed during negotiations, or only gave room to precontractual liability in the cases regulated in the Commercial Code or in the invalidity cases of the Civil Code.[39] Others, however, recognised that, at least theoretically, liability could arise in the negotiations that preceded an offer,[40] particularly for breaking them off.[41]

The next milestone in the reception process was a book published in 1979,[42] where the author recognised that breaking off negotiations is a trigger for precontractual liability if there is negligence or fraud, and where the works of Jhering, Faggella and Saleilles (among other German, Italian and French legal scholars) were analysed. The author did not refer to *confianza* as the basis of this liability but rather to the breach of a duty of good faith.[43] In a 1990 judgment, the Court of Appeal of Santiago referred to this book as the classic work on the subject.[44]

From the mid-nineties onwards an increasing number of judgments referred to precontractual liability for breaking off negotiations and several specialised books, articles and case notes were published on precontractual liability in general and on breaking off negotiations in particular. These will be referred to in the Chilean law chapter, where the continued reception of European ideas, particularly French and German, will be highlighted.[45] For now, it suffices to say that the notion of *confianza* has been increasingly used to explain this liability.[46]

---

38 e.g. Hernán Larraín Ríos, *Lecciones de Derecho Civil* (Editorial Jurídica de Chile, 1994) p. 257.

39 See arts. mentioned in (nn. 27, 28, 31) above; e.g. Tapia Suárez (n. 27) pp. 365–366, 411; Fuentes (n. 27) p. 43; Avelino León Hurtado, *La Voluntad y la Capacidad en los Actos Jurídicos* (4th edn., Editorial Jurídica de Chile, 1991) pp. 58, 60; Alessandri Rodríguez (n. 27) pp. 156–159.

40 Raúl Varela, *Derecho Comercial: Obligaciones y Contratos*, vol. III (Editorial Universitaria S.A., 1966) pp. 8–9.

41 Mario Rossel, 'La Indemnización de Perjuicios en la Formación del Consentimiento y en el Contrato de Transporte Terrestre' (Licenciado en Ciencias Jurídicas y Sociales thesis, Universidad de Chile, 1966) pp. 28 ff., following Faggella and Saleilles, but concluding that because Chilean legislation does not expressly recognise this liability, it cannot arise in Chilean law.

42 Hugo Rosende Álvarez, *Algunas Consideraciones sobre la Responsabilidad Precontractual* (Ediciones Universitarias de Valparaíso, 1979), with a prologue by the renowned Chilean professor Fernando Fueyo.

43 Rosende Álvarez (n. 42) p. 79.

44 CA Santiago, 27 June 1990, *Sociedad Industrial y Comercial Fabril Maderera Patagonia Ltda. con Ministro de Bienes Nacionales*, Gaceta Jurídica 1990 no. 121.

45 Ch. 5 s. I.

46 Ch. 5 s. II 1.

II. FREEDOM AND LIABILITY

Before analysing the selected jurisdictions and the contrasting jurisdiction, it is important to understand that they all have the same starting point but reach a different outcome with regard to the paradigm case.

They all start from the same guiding principle: freedom of contract or, rather, a negative freedom of contract ('freedom from contract')[47] which leads to freedom to break off negotiations.[48] In each of the selected jurisdictions it is possible to say that the principle of good faith balances this freedom and, consequently, that a party who breaks off negotiations may be held liable.[49] It appears that the division between the selected jurisdictions, on the one hand, and the contrasting jurisdiction, on the other hand, begins here, because the latter does not recognise a general principle of good faith.[50] This book will argue, however, that the recognition (or not) of a principle of good faith does not necessarily have to influence the recognition of precontractual liability, i.e. that this liability can be detached from good faith and can operate in a system, like the contrasting jurisdiction, that only recognises good faith in particular situations.

It is important to bear in mind several points. First, in the selected jurisdictions, liability for breaking off negotiations is only imposed in exceptional circumstances,[51] and the imposition of liability in the paradigm case is subject to exacting requirements precisely because it is the case scenario where it is most difficult to justify the granting of relief.[52] At the same time, it is the case which best evidences the balance that must be found between the freedom to break off and the protection of reliance.[53] This leads to a second point, which is that, unless one is bound by contract or by law to enter into a contract, the freedom not to contract always remains. Thus, the freedom to break off negotiations also always remains. In the selected jurisdictions, the question raised by precontractual liability for breaking off negotiations does not relate to whether one party can be forced to enter into a contract he does

---

47 Nili Cohen, 'Pre-Contractual Duties: Two Freedoms and the Contract to Negotiate' in Jack Beatson and Daniel Friedmann (eds.), *Good Faith and Fault in Contract Law* (Clarendon Press, 1995) p. 27.

48 In Germany, Basil Markesinis, Hannes Unberath and Angus Johnston, *The German Law of Contract: A Comparative Treatise* (2nd edn., Hart, 2006) p. 99; in France, new art. 1112 Cciv; in Chile, Enrique Barros Bourie, *Tratado de Responsabilidad Extracontractual* (Editorial Jurídica de Chile, 2006) p. 1008; in English law, H.G. Beale (ed.), *Chitty on Contracts*, vol. I (33rd edn., Sweet & Maxwell/Thomson Reuters, 2018) para. 2-201.

49 Ingeborg Schwenzer, Pascal Hachem and Christopher Kee, *Global Sales and Contract Law* (OUP, 2012) p. 280.

50 See details in Ch. 7, s. II 1 below.

51 *Ius Commune* (n. 1) p. 431.

52 See Preface text to (n. 5).

53 Similarly, Schwenzer, Hachem and Kee (n. 49) p. 280.

not want, but to whether compensation can be sought by the other party. Although the argument can be made that imposing liability on the party that breaks off forces him, to some extent, to decide to contract rather than pay damages, there is little to support it. This leads to a third point, that the extent of the compensation is limited and does not correspond to the protection of the interest in the benefits that the contract would have produced but to the protection of the interest of the party that has relied on an expectation generated by the other party.[54]

This book will show that if these points are kept in mind, the reservations that jurisdictions, such as the contrasting one, have towards precontractual liability for breaking off negotiations, particularly in the paradigm case, might be overcome.

54 For details see Ch. 6 s. IV below.

CHAPTER 3

RELIANCE IN THE BREAKING-OFF OF NEGOTIATIONS IN GERMAN LAW

According to the theory of *culpa in contrahendo*,[1] from the moment that negotiating parties enter into contractual negotiations, a special relationship (*Sonderrechtsverhältnis*) arises between them by virtue of the law, which imposes on both parties duties of protection and loyalty (*Schutzpflichten*).[2] The culpable violation of these duties may give rise to liability for *culpa in contrahendo* which is governed by the rules of contractual liability (§§276ff BGB).[3] In the current German legal scholarship, the notion of precontractual liability imposed by law is rationalised as a reliance-based 'relationship of obligation' imposed by law (*gesetzliches Schuldverhältnis*).[4] The reliance basis of the doctrine of precontractual liability has also been recognised by the courts. For instance, the *Bundesgerichtshof* has stated that this doctrine is ultimately based upon 'reliance that does not materialize' (*enttäuschtes Vertrauen*).[5] The idea underlying the judgments that refer to *culpa in contrahendo* liability, in its different groups of cases, is that of a general duty to answer for the disappointed trust (*enttäuschtes Vertrauen*) of others in the valid conclusion of a contract.[6] Indeed, in cases of liability for breaking off negotiations there is an

---

1 Explained in Ch. 2 s. I 2 (a).

2 Stephan Lorenz and Wolfgang Vogelsang, case 1, in John Cartwright and Martijn Hesselink (eds.), *Precontractual Liability in European Private Law* (CUP, 2008) p. 33; Hugh Beale and others, *Ius Commune Casebooks for the Common Law of Europe: Cases, Materials and Text on Contract Law* (3rd edn., Hart, 2019) p. 374; BGH, 16 March 1954, LM §276 BGB (Fa) no. 3, translated extract in Arthur von Mehren, 'The Formation of Contracts' in *International Encyclopedia of Comparative Law*, vol. VII (JCB Mohr (Paul Siebeck) and Martinus Nijhoff Publishers, 1992) para. 121.

3 *Ius Commune* (n. 2) p. 437; Lorenz and Vogelsang, case 1, in Cartwright and Hesselink (n. 2) p. 33.

4 Basil Markesinis, Hannes Unberath and Angus Johnston, *The German Law of Contract: A Comparative Treatise* (2nd edn., Hart, 2006) pp. 92, 119.

5 BGH, 12 December 1980, NJW 1981, 1036, as quoted by Werner F. Ebke, 'Federal Republic of Germany' in ICC (ed.), *Formation of Contracts and Precontractual Liability* (ICC Publishing, 1990) p. 48 fn. 18.

6 Dário Moura Vicente, *Da Responsabilidade Pré-Contratual em Direito Internacional Privado* (Almedina, 2001) pp. 250, 336.

expectation as to the future conclusion of a contract that has been disappointed.[7] Some authors have gone as far as to conceive *culpa in contrahendo* as a possible ground of 'reliance liability' (*Vertrauenshaftung*) which would be a 'third way' (*dritte Spur*) between contract and delict.[8]

Although the principles of *culpa in contrahendo* were codified in 2001[9] ('the 2001 reform') and, consequently, precontractual liability now has a statutory basis in German law (§§241(2), 280(1), 311(2)(3) BGB), these paragraphs must be interpreted in relation to the case law which preceded the 2001 reform as, with the codification of these provisions, the legislator intended neither to change the rules of *cic* that had been previously developed by the courts nor to impede their further development by future case law.[10] These paragraphs state:

> §311: Obligations created by legal transaction and similar obligations (2) An obligation with duties in accordance with §241(2) also arises as a result of 1. entry into contractual negotiations, 2. preparations undertaken with a view to creating a contractual relationship if one party permits the other party to affect his rights, his legally protected interest or other interests or entrusts them to that party, or 3. similar business contact. (3) An obligation with duties under §241(2) may also come into existence in relation to persons who are not themselves intended to be parties to the contract. Such an obligation comes into existence in particular if the third party, by laying claim to being given a particularly high degree of trust, substantially influences the pre-contract negotiations or the entering into of the contract.
>
> §241: Duties arising from an obligation (2) An obligation may also, depending on its contents, oblige each party to take account of the rights, legal interests and other interests of the other party.

---

7 e.g. BGH, 14 July 1967, LM §276 BGB (Fa) no. 23, translated extract in Arthur von Mehren and James Gordley, *The Civil Law System: An Introduction to the Comparative Study of Law* (2nd edn., Little, Brown and Company, 1977) p. 842; BGH, 22 February 1989, NJW-RR 1989, 627 (*The newspaper* case), translation in James Gordley and Arthur von Mehren, *An Introduction to the Comparative Study of Private Law: Readings, Cases, Materials* (CUP, 2006) pp. 444–447.

8 Canaris, 'Ansprüche wegen "positiver Vertragsverletzung" und "Schutzwirkung für Dritte" bei nichtigen Verträgen' [1965] JZ 475, as cited by Moura Vicente (n. 6) 337; see text to (n. 65) below.

9 Modernization of the Law of Obligations Act of 26 November 2001, which entered into force on 1 January 2002; Reinhard Zimmermann, *The New German Law of Obligations: Historical and Comparative Perspectives* (OUP, 2005) p. 1.

10 Lorenz and Vogelsang, case 1, in Cartwright and Hesselink (n. 2) p. 34; Markesinis, Unberath and Johnston (n. 4) p. 93; Zimmermann (n. 9) p. 3; Clara Asúa González and José Javier Hualde Sánchez, 'Codificación de la *Culpa in Contrahendo* en el Derecho Alemán' in Antonio Cabanillas Sánchez and others (eds.), *Estudios Jurídicos en Homenaje al Profesor Luis Díez-Picazo*, vol. II (Thomson Civitas, 2003) p. 1418.

> §280: Damages for breach of duty (1) If the obligor breaches a duty arising from the obligation, the obligee may demand damages for the damage caused thereby. This does not apply if the obligor is not responsible for the breach of duty.[11]

From the outset, it is possible to see that the notion of *Vertrauen*, which can be translated as trust or reliance, has a paramount place in the German view of precontractual liability and particularly in the breaking-off of negotiations. The extent of the role it plays and its interaction with other well-known doctrines of the German legal system will be analysed below. The chapter will begin by looking at the precontractual relationship (which is a relationship of reliance) and the precontractual duties that emanate from it (section I). It will continue with the analysis of the requirements of precontractual liability for breaking off negotiations, focusing on the reliance element (section II). It will argue that reliance (*Vertrauen*) is the theoretical basis of this liability, although the chapter will also explore other theoretical bases which have been put forward, particularly good faith and *venire contra factum proprium* (section III). The chapter will finally analyse the distinct situation of breaking off negotiations for the conclusion of a formal contract and lack of formality cases, as these are some of the most controversial cases in this area, and also have a strong reliance element (section IV). The chapter will argue that reliance is the key element for there to be *culpa in contrahendo* liability for breaking off negotiations in German law.

I. THE PRECONTRACTUAL RELATIONSHIP AND PRECONTRACTUAL DUTIES

What has been described as a 'special relationship of trust' arises when negotiating parties start to negotiate and which requires them to consider each other's interests.[12] This relationship imposes on each negotiating party special duties of care, the negligent violation of which can lead to precontractual liability.[13] The reliance basis of this relationship and the duties that it entails regarding the breaking-off of negotiations will be analysed below.

---

[11] Translations from *Ius Commune* (n. 2) pp. 426 and from the German Federal Ministry of Justice website <http://www.gesetze-im-internet.de/englisch_bgb/> accessed 19 April 2019.

[12] Hein Kötz, *European Contract Law* (Gill Mertens and Tony Weir tr., 2nd edn., OUP, 2017) p. 33.

[13] B.S. Markesinis, Werner Lorenz and Gerhard Dannemann, *The German Law of Obligations, Volume I The Law of Contracts and Restitution: A Comparative Introduction* (Clarendon Press, 1997) p. 64.

1. THE PRECONTRACTUAL RELATIONSHIP

Even before the 2001 reform, the courts had already developed the idea that the beginning of contractual negotiations led to the creation of a contract-like relationship of trust (*vertragsähnliches Vertrauensverhältnis*), from which mutual protective obligations originate.[14]

For example, the *Reichsgericht*, in a 1928 judgment, stated that:

> the courts, (…), have recognized that the stage of contractual negotiations, even when they do not lead to the conclusion of a contract, engender a relationship of trust between the parties similar to that arising from a contract, so that the parties are required to observe the customary standard of care.[15]

Along the same lines and in an emblematic case dealing with the breaking-off of negotiations, the *Bundesgerichtshof* held, in a 1970 judgment, that even at the stage of negotiations for the conclusion of a contract, negotiating parties owe each other a duty to have reasonable regard for the legitimate interests of the other party, in view of the relationship of trust created by the negotiations, which is analogous to that existing in a contractual relationship.[16] Later on, the *Bundesgerichtshof* stated that precontractual liability ultimately results from a 'relationship of mutual trust and confidence' (*gegenseitiges Vertrauensverhältnis*).[17] The relevance of the existence of a relationship of trust and confidence in the precontractual stage for the configuration of precontractual liability in German law, was noticed by comparative legal scholars at the early stages of the development of the theory. For example, in the sixties, Kessler and Fine wrote that 'Once parties enter into negotiations for a contract, the sweeping language of the cases informs us, a relationship of trust and confidence comes into existence, irrespective of whether they succeed or fail'.[18] More recent legal scholars have reaffirmed this finding.[19]

---

14 Peer Zumbansen, 'The Law of Contracts' in Mathias Reimann and Joachim Zekoll (eds.), *Introduction to German Law* (2nd edn., Kluwer Law International, 2005) p. 196.

15 RG, 1 March 1928, RGZ 120, 249, 251, translated extract in Arthur von Mehren, *The Civil Law System: Cases and Materials for the Comparative Study of Law* (Prentice-Hall, 1957) p. 491.

16 BGH, 10 July 1970, NJW 1970, 1840 (*The letter* case), translation in *Ius Commune* (n. 2) p. 436. BGH 14 July 1967 (n. 7) also refers to a 'contract-like relationship of trust'.

17 BGH, 12 November 1986, BGHZ 99, 101, quoted by Ebke (n. 5) pp. 39, 48 fn. 18.

18 Friedrich Kessler and Edith Fine, 'Culpa in Contrahendo, Bargaining in Good Faith, and Freedom of Contract: A Comparative Study' (1964) 77 HarvLRev 401, p. 404; e.g. BGH, 20 June 1952, BGHZ 6, 330, translation in Markesinis, Unberath and Johnston (n. 4) pp. 607–609; RG 1 March 1928 (n. 15); RG, 28 November 1923, RGZ 107, 357, 360–363; RG, 5 April 1922, RGZ 104, 265; RG, 24 September 1918, RGZ 95, 58, 60–61.

19 e.g. Nigel Foster and Satish Sule, *German Legal System and Laws* (4th edn., OUP, 2010) p. 471; Bertrand de Coninck, 'Le Droit Commun de la Rupture des Négociations Précontractuelles' in Marcel Fontaine (ed.), *Le Processus de Formation du Contrat: Contributions Comparatives et Interdisciplinaires à L'Harmonisation du Droit Européen* (Bruylant LGDJ, 2002) p. 54;

Although this relationship is often referred to as 'of trust and confidence', the content of these notions sometimes varies regarding their orientation. Generally, the object of the trust and confidence is that each of the negotiating parties is able to rely on the fact that the other party will not violate the duties that arise from the precontractual relationship.[20] Here, the trust dimension of reliance is evidenced in that the negotiating parties place trust or confidence on each other (on their persons) and on their conduct throughout the negotiations. Although they are not yet bound by a contract, they are not complete strangers;[21] they are involved in a relationship that entitles them to rely on one another and imposes duties on each of them as to their conduct during the negotiations, particularly the duty to take each other's interests into account. In this way, Larenz stated that the mere fact of beginning negotiations gives rise to special duties of care and consideration between the parties; an expectation of honest treatment (*Redlichkeitserwartung*) arises and this expectation deserves protection by the legal order as, without it, smooth commercial intercourse (*ein reibungsloser Geschäftsverkehr*) would be impossible.[22] However, the expectation dimension of reliance is also present in that, because a relationship of trust and confidence exists between the negotiating parties, one party is liable if he negligently created the expectation in the other that a contract would be concluded, although he knew or should have known that the expectation could not be realised.[23]

It is important to understand that this idea of a relationship forming between the negotiating parties from the moment that they enter into negotiations is necessary in German law in order to bring the precontractual stage closer to the contractual sphere and, thus, be able to sustain that precontractual liability is governed by the rules of contractual relations.[24]

It was established early on that this liability cannot be governed by the law of delict.[25] The German law of delict presents certain characteristics that have been

---

Alfredo Mordechai Rabello, 'The Theory Concerning Culpa in Contrahendo Precontractual Liability: From Roman Law to the German Legal System – A Hundred Years After the Death of Jhering' in Alfredo Mordechai Rabello (ed.), *European Legal Traditions and Israel* (Harry and Michael Sacher Institute for Legislative Research and Comparative Law, Hebrew University of Jerusalem, 1994) p. 144; Ebke (n. 5) p. 39.

20 Clara Asúa González, *La Culpa in Contrahendo: Tratamiento en el Derecho Alemán y Presencia en Otros Ordenamientos* (Universidad del País Vasco, 1989) pp. 61, 62.

21 Asúa (n. 20) p. 62.

22 Larenz, *Lehrbuch des Schuldrechts*, vol. I Allgemeiner Teil (13th edn., 1982) §9 I p. 101, as cited by von Mehren (n. 2) para. 122.

23 Kessler and Fine (n. 18) p. 404; e.g. RG, 19 January 1934, RGZ 143, 219, English translation in Gordley and von Mehren (n. 7) pp. 443–444.

24 See text to (n. 3) above.

25 Asúa (n. 20) p. 37; Béatrice Jaluzot, *La Bonne Foi dans les Contrats: Étude Comparative des Droit Français, Allemand et Japonais* (Dalloz, 2001) p. 529.

described as 'inadequacies', 'shortcomings' or 'weaknesses'.[26] A first weakness, which is decisive in the scenario of *cic* liability for broken negotiations, is that pure economic loss (which is the type of loss generally caused in situations of liability for broken negotiations) is not recoverable (§823(1) BGB) unless the damage is caused wilfully and in a manner contrary to public policy (§826 BGB). Therefore, wasted expenditure and forgone opportunities caused in cases of liability for broken negotiations will not generally be recoverable in delict.[27] A second shortcoming of the German law of delict, which is decisive in *cic* liability for personal injury cases, is that there is no real vicarious liability, as §831(1) BGB allows the employer to exonerate himself from liability by showing that he carefully selected and supervised his employee, whereas, in contract, §278 BGB imputes the negligence of the employee to the employer without the possibility of exoneration for the latter.[28] The contractual regime presents a further advantage in that it shifts the burden of proof to the defendant in respect of the presence of fault,[29] or rather in respect of the absence of fault, as §280(1) second sentence BGB[30] imposes liability for presumed fault, which means that it is for the debtor to show that he has not been at fault in order to escape liability.[31]

Consequently, the more favourable contractual regime[32] was an important incentive for the German courts to establish the existence of a relationship of mutual trust between the negotiating parties, similar to a contractual relationship, in order to apply the contractual regime to cases of *culpa in contrahendo*.[33] The need to resort to the notion of a contract-like relationship between negotiating parties is not present in jurisdictions such as France and Chile, which, unlike

---

26 Jan Peter Schmidt, 'Sentencias famosas: Alemania. Sobre el caso de los "rollos de linóleo"' (2013) 24 Revista de Derecho Privado Universidad Externado de Colombia 329; Jan von Hein, 'Culpa in Contrahendo' in Jürgen Basedow and others (eds.), *The Max Planck Encyclopedia of European Private Law*, vol. I (OUP, 2012) p. 430; *Ius Commune* (n. 2) p. 437; Basil S. Markesinis and Hannes Unberath, *The German Law of Torts: A Comparative Treatise* (4th edn., Hart Publishing, 2002) p. 59; Werner Lorenz, 'Germany' in Ewoud H. Hondius (ed.), *Precontractual Liability: Reports to the XIIIth Congress International Academy of Comparative Law, Montreal, Canada, 18–24 August 1990* (Kluwer Law, 1991) p. 163; Ebke (n. 5) p. 42; Kessler and Fine (n. 18) p. 406.

27 von Mehren, 'The Formation of Contracts' (n. 2) para. 121.

28 Markesinis, Unberath and Johnston (n. 4) pp. 95, 450.

29 von Hein (n. 26) p. 431.

30 See text to (n. 11) above.

31 Markesinis, Unberath and Johnston (n. 4) p. 446; Peter Huber, 'Contract Formation and Non-Performance in German Law' in Reiner Schulze and Fryderyk Zoll (eds.), *The Law of Obligations in Europe: A New Wave of Codifications* (Sellier, 2013) p. 202.

32 Markesinis, Unberath and Johnston (n. 4) p. 96, point out that there used to be another advantage in the application of the contractual regime regarding the prescription period: contractual claims had a 30-year period whereas delictual claims had a 3-year period. Today, however, the period is 3 years in both cases (§195 BGB).

33 *Ius Commune* (n. 2) p. 437. Also, Peter Jung, 'La Protection de la Confiance en Droit Allemand des Contrats' in Bénédicte Fauvarque-Cosson and Peter Jung (eds.), *La Confiance: 11èmes Journées Bilatérales Franco-allemandes, Paris, 22 et 23 Novembre 2012* (Société de Législation Comparée, 2013) p. 35.

German law, have a general principle of delictual liability covering situations of pure economic loss.[34]

2. PRECONTRACTUAL DUTIES

The 2001 reform codified the judge-made law concept of *culpa in contrahendo* developed from the principle of reliance; particularly in §241(2) BGB, where it established the previously implied duty to take account of the rights, legal interests and other interests of the other party, and in §311(2)(3) BGB, where it provided that this duty also arises out of obligations similar to legal transactions.[35] In other words, the reform recognised the notion of a precontractual relationship that gives rise to precontractual duties.[36] Although the codification does not contain all the details and requirements of *culpa in contrahendo* that have been developed in the case law, these provisions do provide a normative basis for the recognition of the precontractual duties which had been previously identified by legal scholars as originating from the precontractual relationship of trust, and for a compensation claim in case of breach of such duties.[37]

According to §311(2)1, from the moment of entering into contractual negotiations, an obligation with duties in accordance with §241(2) arises. In §241(2), the Code, for the first time, expressly provided for an abstract and general obligation, mutually owed between the parties, to respect the rights and interests of the other party, depending on the content of the relationship of obligation, thereby confirming the previous practice of the courts of implying protective obligations (*Schutzpflichten*) into contracts.[38] The protective obligation (*Schutzpflicht*), in abstract terms, means that one party should not violate the rights and interests of the other party and, broadly speaking, is derived from the principle of *neminem laedere*.[39]

It is important to realise that, although *Schutzpflichten* have traditionally been linked to the protection against bodily harm, *Schutzpflichten* based upon a special relationship between the parties are not restricted to the protection of rights (such as bodily integrity), since the more significant branch in the

[34] Moura Vicente (n. 6) pp. 256–257; Hélène Aubry, *L'Influence du Droit Communautaire sur le Droit Français des Contrats* (PUAM, 2002) p. 327. See Ch. 4 text following (n. 16) and Ch. 5 text following (n. 23) below.

[35] Carsten Herresthal, '10 Years after the Reform of the Law of Obligations in Germany – The Position of the Law of Obligations in German Law' in Reiner Schulze and Fryderyk Zoll (eds.), *The Law of Obligations in Europe: A New Wave of Codifications* (Sellier, 2013) p. 191.

[36] Carlo Castronovo, 'Precontractual Liability' in José Lebre de Freitas and others (eds.), *Estudos em Homenagem ao Professor Doutor Carlos Ferreira de Almeida*, vol. II (Almedina, 2011) p. 231.

[37] Zumbansen (n. 14) p. 196; Asúa and Hualde (n. 10) pp. 1419–1420.

[38] Markesinis, Unberath and Johnston (n. 4) pp. 128, 447.

[39] Markesinis, Unberath and Johnston (n. 4) p. 126.

development of the notion of *Schutzpflichten* has been the gradual increase in recognition of duties aimed at the protection of financial interests, particularly the protection against pure economic loss.[40] These protective duties may arise in the precontractual context and, depending on the case, they may consist of duties not to harm the other party's person or property, to provide the other party with certain types of information, and not to break off very advanced negotiations.[41]

Therefore, the variety of *culpa in contrahendo* case groups that have been developed in the case law are generally grouped under either duties of protection or duties of loyalty (also referred to as duties to respect the trust of others), and one subgroup within the latter is formed by cases of broken negotiations.[42] Another classification distinguishes between duties of information or disclosure (*Aufklärungs- und Auskunftspflichten*) and duties of conservation or to exercise proper care (*Obhuts- und Fürsorgepflichten*),[43] with broken negotiations cases falling into the broadly understood duty of information which has as one of the possible criteria to determine its extension the trust or reliance that has been raised in the other party.[44]

In cases of breaking off negotiations, these duties of loyalty (or information) may be characterised as duties of care based upon mutual reliance,[45] emanating from the special relationship of trust that arises between the negotiating parties as soon as they enter into contractual negotiations. The duty to have regard for the legitimate interests of the other party includes an obligation not to break off negotiations without good reason once one party has induced or encouraged in the other a confident expectation that the contract will definitely be concluded.[46] The culpable violation of such a duty may give rise to liability for *culpa in contrahendo*, according to the requirements that will be analysed in the next section.

II. THE REQUIREMENTS OF PRECONTRACTUAL LIABILITY FOR BREAKING OFF NEGOTIATIONS

Legal scholars have listed the requirements for a successful claim of *culpa in contrahendo* for breaking off negotiations and, amongst these elements, the

---

40 Lorenz (n. 26) p. 177.

41 *Ius Commune* (n. 2) p. 426.

42 Michael Tegethoff, '*Culpa in Contrahendo* in German and Dutch Law – a Comparison of Precontractual Liability' (1998) 5 Maastricht Journal of European and Comparative Law 341, p. 353; de Coninck (n. 19) pp. 55–56.

43 Florian Faust and Volker Wiese, 'Protecting Legitimate Expectations The German Perspective' in Bénédicte Fauvarque-Cosson (ed.), *La Confiance Légitime et L'Estoppel*, vol. 4 (Societé de Législation Comparée, 2007) pp. 123–124.

44 Asúa (n. 20) pp. 63–64.

45 Lorenz (n. 26) p. 177.

46 *The letter* case (n. 16) p. 436; Asúa (n. 20) pp. 155–156.

notions of reliance and expectation are prominent. These requirements are (i) that the negotiating parties entered into a precontractual relationship, having entered into negotiations with a view to concluding a contract; (ii) that one negotiating party, negligently or intentionally, created an expectation in the other that a contract would be (and not merely might be) concluded; (iii) that the claimant was induced to rely on this expectation by the defendant, incurring expenses or forgoing opportunities in a way which was detrimental for him; and (iv) that the defendant broke off the negotiations without a justifiable reason.[47] The elements set out in numbers (ii) and (iii) can be jointly described as the requirement of expectation-based reliance.

The requirement of reliance, particularly in its expectation-dimension, also features prominently in the case law of the *Bundesgerichtshof* on liability for breaking off negotiations. For instance, in a 1967 judgment, it held that

> [A] fault in contractual negotiations that renders one liable for damages can also exist in that one party awakes in the other confidence in the imminent coming into existence of a contract – subsequently not concluded – and thus causes the latter party to incur expenses (…).[48]

Then, in a 1975 judgment, the court again referred to the expectation-dimension of reliance, stating that

> [T]he groundless breaking off of contractual negotiations gives rise to an obligation to compensate for harm caused by violation of trust if the person who breaks off the negotiations had previously, by his conduct, awakened or supported the confidence that the contract would certainly come into existence (…).[49]

According to this case law, three conditions must be met for liability for breaking off negotiations to arise: (i) one negotiating party must have led the other to believe that the conclusion of the contract was certain; (ii) expenses were incurred by the latter in view of the future conclusion of the contract; and

---

47 Joachim Dietrich, 'Classifying Precontractual Liability: A Comparative Analysis' (2001) 21 Legal Studies 153, pp. 177 ff. Also, Moura Vicente (n. 6) p. 249; Asúa (n. 20) pp. 71, 156.

48 BGH 14 July 1967 (n. 7).

49 BGH, 12 June 1975, NJW 1975, 1774, English translation in Markesinis, Unberath and Johnston (n. 4) pp. 609–610; in Raymond Youngs, *Sourcebook on German Law* (2nd edn., Cavendish, 2002) pp. 393–395; and in The University of Texas at Austin's website <www.utexas.edu/law/academics/centers/transnational/work_new/german/case.php?id=1489>. Other examples are: BGH, 6 February 1969, LM §276 BGB (Fa) no. 28, translated extract in von Mehren and Gordley (n. 7) p. 843; *The letter* case (n. 16); *The newspaper* case (n. 7); earlier, RG 19 January 1934 (n. 23); RG 1 March 1928 (n. 15).

(iii) subsequently, the party who led the other to believe in the conclusion of the contract broke off the negotiations without a good reason.[50]

The precontractual relationship of trust that arises when negotiations are entered into and the precontractual duties that emanate from it have been dealt with above;[51] therefore, the remaining requirements will be examined below, placing particular emphasis on the reliance element.

1. THE (CULPABLE) CREATION OF AN EXPECTATION AND INDUCEMENT OF RELIANCE

The theory of *culpa in contrahendo* protects the aggrieved party's reliance interest (*Vertrauensschaden*) and it is said that the scope of this liability 'mirrors its rationale which is not to be found in a party's refraining from a bargain but in his creation of legitimate expectations within the other party that a contract would be brought about'.[52] The *Reichsgericht*[53] and the *Bundesgerichtshof*[54] have accepted the view that liability arises when, during the course of negotiations, one party arouses in the other the trust that the conclusion of the negotiated contract is imminent and the latter is thereby induced to incur expenditure.[55]

Within this requirement of the creation of an expectation of the future conclusion of the negotiated contract and the inducement of reliance on such an expectation by the defendant in the claimant, it is necessary to determine whether an element of fault is required in order to incur in this type of liability and, if so, where it is to be found. It is also crucial to determine the content of the expectation and to explore which criteria can establish the reasonableness or legitimacy of the claimant's reliance on the expectation created by the defendant.

(a) A Fault-Based Liability

Starting from von Jhering's theory, *culpa in contrahendo* has been established by German courts as a general fault-based remedy for loss occurring in the context of contractual negotiations,[56] applying §276 BGB.[57] This paragraph of the Code

---

50 Markesinis, Unberath and Johnston (n. 4) p. 100. Also, Cornelia Feldmann and Manfred Löwisch, '§311' in Heinz-Peter Mansel (ed.), *J. von Staudingers Kommentar zum Bürgerlichen Gesetzbuch*, vol. Buch 2: Recht der Schuldverhältnisse (Sellier, 2012) para. 134.

51 This Ch. s. I.

52 Lorenz and Vogelsang, case 1, in Cartwright and Hesselink (n. 2) p. 36. Also Kessler and Fine (n. 18) p. 404.

53 e.g. RG 19 January 1934 (n. 23).

54 e.g. BGH 16 March 1954 (n. 2); BGH 14 July 1967 (n. 7); and judgments cited in (n. 49) above.

55 BGH 16 March 1954 (n. 2).

56 Markesinis, Unberath and Johnston (n. 4) pp. 94–95; Asúa (n. 20) pp. 79 ff.

57 e.g. RG 19 January 1934 (n. 23); Huber (n. 31) p. 202; Lorenz (n. 26) p. 166.

lays down fault as the basis of liability in the law of obligations generally.[58] Thus, it is said that liability for *culpa in contrahendo*, in keeping with the generally applicable principle governing contractual liability in German law, presupposes fault (at least negligence) and that since the standards of negligence are objective, 'it is sufficient that the party to be held liable deviated from the standards of care and fairness expected under the circumstances'.[59]

Therefore, only a party who by his fault has made the other party expect that a contract will certainly be concluded, but then without good reason (*ohne triftigen Grund*) or for non-pertinent motives (*sachfremde Erwägungen*) breaks off the negotiations, is liable.[60] This fault is manifested in the fact that a person negligently or fraudulently created the expectation on the part of another that a contract would be concluded, although he knew or should have known that this expectation could not be fulfilled.[61] In this way, in a 1962 judgment, the *Bundesgerichtshof* held that compensation is only awarded where one party 'through his earlier behavior, has wrongfully [culpably] (*schuldhaft*) aroused or nourished the trust that the contract was certain to be concluded'.[62] Along the same lines, in *The letter* case, the court stated that the culpable breach of the duty to have reasonable regard for the legitimate interests of the other party, including an obligation not to break off negotiations without good reason once that party has induced or encouraged in the other a confident expectation that the contract will definitely be concluded, may give rise, on the basis of the doctrine of *culpa in contrahendo*, to liability to compensate the other party for the damage suffered by him as a result of its reliance on that expectation.[63]

However, it must be noted that, previously to the 2001 reform, some German authors[64] took a different view, in that they considered that liability for breaking off negotiations should not be based on the doctrine of *culpa in contrahendo* and, consequently, on fault, but on the protection of reliance (*Vertrauenshaftung*).[65] In their opinion, the absence of a duty to conclude a contract implied that

---

58 Markesinis, Unberath and Johnston (n. 4) p. 95.

59 Kessler and Fine (n. 18) p. 406. Also Markesinis, Unberath and Johnston (n. 4) pp. 99, 448.

60 *Ius Commune* (n. 2) pp. 437.

61 Ebke (n.5) p. 42; Kessler and Fine (n. 18) p. 404.

62 BGH, 17 May 1962, BB 1962, 816, quoted by von Mehren, 'The Formation of Contracts' (n. 2) para. 121. Also, BGH 14 July 1967 (n. 7); RG 19 January 1934 (n. 23) p. 444.

63 BGH 10 July 1970 (n. 16) p. 436.

64 e.g. Ballerstedt, Canaris and Larenz, cited by Hugh Beale and others, *Ius Commune Casebooks for the Common Law of Europe: Cases, Materials and Text on Contract Law* (Hart, 2002) p. 254.

65 *Ius Commune* (n. 2) p. 437; Beale and others (n. 64) p. 254. Some Spanish legal scholars, e.g. María Paz García Rubio and Marta Otero Crespo, 'La Responsabilidad Precontractual en el Derecho Contractual Europeo' (2010) 2 InDret Revista para el Análisis del Derecho 1, pp. 4, 26, refer to *cic* liability in German law in terms of *Vertrauenshaftung*. This view is also explained in Asúa (n. 20) p. 162.

breaking off negotiations could never constitute fault and, therefore, liability should not be based on the violation of a pre-contractual duty.[66]

Under this approach there is a strong analogy with §122 BGB, according to which, if the mistaken party avoids the contract, the other party (as long as he is innocent) can claim his reliance interest, but capped at the value of the expectation interest. Although this paragraph compensates the other party's reliance interest in the case of a failed contract, it establishes a strict liability[67] as it does not depend on a negligent or otherwise blameworthy behaviour of the party avoiding the declaration.[68] Paying compensation to the other party is the 'price' to be paid for having the contract set aside.[69] Thus, it is argued that in §122 the underlying principle is not the fault-based doctrine of *culpa in contrahendo* but the reliance principle.[70] However, *culpa in contrahendo* and §122 are connected by the principle that justified reliance is entitled to legal protection.[71]

Some of the *Bundesgerichtshof's* Senates adopted this *Vertrauenshaftung* approach.[72] For instance, in a 1969 decision, the *Bundesgerichtshof* held that damages were recoverable if the breaking-off of negotiations was 'without plausible or weighty ground' (*ohne triftigen Grund*) and the injured party's reliance on the ultimate conclusion of the contract was reasonable and induced by the other party's conduct.[73] In this case, the court drew an express analogy to §122 BGB and based its decision on the disappointment of trust:

> If thereafter he refuses to contract without an appropriate ground and thus disappoints the trust that has been awakened in the other's party, the factual and legal situation is similar to a case in which a contract has, (...), come into existence, but one party later impugns it because of error.[74]

In a 1975 decision, the *Bundesgerichtshof* held that 'The basis of liability for fault in contractual negotiations is disappointed trust'.[75] And in *The newspaper* case, the *Bundesgerichtshof* maintained this view, holding that liability for losses suffered at the precontractual stage arises only if one of the parties, in the course

66 Beale and others (n. 64) p. 254.
67 Markesinis, Unberath and Johnston (n. 4) p. 94; Reinhard Zimmermann, *Roman Law, Contemporary Law, European Law: The Civilian Tradition Today* (OUP, 2001) p. 89.
68 Faust and Wiese (n. 43) p. 122; *Ius Commune* (n. 2) p. 476.
69 Markesinis, Unberath and Johnston (n. 4) p. 94.
70 *Ius Commune* (n. 2) p. 476.
71 von Mehren (n. 2) para. 26.
72 e.g. BGH 6 February 1969 (n. 49), BGH 12 June 1975 (n. 49), BGH 22 February 1989 (n. 7).
73 BGH 6 February 1969 (n. 49), as quoted by von Mehren, 'The Formation of Contracts' (n. 2) para. 121.
74 BGH 6 February 1969 (n. 49).
75 BGH 12 June 1975, translation in Youngs (n. 49) p. 395. The translation in The University of Texas at Austin's website (n. 49) refers to 'disappointed expectations'.

of the negotiations, creates the impression in the other party, and the latter actually and reasonably relies upon it, that the contract will be concluded, but nevertheless breaks off the negotiations without reasonable grounds.[76] The court used the language of 'trust' (*Vertrauen*) stating that

> A duty to pay compensation only exists when a partner to the negotiations is accountable for awakening in the other party the trust – justifiable from his point of view – that a contract will certainly come to be, and then breaks off contractual negotiations without a sufficient reason (...).[77]

Therefore, according to this decision, precontractual liability can arise as a result of the disappointment of an expectation of the future conclusion of the negotiated contract where negotiations are broken off without good reason, it not being necessary to show any culpable creation of such an expectation.[78]

Thus, it can be seen that the difference between the *culpa in contrahendo* and the *Vertrauenshaftung* approach is that only under *culpa in contrahendo* is fault required, but the other elements of liability remain the same under both views (one party has made the other expect that a contract will certainly be concluded and has broken off the negotiations without good reason).[79] It has been pointed out that the practical importance of this difference is very limited because it is difficult to imagine a situation where a party who breaks off negotiations without a good reason, after having induced the other party to believe that a contract would certainly be concluded, has not acted at least negligently.[80]

Some authors, commenting on *The newspaper* decision, have indicated that, although according to this judgment it is not necessary to show a culpable creation of the expectation, it is still necessary to show a legitimate or justifiable expectation (*berechtigte Vertrauen*) on the part of the claimant that a contract will be concluded, and that it is difficult to conceive of situations where such an expectation might be established without words or conduct on the part of the defendant which, objectively seen, could reasonably give rise to such an expectation.[81] Therefore, engaging in such conduct by the defendant, where the conclusion of the contract is not a certainty (unless there is a good reason that justifies the defendant's breaking-off), must surely be negligent.[82]

Consequently, although the discussion between a fault-based or a reliance-based approach can maintain a theoretical relevance, in practice it has none

76 BGH 22 February 1989 (n. 7), as explained by Ebke (n. 5) p. 43.
77 BGH 22 February 1989 (n. 7) p. 446.
78 Dietrich (n. 47) p. 178.
79 Beale and others (n. 64) p. 255.
80 Beale and others (n. 64) p. 255.
81 Dietrich (n. 47) p. 178.
82 Dietrich (n. 47) p. 178.

today, because since the 2001 reform it is undeniable that *culpa in contrahendo* is a fault-based liability[83] and as liability for breaking off negotiations is a type of *cic* liability, it is also undeniably fault-based.[84] Furthermore, the fact that *culpa in contrahendo* is a fault-based liability does not exclude the operation of reliance; quite the contrary, reliance is an essential requirement in the configuration of *cic* liability for the breaking-off of negotiations.[85] Inducing reliance on an expectation of the future conclusion of the negotiated contract is the key aspect of precontractual liability for broken negotiations and whether this can be termed as 'culpable' is of secondary importance in that it most likely can (even if not in a technical sense).[86]

(b) The Place of Fault

Having established that *culpa in contrahendo* is a fault-based liability which requires reliance, it must be pointed out that there is still some room for debate as to where the fault lies: whether in awakening an expectation of the future conclusion of the contract under negotiation where there is no sound basis for a contract being finally concluded, or whether in the subsequent breaking-off of the negotiations without good reason once a culpable creation of such an expectation has taken place.[87]

Some scholars even state that fault only relates to the breaking-off and not to the inducement of reliance in the other party[88] and they base this on cases such as *The newspaper* where negligence in the creation of the expectation was not required but where breaking off negotiations without reasonable grounds was still required for liability to arise.[89] Therefore, according to this view, one party must not induce the other to incur expenses by encouraging his hopes that a contract will be concluded (even though, from an objective point of view, this hope is completely futile), regardless of whether the legitimate expectations of the other party were raised culpably or not.[90] It must be emphasised that, even according to this view, this is not a case of strict liability (as argued by the

83 Breach of a precontractual duty must be due to negligence or intention (§280(1) and §276 BGB considered jointly with §311(2) BGB), Faust and Wiese (n. 43) p. 124; Huber (n. 31) p. 202; Markesinis, Unberath and Johnston (n. 4) p. 313.

84 *Ius Commune* (n. 2) p. 437.

85 See text following (n. 47) above.

86 Markesinis, Unberath and Johnston (n. 4) p. 101, referring to *The newspaper* case (n. 7), point out that it is disputed whether fault 'in the technical sense' is necessary.

87 Dietrich (n. 47) p. 177.

88 e.g. Reinhard Zimmermann and Dirk Verse, case 3, in Reinhard Zimmermann and Simon Whittaker (eds.), *Good Faith in European Contract Law* (CUP, 2000) p. 237.

89 Dietrich (n. 47) p. 178, referring to BGH 22 February 1989 (n. 7).

90 Lorenz and Vogelsang, case 1, in Cartwright and Hesselink (n. 2) p. 35, referring to BGH 22 February 1989 (n. 7).

Vertrauenshaftung writers mentioned above)[91] since the *culpa* (fault) necessary for a claim in *culpa in contrahendo* is established by the fact of breaking off negotiations without a good reason.[92]

It has been argued that the relevance of distinguishing between fault in the creation of an expectation that a contract will be concluded and fault in the breaking-off of negotiations after having created this expectation might be a 'moot point', in that both the creation of an expectation and its subsequent disappointment are needed in order for liability to arise, and that culpability may be found in a combination of both of these elements.[93] However, it is suggested that distinguishing between fault at the level of the creation of the expectation and fault at the level of the breaking-off might be relevant in order to assess whether the requirements of *cic* liability for breaking off negotiations are satisfied.

In this way, it appears that fault will normally be found in the culpable creation of an expectation that a contract will be concluded and in the subsequent breaking-off without a good reason. But, as established in *The newspaper* case,[94] liability for breaking off negotiations could also arise where fault is only present in the breaking-off (lack of a good reason) and not in the creation of the expectation. Liability will not normally arise in the opposite case, i.e. where fault is present in the creation of the expectation (negligent inducement of reliance) but not in the breaking-off (because there is a good reason for breaking off).[95] This is due to the fact that *culpa in contrahendo* liability requires the presence of both elements: creation of an expectation and breaking off negotiations without good reason. Therefore, if there is a good reason for breaking off, even if the expectation of the future conclusion of the contract was created negligently, there would be, in principle, no liability.

Nevertheless, it is suggested that fault in the creation of the expectation has the potential of influencing the courts' assessment of the 'goodness' or 'badness' of the reason for breaking off[96] and, in this way, expectation-based reliance could influence the assessment of the motive. Ultimately, this is because the basis of *cic* liability for breaking off negotiations is expectation-based reliance. Thus, it is proposed that in certain cases (which will most likely be exceptional) a negligently induced expectation of the conclusion of the negotiated contract could outweigh the normally 'good' reason for breaking off; i.e. the strength

91 See (n. 64) above.

92 Lorenz and Vogelsang, case 1, in Cartwright and Hesselink (n. 2) p. 35.

93 Dietrich (n. 47) pp. 177–178.

94 BGH 22 February 1989 (n. 7).

95 In exceptional cases, *dolus* (intentional conduct) in the creation of the expectation can lead to liability even if there was a good reason to break off: see text to (n. 193) below in relation to breaking off negotiations for the conclusion of a formal contract.

96 See in this section, sub-s. 2 below.

of expectation-based reliance could allow the judges to consider as 'bad' or as 'non-exculpating' a reason which would normally be considered as 'good' (and which would have excluded liability). The following hypothetical example is proposed: two businessmen (A and B) have been negotiating for some time the sublease of a machine by A to B. The machine is owned by C (the current lessor) who is not involved in the negotiations. The negotiations are well advanced and the future sublessee (B) has incurred significant expenses under the expectation that the contract will be concluded, expectation which has been negligently induced by the current lessee and future sublessor (A) who has constantly assured B that the contract will be concluded as soon as he obtains permission to sublet from C; permission which he assures B he is sure to obtain. Before they conclude the sublease, A informs B that he cannot continue the negotiations because C has denied his permission. Although the reason for breaking off appears to be a good reason, as A is legally impeded from subletting without C's permission (§540 BGB), the relevance of B's reliance on the expectation created by A's negligence could, in theory, allow the court to find that the negotiations have been broken off without good reason and that the requirements of *culpa in contrahendo* liability have been met.

It can be concluded that, although distinguishing between fault in the creation of an expectation of the future conclusion of the negotiated contract and fault in breaking off is not usually relevant, as the fault requirement is normally found in a combination of these elements, the distinction may be relevant in cases where fault in the breaking-off suffices, in cases where fault (in the form of *dolus*) in the creation of the expectation suffices, and in cases where fault in the creation of the expectation could potentially influence the assessment of the reason for breaking off and the ultimate finding of liability.

(c) *The Content of the Expectation*

In German law it is emphasised that the expectation or belief which must be created by one negotiating party in the other is that the contract will be concluded with certainty.[97] In *The newspaper* case, the court stated that in order for the risk to be shifted, the claimant needed to show more than merely an expectation that the contract might be concluded, but instead had to show that the defendant had induced the belief that the contract would, with certainty, be concluded.[98] The court held that:

> An express declaration is not required. But the defendant must at least have made its firm will to conclude a contract to appear clearly. That could be accepted, for example,

97 Dietrich (n. 47) p. 181; *Ius Commune* (n. 2) p. 464; BGH 14 July 1967 (n. 7); BGH 12 June 1975 (n. 49).

98 Dietrich (n. 47) p. 181, explaining BGH 22 February 1989 (n. 7).

> if the third defendant had encouraged the plaintiff to take measures that would only be of use if a contract should arise (...).[99]

It has been pointed out that this requirement in German law may go even further than in other jurisdictions, but that, alternatively, it may be understood that the required expectation or belief varies according to the nature of the reliance of the claimant.[100] Therefore, in some situations (for instance, where the defendant has requested specific, onerous tasks or where the claimant has acted in part performance of the anticipated contract with the defendant's knowledge) a lesser expectation may suffice, whereas in other situations (for example, where the claimant has incurred preliminary expenses of his own accord) the expectation induced by the defendant may need to be one of the certain conclusion of the negotiated contract.[101] Other scholars have also argued for flexibility in the requirement that the expectation is that the negotiated contract will definitely be entered into, indicating that a party is liable for *culpa in contrahendo* if he led the other party legitimately to believe 'that a contract would (almost) certainly be concluded' but then, without good reason, refused to go ahead.[102]

It seems that this alternative, more flexible understanding of the content of the expectation as to the future conclusion of the negotiated contract is the better approach for protecting the reliance interest of the aggrieved party.

(d) The Reliance Must Be Justified (Positive Criteria)

The claimant's reliance on an expectation of the future conclusion of the negotiated contract must be legitimate or reasonable,[103] i.e. it must have been justified in the circumstances of the case, and it must have been induced by a representation, silence or conduct of the party who subsequently breaks off the negotiations.[104]

In many cases there are objective circumstances which can be categorised as positive criteria for founding the reasonableness of the reliance and, hence, for finding liability. For instance, the long duration of the negotiations or the very advanced stage that they have reached seem to be decisive[105] or, at least, relevant objective factors. However, *culpa in contrahendo* liability is not established by

---

99 BGH 22 February 1989 (n. 7) p. 447. See also text to (n. 77) above.

100 Dietrich (n. 47) p. 181.

101 Dietrich (n. 47) p. 181.

102 Lorenz and Vogelsang, case 7, in Cartwright and Hesselink (n. 2) p. 203.

103 e.g. BGH 6 February 1969 (n. 49), as cited by von Mehren (n. 2) para. 121, refers to a 'reasonable reliance'; BGH 12 June 1975, translation in Youngs (n. 49) p. 393, to a 'justified expectation'; BGH 22 February 1989 (n. 7) p. 446 to a 'justifiable trust'.

104 *Ius Commune* (n. 2) p. 464.

105 *Ius Commune* (n. 2) p. 464.

the mere lengthy prolongation of the negotiations.[106] An example of an objective factor justifying the belief in the future conclusion of the negotiated contract is the advanced stage of negotiations where agreement on the essential terms of the future contract has been reached.[107] Nevertheless, it must be noted that the *Bundesgerichtshof* does not require agreement on all essential points of the contract for there to be *culpa in contrahendo* liability.[108] In this way, in *The letter* case, the court held that 'The fact that the parties had not yet agreed all the details of the contract to be concluded does not of itself preclude liability in damages (...)'.[109] Knowledge that the other party has incurred expenses relying on the expectation of the future conclusion of the negotiated contract is also a relevant factor,[110] but liability does not arise from the mere fact of knowing that the other party has already incurred considerable expenses.[111]

The test for determining the legitimacy of the expectation that a contract will be concluded is said to be both objective and subjective. Subjective in that it entails a belief in the future conclusion of the contract and objective in that the belief must be founded on objective circumstances.[112] Consequently, if there are no objective reasons for the aggrieved party's belief, he cannot legitimately assume that a contract is very likely to be concluded.[113] However, some argue that the assessment is entirely objective in that the trust or belief must not be understood as a real and personal one, but as a 'general expectation of honesty' (*allgemeine Redlichkeitserwartung*) of a negotiating party, the protection of which is essential to the fluidity of trade.[114] Others have even concluded that the *Bundesgerichtshof* does not determine when trust has been improperly aroused under an objective test but requires that a 'special trust' has been created.[115] It seems that despite the differences in defining the test for the legitimacy of the trust or belief, the end-result is the same because the objective circumstances of the case are those which allow the judges to determine the reasonableness or legitimacy of the reliance.

It can be seen that there is some ambiguity as to defining the criteria that entitle a negotiating party to reasonably rely on the expectation of the future

---

106 Markesinis, Unberath and Johnston (n.4) p. 101; e.g. BGH, 7 December 2000, NJW-RR 2001, 381; *The newspaper* case (n. 7) p. 446.
107 Lorenz and Vogelsang, case 7, in Cartwright and Hesselink (n. 2) p. 204.
108 *Ius Commune* (n. 2) p. 465.
109 BGH 10 July 1970 (n. 16) p. 436.
110 BGH, 18 October 1974, NJW 1975, 43, translated text in *Ius Commune* (n. 2) pp. 399–401.
111 *Ius Commune* (n. 2) p. 437; von Mehren (n. 2) para. 121; e.g. RG, 24 February 1931, RGZ 132, 26; BGH 17 May 1962 (n. 62); BGH 14 July 1967 (n. 7).
112 Lorenz and Vogelsang, case 7, in Cartwright and Hesselink (n. 2) p. 204.
113 Lorenz and Vogelsang, case 7, in Cartwright and Hesselink (n. 2) p. 204.
114 Larenz (n. 22) p. 106, as quoted by Moura Vicente (n. 6) p. 337.
115 Nirk, 'Culpa in Contrahendo – Eine geglückte richterliche Rechtsfortbildung – Quo Vadis?' in Hefermehl (ed.), *Festschrift Philipp Möhring* (1975) 76, as cited by von Mehren (n. 2) para. 122.

conclusion of the negotiated contract, and this has been the subject of criticism by German legal scholars. Medicus, for instance, stated that the *Bundesgerichtshof* 'has not (…) given an exact general formulation of the circumstances in which a negotiating party is able to rely on the conclusion of the contract'.[116] Nevertheless, it is clear that there are some objective circumstances which, if present in a particular case, allow the courts to find that the claimant legitimately relied on the expectation of the future conclusion of the negotiated contract, induced by the defendant.

To sum up the analysis of the reliance element, it can be concluded that the culpable disappointment of legitimate reliance is the basis and key requirement of *culpa in contrahendo* liability for broken negotiations.[117] The emphasis in the case law and in the writings of legal scholars is mainly on the expectation dimension of reliance, i.e. in the creation of an expectation that a contract will be concluded and inducement of reliance on such an expectation.[118] However, the trust dimension is also present in the relationship of trust and confidence that arises between negotiating parties, which allows each party to place trust on the conduct of the other.[119]

2. BREAKING OFF WITHOUT A JUSTIFIED REASON (NEGATIVE CRITERION)

In addition to the precontractual relationship and the reliance requirement analysed above,[120] the lack of a good reason for breaking off is required for precontractual liability to arise. This negative criterion (the reason for breaking off being unwarranted) serves to establish liability. Consequently, if a negotiating party legitimately relied on the expectation that a contract would be concluded, created by the other party's conduct, it is crucial to determine whether the reasons asserted by such party (who then broke off the negotiations) for breaking them off are well-founded; the onus of proof lying with the party who broke off.[121]

The breaking-off is generally considered well-founded if, for the party who broke off, the conclusion of the contract under the circumstances of the case would be 'unconscionable'.[122] An example would be where the reason given by

116 Medicus, 'Verschulden bei Vertragsverhandlungen' in Bundesminister der Justiz (ed.), *Gutachten und Vorschläge zur Überarbeitung des Schuldrechts I* (Haymanns 1981) 496, quoted by von Mehren (n. 2) para. 122.

117 e.g. Jung (n. 33) p. 48; de Coninck (n. 19) pp. 58–59.

118 e.g. cases cited in (n. 49) above.

119 See this Ch. s. I 1 above.

120 In ss. I and II 1 of this Ch.

121 Lorenz and Vogelsang, case 7, in Cartwright and Hesselink (n. 2) p. 204.

122 Lorenz and Vogelsang, case 7, in Cartwright and Hesselink (n. 2) p. 204.

the party breaking off would also frustrate an already concluded contract.[123] A better offer from a third party may be regarded as a good reason for breaking off, but where negotiations have extended over a long period of time or where one party has requested the other to incur precontractual expenses, a better offer from another party may not always justify the breaking-off.[124] It is stated that, in general, the standard for accepting a good reason to break off negotiations should not be 'pitched too high'.[125]

German courts have taken the view that in situations where one negotiating party has led the other to count on the conclusion of the contract, it is a breach of duty to break off negotiations and put forward 'either no reason at all, or only reasons which are irrelevant or factitious'.[126] In several judgments the *Bundesgerichtshof* has referred to breaking off negotiations 'without good reason'[127] or 'without a sufficient reason'.[128] In a 1969 decision, the *Bundesgerichtshof* held that damages were recoverable if the breaking-off was 'without plausible or weighty ground (*ohne triftigen Grund*)'[129] and in later judgments it has referred to its 1969 decision and repeated the *ohne triftigen Grund* formula.[130] Legal scholars have criticised the 'plausible or weighty ground' test as vague and without content[131] and have provided different answers to the question of what is a plausible or weighty ground (*triftigen Grund*).[132] Some, for example, find such a ground only where the basic assumptions on which a party negotiated have disappeared.[133] Others suggest that an acceptable ground for breaking off should be found only in circumstances that would excuse a party under a legal duty to contract from concluding the contract.[134]

Although it is not entirely clear what exactly will constitute a good reason for breaking off negotiations, it has been noted that it seems that any grounds which would justify avoidance of a completed contract will also justify a refusal

---

123 Lorenz and Vogelsang, case 7, in Cartwright and Hesselink (n. 2) p. 204; *Staudinger* (n. 50) para. 137.

124 Zimmermann and Verse, case 3, in Zimmermann and Whittaker (n. 88) p. 237.

125 Zimmermann and Verse, case 3, in Zimmermann and Whittaker (n. 88) p. 237. See text to (n. 96) above for the possible influence of fault in the creation of an expectation in the assessment of the reason for breaking off.

126 Kötz (n. 12) p. 37, citing, e.g. BGH, 8 June 1978, BGHZ 71, 386; BGH, 7 February 1980, BGHZ 76, 343; BGH, 29 March 1996, [1996] NJW 1884.

127 e.g. BGH 10 July 1970 (n. 16) p. 436; BGH 12 June 1975 (n. 49), as translated in Markesinis, Unberath and Johnston (n. 4) pp. 609–610.

128 e.g. BGH 22 February 1989 (n. 7) p. 446.

129 BGH 6 February 1969 (n. 49), quoted by von Mehren (n. 2) para. 121.

130 e.g. BGH 18 October 1974 (n. 110); BGH, 9 November 2012, NJW 2013, 928.

131 e.g. Stoll, 'Tatbestände und Funktionen der Haftung für Culpa in Contrahendo' in Ficker (ed.), *Festschrift Ernst von Caemmerer* (1978) 449, as cited by von Mehren (n. 2) para. 122.

132 von Mehren (n. 2) para. 122.

133 Nirk (n. 115) p. 84, cited by von Mehren (n. 2) para. 122.

134 Stoll (n. 131) p. 450, cited by von Mehren (n. 2) para. 122.

to enter into a contract; thus, a good reason for breaking off negotiations will generally be found where a contract fails due to any impediment originating from the claimant's sphere.[135] It has also been pointed out that it appears that even if there is a good reason for breaking off, the 'guilty' party is still under an obligation to 'warn' the other party that he no longer intends to continue with the negotiations, if he has led the other party to believe that he will conclude the contract and knows that the other party has relied on that, incurring expenses.[136] Finally, reasons that have nothing to do with the negotiations cannot justify the breaking-off.[137]

III. OTHER THEORETICAL BASES OF PRECONTRACTUAL LIABILITY FOR BREAKING OFF NEGOTIATIONS

In cases of broken negotiations, reliance-based *culpa in contrahendo* is not the only doctrine that has a role to play, as other fundamental principles of German law, such as good faith and *venire contra factum proprium*, have also been used as bases to explain the imposition of precontractual liability in such cases. German law, unlike French law, has not developed an 'overarching theory' of abuse of rights (despite having a provision on abuse of rights in §226 BGB)[138] and, consequently, this doctrine has not been advanced as a possible basis of this type of liability, although a reference to the 'inadmissible exercise of legal rights' has been made in at least one judgment relating to lack of formality cases.[139] In German law, preference has been given to the principle of good faith, which was developed at an earlier stage and much more extensively than in French law.[140] This section will therefore explore the role that good faith and *venire contra factum proprium* play in the imposition of *culpa in contrahendo* liability for breaking off negotiations and how they interact with its reliance basis.

---

135 Dietrich (n. 47) p. 179.

136 Markesinis, Unberath and Johnston (n. 4) p. 101; e.g. BGH, 29 March 1996, NJW 1996, 1884, translated text in Markesinis, Unberath and Johnston (n. 4) pp. 610–612.

137 *Ius Commune* (n. 2) p. 465; *Staudinger* (n. 50) para. 137; e.g. BGH 7 February 1980 (n. 126).

138 Simon Whittaker and Reinhard Zimmermann, 'Coming to Terms with Good Faith' in Zimmermann and Whittaker (n. 88) p. 694. See Ch. 4 s. II 2 below for the abuse of rights analysis in French law.

139 Jaluzot (n. 25) p. 367, referring to BGH, 27 October 1967, BGHZ 48, 396, translation in Markesinis, Unberath and Johnston (n. 4) pp. 593–594. Also, see text to (n. 210) below.

140 Whittaker and Zimmermann (n. 138) p. 694; Whittaker and Zimmermann, 'Good Faith in European Contract Law: Surveying the Legal Landscape' in Zimmermann and Whittaker (n. 88) pp. 23, 33.

1. GOOD FAITH

Good faith (*Treu und Glauben*) has a historical connection with the development of the doctrine of *culpa in contrahendo* in German law. Because the drafters of the BGB did not incorporate *cic* into the code as a general provision, the courts and legal scholars, in developing a general doctrine of *cic* from the few provisions of the code that assimilated Jhering's idea of *cic* liability, needed to find a legal basis in the BGB that supported this development.[141] This purpose was served by §242 BGB and *culpa in contrahendo* became 'anchored' in the principle of good faith.[142]

German law has a general clause of good faith in §242 BGB which permeates the whole law of contracts.[143] Despite its wording, which is limited to the manner of performance of the debtor,[144] the principle of good faith contained in §242 is considered to apply to the precontractual stage.[145] §242 has been used as a legal basis to give rise to a host of ancillary or supplementary duties that may arise under a contract (for instance, duties of information, documentation, cooperation, protection, disclosure) and that can also arise in the precontractual stage.[146] In this way, it is said that liability for breaking off negotiations derives from the breach by a negotiating party of its duties to act in good faith towards the other.[147] Under this view, the precontractual duties that emanate from the precontractual relationship are considered to ultimately derive from the principle of good faith.[148] After the 2001 reform, it has been said that the duty of bargaining in good faith as the basis of the doctrine of *culpa in contrahendo* has been established by virtue of the law (§241(2) in combination with §311(2) BGB).[149]

Even if it is considered that the principle of good faith is the basis of liability for breaking off negotiations, it must be realised that good faith interacts with the notion of reliance. Thus, it is considered that the protection of legitimate reliance is based on the principle of good faith,[150] that *Vertrauen* is the ultimate

---

141 See Ch. 2 s. I 2 (a) above.

142 Kessler and Fine (n. 18) p. 404.

143 Markesinis, Unberath and Johnston (n. 4) pp. 121, 119.

144 '§242: Performance in accordance with the principle of good faith. The debtor must perform his obligation in accordance with the requirements of good faith, taking into account the prevailing practice'; translation from *Ius Commune* (n. 2) p. 829. Also, Stefan Vogenauer, '"General Principles" of Contract Law in Transnational Instruments' in Louise Gullifer and Stefan Vogenauer (eds.), *English and European Perspectives on Contract and Commercial Law: Essays in Honour of Hugh Beale* (Hart Publishing, 2014) pp. 296–297.

145 Markesinis, Unberath and Johnston (n. 4) pp. 24, 99.

146 Whittaker and Zimmermann (n. 140) p. 24.

147 Markesinis, Unberath and Johnston (n. 4) p. 99.

148 Moura Vicente (n. 6) p. 249; see this Ch. s. I above.

149 Lorenz and Vogelsang, case 6, in Cartwright and Hesselink (n. 2) p. 173.

150 Jung (n. 33) p. 43.

element protected by good faith and that *Vertrauen* is often constituted by the expectations of the parties.[151] Indeed, the protection of reliance has an important place in the application of §242.[152] Consequently, it is said that a party is entitled to rely on the conclusion of a future contract only if the other party is in breach of his duty to bargain in good faith, i.e. if he has (i) entered into, (ii) continued with or (iii) broken off the negotiations in contravention of the standard of good faith.[153] In the case of breaking off negotiations, the party who ends them is in breach of his duty to bargain in good faith if in the course of the negotiations he made the other party believe that a contract would certainly be concluded, but then, without good reason, refuses to go ahead.[154] Breaking off negotiations after having induced in the other party expectation-based reliance, amounts to a breach of good faith. Therefore, it can be seen that the liability of the party who breaks off negotiations in a manner contrary to good faith is a liability not for the breaking-off, but for breaking off after inducing the other party's reliance that the contract would be concluded.[155] It is important to note that when phrasing this liability in terms of breach of the duty to bargain in good faith, the two essential elements that are required for *culpa in contrahendo* liability to arise in the breaking-off of negotiations do not change (creation of an expectation that a contract will be concluded and breaking off without good reason after having created this expectation in the other party).

Hence, it appears that good faith is not truly the basis of *culpa in contrahendo* liability for breaking off negotiations. While some authors, in their comparative analysis of precontractual negotiations, describe all the different scenarios of precontractual liability (including the breaking-off of negotiations) as types of conduct contrary to precontractual good faith, in the particular case of Germany they point out that none of the different dogmatic bases of precontractual duties that have been suggested by legal scholars, among which are *Treu und Glauben* (good faith) and the *Vertrauensprinzip* (reliance principle), can be said to have been generally accepted.[156] Others lean towards the reliance basis, stressing that, even though, in a way, liability for *culpa in contrahendo* can also be seen as an emanation of §242 BGB (because the close relationship between negotiating parties is considered, in good faith, to give rise to special duties), when discussing *culpa in contrahendo*, German legal authors do not usually refer to 'good faith' but rather to '[reasonable] reliance'.[157] This is reaffirmed by the

---

151 Jaluzot (n. 25) pp. 86–87. Similarly, Whittaker and Zimmermann (n. 140) p. 31.
152 Jaluzot (n. 25) p. 147.
153 Lorenz and Vogelsang, case 1, in Cartwright and Hesselink (n. 2) p. 35; e.g. BGH, 10 January 1996, WM 1996, 738.
154 Lorenz and Vogelsang, case 1, in Cartwright and Hesselink (n. 2) p. 35; e.g. *The letter* case (n. 16) p. 436.
155 *Ius Commune* (n. 2) p. 437.
156 *Ius Commune* (n. 2) pp. 426, 427.
157 Whittaker and Zimmermann (n. 140) p. 27 fn. 115.

previous analysis of the requirements of liability for breaking off negotiations (creation of an expectation and breaking off without good reason), which are not phrased in terms of breach of a good faith duty and where the notion of good faith is hardly mentioned, whereas the notion of reliance is repeatedly used.[158]

This distancing from good faith can be explained by the fact that *culpa in contrahendo* is one of many institutions originally based on the general good faith clause that 'started to lead an independent life',[159] even before the 2001 reform. Thus, not only in the case of *culpa in contrahendo* but also in relation to other legal doctrines, it is said that:

> §242 BGB is often needed merely for a transitory phase until a new rule is sufficiently well established to be able to stand on its own legs: so that 'figuratively speaking, the statutory foundation of §242 could be withdrawn without any risk of having the judge-made edifice collapse'.[160]

Following from this development, and before the 2001 reform, it was said that the approach of German law combined the application of the principle of good faith with an independent notion of *culpa in contrahendo*, in that good faith was the legal basis (§242 BGB) for the recognition of a precontractual duty, but *culpa in contrahendo* provided the legal basis (§276 BGB) for the remedy of its breach.[161] However, the courts rarely followed this tiered argument given by legal scholars and usually based the doctrine of *cic* and precontractual duties directly on §276 without resorting to §242.[162] Therefore, it was stated that precontractual liability in German law was less and less linked to good faith.[163] Today, after the 2001 reform which codified the case law on *culpa in contrahendo*,[164] it is even clearer that it is no longer necessary to find its basis in §242 BGB,[165] notwithstanding the fact that the origin of *cic* in German law can still be historically related to the precept of good faith.[166]

Nevertheless, it is relevant to determine whether good faith still has a role to play in defining the precontractual duties whose breach is remedied by *culpa in*

---

158 See this Ch. s. II above.

159 Whittaker and Zimmermann (n. 140) p. 31.

160 Whittaker and Zimmermann (n. 140) p. 32, quoting Hein Kötz, 'Towards a European Civil Code: The Duty of Good Faith' in Peter Cane and Jane Stapleton (eds.), *The Law of Obligations: Essays in Celebration of John Fleming* (Clarendon Press, 1998) p. 250.

161 Editors' comparative observations to case 1, Zimmermann and Whittaker (n. 88) p. 204. Also Jaluzot (n. 25) pp. 524–525.

162 Jaluzot (n. 25) pp. 361, 368, 525.

163 Jaluzot (n. 25) p. 368.

164 See text to (n. 11) above; Markesinis, Unberath and Johnston (n. 4) p. 24.

165 Zimmermann (n. 9) pp. 3–4; Martijn W. Hesselink, 'The Concept of Good Faith' in Arthur S. Hartkamp and others (eds.), *Towards a European Civil Code* (4th edn., Kluwer Law International, 2011) p. 645.

166 See Ch. 2 s. I 2 (a) above.

contrahendo,[167] or whether the configuration of these duties is today possible without resorting to the notion of good faith, on the basis of §241(2) BGB. This will be analysed in Chapter 6, where it will be argued that although good faith historically served to explain the development and expansion of the doctrine of *culpa in contrahendo*, the latter is not inextricably linked with the former and can function independently from it.[168]

2. *VENIRE CONTRA FACTUM PROPRIUM*

Liability for broken negotiations can also be seen as flowing from the prohibition of going against one's own actions, *venire contra factum proprium*, as deduced from §242 BGB. Under this rationale, liability will be imposed where one negotiating party, by his conduct, created in the other the expectation that the negotiated contract would be concluded and subsequently contradicted his previous conduct by breaking off negotiations without a good reason.[169]

The concept of *venire contra factum proprium* is generally thought to be embedded in the broader principle of good faith (§242), which is one of the 'blanket clauses' (*Generalklauseln*) of the BGB.[170] For this reason, it is said that the concept of *venire contra factum proprium* appears vague and in need of interpretation in order to be rendered more precise.[171] The rationale behind *venire contra factum proprium* is controversial, particularly its justification in the principle of good faith, which is why the prohibition of *venire contra factum proprium* nowadays is frequently attributed to the protection of legitimate expectations[172] and legitimate reliance.[173] The prohibition of *venire contra factum proprium* is also linked to the notion of abuse of rights (which in turn is another emanation of good faith) in that a person exercising a right must not contradict his own previous conduct, provided that he had induced reliance in the debtor.[174]

In order to apply the concept of *venire contra factum proprium*, the following elements are required: (i) a conduct by one person which induced someone else's reliance; and (ii) a subsequent conduct by the first person which conflicts with its previous conduct and which would destroy arrangements the second person

167 As was held before the reform by, e.g. Zimmermann and Whittaker (n. 88) p. 257 in their comparative observations to case 3; Zimmermann and Verse, case 1, in Zimmermann and Whittaker (n. 88) p. 173; Asúa (n. 20) pp. 62–64.

168 See Ch. 6 s. III 3 below.

169 e.g. Zimmermann and Verse, case 3, in Zimmermann and Whittaker (n. 88) p. 237; Tegethoff (n. 42) p. 356; Mordechai Rabello (n. 19) p. 151.

170 Faust and Wiese (n. 43) p. 116; Whittaker and Zimmermann (n. 140) pp. 24–25.

171 Faust and Wiese (n. 43) p. 116.

172 Faust and Wiese (n. 43) p. 116 citing, e.g. Hohloch, Larenz and Wolf, Roth.

173 Jung (n. 33) p. 38.

174 Markesinis, Unberath and Johnston (n. 4) p. 123.

could have reasonably made.[175] These elements can normally be found in cases of broken negotiations where the party who broke off had previously induced reliance in the other as to the future conclusion of the negotiated contract.

However, situations which are considered to fall under the principle of *venire contra factum proprium* lead to liability for the expectation interest (resulting in the party who contradicted itself being bound), whereas situations covered under the principle of *culpa in contrahendo* normally lead to liability for the reliance interest.[176] In this way, it can be seen that the notion of *venire contra factum proprium* is not an appropriate basis of liability for broken negotiations. Nevertheless, sometimes it is difficult to determine whether to apply the rules of *culpa in contrahendo* or the principle of *venire contra factum proprium* and this is particularly evident in lack of form cases.[177]

Therefore, to conclude this section, it is suggested that neither good faith nor *venire contra factum proprium* are the true bases of *culpa in contrahendo* liability for breaking off negotiations in German law. Although *venire contra factum proprium* has a reliance-based rationale which could be equated to that found in cases of liability for broken negotiations, the remedy it leads to is not the appropriate one for these cases. And although good faith might have a role to play in defining the duties whose breach would lead to *culpa in contrahendo* liability, at the core of this liability is the reliance element which is its true basis.

IV. BREAKING OFF NEGOTIATIONS FOR THE CONCLUSION OF A FORMAL CONTRACT AND LACK OF FORMALITY CASES

The breaking-off of negotiations subcategory of *culpa in contrahendo* cases generally relates to negotiations for the conclusion of a consensual contract, which does not require any type of formality to be valid. However, the negotiations that are subsequently broken off could also relate to the future conclusion of a 'formal contract', i.e. a contract which is binding only if a certain formal requirement is met.[178] In this scenario, *culpa in contrahendo* liability is also possible and it will be argued that the reliance element acquires an even greater relevance. Cases of 'breaking off negotiations for the conclusion of a formal contract' must be distinguished from what will be called 'lack of formality' cases in that, in the latter, an agreement has been reached, whereas, in the former, the parties are still

175 Faust and Wiese (n. 43) p. 116, citing BGH, 6 March 1985, NJW 1985, 2589.
176 Faust and Wiese (n. 43) p. 124; *Ius Commune* (n. 2) pp. 437, 457; see Ch. 6 s. IV 1 (a) below.
177 Faust and Wiese (n. 43) pp. 118, 124. See text to (n. 211) below.
178 *Ius Commune* (n. 2) p. 465.

at the stage of negotiating an agreement.[179] Nevertheless, both types of cases fall into the broader category of *culpa in contrahendo* for failed contracts.[180] Lack of formality cases also fall into the broader category of *culpa in contrahendo* liability derived from the flawed conclusion of a contract leading to its invalidity.[181] It will be shown that although in lack of formality cases good faith plays a very relevant role, reliance is still significant.

1. BREAKING OFF NEGOTIATIONS FOR THE CONCLUSION OF A FORMAL CONTRACT

Even though German law is based on the principle of consensualism, it has rules on formalities which are meant to protect the parties 'by ensuring that they enter legal transactions only after serious consideration of the consequences of their acts'.[182] One type of formality is the notarial authentication (*notarielle Beurkundung*)[183] and among the transactions subject to this formality is the contract of sale of land (§311b(1) BGB). The focus of this section will be on this contract as it is very relevant in practice and in the case law.

When negotiations conducted in view of concluding a formal contract (such as the sale of land) are broken off by one party, it has been suggested that the party breaking off cannot be made liable because the other party is never justified in relying on the imminent conclusion of such a contract, since he should know that there will be no binding contract before the formal requirement is fulfilled.[184] It has also been argued that liability in such a case would undermine the purpose of the form requirement, which is to protect a party from over-hasty decisions,[185] particularly in cases of potentially 'dangerous' transactions such as the sale of land.[186]

However, the *Bundesgerichtshof* has held that a party who breaks off negotiations for the conclusion of a formal contract can be liable in *culpa in contrahendo*. For example, in a 1967 decision, it held that:

> The (...) purposes of the formal requirements of BGB §313 [now §311b(1) BGB] (...), in negotiations for the conclusions of contracts for the sale of realty do not exempt the parties from the duties that arise for them from entering into contractual negotiations

---

179 *Ius Commune* (n. 2) pp. 476–477.
180 Markesinis, Unberath and Johnston (n. 4) pp. 99 ff.
181 Markesinis, Unberath and Johnston (n. 4) pp. 99–100. *Ius Commune* (n. 2) p. 474, refers to these cases as of 'knowingly or carelessly entering an invalid contract', emphasising the breach of a duty to inform or warn the other party of the invalidity.
182 Markesinis, Unberath and Johnston (n. 4) p. 81.
183 Markesinis, Unberath and Johnston (n. 4) p. 83.
184 *Ius Commune* (n. 2) p. 465.
185 *Ius Commune* (n. 2) p. 465.
186 Markesinis, Unberath and Johnston (n. 4) p. 84.

> and from the thus created contract-like relationship of trust. Each party owes the other the fulfillment of the duties of informing and clarifying (...) and can in the event of a faulty violation of these duties be liable to compensate for the reliance interest (...).[187]

It has been argued that liability can arise in this scenario because the party breaking off is not liable for the breaking-off itself, but for inducing the other party to act on the belief that a contract would be concluded, i.e. the fault lies in inducing reliance, not in refusing to conclude the contract. And, in providing compensation of the reliance interest, this liability does not undermine the form requirement.[188]

Nevertheless, some legal scholars have disapproved of these decisions in very strong terms and have suggested that in cases where the result would be truly unbearable, §242 BGB could provide a solution.[189] The *Bundesgerichtshof*, in a 1996 judgment,[190] applied these ideas in deciding whether a claim for compensation for loss in the breaking-off of negotiations for the conclusion of a contract of sale of land could be successful, and sought to solve the problem by referring to the line of cases where good faith has been used 'to do away with formal requirements'.[191] It made clear that in the case of negotiations for a formal contract, the conduct of the party breaking off only gives rise to liability if he has deliberately failed in his duty to bargain in good faith,[192] which amounts to requiring *dolus* for a claim based on *culpa in contrahendo*.[193] Thus, it is said that liability will only arise if breaking off negotiations can be regarded as a particularly grave breach of the other party's trust and that, at the very least, this presupposes intentional conduct.[194] The court held that:

> In so far as this follows from the defendant's conduct being a particularly serious breach of good faith, only an intentional violation of the duty of good faith can as a rule be considered as a basis for a claim to compensation for harm under *culpa in contrahendo*, as it amounts to a person pretending to be ready to conclude a contract when he is not (...).[195]

---

187 BGH 14 July 1967 (n. 7). Similarly, BGH 10 July 1970 (n. 16) p. 436.

188 *Ius Commune* (n. 2) p. 465.

189 e.g. Medicus (n. 116) pp. 192, 499, as cited in *Ius Commune* (n. 2) pp. 465–466.

190 BGH 29 March 1996 (n. 136).

191 Markesinis, Unberath and Johnston (n. 4) p. 101. This line of cases is analysed in this s. IV, sub-s. 2 below.

192 Lorenz and Vogelsang, case 3, in Cartwright and Hesselink (n. 2) p. 99, referring to BGH 29 March 1996 (n. 136).

193 Zimmermann and Verse, case 3, in Zimmermann and Whittaker (n. 88) p. 237, referring to the same judgment.

194 Markesinis, Unberath and Johnston (n. 4) p. 101.

195 BGH 29 March 1996 (n. 136) p. 611. Similarly, BGH 9 November 2012 (n. 130) refers to a particularly serious (and usually intentional) breach of a duty of loyalty.

This seems to be the current view.[196] In these cases, the extreme relevance of the reliance element is evidenced, as its presence influences the courts in providing relief in situations where normally there would not be any liability. This supports the claim that, ultimately, the essential element for there to be precontractual liability for breaking off negotiations is the notion of reliance. It is also important to realise that in these cases fault is not required at the level of the breaking-off but at the level of the creation of the expectation. However, it seems that negligence will not suffice and that an increased degree of fault is required in order to reconcile the imposition of liability with the purpose of the form requirement.[197]

2. LACK OF FORMALITY CASES

In these cases an agreement has been reached but without fulfilling the form required for the contract to be valid. Where form is required, its absence will typically make the transaction void (§125 BGB). Nevertheless, a considerable amount of case law has developed in relation to the absence of form in the context of §311b(1) BGB, which has tried to mitigate the rigour of the rule of nullity in certain deserving cases.[198] This line of cases has used good faith 'to do away with formal requirements'[199] in order to protect the party who was induced by the other party to trust that no form was required or that the form would be fulfilled.[200] In these cases, although good faith plays a key role, reliance remains prominent in that one party made the other rely on the conclusion of the contract and then refused to fulfil the required formality. Therefore, along with the principle of good faith, there is a 'strong reliance element'.[201]

According to this case law, in situations where the vendor intentionally or even negligently induced the purchaser to believe that no form was needed, to allow the vendor to reclaim the property, or to deny the purchaser his claim to performance because of the lack of form, could be contrary to good faith.[202]

---

196 *Staudinger* (n. 50) para. 136.

197 Markesinis, Unberath and Johnston (n. 4) p. 101. Also, Peter Mankowski and Michael Müller, 'Formation' in Stefan Leible and Matthias Lehmann (eds.), *European Contract Law and German Law* (Kluwer Law International, 2014) p. 113.

198 Markesinis, Unberath and Johnston (n. 4) p. 85. Also, Konrad Zweigert and Hein Kötz, *Introduction to Comparative Law* (Tony Weir tr., 3rd rev. edn., Clarendon Press, 1998) p. 375.

199 See (n. 191) above. This type of cases may also be classified within the violation of a duty to bargain in good faith, particularly of the precontractual duty to contribute to the conclusion of a valid contract: Lorenz (n. 26) p. 171.

200 Asúa (n. 20) pp. 158, 160; Zimmermann and Whittaker (n. 88) p. 290, in their comparative observations to cases 4 and 5.

201 Lorenz (n. 26) p. 167.

202 Markesinis, Unberath and Johnston (n. 4) p. 85.

Most of these cases have to do with the question whether, according to the principle of good faith (§242 BGB), a party is entitled to specific performance despite the absence of form (i.e. whether the other party's claim of lack of form is contrary to good faith), and the problem of a claim for damages based upon *culpa in contrahendo* is only dealt with subsidiarily.[203] Particularly in §242-relief cases, 'reliance is essential'.[204]

This line of cases started in 1927 with the *Edelmann* decision of the *Reichsgericht*, which held that a plea of violation of good faith or malice 'requires that a party who opposes a plea of lack of form must have been mistaken concerning the legal requirement of form and that this mistake was caused wilfully or negligently (§276 BGB) by the other party to the transaction'.[205] The claim failed on the facts of the case because both parties were aware of the need to observe the formalities. The court reasoned that the defendant's word as a nobleman could not have induced the claimant's reliance on a valid contract since the claimant knew that pre-emption clauses require certification by a notary.[206] Additionally, the court found that the defendants could not be said to have acted culpably at the time when the disputed promises were made, as they had the serious intention at that time to honour their promises and made such promises with this intention in mind.[207]

In 1967, the *Bundesgerichtshof* issued a contrasting decision in a case with very similar facts to the *Edelmann* decision.[208] The court considered that, even though the claimant knew of the lack of formality, the defendant's behaviour was sufficient to make the claimant rely on the validity of the contract. The court also held that, as in cases where one party makes the other erroneously believe that a contract is not subject to form requirements, the defendant was barred by good faith (§242 BGB) from denying its contractual liability since such a denial would amount to *venire contra factum proprium*.[209] The court stated that to argue that the defective form of the contract renders it null and void 'constitutes an inadmissible exercise of its legal rights'.[210]

---

203 Lorenz and Vogelsang, case 11, in Cartwright and Hesselink (n. 2) p. 318. See also text to (n. 226) below.

204 Arthur von Mehren, 'Formal Requirements' in *International Encyclopedia of Comparative Law*, vol. VII (JCB Mohr (Paul Siebeck) and Martinus Nijhoff Publishers, 1998) ch. 10 paras. 183, 211–214, pointing out that German law takes into account several interdependent factors, such as the awareness of the formal requirement, the egregious conduct of one party and the extent of reliance of the other.

205 RG, 21 May 1927, RGZ 117, 121 (*Word as a nobleman*), translation in Markesinis, Unberath and Johnston (n. 4) pp. 591–593, 592.

206 Faust and Wiese (n. 43) p. 117.

207 RG 21 May 1927 (n. 205), as translated in Markesinis, Unberath and Johnston (n. 4) p. 592.

208 BGH 27 October 1967 (n. 139).

209 Faust and Wiese (n. 43) p. 118, explaining BGH 27 October 1967 (n. 139).

210 BGH 27 October 1967 (n. 139).

There is some doubt as to whether in these types of cases the principle of *venire contra factum proprium* should lead to the expectation interest, because these cases could also be dealt with under the principle of *culpa in contrahendo*.[211] In this 1967 case, the court upheld the ruling that the defendant be condemned to convey the premises to the claimant, ordering specific enforcement of the contract.[212] The court also clarified when a contract of sale which is void for lack of form will be binding according to good faith, stating that 'the practice is that this is only the case if not to recognise the contract as valid would lead to a result which would be unbearable for the purchaser and would not only affect him harshly'.[213] These conditions were regarded as fulfilled in this case, as there was a strong reliance element[214] in that one contracting party had given up his own way of life in reliance on the promise made by the other or had assumed a new way of life, which he would have to give up, if the existence of the contract was denied.[215] This decision stands out as an example of bold judicial intervention which set aside the rules of formalities, using an abuse of rights argument that served to justify a cause of action to protect the performance interest.[216]

These two decisions of the *Reichsgericht* and of the *Bundesgerichtshof*[217] have been subject to much criticism by German legal scholars, as, although it is generally accepted that in cases of lack of form the fraudulent or malicious behaviour of one party gives rise to liability for the expectation interest if the other party is not aware of the form requirement,[218] it is highly questionable whether the defendant should also be held liable in cases where the defendant exploited his social or commercial superiority in order to make the claimant refrain from observing a form requirement of which the claimant knew.[219]

It has been the consistent practice of the *Bundesgerichtshof* that specific performance of the contract may only be ordered if the invalidity of the contract for lack of formality would create an 'absolutely unbearable result'

211 Faust and Wiese (n. 43) p. 118; see text to (n.177) above.

212 BGH 27 October 1967 (n. 139).

213 BGH 27 October 1967 (n. 139), as translated in Markesinis, Unberath and Johnston (n. 4) p. 594.

214 A 'relationship of trust' according to Jung (n. 33) p. 39.

215 BGH 27 October 1967 (n. 139), as per translation in Markesinis, Unberath and Johnston (n. 4) p. 594.

216 Markesinis, Unberath and Johnston (n. 4) pp. 85, 124.

217 RG 21 May 1927 (n. 205) and BGH 27 October 1967 (n. 139).

218 Faust and Wiese (n. 43) p. 118, citing Canaris, *Die Vertrauenshaftung im deutschen Privatrecht* (1971) 277, and Hertel, '§125' in *Staudinger Kommentar zum BGB* (2004) para. 112.

219 Faust and Wiese (n. 43) p. 118, citing Larenz and Wolf, *Allgemeiner Teil des Bürgerlichen Rechts* (9th edn., 2004) §27 para. 73, and Reinicke, [1968] NJW 43. Also von Mehren (n. 204) para. 211.

(*schlechthin untragbares Ergebnis*) for the innocent party and not merely a 'harsh one' (*nicht bloß ein hartes Ergebnis*).[220] This is considered to be the case only: (i) if there is a very strong breach of the duty of regard and loyalty by the party claiming the lack of form; or (ii) if the invalidity of the contract would seriously endanger the innocent party's economic viability.[221] The distinction between 'an absolutely unbearable result' and a result which is 'harsh but not unbearable' is disapproved of by most legal scholars because no clear borderline can be drawn.[222]

A 1972 judgment[223] gives a good illustration of what the courts have in mind when deciding these cases, as the *Bundesgerichtshof* considered that the particular and exceptional circumstances of the case (the advanced years of the claimant, the purpose of the transaction, and the fact that compensation for damages would be an inadequate remedy given the possibility of imminent death) all 'weighed heavily' in favour of allowing the claimant to insist on the conveyance of the property.[224] The court highlighted the strong reliance element in the case in that the claimant was an ordinary craftsman and member of the housing cooperative (the defendant), whom he trusted with the choice of a correct and legally sound form for their contract and, consequently, trusted in the validity of the contract.[225]

A party arguing the lack of form of an agreement may be liable for damages on the ground of *culpa in contrahendo* if the invalidity of the contract is in fact harsh but not unbearable for the other party, but this action only lies in exceptional circumstances.[226] Liability on the ground of *culpa in contrahendo* only arises if the party asserting the lack of form was under a duty to take care of the other party's interest in the validity of the contract (*Betreuungspflicht*) and, thus, should have informed the other party of the formality requirements.[227] This duty of care is breached where one party knew or should have known of the formal requirement and the other party did not know and was not under a duty

---

220 Lorenz and Vogelsang, case 11, in Cartwright and Hesselink (n. 2) p. 318; e.g. BGH 27 October 1967 (n. 139); see text to (n. 213) above.

221 Lorenz and Vogelsang, case 11, in Cartwright and Hesselink (n. 2) p. 318. Also, von Mehren (n. 204) para. 209; e.g. BGH, 23 June 1994, DTZ 1994, 339; BGH, 27 June 1988, NJW 1989, 166; BGH, 19 November 1982, BGHZ 85, 315, 319; BGH 27 October 1967 (n. 139); BGH, 3 December 1958, BGHZ 29, 6, 10.

222 Lorenz and Vogelsang, case 11, in Cartwright and Hesselink (n. 2) pp. 318–319 fn. 26, citing, e.g. Larenz and Wolf, *Allgemeiner Teil des Bürgerlichen Rechts* (8th edn., 1997) §27 para. 47. Also Lorenz (n. 26) p. 167 fn. 18.

223 BGH, 21 April 1972, NJW 1972, 1189, translation in Markesinis, Unberath and Johnston (n. 4) pp. 595–597, and in *Ius Commune* (n. 2) pp. 401–402.

224 Markesinis, Unberath and Johnston (n. 4) p. 86.

225 BGH 21 April 1972 (n. 223). Also, von Mehren (n. 204) para. 213.

226 Lorenz and Vogelsang, case 11, in Cartwright and Hesselink (n. 2) p. 319; Lorenz (n. 26) p. 167.

227 Lorenz and Vogelsang, case 11, in Cartwright and Hesselink (n. 2) p. 319.

to inquire regarding formal requirements, and the former negligently failed to inform the latter.[228]

This was the situation in a 1965 case,[229] where the *Bundesgerichtshof* held that *venire contra factum proprium* was inapplicable because the claimant did not act maliciously or fraudulently and because the eviction did not put an intolerable burden on the defendants, but found that the claimant had negligently violated a duty to inform the defendants of the formality requirement and was, therefore, liable under *culpa in contrahendo*.[230] This information duty has been approved of where one party knows that the other is commercially inexperienced and that he relies on his legal expertise in relation to the perfection of the contract (such as in the 1965 case).[231] In this case, emphasis was placed on the existence of a relationship of trust between the parties.[232] Accordingly, the reason for *culpa in contrahendo* liability is not to be found in the refusal to perfect the contract but in the fact that one party has made the other party legitimately believe that a valid contract has already been concluded.[233] However, this 1965 decision has been heavily criticised in the legal literature because it provided for compensation of the expectation interest; and this, even if only in monetary form, is said to circumvent the form requirement.[234]

In a 1974 case, the *Bundesgerichtshof* found that neither relief under §242 BGB nor under *culpa in contrahendo* could be provided. It agreed with the lower courts that relief under §242 was inapplicable because the financial consequences of the nullity were harsh but not intolerable and held that '[f]rom the point of view of good faith the present conduct of the defendants did not conflict with their past conduct';[235] hence, there was no *venire contra factum proprium*. As to the claim for damages, it was dismissed because the requirement that fault was committed by the defendant was not satisfied. Additionally, the court held that precedents, such as its 6 February 1969 judgment, where the court drew an analogy to §122 BGB in a case of compensation for *culpa in contrahendo*,[236] cannot be applied to situations where the law lays down

228 von Mehren (n. 204) para. 215.

229 BGH, 29 January 1965, NJW 1965, 812, translation in Hugh Beale and others, *Ius Commune Casebooks for the Common Law of Europe: Cases, Materials and Text on Contract Law* (2nd edn., Hart, 2010) pp. 420–422.

230 Referring to this case, Faust and Wiese (n. 43) p. 125; von Mehren (n. 204) para. 216.

231 Lorenz and Vogelsang, case 11, in Cartwright and Hesselink (n. 2) p. 319.

232 BGH 29 January 1965 (n. 229), as translated in Beale and others (n. 229) p. 421; von Mehren (n. 204) para. 215.

233 Lorenz and Vogelsang, case 11, in Cartwright and Hesselink (n. 2) p. 319.

234 Faust and Wiese (n. 43) p. 125, citing Flume, *Allgemeiner Teil des Bürgerlichen Rechts II* (4th edn., 1992) §15 III 4c dd, and Larenz, 'Bemerkungen zur Haftung für "culpa in contrahendo"' in *Festschrift für Ballerstedt* (1975) 397, 404 ff. For details of the compensation awarded, see Ch. 6, text to (nn. 247, 248) below.

235 BGH 18 October 1974 (n. 110) p. 400.

236 See text to (n. 74) above.

a formal requirement and that requirement is not met.[237] This decision serves to emphasise that the blameworthiness of each of the parties' conduct, in causing a formally defective contract to be concluded and relied upon, is decisive when seeking relief under *culpa in contrahendo*.[238]

As can be seen, both in cases of breaking off negotiations for the conclusion of a formal contract and in lack of formality cases (and within this second category both in §242-relief cases that lead to specific performance, and in *culpa in contrahendo*-relief cases that lead to damages), reliance plays a fundamental role, as the courts, due to the presence of a strong reliance element which needs protection, have found a way to provide remedies in situations where normally no protection would have been provided.

V. CONCLUSIONS

Reliance on an induced belief or expectation of the future conclusion of the negotiated contract is an essential requirement of *culpa in contrahendo* liability for breaking off negotiations in German law and it is also the theoretical basis of this liability. Although the focus is on the expectation dimension of reliance (the justified belief in the future conclusion of the contract), the trust dimension of reliance is also present in the relationship of mutual trust and confidence (*gegenseitiges Vertrauensverhältnis*) which arises between negotiating parties from the moment they enter into contractual negotiations. The reliance element is also crucial in cases of broken negotiations for the conclusion of a formal contract and in lack of formality cases, although in the latter good faith also plays a fundamental role. In general, regarding liability for breaking off negotiations, good faith appears to play a role in defining the precontractual duties of the parties which must not be breached.

237 BGH 18 October 1974 (n 110) pp. 400–401.

238 von Mehren (n. 204) para. 215.

CHAPTER 4

RELIANCE IN THE BREAKING-OFF OF NEGOTIATIONS IN FRENCH LAW

After several projects to reform the French law of contract and obligations were prepared by academics and by the Ministry of Justice,[1] *Ordonnance* no. 2016-131 of 10 February 2016 on the reform of the law of contract, the general regime of obligations and proof of obligations was published on 11 February 2016 in the Official Journal ('the 2016 reform').[2] This substantial reform of the *Code civil* came into force on 1 October 2016 and is applicable to contracts entered into from that date onwards.[3] *Loi* no. 2018-287 of 20 April 2018 ratified *Ordonnance* no. 2016-131 of 10 February 2016 but modified some of the articles of the *Code civil* introduced by the *Ordonnance*. *Loi* no. 2018-287 entered into

---

1 *Avant-projet de réforme du droit des obligations et de la prescription* ('*Avant-projet Catala*'), English translation in John Cartwright, Stefan Vogenauer and Simon Whittaker (eds.), *Reforming the French Law of Obligations: Comparative Reflections on the Avant-projet de réforme du droit des obligations et de la prescription ('the Avant-projet Catala')* (Hart Publishing, 2009); *Projet Terré pour une réforme du droit des contrats* ('*Projet Terré Contrats*'), text in François Terré (ed.), *Pour une Réforme du Droit des Contrats* (Dalloz, 2009); *Ministère de la Justice, Projet de réforme du droit des contrats* (July 2008, May 2009) ('*2008 Projet de réforme*' and '*2009 Projet de réforme*'), 2009 Project in <http://droit.wester.ouisse.free.fr/textes/TD_contrats/projet_contrats_mai_2009.pdf> accessed 27 April 2019; *Avant-Projet de Reforme du Droit des Obligations, Document de Travail* (23 October 2013) ('*Document de Travail*'); *Projet d'ordonnance du portant réforme du droit des contrats, du régime général et de la preuve des obligations* (25 February 2015) ('*Projet d'ordonnance*') in <http://www.justice.gouv.fr/publication/j21_projet_ord_reforme_contrats_2015.pdf> accessed 27 April 2019, English translation by John Cartwright, Bénédicte Fauvarque-Cosson and Simon Whittaker, in <http://www.textes.justice.gouv.fr/art_pix/Draft-Ordonnance-for-the-Reform-of-the-Civil-Codepdf.pdf> accessed 27 April 2019.

2 Text available in <https://www.legifrance.gouv.fr/affichTexte.do;jsessionid=74426F020D26B97B1D83F5A7C97B077D.tplgfr28s_1?cidTexte=JORFTEXT000032004939&dateTexte=&oldAction=rechJO&categorieLien=id&idJO=JORFCONT000032003864> accessed 27 April 2019; English translation by John Cartwright, Bénédicte Fauvarque-Cosson and Simon Whittaker, commissioned by the *Direction des affaires civiles et du sceau, Ministère de la Justice, République française*, available in <http://www.textes.justice.gouv.fr/art_pix/THE-LAW-OF-CONTRACT-2-5-16.pdf> accessed 27 April 2019, and in John Cartwright, Bénédicte Fauvarque-Cosson and Simon Whittaker, 'Appendix' in John Cartwright and Simon Whittaker (eds.), *The Code Napoléon Rewritten: French Contract Law after the 2016 Reforms* (Hart Publishing, 2017) pp. 409 ff.

3 art. 9 *Ordonnance* no. 2016-131 (n. 2).

force on 1 October 2018.[4] The reform introduced significant modifications to the law of contract and obligations in general, but the most relevant for this book are the new general 'Introductory Provisions',[5] amongst which new article 1104 expressly establishes that contracts must be negotiated in good faith,[6] and the new chapter on 'Formation of Contracts',[7] where new article 1112 expressly recognises liability for breaking off negotiations.[8] The text of article 1112 as introduced by *Ordonnance* no. 2016-131 is the following:

> The commencement, continuation and breaking-off of precontractual negotiations are free from control. They must mandatorily satisfy the requirements of good faith.
>
> In case of fault committed during the negotiations, the reparation of the resulting loss is not calculated so as to compensate the loss of benefits which were expected from the contract that was not concluded.[9]

The text of article 1112 as modified by article 3 of *Loi* no. 2018-287 is the following:

> The commencement, continuation and breaking-off of precontractual negotiations are free from control. They must mandatorily satisfy the requirements of good faith.
>
> In case of fault committed during the negotiations, the reparation of the resulting loss is not calculated so as to compensate neither the loss of benefits which were expected from the contract that was not concluded nor the loss of the chance to obtain such benefits.[10]

---

4 Text of *Loi* no. 2018-287 available in <https://www.legifrance.gouv.fr/affichTexte.do;jsessionid=2174D458B6D96120439528DDB7AF99C1.tplgfr30s_3?cidTexte=JORFTEXT000036825602&categorieLien=id> accessed 27 April 2019.

5 Ch. I of Sub-Title I ('Contract') of Title III ('The Sources of Obligations').

6 See text to (n. 210) below.

7 Ch. II of Sub-Title I of Title III.

8 It is said that new arts. 1112 and 1112-1 Cciv together acknowledge precontractual liability in French written law but without mentioning it explicitly: Pietro Sirena, 'The New Design of the French Law of Contract and Obligations: An Italian View' in John Cartwright and Simon Whittaker (eds.), *The Code Napoléon Rewritten: French Contract Law after the 2016 Reforms* (Hart Publishing, 2017) p. 357.

9 Translation from Cartwright, Fauvarque-Cosson and Whittaker (n. 2) p. 414. Text in French: '*L'initiative, le déroulement et la rupture des négociations précontractuelles sont libres. Ils doivent impérativement satisfaire aux exigences de la bonne foi.*
En cas de faute commise dans les négociations, la réparation du préjudice qui en résulte ne peut avoir pour objet de compenser la perte des avantages attendus du contrat non conclu.'

10 Text in French: '*L'initiative, le déroulement et la rupture des négociations précontractuelles sont libres. Ils doivent impérativement satisfaire aux exigences de la bonne foi.*
En cas de faute commise dans les négociations, la réparation du préjudice qui en résulte ne peut avoir pour objet de compenser ni la perte des avantages attendus du contrat non conclu, ni la perte de chance d'obtenir ces avantages.' As can be seen, art. 3 of *Loi* no. 2018-287 only modified the second para. of art. 1112, clarifying the extent of compensation (see Ch. 6 (n. 204) below), and according to art. 16 I of *Loi* no. 2018-287, the amendments made by this

This is the first article of Sub-section 1 ('Negotiations') of Section I ('Conclusion of Contracts') of Chapter II,[11] which contains two other articles that may also give rise to other cases of precontractual liability: article 1112-1 on the general duty of precontractual information (expressly introducing the notion of *confiance* between contracting parties) and article 1112-2 on the use or disclosure of confidential information. This Sub-section codified the rules that had been developed by the case law, which, consequently, should remain authoritative.[12] Unlike some of its corresponding articles in the reform projects,[13] article 1112 does not expressly indicate that reparation must be made on the basis of delictual liability.[14] Nevertheless, since *la jurisprudence* (the case law) and *la doctrine*

law to art. 1112 are of an interpretative nature. For details as to the extent of compensation in French law, see Ch. 6 s. IV 1 (a) below.

11 The other Sub-ss. of S. I are no. 2 ('Offer and Acceptance'), no. 3 ('Pre-emption Agreements and Unilateral Promises') and no. 4 ('Special Provisions Governing Contracts made by Electronic Means').

12 Ministère de la Justice, *Rapport au Président de la République relatif à l'ordonnance n° 2016-131 du 10 février 2016 portant réforme du droit des contrats, du régime général et de la preuve des obligations* (Journal Officiel 2016) p. 9; Bruno Dondero, 'La Réforme du Droit des Contrats: Ordonnance n° 2016-131 du 10 Février 2016' (2016) 19 JCP éd E 1283 no. 26, referring to new art. 1112; Laurent Leveneur, 'Présentation Générale de la Réforme du Droit des Contrats, du Régime Général et de la Preuve des Obligations' (2016) 5 CCC dossier 2 no. 27; Peter Rosher, 'French Contract Law Reform' (2016) 17 Business Law International 59, 70; Jan Smits and Caroline Calomme, 'The Reform of the French Law of Obligations' (2016) 23 Maastricht Journal 1040, p. 1046; Birke Häcker, '*La Troisième Jeunesse du Code Civil*: A German Lawyer Looks at the Reform of French Contract Law' in John Cartwright and Simon Whittaker (eds.), *The Code Napoléon Rewritten: French Contract Law after the 2016 Reforms* (Hart Publishing, 2017) p. 395.

13 e.g. art. 1111 *Projet d'ordonnance* (n. 1) ('The commencement, continuation and breaking-off of precontractual negotiations are free from control. They must satisfy the requirements of good faith. The person who is at fault in the conduct or breaking-off of the negotiations must make reparation on the basis of extra-contractual liability. Damages are not calculated so as to compensate the loss of profits which were expected from the contract that has not been concluded'); art. 11 *Document de Travail* (n. 1) ('principle of freedom of precontractual negotiations', the text of the art. is the same as of the aforementioned art. 1111); art. 16 of the *2009* and art. 20 of the *2008 Projet de réforme* (n. 1) share the same text: 'The commencement, continuation and breaking-off of precontractual negotiations are free from control. The person who is at fault in the conduct or breaking-off of the negotiations must make reparation on the basis of delictual liability. The fault is especially established when one party has commenced or has continued negotiations without intention of reaching an agreement. Damages are not calculated so as to compensate the loss of profits which were expected from the contract that has not been concluded'.

14 In this aspect, it resembles art. 24 *Projet Terré Contrats* (n. 1) ('The commencement, continuation and breaking-off of negotiations are free, but they must satisfy the requirements of good faith. Fault in the exercise of the ability to break off is a source of liability. It is especially established when one party has commenced or has continued negotiations without having a real intention of reaching an agreement. In no case can damages compensate the loss of profits which were expected from the contract that has not been concluded'); and art. 1104 *Avant-projet Catala* (n. 1) ('The parties are free to begin, continue and break off negotiations, but these must satisfy the requirements of good faith. A break-down in negotiations can give rise to liability only if it is attributable to the bad faith or fault of one of the parties').

(the writings of legal scholars) have from early on established that precontractual liability has a delictual nature,[15] it will continue to be of this nature, unless there is a contractual regulation of the precontractual phase.[16] Therefore, it will continue to be governed by the general principle of delictual liability established in new articles 1240 and 1241 Cciv (they correspond, respectively, to previous articles 1382 and 1383, whose numeration has changed but not their text) which state that:

> Article 1240: Any human action whatsoever which causes harm to another creates an obligation in the person by whose fault it occurred to make reparation for it.
>
> Article 1241: Everyone is liable for harm which he has caused not only by his action, but also by his failure to act or his lack of care.[17]

These articles deal with the law of civil delict and quasi-delict (*délit* and *quasi-délit*), classification which respectively reflects the distinction between intentional fault and unintentional fault (also characterised as recklessness or negligence), which is identified in article 1241 Cciv.[18] The law of delict and quasi-delict is

---

15 e.g. Cass com, 20 March 1972, Bull civ IV no. 93, JCP 1973 II 17543, note Schmidt (*Gerteis c Vilbert-Lourmat*) (*The Hydrotile machine*), translation in Hugh Beale and others, *Ius Commune Casebooks for the Common Law of Europe: Cases, Materials and Text on Contract Law* (3rd edn., Hart, 2019) pp. 437–439; in James Gordley and Arthur von Mehren, *An Introduction to the Comparative Study of Private Law: Readings, Cases, Materials* (CUP, 2006) pp. 440–441; and in Arthur von Mehren and James Gordley, *The Civil Law System: An Introduction to the Comparative Study of Law* (2d edn., Little, Brown and Company, 1977) p. 846; Cass civ 3, 3 October 1972, Bull civ III no. 491, RTDciv 1977, 127, note Durry (*Monoprix*), translation in *Ius Commune* (n. 15) p. 439; Cass com, 11 January 1984, Bull civ IV no. 16; Cass com, 7 April 1998, D 1999, 514, note Chauvel, JCP éd E 1999, 579, note Schmidt-Szalewski (*Sté Laboratoires Sandoz c Sté Poleval*); CA Paris, 10 March 2000, JCP 2001 II 10470, note Violet; Cass com, 12 February 2002, CCC 2002, no. 90, note Leveneur; Olivier Deshayes and Grégory Maître, case 1, in John Cartwright and Martijn Hesselink (eds.), *Precontractual Liability in European Private Law* (CUP, 2008) p. 28; Jacques Ghestin, *Traité de Droit Civil: La Formation du Contrat*, vol. I Le contrat – Le Consentement (4th edn., LGDJ, 2013) p. 530; François Terré, Philippe Simler and Yves Lequette, *Droit Civil: Les Obligations* (11th edn., Dalloz, 2013) p. 203; Philippe Malaurie, Laurent Aynès and Philippe Stoffel-Munck, *Droit des Obligations* (8th edn., LGDJ, 2016) p. 268.

16 *Rapport au Président* (n. 12) p. 9. Also, Ruth Sefton-Green, 'Formation of Contract: Negotiation and the Process of Agreement' in John Cartwright and Simon Whittaker (eds.), *The Code Napoléon Rewritten: French Contract Law after the 2016 Reforms* (Hart Publishing, 2017) pp. 60 and, notably, 64; Esther Arroyo Amayuelas, 'A Spanish Perspective on the General Theory of Contract' in John Cartwright and Simon Whittaker (eds.), *The Code Napoléon Rewritten: French Contract Law after the 2016 Reforms* (Hart Publishing, 2017) p. 372.

17 Translation from Cartwright, Fauvarque-Cosson and Whittaker (n. 2) p. 446.

18 Jean-Sébastien Borghetti, 'The Definition of *la faute* in the *Avant-projet de réforme*' in John Cartwright, Stefan Vogenauer and Simon Whittaker (eds.), *Reforming the French Law of Obligations: Comparative Reflections on the Avant-projet de réforme du droit des obligations et de la prescription ('the Avant-projet Catala')* (Hart Publishing, 2009) p. 273.

based on a single principle of the utmost generality: any fault which causes damage is actionable.[19] For liability to arise under these articles, the fulfilment of three cumulative conditions is required: fault, harm and causation between fault and harm.[20] Therefore, these requirements must be met and proved for liability for breaking off negotiations to arise.[21]

Particular emphasis will be placed on the analysis of the fault requirement, as it is within the configuration of precontractual fault that the reliance element is present in the French view of precontractual liability for breaking off negotiations. The reliance element is embodied in the notions of '*croyance légitime*' (legitimate belief) and '*confiance légitime*' (legitimate confidence or trust) found in the case law[22] and in the writings of legal scholars[23] relating to this liability.

The chapter will begin with an analysis of precontractual fault (section I). It will continue with an examination of the theoretical bases of liability for breaking off negotiations, arguing in favour of *croyance légitime* and *confiance légitime* as opposed to the more traditional notions of abuse of rights and good faith (section II). It will then look at the positive and negative criteria for the finding of liability (section III). It will continue with the analysis of breaking off negotiations for the conclusion of formal contracts and lack of formality cases, in order to compare the situation in France with the developments of German law in this area (section IV). The chapter will argue that reliance is a relevant

---

19 Barry Nicholas, *The French Law of Contract* (2nd edn., Clarendon, 1992) p. 30.

20 Deshayes and Maître, case 1, in Cartwright and Hesselink (n. 15) p. 28.

21 Joanna Schmidt, *Négociation et Conclusion de Contrats* (Dalloz, 1982) p. 105; Hélène Aubry, *L'influence du Droit Communautaire sur le Droit Français des Contrats* (PUAM, 2002) pp. 327–328.

22 e.g. Cass com, 31 March 1992, Bull civ IV no. 145 p. 102; CA Riom, 10 June 1992, RTDciv 1993, 343, note Mestre, appeal rejected by Cass com, 11 October 1994, no. 92-17860 (*SA Auto 26 c SA Rover-France*); Cass com, 26 November 2003, Bull civ IV no. 186, JCP éd E 2004, 738, note Stoffel-Munck (*Manoukian c X et Les Complices*), translation in *Ius Commune* (n. 15) p. 430.

23 e.g. Joanna Schmidt, 'La Sanction de la Faute Précontractuelle' (1974) 72 RTDciv 46, pp. 53–54; Schmidt (n.21) p. 108; Joanna Schmidt, 'L'évolution de la Responsabilité Précontractuelle en Droit Français' in Günter Weick (ed.), *Entwicklung des Deliktsrechts in rechtsvergleichender Sicht* (Metzner, 1987) p. 148; Joanna Schmidt, 'La Période Précontractuelle en Droit Français' (1990) 42 Revue Internationale de Droit Comparé 545, p. 551; Patrice Jourdain, 'Rapport Français' in Association Henri Capitant (ed.), *La Bonne Foi: (Journées Louisianaises) Tome XLIII 1992* (Litec, 1994) p. 128; Patrick Chauvel, 'Note on Cass com 7 January 1997 and 22 April 1997' D 1998 Jur 45, para. 11; Philippe Stoffel-Munck, *L'Abus dans le Contrat: Essai d'une Théorie* (LGDJ, 2000) pp. 111, 207; Denis Mazeaud, 'La Confiance Légitime et L'Estoppel: Rapport Français' in Bénédicte Fauvarque-Cosson (ed.), *La Confiance Légitime et L'Estoppel*, vol. 4 (Societé de Législation Comparée, 2007) pp. 251–252; Philippe Stoffel-Munck, 'Thème 1: Les Pourparlers' (Séminaire en Droit des Contrats, Master 2 Droit Privé Général, Université Paris 1 Panthéon Sorbonne, 2011) p. 4; Bertrand Fages, 'Existe-t-il un *Vertrauensschutz* en Droit Français des Contrats?' in Bénédicte Fauvarque-Cosson and Peter Jung (eds.), *La Confiance: 11èmes Journées Bilatérales Franco-allemandes, Paris, 22 et 23 Novembre 2012* (Société de Législation Comparée, 2013) pp. 24–25.

element for there to be liability for breaking off negotiations in French law, although not to the extent that it is in German law.

I. PRECONTRACTUAL FAULT

Liability for breaking off negotiations can only arise if there is precontractual fault.[24] This is expressly recognised in new article 1112, which refers to 'fault committed during the negotiations.'[25] It is therefore necessary to analyse the meaning of precontractual fault, the need (or not) for it to be qualified, and the place where it is found in the breaking-off of negotiations, in order to subsequently understand the relation and interaction of fault with other doctrines which are traditionally (or even recently) referred to as bases of precontractual liability (*croyance légitime* and *confiance légitime*, *abus de droit*, good faith).

1. THE MEANING OF PRECONTRACTUAL FAULT

There is no specific definition of 'precontractual fault' and it must be subsumed under the general definition of delictual fault.[26] New article 1112, unlike some of its predecessors in the reform projects,[27] does not provide examples of precontractual fault. Fault is not defined by the *Code civil*[28] and the 2016 reform has not changed this, despite the fact that some of the reform projects provided definitions of civil fault.[29] The *Cour de cassation* has preferred not to tie itself to

---

24 Schmidt, 'La Sanction de la Faute Précontractuelle' (n. 23) p. 52; Sefton-Green (n. 16) p. 60.

25 See text of art. 1112 Cciv in text to (n. 10) above.

26 Joanna Schmidt-Szalewski, 'France' in ICC (ed.), *Formation of Contracts and Precontractual Liability* (ICC Publishing, 1990) p. 95; 'France' in Ewoud H. Hondius (ed.), *Precontractual Liability: Reports to the XIIIth Congress International Academy of Comparative Law, Montreal, Canada, 18–24 August 1990* (Kluwer Law, 1991) p. 150; 'La Période Précontractuelle en Droit Français' (n. 23) p. 550.

27 e.g. art. 16 of the 2009 and art. 20 of the 2008 *Projet de réforme* (n. 13) and art. 24 *Projet Terré Contrats* (n. 14) all mention as an example of precontractual fault, commencing or continuing negotiations without intention of reaching an agreement.

28 Borghetti (n. 18) p. 273.

29 e.g. art. 1352(2) *Avant-projet Catala* (n. 1) ('Fault consists of breach of a rule of conduct imposed by legislation or regulation or failure to conform to a general duty of care and diligence'); art. 5 *Projet Terré pour une réforme du droit de la responsabilité civile* ('*Projet Terré Responsabilité*') ('Fault consists in, voluntarily or negligently, committing an unlawful act. An act is unlawful when it violates a rule of conduct imposed by law or by the general duty of care and diligence'), text in François Terré (ed.), *Pour une Réforme du Droit de la Responsabilité Civile* (Dalloz, 2011). A new draft project on the reform of civil liability (*Projet de réforme de la responsabilité civile*) was published by the French Ministry of Justice on 13 March 2017 ('2017 Project on the reform of civil liability'), text available at <http://www.justice.gouv.fr/publication/Projet_de_reforme_de_la_responsabilite_civile_13032017.pdf> accessed 27 April 2019. Art. 1242 of the 2017 Project on the reform of civil liability states that

a particular definition and academic writers have not reached agreement on this issue either.[30] This is an area where French law seems to lack conceptual clarity, as the different explanations provided by *la doctrine* are somewhat hazy and not clearly distinguishable from each other.

Nevertheless, three main views can be identified. The first defines fault under a breach of duty model. Planiol suggested that fault should be defined as breach of a pre-existing obligation.[31] However, the use of the term 'obligation' has been criticised, as this term today is used in reference to the contractual context.[32] Therefore, a number of writers argue that the term 'obligation' should be replaced with that of 'duty' and state that delictual fault consists in the breach of a pre-existing duty.[33] But even here there is disagreement as to whether fault should be defined as the breach of a 'legal duty'[34] or just 'a duty'.[35] The definition of delictual fault as the non-performance of a pre-existing legal duty has been criticised for being inaccurate and vague.[36]

Despite this criticism, it must be noted that even though the concept of duty is not used to define and control the circumstances in which liability for fault may arise (in contrast to the 'duty of care' in the English tort of negligence),[37] this concept is sometimes used to define what fault may be.[38] Therefore, 'while delictual fault may exist in the absence of breach of a duty, breach of a duty will constitute delictual fault'.[39] However, the courts and in particular the *Cour de cassation* do not always specify the nature of the duty that has been breached when they make a finding of fault.[40]

'*[c]onstitue une faute la violation d'une prescription légale ou le manquement au devoir général de prudence ou de diligence*'. ('Fault consists in the violation of a legal rule or the breach of the general duty of care and diligence'). The previous draft project on the reform of civil liability, launched on 29 April 2016 by the French Ministry of Justice (*Avant-projet de loi réforme de la responsabilité civile*), text available at <http://www.textes.justice.gouv.fr/art_pix/avpjl-responsabilite-civile.pdf> accessed 27 April 2019, stated in its art. 1242 that '*[c]onstitue une faute la violation d'une règle de conduite imposée par la loi ou le manquement au devoir général de prudence ou de diligence*'. ('Fault consists in the violation of a rule of conduct imposed by law or the breach of the general duty of care and diligence').

30 Borghetti (n. 18) pp. 273, 278.

31 Marcel Planiol, *Traité Élémentaire de Droit Civil*, vol. II (3rd edn., LGDJ, 1949) p. 324.

32 Borghetti (n. 18) p. 278.

33 Borghetti (n. 18) p. 278. Some still prefer to refer to breach of an obligation, e.g. Aubry (n. 21) p. 332.

34 e.g. Deshayes and Maître, case 1, in Cartwright and Hesselink (n. 15) p. 28.

35 e.g. Geneviève Viney and Patrice Jourdain, *Traité de Droit Civil: Les Conditions de la Responsabilité* (4th edn., LGDJ, 2013) pp. 445, 450–451.

36 Malaurie, Aynès and Stoffel-Munck (n. 15) p. 43.

37 See Ch. 7 s. III 2 (b) below.

38 John Bell, Sophie Boyron and Simon Whittaker, *Principles of French Law* (2nd edn., OUP, 2008) p. 365.

39 Bell, Boyron and Whittaker (n. 38) p. 365.

40 Borghetti (n. 18) p. 279.

A second view, supported by authors who criticise the definition of fault as breach of a duty,[41] defines fault as contravention of a diligence standard, as behaviour different from that of a reasonably diligent person.[42] Fault is thus generally regarded as conduct below the standard of a reasonable man (*un homme normalement avisé*) in the same situation as the defendant.[43] This standard was also characterised as the 'good father of a family' (*bon père de famille*).[44] The assessment of fault is abstract and objective, made by comparing the conduct of the party under scrutiny with the behaviour of a normally diligent man placed in the same circumstances.[45] However, while in principle the courts take an objective standard in deciding what a reasonable man ought to do in any particular circumstance, the looseness of this definition allows considerable room for manoeuvre.[46]

Finally, a third view adopts a reconciliation approach. Some authors point out that the clash between the two previous definitions of fault is less a matter of substance than of terminology.[47] They try to reconcile the definitions of fault by stating that the authors who take the second view (fault as a departure from an expected conduct), necessarily refer to a norm (which is expressed in the conduct of a good father of a family) and, in this way, they are actually defining fault as breach of a rule.[48] According to this view, it seems that almost all French legal scholars agree on a definition of fault as breach of a norm recognised by the law[49] or breach of a general norm of behaviour.[50]

Consequently, many authors consider that there is a 'general norm of social conduct requiring individuals to behave with care and diligence in all circumstances',[51] which is sometimes called a 'general rule of civility'[52]

41 e.g. Noël Dejean de la Bâtie, 'Responsabilité Délictuelle' in André Ponsard and Ibrahim Fadlallah (eds.), *Aubry et Rau: Droit Civil Français*, vol. VI-2 (8th edn., Librairies Techniques, 1989) p. 44 fn. 9.

42 Borghetti (n. 18) p. 278.

43 e.g. Henri Mazeaud, Léon Mazeaud and André Tunc, *Traité Théorique et Pratique de la Responsabilité Civile Délictuelle et Contractuelle*, vol. I (6th edn., Éditions Montchrestien, 1965) 504; Dejean de la Bâtie (n. 41) p. 45; Paula Giliker, 'A Role for Tort in Pre-Contractual Negotiations? An Examination of English, French, and Canadian Law' (2003) 52 ICLQ 969, 979.

44 Borghetti (n. 18) p. 278.

45 Malaurie, Aynès and Stoffel-Munck (n. 15) p. 44; François Chabas, *Discursos y Conferencias sobre Responsabilidad Civil* (Publicaciones Programa de Doctorado en Derecho, Facultad de Derecho, Universidad de Chile, 2014) p. 19; Aubry (n. 21) p. 333; Chauvel (n. 23) para. 9; Schmidt (n. 21) p. 107; Schmidt, 'La Sanction de la Faute Précontractuelle' (n. 23) p. 52.

46 Bell, Boyron and Whittaker (n. 38) p. 365.

47 Viney and Jourdain (n. 35) p. 445.

48 Borghetti (n. 18) p. 278.

49 Borghetti (n. 18) p. 278.

50 Viney and Jourdain (n. 35) p. 457; Deshayes and Maître, case 1, in Cartwright and Hesselink (n. 15) p. 28.

51 Viney and Jourdain (n. 35) p. 457.

52 Jean Darbellay, *Théorie Générale de L'Illicéité en Droit Civil et en Droit Pénal* (Éditions Universitaires, 1955) p. 161.

or a 'fundamental rule of behaviour' implicit in articles 1382 and 1383 (new articles 1240 and 1241) Cciv.[53] The path taken by courts and writers in France is that a negotiator's liability for misconduct is based on breach of the general duty of care[54] and the generality of article 1240 (formerly article 1382) Cciv allows the courts, with the assistance of *la doctrine*, to regulate precontractual behaviour and impose a minimum standard of conduct outside the contractual regime.[55]

Precontractual fault is therefore defined in relation to an abstract model, the standard of the 'reasonable negotiator' who acts in an honest and loyal manner.[56] In the negotiation phase, precontractual fault can be found in three main types of wrongful behaviour: (i) to enter into or maintain negotiations without a real intention to conclude a contract; (ii) to behave wrongfully towards the other party during the negotiations; and (iii) to suddenly break off the negotiations when the other party had good reason to think that the contract was going to be concluded.[57] This third situation is the 'usual case' of fault in breaking off negotiations, i.e. where the belief in the success of the negotiations has legitimately arisen in the victim of the break-off and the author of the break-off cannot justify it by a legitimate reason.[58] It is in this scenario where the expectation-dimension of reliance is recognised. These examples are very general and the existence of fault is left to the judge's interpretation, according to the particular circumstances of the case.[59] The criteria to determine whether there is a culpable breaking-off are not established by the *Cour de cassation*; it is a question of fact over which the *Cour* does not have control.[60] The *Cour*, however, exercises its control over the legal characterisation of the blameworthy behaviour.[61]

2. THE NEED FOR A 'QUALIFIED' FAULT?

The *Code civil* adopts a wide concept of '*faute*' that covers both intentionally and negligently committed harm.[62] In cases of breaking off negotiations, since

53 Marc Puech, *L'Illicéité dans la Responsabilité Civile Extracontractuelle* (LGDJ, 1973) pp. 45–46. This is explained by Borghetti (n. 18) pp. 278–279.
54 Hein Kötz, *European Contract Law* (Gill Mertens and Tony Weir tr., 2nd edn., OUP, 2017) p. 33.
55 Paula Giliker, *Pre-contractual Liability in English and French Law* (Kluwer Law International, 2002) p. 122.
56 Joanna Schmidt-Szalewski, 'Note on Cass com 7 April 1998' JCP éd E 1999, 579; Patrick Chauvel, 'Note on Cass com 7 April 1998' D 1999, 514, para. 12.
57 Deshayes and Maître, case 1, in Cartwright and Hesselink (n. 15) p. 29.
58 Stoffel-Munck, 'Les Pourparlers' (n. 23) p. 4.
59 Deshayes and Maître, case 1, in Cartwright and Hesselink (n. 15) p. 29. See this Ch. s. III 1 below.
60 Schmidt, 'La Sanction de la Faute Précontractuelle' (n. 23) p. 52.
61 Schmidt (n. 21) p. 111; Dejean de la Bâtie (n. 41) p. 45.
62 Giliker (n. 55) p. 120; see text to (n. 18) above.

'precontractual fault' is subsumed under the general notion of 'delictual fault',[63] the gravity of the fault does not matter, i.e. it is not necessary for the claimant to show either an intentional or a serious wrongdoing on the part of the defendant because, in theory, even the slightest fault may lead to liability.[64] However, because liability for breaking off negotiations is a specific area of delictual liability, it could be asked whether a certain particularity, in the form of a supplementary requirement, should exist? This would translate into the need for a 'qualified fault': either an intention to cause harm or acting in bad faith, during the negotiations.[65] There is nothing in article 1240 (formerly article 1382) to suggest such a requirement, but the courts have considered whether liability in the absence of such an intention would extend precontractual liability too far.[66]

The *Cour de cassation*, in its 1972 judgment in the *Monoprix* case, established that delictual liability for breaking off negotiations does not require negotiations to have been broken off with an intention to cause harm to the other party; it considered that negligence was sufficient.[67] In this case negotiations for the purchase of land had been lengthy, the prospective buyer (a supermarket company) had requested the owner of the land to do works on the property, and subsequently withdrew from the negotiations.[68] The court decided that even though the party breaking off had no wrongful intention, its behaviour in pursuing the negotiations was sufficient to hold it liable for delictual liability.[69] Therefore, the existence of an intention to cause harm is a sufficient but not necessary condition for the imposition of precontractual liability.[70]

Nevertheless, a later judgment of the *Cour de cassation* contradicted *Monoprix* in that, in the absence of an intention to cause harm (*volonté de nuire*), it appeared to require at least bad faith in the course of negotiations.[71] This decision received little support from *la doctrine*, which chose to distinguish it on its facts,[72] and has not been followed by the *Cour de cassation*.[73] The defendant

63 See this Ch. s. I sub-s. 1 above.

64 Deshayes and Maître, case 1, in Cartwright and Hesselink (n. 15) p. 28; Schmidt-Szalewski, 'France' in Hondius (n. 26) p. 150; Schmidt, 'La Période Précontractuelle en Droit Français' (n. 23) p. 550.

65 As explained by Chauvel (n. 23) para. 5.

66 Giliker (n. 55) p. 124.

67 Cass civ 3 October 1972 (n. 15).

68 Bell, Boyron and Whittaker (n. 38) p. 306.

69 Deshayes and Maître, case 8, in Cartwright and Hesselink (n. 15) p. 238.

70 e.g. Ghestin (n. 15) p. 562; Giliker (n. 55) p. 125; Chauvel (n. 23) para. 6.

71 Cass civ 1, 12 April 1976, Bull civ I no. 122 p. 98, RTDciv 1977, 127, note Durry.

72 Giliker (n. 55) p. 124; e.g. Georges Durry, 'Note on Cass civ 3 October 1972 and Cass civ 12 April 1976' RTDciv 1977, 127, 129.

73 e.g. Cass com, 12 October 1993, no. 91-19456; Cass com, 22 February 1994, Bull civ IV no. 79 p. 61 (a *légèreté blâmable* was sufficient to find an abuse of the right to break off negotiations); Cass com, 11 July 2000, Bull Joly 2000 no. 288, note Saintourens, PA 2001 no. 57 p. 19, note Dagorne-Labbé.

was an elderly man who had entered negotiations with the claimant (a property developer) for the sale of his land and the negotiations failed due to the refusal of his co-owner to approve the sale. The claimant was unaware of the existence of the co-owner and argued that the defendant was at fault in failing to inform him of this fact. The defendant had agreed in principle to sell his land to the claimant and although no price had been agreed yet, the claimant had proceeded to purchase a neighbouring lot and had had an architect draw up plans for both properties.[74]

Due to the circumstances of the case, considerations of justice rather than of authority prevailed in this judgment,[75] as the *Cour* was not prepared to condemn the defendant (who believed he was the sole owner) and relied on his lack of malicious intent and that he was not in bad faith in agreeing to the sale in principle, in order to justify a 'sympathetic treatment of his plight'.[76] The outcome of the case was fair, because the claimant should not have taken the enormous risk of buying the neighbouring lot without checking the title of the land (as he could easily have done) and he should not have relied on what was said by the defendant (an elderly man inexperienced in land deals).[77] The case could also be viewed as an example of the attitude of the courts in imposing more stringent requirements for the configuration of fault where the claimant is a professional.[78]

This case is an example of the use of the notion of 'bad faith' (*mauvaise foi*) in precontractual liability cases. The difficulty with this notion is that it does not have a precise definition, thus its content has had to be defined by *la doctrine*, and its characterisation is left to the appreciation of the judges.[79] A further difficulty is that it can take either a subjective or an objective meaning.[80] It has been argued that in this case the court is referring to a subjective notion of bad faith.[81] In this way, it can be understood that most authors conclude from precontractual liability cases[82] that a party is liable for breaking off negotiations not only if he intended to harm the other party, but also if he 'acted in bad faith', as they are referring to objective bad faith, which becomes merged or confused with the notion of '*faute*' in terms of negligence.[83] It is bad faith, in particular, to

74 Facts explained in Schmidt (n. 21) p. 109.
75 Schmidt (n. 21) pp. 109–110.
76 Giliker (n. 55) pp. 124–125.
77 Durry (n. 72) p. 129.
78 Schmidt (n. 21) p. 110; see text following (n. 279) below.
79 Béatrice Jaluzot, *La Bonne Foi dans les Contrats: Étude Comparative des Droit Français, Allemand et Japonais* (Dalloz, 2001) p. 368.
80 Subjective bad faith is based on the notion of intention, Jaluzot (n. 79) pp. 94–96.
81 Chauvel (n. 23) paras. 7–8.
82 e.g. *Hydrotile* (n. 15); *Monoprix* (n. 15); Cass civ 12 April 1976 (n. 71); Cass com, 22 April 1997, D 1998 Jur 45, note Chauvel (*Mabo & Co c Iveco France & Co*); *Manoukian* (n. 22).
83 Yannick Dagorne-Labbé, 'Note on Cass com 11 July 2000' PA 2001 no. 57 p. 19.

break off negotiations all of a sudden, without a good reason, at a point where the other party could reasonably expect the conclusion of the contract.[84]

To conclude, fault has not been specially qualified with regard to breaking off negotiations, it simply corresponds to the application of articles 1240 and 1241 (formerly articles 1382 and 1383) Cciv,[85] and breaking off can be blameworthy even if it is due to a simple negligence.[86]

3. THE PLACE OF PRECONTRACTUAL FAULT

Where one party breaks off the negotiations and the other party had good reason to trust that the contract was to be concluded, it is necessary to understand where the fault lies: in the breaking-off itself, in the circumstances that lead to the breaking-off, in the inducement of reliance on an expectation, or in a combination of these criteria.

Since the decision of the *Cour de cassation* in *Manoukian*, which referred to 'the circumstances constituting fault in the exercise of the right unilaterally to break off precontractual negotiations',[87] it has been argued that it is not the breaking-off itself that constitutes an abuse or fault but the circumstances which lead to it.[88] It is said that, in *Manoukian*, the fault lies in having led the other party to believe (*avoir laissé croire*) that the outcome of the negotiations would be successful,[89] while remaining silent about the fact that an agreement had already been concluded with a third party.[90] Deshayes distinguishes between 'fault for breaking off' (*faute de rupture*) and 'fault during the breaking-off' (*faute dans la rupture*) or 'fault in negotiating' (*faute de négociation*) and argues that the former does not exist and that only the latter is conceivable; fault which is foreign to the break-off but committed or revealed in relation to it.[91] Even before *Manoukian*, some authors argued that because it expresses the exercise of a freedom, the

---

84 *Ius Commune* (n. 15) p. 440; e.g. Terré, Simler and Lequette (n. 15) pp. 201–202; Ghestin (n. 15) pp. 537–538; Anne Danis-Fatôme, *Apparence et Contrat* (LGDJ, 2004) p. 481; Jourdain (n. 23) p. 128.

85 Chauvel (n. 23) para. 8.

86 Schmidt (n. 21) p. 111; Schmidt, 'La Période Précontractuelle en Droit Français' (n. 23) p. 550; Danis-Fatôme (n. 84) p. 481; Bertrand de Coninck, 'Le Droit Commun de la Rupture des Négociations Précontractuelles' in Marcel Fontaine (ed.), *Le Processus de Formation du Contrat: Contributions Comparatives et Interdisciplinaires à L'Harmonisation du Droit Européen* (Bruylant LGDJ, 2002) p. 25.

87 Cass com 26 November 2003 (n. 22).

88 *Ius Commune* (n. 15) p. 433.

89 Philippe Stoffel-Munck, 'Note on Cass com 26 November 2003' JCP éd E 2004, 738; see text to (n. 124) below.

90 François Guy Trébulle, 'Note on Cass com 26 November 2003' Droit des Sociétés no. 3 2004 no. 37.

91 Olivier Deshayes, 'Le Dommage Précontractuel' (2004) 2 RTDcom 187, para. 16. This distinction is criticised as artificial by Ghestin (n. 15) p. 566.

breaking-off cannot in itself constitute a fault, and that it is the blameworthy character of the implementation of the negotiations that can justify the existence of an obligation to compensate.[92]

The *Cour de cassation* confirmed *Manoukian* in a 2006 judgment[93] and commenting on this case in its annual report, the court observed that the right of the parties to break off negotiations freely leads to the exclusion of any causal relation between the loss of a chance to benefit from the negotiated contract and the circumstances of the breaking-off where the fault lies.[94] This has been interpreted by some in terms that the decision to break off in itself can never constitute fault[95] and that fault lies in the manner of the breaking-off.[96] However, before *Manoukian*, in cases where the breaking-off was done in a sudden, abrupt or unpredictable manner it could be argued that the breaking-off itself constituted fault.[97] And, after *Manoukian*, Ghestin still argues that in most cases it is the decision itself to break off that is culpable (to have broken off in a blameworthy or abusive way), but that its culpable character is recognised and characterised in relation to the circumstances or reasons for this decision.[98]

The *Manoukian* line of case law has been reaffirmed by new article 1112(2) Cciv in that the fault lies in the exercise of the right to break off and not in the breaking-off itself.[99] Thus, it seems that the place of fault is found in the circumstances which lead to the breaking-off and not in the breaking-off itself. However, it is still possible to consider that the fault lies in the conduct, during the negotiations, of the party who ultimately breaks them off, in inducing a *croyance* or *confiance légitime* in the other party, and that this fault can be evidenced in the presence of certain typical objective circumstances.[100]

---

92 e.g. Aubry (n. 21) p. 333.

93 Cass civ 3, 28 June 2006, Bull civ III no. 164 p. 136, JCP 2006 II 10130, note Deshayes. Also in Cass civ 3, 7 January 2009, Bull civ III no. 5, RTDciv 2009, 113, note Fages; Cass com, 18 September 2012, Bull civ IV no. 163; Cass civ 3, 19 September 2012, Revue des Contrats 2013 no. 1 p. 98, note Deshayes.

94 Cour de cassation, *Rapport Annuel 2006* (La Documentation Française 2006) 399–400, at <https://www.courdecassation.fr/publications_26/rapport_annuel_36/rapport_2006_2284/> accessed 27 April 2019.

95 Olivier Deshayes, 'Note on Cass com 18 September 2012 and Cass civ 19 September 2012' Revue des Contrats 2013 no. 1 p. 98, 99; Olivier Deshayes, 'Note on Cass civ 28 June 2006' JCP 2006 II 10130, p. 1511; Deshayes (n. 91) para. 36.

96 Olivier Deshayes, 'La Rupture des Pourparlers' (2008) 203 PA 4.

97 Chauvel (n. 23) para. 13; Jaluzot (n. 79) p. 363; e.g. Cass com 22 April 1997 (n. 82); Cass com, 7 January 1997, D 1998 Jur 45, note Chauvel (*Eurolocatique & Co c Banque franco-allemande*); CA Rennes, 29 April 1992, Bull Joly 1993 no. 132, note Daigre.

98 Ghestin (n. 15) pp. 562–563.

99 According to *Rapport au Président* (n. 12) p. 9.

100 This 'reliance view' is analysed in this Ch. s. II 1 below and these circumstances are analysed in this Ch. s. III 1 below.

II. THEORETICAL BASES OF PRECONTRACTUAL LIABILITY FOR BREAKING OFF NEGOTIATIONS

At least three different doctrines of French private law have been put forward as possible bases for the delictual liability arising from breaking off negotiations: abuse of rights, good faith and *croyance légitime/confiance légitime*. This section will argue that the appropriate basis of this liability is 'reliance' expressed in terms of *croyance légitime/confiance légitime*. This section will also look at the abuse of rights and good faith explanations, analysing how they interact with the notion of reliance and why they should yield to the reliance account. From the outset, it must be noted that this is not an area of great conceptual clarity in that there are no clear-cut definitions of the concepts and they often intertwine.[101]

1. *CROYANCE LÉGITIME/CONFIANCE LÉGITIME*

Under this basis, the party who breaks off negotiations is not liable for breaking off but for inducing and then disappointing the other party's reliance that the negotiated contract would be concluded.[102] The claimant can thus argue that the defendant had induced in him an 'excessive confidence' that they were going to conclude the contract.[103] The concepts of '*croyance légitime*' (legitimate belief) and '*confiance légitime*' (legitimate confidence or trust) have been proposed by some French authors as criteria for revealing the fault of the party breaking off negotiations.[104] It is through the use of these concepts that the notion of reliance is recognised in precontractual liability for breaking off negotiations in French law, as it is held that '[t]he concept of "legitimate belief" may be related to a certain extent to the common law concept of *reliance*'.[105] These concepts are generally used interchangeably[106] but some authors prefer to use the notion of *confiance légitime* rather than *croyance légitime*.[107] Sometimes these notions are used within other doctrines, such as the doctrines of appearance, coherence and legitimate expectations. The meaning, operation and relevance of these notions

---

101 e.g. abuse, fault, good faith, bad faith, are all 'neighbour' notions which are difficult to define, Malaurie, Aynès and Stoffel-Munck (n. 15) p. 257.

102 *Ius Commune* (n. 15) p. 433. See text to (n. 100) above.

103 Horatia Muir-Watt, Ruth Sefton-Green and Stéphane Reifegerste, case 3, in Reinhard Zimmermann and Simon Whittaker (eds.), *Good Faith in European Contract Law* (CUP, 2000) p. 240.

104 Deshayes and Maître, case 7, in Cartwright and Hesselink (n. 15) p. 202; e.g. authors cited in (n. 23) above.

105 Deshayes and Maître, case 7, in Cartwright and Hesselink (n. 15) p. 202 fn. 19 (also case 5, p. 145 fn. 12).

106 e.g. Ghestin (n. 15) pp. 536–537; Stoffel-Munck (n. 89); Danis-Fatôme (n. 84) p. 479.

107 e.g. D. Mazeaud (n. 23).

and their relation to the concept of 'reliance' in the configuration of liability for breaking off negotiations is analysed below.

(a) Croyance Légitime

The criterion of 'legitimate belief' tends to focus on the victim of the break-off, in that as soon as the victim had good reasons to believe that the negotiated contract was to be concluded, breaking off should be considered wrongful.[108] The belief relates to the future conclusion of the contract (to the expectation dimension of reliance). However, any belief will not do; the belief must be legitimate or reasonable.

The *croyance légitime* may be induced by the conduct of the party who breaks off the negotiations.[109] Examples are: (i) dangling the prospect of the certain conclusion of the contract to the disappointed party;[110] (ii) acting as if the transaction was already made (for instance by letting the other party begin performance, or by accepting partial performance;[111] or by presenting the other negotiating party as his associate),[112] and (iii) the existence of an established climate of trust ('*climat de confiance*') between the negotiating parties.[113]

The *croyance légitime* may also be induced by the existence of certain objective circumstances which influence the assessment of the legitimate belief in the ultimate success of the negotiations, among which the length and high level of advancement of the negotiations must be highlighted.[114] The more advanced the negotiations, the more the *croyance* of the other party in the success of the negotiations is legitimised and the more necessary it will become to provide a serious and objective motive to break off without incurring liability.[115] On the contrary, there are elements which are unfavourable to the finding of a *croyance légitime*, such as the existence of contextual risks or unexpected obstacles ('*aléas*') or the known existence of negotiations with third parties.[116] In the *Adjani* case, the court found that there had been no wrongful breaking-off because:

> [N]othing permits one to say that Mlle Adjani led the *Société Sofracima* to believe with certainly that she would give her consent and sign the contract, (...) shows the reticence

108 Deshayes and Maître, case 7, in Cartwright and Hesselink (n. 15) p. 202 fn. 19.
109 This para. follows Stoffel-Munck, 'Les Pourparlers' (n. 23) p. 4.
110 e.g. Cass com, 15 October 2002, no. 00-13738; CA Rennes, 8 July 1929, DH 1929 p. 548. Also, Schmidt, 'La Sanction de la Faute Précontractuelle' (n. 23) p. 53.
111 e.g. CA Paris 10 March 2000 (n. 15).
112 e.g. Cass com 11 July 2000 (n. 73).
113 e.g. CA Riom 10 June 1992 (n. 22).
114 e.g. Cass com, 18 January 2011, no. 09-14617; *Manoukian* (n. 22); CA Riom 10 June 1992 (n. 22); CA Rennes 29 April 1992 (n. 97). See this Ch. s. III 1 below.
115 Stoffel-Munck, 'Les Pourparlers' (n. 23) p. 7.
116 Stoffel-Munck, 'Les Pourparlers' (n. 23) p. 6.

> of Mlle Adjani, her refusal to commit herself, and the absence of all the things necessary for her to agree to the proposal.[117]

The courts have expressly recognised the influence of this 'legitimate belief' on the fulfilment of the fault requirement in some cases of liability for broken negotiations.[118] Thus, some judgments have established that fault consists in making the other party legitimately believe (*faire croire légitimement*) that they were about to conclude the contract.[119] For instance, the Court of Appeal of Riom held that:

> [W]hen (...) [negotiations] have reached a length and level of intensity such that one party may legitimately believe that the other is about to conclude the contract and in readiness encourages him to incur certain expenses, breaking off such negotiations is wrong, causes loss and gives rise to reparation.[120]

This judgment requires a combination of inducement of reliance by the conduct of the defendant and the presence of objective circumstances, such as the length and level of intensity of the negotiations, in order to found the legitimacy of the *croyance* of the claimant. Other judgments place emphasis on the conduct of the author of the break-off rather than on the belief of the victim of the break-off and refer to the conduct of suggesting or leading the other party to believe (*laisser croire*) that the author of the break-off would contract.[121] Hence, fault generally consists in a sudden U-turn, putting an end to lengthy negotiations which had led the other party to believe in the upcoming conclusion of the contract.[122]

The *Manoukian* judgment[123] (in the particular scenario of parallel negotiations) provides an example of the expectation-based reliance involved in *croyance légitime*, in that the *Cour de cassation*, upholding the decision of the Paris *cour d'appel*, considered that the claimant was entitled to believe that the defendants would conclude the contract. The court placed emphasis on the facts that a draft agreement settling most of the differences between them had been reached, and that the defendants had delayed informing the claimant that a

---

117 CA Paris, 13 December 1984, RTDciv 1986, 97, note Mestre (*Société Sofracima c Isabelle Adjani*), translated text from Gordley and von Mehren (n. 15) p. 443. See text to (n. 144) below. Similarly, Cass com, 5 May 2009, no. 08-10474.

118 Deshayes and Maître, case 7, in Cartwright and Hesselink (n. 15) p. 202; e.g. Cass com 31 March 1992 (n. 22).

119 Danis-Fatôme (n. 84) p. 483.

120 CA Riom 10 June 1992 (n. 22), translated quote by Giliker (n. 55) p. 124. Also, Cass civ 3, 7 October 1997, no 96-10380.

121 Danis-Fatôme (n. 84) p. 483 fn. 401; e.g. Cass com 31 March 1992 (n. 22); CA Paris 10 March 2000 (n. 15); *Manoukian* (n. 22); Cass com, 13 October 2009, no. 08-16634.

122 Malaurie, Aynès and Stoffel-Munck (n. 15) p. 268.

123 Cass com 26 November 2003 (n. 22).

contract had already been concluded with a third party, while letting him believe that the delay in concluding the contract with him was only due to a formality.[124]

(b) Confiance Légitime

The 'legitimate belief' can also be phrased in terms of legitimately trusting that the negotiated contract will be concluded and, so, the notion of *croyance légitime* merges with that of *confiance légitime* regarding liability for broken negotiations. Hence, all that has been said in (a) above in relation to *croyance légitime* is applicable to *confiance légitime.* However, it is important to analyse the particular views on the notion of *confiance légitime* developed by some French legal scholars who base this liability on this notion.

Professor Schmidt-Szalewski has proposed the principle of '*confiance légitime trompée*' (betrayed legitimate trust) as the criterion of fault in the imposition of liability for broken negotiations.[125] This concept was first used by Emmanuel Lévy to explain the basis of liability in general, and a specific example he gave was the *confiance* inspired in the offeree by the promise made by the offeror that he would maintain his offer; *confiance* which was deceived if the offeror did not maintain his offer, making him liable.[126] Schmidt-Szalewski's criterion of *confiance légitime trompée*, which defines precontractual fault, is an illustration of the general notion of delictual fault.[127] Fault consists in deceiving the trust (*tromper la confiance*) in the conclusion of the negotiated contract created in one of the negotiating parties.[128] The degree of trust between the parties increases as negotiations develop towards reaching an agreement.[129] This criterion, however, presents the danger of leading to the admission of too broad a liability to the detriment of the principle of freedom of contract.[130] It is, therefore, necessary to control the application of the notion of *confiance* and to admit its consequences only if the analysis of the facts of the case shows the existence of a 'serious, legitimate, and foreseeable' confidence (*confiance*) created by the conduct of one of the negotiating parties.[131] The appreciation of the legitimacy of *confiance*

---

124 John Cartwright, 'Cour de Cass, 26.11.2003 – "*Perte de Chance*" (Expectation Interest) and Liability of a Third Person in Case of Breaking Off Negotiations: English Case Note' (2005) 13 ERPL 455, p. 457; *Ius Commune* (n. 15) p. 431.

125 See references to Schmidt in (nn. 21, 23) above.

126 Emmanuel Lévy, *La Vision Socialiste du Droit* (Marcel Giard, 1926) pp. 61–63, 80; Emmanuel Lévy, *Les Fondements du Droit* (Librairie Félix Alcan, 1933) p. 51.

127 Schmidt, 'La Période Précontractuelle en Droit Français' (n. 23) p. 554.

128 Schmidt, 'La Sanction de la Faute Précontractuelle' (n. 23) p. 57.

129 Schmidt, 'L'évolution de la Responsabilité Précontractuelle en Droit Français' (n. 23) p. 149; 'La Période Précontractuelle en Droit Français' (n. 23) p. 551. Also, Terré, Simler and Lequette (n. 15) pp. 201–202.

130 Schmidt (n. 21) p. 108.

131 Schmidt (n. 21) p. 108. Translation of Schmidt in Arthur von Mehren, 'The Formation of Contracts' in *International Encyclopedia of Comparative Law*, vol. VII (JCB Mohr (Paul Siebeck) and Martinus Nijhoff Publishers, 1992) para. 123.

can be compared with the 'excusable' character of mistake, in that the analysis must rest on circumstances of fact.[132] Two factors are particularly relevant in determining the legitimacy of *confiance*: the more or less advanced character of the negotiations and the position of the victim of the break-off (whether he is a professional or a layman).[133] Through the notion of *confiance*, French law admits, in an implicit manner, an analogous notion to that of 'substantial reliance' in the doctrine of estoppel used by US courts in the treatment of problems of precontractual liability, where a promise is broadly understood as 'any conduct that brings about an expectation of a contract'.[134]

It is suggested that in Schmidt-Szalewski's criterion of *confiance légitime trompée* the notion of reliance manifests in both its dimensions. The trust-dimension is present in the trust between the parties which increases as negotiations develop, and the expectation-dimension is present in the legitimate confidence in the future conclusion of the negotiated contract which is deceived. One or both dimensions are highlighted in some authors' interpretation of Schmidt-Szalewski's criterion. For instance, Giliker's analysis focuses on the trust dimension: liability will be imposed where the defendant has broken a relationship of trust or mutual confidence between the parties; confidence which does not arise easily. Freedom of contract remains the governing principle but intervention will be justified where the parties are in a close relationship of trust. There is a line that must be drawn between the period where negotiating parties act at their own risk and the stage where negotiations have advanced to a point where a relationship of trust and confidence exists. In the latter stage a party is at fault in breaking off negotiations abruptly and without warning.[135] Danis-Fatôme highlights that the existence of negotiations creates a reciprocal *confiance* between the negotiating parties.[136] Muir-Watt considers both dimensions of reliance, stating that an abusive break-off of negotiations disappoints the *confiance légitime* that the other party could place if not in the success of the negotiations, at least in the relationship that they imply.[137] Deshayes focuses on the expectation dimension, referring to the protection of the legitimate *confiance* that the words or conduct of the party breaking off have given rise to in the other party.[138]

132 Schmidt (n. 21) p. 108.
133 Schmidt (n. 21) p. 108.
134 Schmidt (n. 21) p. 108 fn. 9; 'L'évolution de la Responsabilité Précontractuelle en Droit Français' (n. 23) p. 149. Translation of Schmidt in von Mehren (n. 131) para. 123 fn. 495.
135 Giliker (n. 55) pp. 130–131, 132; Giliker (n. 43) p. 984.
136 Danis-Fatôme (n. 84) p. 484.
137 Horatia Muir-Watt, 'Les Pourparlers: De la Confiance Trompée à la Relation de Confiance' in Pauline Rémy-Corlay and Dominique Fenouillet (eds.), *Les Concepts Contractuels Français à L'heure des Principes du Droit Européen des Contrats* (Dalloz, 2003) p. 61.
138 Deshayes (n. 91) para. 31. Also de Coninck (n. 86) p. 52.

Confiance légitime trompée, which is the criterion of precontractual fault, plays a moralising role in the negotiations period.[139] Hence, liability will arise when, in the interest of justice, the law intervenes to protect the trust developed between the negotiating parties, where the claimant could reasonably expect the negotiated contract to be concluded, by providing a remedy for the detrimental reliance suffered.[140]

The notion of *confiance légitime* can be found underlying most judgments that relate to liability for broken negotiations,[141] particularly in case law which refers to the advanced stage of negotiations and the suddenness with which an established relationship was terminated.[142] For instance, in a 2003 decision, the *Cour de cassation* held that the defendant had provoked in the claimant a *confiance* in the conclusion of the negotiated contract and that the negotiations were sufficiently advanced for him to legitimately believe that they would succeed.[143] In contrast, the *Adjani* case, where the liability of an actress for wrongful breaking-off of negotiations was rejected because there was nothing to allow to say that she had maintained the film company in the certainty that she would sign the contract, is an example of a case where the lack of legitimate *confiance* in the conclusion of the contract entails the rejection of liability.[144] In a judgment of the Court of Appeal of Pau the criterion of *confiance* was implicitly recognised, in that the court rejected liability because it found that the negotiations were too weak, implying that they could not give rise to a sufficiently founded *confiance* in the conclusion of the contract.[145]

Although most of the case law relating to liability for broken negotiations developed from the 1970s onwards,[146] there are older cases imposing delictual liability for broken negotiations based on an implicit notion of *confiance légitime*. For instance, in an 1883 decision of the Court of Appeal of Paris it was found that the abrupt termination of negotiations, one party having given

139 Schmidt, 'La Période Précontractuelle en Droit Français' (n. 23) p. 566. Also, Dagorne-Labbé (n. 83).

140 Giliker (n. 55) p. 132; Clara Asúa González, *La Culpa in Contrahendo: Tratamiento en el Derecho Alemán y Presencia en Otros Ordenamientos* (Universidad del País Vasco, 1989) p. 240.

141 Schmidt, 'L'évolution de la Responsabilité Précontractuelle en Droit Français' (n. 23) p. 149; Danis-Fatôme (n. 84) p. 482.

142 Giliker (n. 55) p. 131; Franck Violet, 'Note on CA Paris 10 March 2000' JCP 2001 II 10470; Dagorne-Labbé (n. 83); Arnaud Lecourt, 'Note on CA Agen 21 August 2002' JCP 2003 II 10162, 1830.

143 Cass com, 25 February 2003, no. 01-12660.

144 CA Paris 13 December 1984 (n. 117); e.g. Danis-Fatôme (n. 84) p. 483; Jacques Mestre, 'Note on CA Paris 13 December 1984' RTDciv 1986, 97, 100.

145 CA Pau, 14 January 1969, D 1969, 716, translated text in Gordley and von Mehren (n. 15) p. 442; Schmidt (n. 21) p. 108 fn. 10.

146 Giliker (n. 55) p. 132.

the other just reason to believe in the strength of their commercial relationship (trust-based reliance), amounted to delictual liability.[147] And in 1893, the Court of Appeal of Dijon imposed liability on the author of the break-off, basing such liability on the assurances as to the future conclusion of the contract that he had made to the other party.[148]

The *Hydrotile machine* case[149] provides an example of the operation of *confiance légitime* in both dimensions of reliance, as, on the one hand, the defendant's knowledge of the claimant's expenses, his retention of an estimate required by the claimant, and his continuance of negotiations had induced the claimant to believe that a contract would ensue (expectation-dimension) and, on the other hand, as negotiations had made considerable progress, the claimant had incurred substantial expenses, in the belief that no obstacle existed to his purchase of the machine. If this latter belief is a consequence of the degree of trust which had developed between the parties (trust-dimension), then it is suggested that both levels of reliance are linked, in that trust in the other negotiating party allows the aggrieved party to believe in the future conclusion of the contract or justifies his *confiance* in the future conclusion of the contract.

(c) Legitimate Expectations

Another notion which is connected to that of *confiance* and has been used to explain liability for broken negotiations is that of *attente légitime* (legitimate expectation). Hélène Aubry proposed a theory according to which the breach of the legitimate expectation of the other party in the future conclusion of the negotiated contract constitutes a fault which gives rise to the application of articles 1382 and 1383 Cciv (new articles 1240 and 1241), and is the basis of the obligation to compensate of the party who breaks off the negotiations.[150]

According to this view,[151] in the period of precontractual negotiations, negotiating parties are no longer strangers because a factual relationship develops between them, and this justifies that their conduct is sometimes subject to the control of the courts. By engaging in precontractual negotiations, each negotiating party relies on his partner and a duty arises to not deceive the trust and the expectations that were raised by entering into the precontractual relationship. The expectation of the other party supposes an act of faith, as there can be no hope without trust (*confiance*), but this expectation must be legitimate

---

[147] CA Paris, 13 February 1883, Gaz Pal 1883, 2, 414, as explained by Giliker (n. 55) p. 122.

[148] CA Dijon, 15 February 1893, Sirey 1894, 2, 144, as explained by Danis-Fatôme (n. 84) pp. 482–483.

[149] Cass com 20 March 1972 (n. 15).

[150] Aubry (n. 21) pp. 323–324, 333.

[151] This para. follows Aubry (n. 21) pp. 323–338 (particularly, pp. 325, 332–336), also pp. 251, 254.

for it to be taken into account by the courts. A legitimate expectation is such that is worthy of being taken into consideration by the law. Judges will have to focus on the events accompanying the precontractual period which are able to arouse the expectation of the future conclusion of the contract in the other party. Two criteria are particularly relevant: the quality of the parties and the level of advancement of the precontractual relation (the *Adjani* decision being an example of a case where the expectation of the future conclusion of the contract was not legitimate).[152] *La doctrine* and *la jurisprudence* take into consideration the notions of *confiance* and legitimate expectations in the characterisation of precontractual fault and, so, the breach of the legitimate expectation of the other party is the basis of the case law regarding liability for broken negotiations.

This notion of legitimate expectations is very similar to that of *confiance/croyance légitime* and leads to the same effects in compensating for delictual liability. The notion of 'legitimate expectation' of French law can be compared to that of 'reliance' of Anglo-American jurisdictions.[153]

(d) *Theory of Appearance*

The criterion of *confiance légitime trompée ou déçue* (deceived or disappointed legitimate trust) can also be found within the theory of '*l'apparence*' which has been proposed by Anne Danis-Fatôme as an alternative pathway to explain precontractual liability for broken negotiations, independently of delictual liability.[154]

According to this view,[155] a partial application of the theory of appearance has been made by French case law in the area of precontractual liability, by using the requirements of the theory of appearance (the notion of *confiance/croyance légitime trompée* as the criterion of fault) to establish the liability of the author of the break-off, but without endorsing its effects by refusing to compensate the damage consisting in the loss of the expected profits from the conclusion of the contract. The courts have imposed liability on the author of the break-off because he deceived the legitimate trust created in the other party of the future conclusion of the contract, having created an appearance of a will to conclude the contract that he did not follow. The courts should fully apply the theory of appearance and grant to the victim of the appearance that which he legitimately believed to obtain, i.e. the expected benefits of the conclusion of the contract. This would lead to the imposition of the effects of the negotiated contract on

152 See text to (n. 144) above.
153 Danis-Fatôme (n. 84) p. 518.
154 Danis-Fatôme (n. 84) pp. 479–480.
155 This para. follows Danis-Fatôme (n. 84) pp. 477–496 (particularly, pp. 480, 483, 486, 489, 493, 494).

the party who created the misleading appearance and broke off the negotiations deceiving the *confiance légitime* of the other party. This solution does not challenge freedom of contract because it does not establish the forced formation of a contract, as the obligations imposed on the author of the break-off do not have a contract as a source, but are imposed on the autonomous basis of the theory of appearance.

Although the theory of appearance is appealing in that it has as a goal protecting legal certainty,[156] a theory which leads to the protection of the expectation interest could only be applicable in cases where one party believed that a contract was indeed concluded, and not in cases (such as the paradigm case) where one party legitimately believed that the contract would be concluded in the future.[157]

Some case law shows that fault can be found where a negotiator created an 'appearance' which led to the other party's belief that the contract was going to be concluded.[158] Whether this belief (*croyance*) is considered to be 'legitimate' depends on different factors such as the importance of the preparatory work, knowledge of such work, the length of the negotiations, the abruptness of the breaking-off and whether the parties are professionals or non-professionals.[159]

(e) *Principles of* Venire Contra Factum Proprium *and of Coherence*

The principles of *venire contra factum proprium* and of coherence have also been linked to the notion of *confiance légitime* and have been proposed as explanations of liability for broken negotiations.

Although the protection of *confiance légitime* is not a general principle of the French law of contract, it has many applications,[160] one of which is the prohibition of contradicting oneself to the detriment of another (*venire contra factum proprium*).[161] The courts are sensitive to the idea that an unpredictable and inconsistent party, whose acts or words are contradictory, and who deceives or misleads in this way the *confiance légitime* of the other party, must assume the consequences of his contradictions. The requirement of contractual coherence has application in the stage of formation of contracts, as the concept of *confiance légitime* is used to temper the principle of precontractual freedom which dominates the negotiation phase.

---

156 Danis-Fatôme (n. 84) p. 493.

157 Regarding reliance-based remedies, see Ch. 6 s. IV 2 below.

158 Deshayes and Maître, case 4, in Cartwright and Hesselink (n. 15) pp. 121–122; e.g. Cass com 11 July 2000 (n. 73); CA Paris 10 March 2000 (n. 15).

159 Deshayes and Maître, cases 4 and 9, in Cartwright and Hesselink (n. 15) pp. 122, 257; Danis-Fatôme (n. 84) p. 484. See this Ch. s. III 1 below.

160 Fages (n. 23) p. 29.

161 The following expresses ideas by D. Mazeaud (n. 23) pp. 250–251.

In several judgments,[162] the *Cour de cassation* has decided that if, due to their duration, their advanced stage or the expenses that they have generated, the negotiations have engendered in the mind of one of the negotiators a *confiance légitime* in the conclusion of the negotiated contract, their brutal and unforeseeable breaking-off entails the delictual liability of the 'unreliable negotiator', whose inconsistent behaviour should be sanctioned.[163]

The principle of coherence (*le principe de cohérence*) has also been put forward to explain different situations of precontractual liability. According to Houtcieff,[164] although the freedom to break off negotiations remains intact, it does not authorise any kind of conduct. Fault in the exercise of the right to break off consists in deceiving the legitimate *confiance* in the future conclusion of the contract created in the other party. If this contradiction causes detriment to the other party, the remedy is delictual damages (not the ineffectiveness of the incoherent act which, he argues, is the remedy in cases of revocation of an offer).

It is interesting to note that the *Projet Terré Contrats* included an article which banned contradictory behaviour and expressly referred to the notion of *confiance légitime*.[165] The 2016 reform, however, has not introduced a similar article into the *Code civil*.[166]

(f) Conclusions

The basis of liability for broken negotiations in French law is found in the notion of *croyance/confiance légitime* (legitimate belief or trust), which may be treated as one notion due to the fact that most judgments and authors use them interchangeably and do not provide a clear distinction between them. This notion also embodies that of legitimate expectations (*attentes légitimes*) in the future conclusion of the contract.

The concept of *croyance/confiance légitime* reflects the notion of reliance in both its dimensions; while *croyance légitime* is more oriented to the expectation-dimension, as it refers to a legitimate belief in the future conclusion of the contract, *confiance légitime* embodies both dimensions, as it refers to a trust developed between the negotiating parties which allows one of them to legitimately expect the future conclusion of the contract.

---

162 e.g. Cass com 22 April 1997, *Mabo c Iveco* (n. 82); *Manoukian* (n. 22).

163 D. Mazeaud (n. 23) pp. 251–252.

164 Dimitri Houtcieff, *Le Principe de Cohérence en Matière Contractuelle*, vol. 2 (PUAM, 2001) paras. 868–869.

165 *Projet Terré Contrats* (n. 1) 'Article 6: A party cannot act in contradiction with his previous statements and conduct on the faith of which the other party has legitimately based himself. Mere tolerance is not enough to render trust legitimate'.

166 See (n. 2) above.

2. *ABUS DE DROIT*

French courts have been cautious in admitting the existence of precontractual liability in order to not unduly restrict the principle of freedom of contract.[167] Under a traditional view, liability for breaking off negotiations is conceived as an exception to the rule that a party is always free to break off, and restrictions on the right to break off are considered as an exception to freedom of contract, which is justified by the abusiveness of the breaking-off.[168] Consequently, attempts have been made to qualify precontractual fault[169] and recourse has been had to the doctrine of abuse of rights (*abus de droit*) as a basis of liability for breaking off negotiations.[170] It will be argued that although this account is present in the writings of part of *la doctrine* and in some judgments, it is not the appropriate basis for this liability as it does not explain its essence.

Ever since the initial suggestions made by French legal scholars at the beginning of the twentieth century that French law should recognise a general theory of 'abuse of rights', no agreement has yet been reached as to its proper limits.[171] The idea of abuse of contractual rights was recognised and seen as supported by article 1134(3) Cciv, which ordered that contracts be performed in good faith.[172] In addition, the idea that other rights associated with contracts (although not arising from them) were capable of being abused, particularly the right to refuse to conclude a contract where this was done in an abrupt fashion, after lengthy negotiations, was also recognised.[173] In this situation, abuse of rights constitutes delictual fault and where it has caused harm it gives rise to damages for delictual liability, based on the generality of articles 1240 and 1241 (formerly articles 1382 and 1383) Cciv.[174]

Thus, some authors and judgments characterise precontractual fault in terms of *abus de droit*.[175] Some commentators have taken the view that if a negotiating party has taken advantage of his freedom to negotiate, he has abused his

---

167 Giliker (n. 55) p. 124; Schmidt-Szalewski, 'France' in Hondius (n. 26) p. 150; CA Riom 10 June 1992 (n. 22).

168 *Ius Commune* (n. 15) p. 433.

169 See this Ch. s. I 2 above.

170 As explained by, e.g., Deshayes and Maître, case 1, in Cartwright and Hesselink (n. 15) p. 28 fn. 24; Aubry (n. 21) p. 325; Jaluzot (n. 79) p. 367.

171 Simon Whittaker and Reinhard Zimmermann, 'Good Faith in European Contract Law: Surveying the Legal Landscape' in Reinhard Zimmermann and Simon Whittaker (eds.), *Good Faith in European Contract Law* (CUP, 2000) p. 34.

172 Whittaker and Zimmermann (n. 171) p. 35. New art. 1104 Cciv is analysed in sub-s. 3 below.

173 Whittaker and Zimmermann (n. 171) p. 35.

174 Whittaker and Zimmermann (n. 171) p. 35; Bell, Boyron and Whittaker (n. 38) p. 374.

175 As indicated by Aubry (n. 21) p. 325.

'right to break off negotiations'[176] and fault is found in the exercise of this right.[177] It might be said that there exists a right to break off negotiations, but that this right is controlled in that liability arises in case of abuse.[178] While a person may in principle freely withdraw from negotiations before a contract is concluded, he may not do so abusively.[179] Ghestin connects the notions of *confiance/croyance légitime* and abuse of right in that when the former legitimately arises, the right to break off is abused.[180] The *Cour de cassation* has sometimes analysed liability for breaking off negotiations in terms of whether there was an abuse of the right to break off, and has considered that that will be the case where the negotiating party committed acts constituting fault in the exercise of such a right.[181] The *Cour* has also referred expressly to the control that it exercises over the abuse of the right to break off negotiations by the defendant.[182] In the *Hydrotile machine* case, the court stated that the judges below had established the '*rupture abusive des pourparlers*' (abusive break-off of negotiations),[183] and in a 1992 judgment the Court of Appeal of Rennes referred to '*l'abus de rupture des pourparlers*' (the abuse in breaking off negotiations).[184]

There is a division in *la doctrine* with regard to the usefulness of the notion of abuse of rights as a basis of liability for breaking off negotiations. Although some argue that cases which have recognised this liability should be explained in terms of abuse of the exercise of the right to break off,[185] others argue that the notion of abuse of the right to break off should be abandoned and other bases of liability (such as *confiance légitime trompée*[186] or legitimate expectation)[187] should be preferred. Schmidt states that it is debatable whether to talk of 'abuse of right' in relation to breaking off negotiations because the author of the break-off does not exercise a 'defined and determined' right but rather a simple freedom to not contract.[188] Chauvel is of a similar view, indicating that the use of the notion of abuse of the right to break off negotiations is relatively uncommon

---

176 As explained by Giliker (n. 55) p. 131; e.g. Georges Durry, 'Note on Cass com 20 March 1972' RTDciv 1972, 779, 780; Terré, Simler and Lequette (n. 15) p. 201; Muriel Fabre-Magnan, *Droit des Obligations*, vol. I: Contrat et Engagement Unilatéral (4th edn., PUF, 2016) p. 270.

177 Ghestin (n. 15) pp. 532–533.

178 Chauvel (n. 23) para. 19.

179 Bell, Boyron and Whittaker (n. 38) p. 298.

180 Ghestin (n. 15) pp. 536–537.

181 e.g. Cass civ 3, 16 October 1973, D 1974 IR 35. As to the degree of fault required, see this Ch. s. I 2 above, especially (n. 73). As to whether the breaking-off itself constitutes an abuse, see this Ch s. I 3 above.

182 Cass com 7 January 1997, *Eurolocatique c Banque franco-allemande* (n. 97); Chauvel (n. 23) para. 19.

183 Cass com 20 March 1972 (n. 15). Also, Cass com 11 July 2000 (n. 73).

184 CA Rennes 29 April 1992 (n. 97).

185 e.g. Ghestin (n. 15) pp. 559–560; Durry, 'Note on Cass com 20 March 1972' (n. 176).

186 e.g. Giliker (n. 55) p. 132.

187 e.g. Aubry (n. 21) p. 325.

188 Schmidt (n. 21) p. 108. Also, Aubry (n. 21) pp. 328, 329.

in the case law,[189] and that it is not clear that the use of this notion is justified, as it is not really an abuse of right but rather an 'abuse of liberty', because before the conclusion of the contract the parties are not bound by any obligation imposed by law or by private agreement.[190] Furthermore, in cases like the paradigm case, it has been argued that an analysis in terms of abuse of right seems hardly useful.[191] It has also been criticised that the understanding of abuse of rights is so flexible that it loses its specific features in relation to bad faith.[192]

Therefore, it seems that the better view is that the concept of abuse of rights 'adds nothing new to the idea of fault'[193] or is confused with delictual fault[194] in the breaking-off of negotiations, and that the concepts of *croyance/confiance légitime* or legitimate expectations are more suited as criteria on which to base the fault of the party breaking off, as they truly reflect the reliance element which is at the essence of this liability. Additionally, the fact that the doctrine of abuse of rights is based on the principle of good faith (which will be argued below is not essential to the configuration of this liability), also supports the rejection of abuse of rights as the basis of this liability.[195]

3. GOOD FAITH

The law of delict holds negotiating parties to a standard of proper conduct,[196] which is generally referred to either positively in terms of a requirement of good faith or negatively in terms of abusing the right to break off negotiations.[197] In this way, good faith (*bonne foi*) or bad faith (*mauvaise foi*) is also suggested as a basis of liability for breaking off negotiations. It will be argued that this standard, although useful in identifying the wrongful conduct of the negotiating parties, is not essential to founding this liability which has reliance at its core.

Before the 2016 reform, article 1134(3) Cciv established that contracts must be performed in good faith and the Cciv had no legal provision expressly establishing good faith in the formation of contracts. An earlier draft of article 1134(3) stated that '[contracts] must be contracted and performed in good faith'[198] but the word 'contracted' (*contractées*) was struck out because

189 Examples of cases that refer to it are: Cass com 11 July 2000 (n. 73); Cass com 7 January 1997 (n. 97); Cass com 22 February 1994 (n. 73).

190 Chauvel (n. 23) para. 19.

191 Stoffel-Munck, *L'Abus dans le Contrat* (n. 23) p. 111.

192 Aubry (n. 21) p. 328.

193 e.g. Schmidt (n. 21) p. 108; Chauvel (n. 23) para. 19; Danis-Fatôme (n. 84) p. 481.

194 Aubry (n. 21) p. 329.

195 The 2016 reform (n. 2) did not introduce an article on abuse of rights, and the 2017 Project on the reform of civil liability (n. 29) does not contemplate such an article either.

196 See text to (n. 55) above.

197 Bell, Boyron and Whittaker (n. 38) p. 305.

198 Bell, Boyron and Whittaker (n. 38) p. 308 fn. 97.

Portalis found it superfluous.[199] Thus, it was said that the omission of creating contracts in good faith was made on formal rather than on substantive grounds.[200] Consequently, many scholars considered that article 1134(3) also applied to the formation of contracts.[201] The courts and *la doctrine* began to 'import, in reliance on the general principle of delictual liability, a requirement of good faith or honesty and fair dealing into the pre-contractual negotiations'.[202] It was argued that the duty of good faith was an integral part of the '*normes générales de comportement*', breach of which led to liability under articles 1382 and 1383 Cciv.[203] By virtue of the law of delict, the negotiating parties were considered to be subject to a duty to negotiate in good faith.[204] It was, therefore, accepted that the principle of good faith extended to the negotiation of contracts, despite the limited terms of the Cciv,[205] and the courts and most contemporary French authors recognised a general duty of precontractual good faith or a duty to negotiate in good faith;[206] good faith understood as a norm of conduct which governs precontractual relations.[207] Thus, while the starting point was that, in principle, negotiating parties were free to break off negotiations without liability at any stage, this was limited by developing a general 'duty of loyalty' during negotiations, a duty to negotiate in good faith.[208]

The 2016 reform did not change this doctrinal and judicial development;[209] on the contrary, it embraced it by introducing new article 1104 Cciv which expressly recognises that 'Contracts must be negotiated, formed and performed in good faith. This provision is a matter of public policy'.[210] This article is further reaffirmed by new article 1112 which expressly establishes that, from their beginning until their end, negotiations must mandatorily satisfy the

199 Jaluzot (n. 79) p. 132.
200 Jacques Mestre, RTDciv 1988, 340.
201 e.g. Jacques Mestre, RTDciv 1989, 739; Dagorne-Labbé (n. 83).
202 Nicholas (n. 19) p. 70.
203 Deshayes and Maître, case 7, in Cartwright and Hesselink (n. 15) p. 200 fn. 16.
204 Nili Cohen, 'Pre-Contractual Duties: Two Freedoms and the Contract to Negotiate' in J. Beatson and Daniel Friedmann (eds.), *Good Faith and Fault in Contract Law* (Clarendon Press, 1995) p. 38.
205 e.g. Whittaker and Zimmermann (n. 171) p. 37; Jourdain (n. 23) p. 122; Jaluzot (n. 79) p. 359. Solène Rowan, 'The New French Law of Contract' (2017) 66 ICLQ 805, p. 807, mentions the extension by the courts of the principle in art. 1134 of the 1804 Code that contracts should be performed in good faith to precontractual negotiations and contract formation as an example of an area of French contract law where the courts had shaped almost entirely new laws.
206 *Ius Commune* (n. 15) p. 425; e.g. Terré, Simler and Lequette (n. 15) p. 201; Juliette Sénéchal, 'Contract Formation and Non-performance in French Law' in Reiner Schulze and Fryderyk Zoll (eds.), *The Law of Obligations in Europe, A New Wave of Codifications* (Sellier, 2013) pp. 346, 351; Ghestin (n. 15) p. 514; Danis-Fatôme (n. 84) p. 481; Jourdain (n. 23) pp. 128, 131; Schmidt (n. 21) p. 107.
207 Jourdain (n. 23) p. 132.
208 e.g. Muir-Watt, Sefton-Green and Reifegerste, case 3, in Zimmermann and Whittaker (n. 103) pp. 240, 241; Sénéchal (n. 206) p. 352; Malaurie, Aynès and Stoffel-Munck (n. 15) p. 268.
209 Rosher (n. 12) p. 70; Rowan (n. 205) p. 814.
210 The 2016 reform (n. 2).

requirements of good faith.[211] Unlike most of its predecessors in the different reform proposals,[212] new article 1104 Cciv indicates that it is a mandatory provision,[213] i.e. parties cannot contract out of the requirements of good faith.[214] It does not, at least expressly, establish good faith as a principle but the fact that it is contained within the new general 'Introductory Provisions'[215] sets the tone of good faith as a guiding principle even if not as an overriding principle.[216]

Therefore, after the 2016 reform, it is still possible to state that delict sets a standard of behaviour to be followed during the negotiation period and that it is possible to identify certain duties which the parties must fulfil to avoid delictual liability,[217] but now these duties have a direct legal basis in new articles 1104 and 1112 Cciv. It is still valid to say that because the notion of good faith has vague contours, the needs of legal technique have required giving it a more defined content and this has been achieved by translating good faith into concrete duties that can be better grasped and given effect to by the law.[218] In this way, French courts accept that negotiations involve a period of risk but that, at a certain point, intervention is necessary to impose duties of good conduct: '*obligations de loyauté et de bonne foi*'[219] (obligations of loyalty and good faith). Therefore, in French law (unlike German law where precontractual duties arise from the moment of entering into contractual negotiations)[220] duties imposing

---

211 See text of art. 1112 in text to (n. 10) above.

212 art. 1104(1) *Avant-projet Catala* (n. 14); art. 18 *2008 Projet de réforme* (n. 1) ('Each of the parties must act in good faith'); art. 6 *2009 Projet de réforme* (n. 1) ('Contracts must be formed and performed in good faith'); art. 3 *Document de Travail* (n. 1) ('Contracts must be formed and performed in good faith'); art. 1103 *Projet d'ordonnance* (n. 1) ('Contracts must be formed and performed in good faith').

213 Similarly, art. 5 *Projet Terré Contrats* (n. 1) ('Contracts are formed and performed in good faith; the parties may not exclude or limit this duty').

214 Fabre-Magnan (n. 176) p. 262.

215 See text to (n. 5) above.

216 Malaurie, Aynès and Stoffel-Munck (n. 15) p. 254; Sefton-Green (n. 16) p. 60; Rowan (n. 205) p. 813; Jean-François Le Coq, 'The Stakes and Objectives of the Reforms of Contract Law, General Regime and Proof of Obligations' (2017) 6 IBLJ 515, p. 521. The *Avant-projet Catala* (n. 14) did not elevate good faith to an overarching general principle of law, unlike art. 18 *2008 Projet de réforme* (n. 212) which codified good faith as a 'guiding' or 'governing principle' of contract law: Stefan Vogenauer, 'The Avant-projet de réforme: An Overview' in John Cartwright, Stefan Vogenauer and Simon Whittaker (eds.), *Reforming the French Law of Obligations, Comparative Reflections on the Avant-projet de réforme du droit des obligations et de la prescription ('the Avant-projet Catala')* (Hart Publishing, 2009) pp. 15, 19. The *2009 Projet de réforme* (n. 1) removed the governing principles section but kept good faith in art. 6 (n. 212). Art. 5 *Projet Terré Contrats* (n. 213) did not explicitly ascribe to good faith the status of 'governing principle': Vogenauer (n. 216) p. 20. Art. 3 *Document de Travail* (n. 212) had as heading '*principe de bonne foi*'. Art. 1103 *Projet d'ordonnance* (n. 212) kept the same text but eliminated the heading.

217 Giliker (n. 55) p. 123.

218 Jourdain (n. 23) p. 122.

219 Giliker (n. 55) p. 105; e.g. *Hydrotile machine* case (n. 15).

220 See Ch. 3, text following (n. 37) above.

standards of honesty and loyalty arise only when negotiations have reached an advanced stage.

The courts have constructed *obligations de loyauté* (obligations of loyalty), *obligations de co-opération* (obligations of cooperation) and *obligations de cohérence* (obligations to be coherent) from the legal basis of good faith[221] (initially article 1134(3) and now new articles 1104 and 1112 Cciv), and this case law is expected to remain relevant.[222] French courts usually infer three types of duties from the general obligation of good faith in the negotiation stage: a duty to inform, a duty of confidentiality and a duty not to behave inconsistently during the negotiations.[223] A duty of transparency of the risks of non-conclusion of the negotiations is also imposed.[224] This duty of transparency, along with the duty of coherence, particularly relates to the *confiance/croyance légitime* basis of liability for breaking off negotiations.[225] A more general classification divides precontractual duties into two main groups: (i) duties that emerge from good faith as an instrument of protection of consent, and (ii) duties that emerge from good faith guaranteeing the efficacy and security of negotiations.[226] This second group is relevant in the paradigm case, as this good faith is aimed at preventing all disloyalty that would lead to the failure of the completion of the negotiations or that would cause harm to the other party.[227]

The courts accept that good faith is required in contractual negotiations so that the defendant will not be permitted to betray the trust legitimately raised in the other negotiating party.[228] The tendency is that French courts increasingly police whether the duty of good faith is respected.[229] This is evidenced in the *Hydrotile* decision, where it was held that the defendant had deliberately not passed on the final estimate intended for the claimant and, without legitimate reason, had abruptly and unilaterally broken off their negotiations, which were at an advanced stage, knowing that the claimant had already incurred considerable expense, and having intentionally kept the claimant in a state of protracted uncertainty, thereby 'infringing the rules of good faith in commercial relations'.[230] The Court of Appeal of Pau had already

221 Whittaker and Zimmermann (n. 171) p. 37; Martijn W. Hesselink, 'The Concept of Good Faith' in Arthur S. Hartkamp and others (eds.), *Towards a European Civil Code* (4th edn., Kluwer Law International, 2011) p. 624.
222 Rowan (n. 205) p. 814.
223 *Ius Commune* (n. 15) p. 426.
224 Muir-Watt (n. 137) p. 59.
225 See this Ch. s. II 1 above.
226 Jourdain (n. 23) p. 122.
227 Jourdain (n. 23) p. 122.
228 Giliker (n. 55) p. 137.
229 *Ius Commune* (n. 15) p. 440.
230 Cass com 20 March 1972 (n. 15), translation from *Ius Commune* (n. 15) p. 438.

acknowledged that negotiating parties owe each other certain obligations of rectitude and good faith in negotiating, which relate not to the conclusion of the eventual contract but to the conduct of the negotiators themselves.[231]

A number of other cases also suggest a good faith basis of precontractual liability. For instance, in a 1997 decision, the *Cour de cassation* found that the defendant had brutally and unilaterally broken off very close negotiations, and had failed to comply with the rules of good faith in commercial relations.[232] Chauvel, commenting on this case,[233] stressed that it is very clear that the terminology of 'good faith' refers to a system of norms which is entirely objective and independent of the state of mind of the party breaking off. He explained that the 'failure to comply with good faith' consists in behaviour which does not conform to that which the judge considers should be adopted by an honest partner who is normally concerned to observe the morality and the customs of business practice, and that the awareness, on the part of the author of the breaking-off, of the failure of his conduct to comply with these norms, does not have to be specially established. In the *Sandoz* case, the *Cour de cassation* found that in withdrawing at a late stage of the negotiation process with no good reason, Sandoz had shown a lack of fairness (*loyauté*).[234]

Because good faith operates as an objective standard, some basic principles which establish a framework for intervention for the courts can be found, and it is possible to identify forms of behaviour which the courts will condemn as contrary to the rules of good faith and loyalty in the negotiation process.[235] Thus, bad faith will consist, in particular, in engaging in negotiations without having a serious intention to contract, in prolonging negotiations when there is no longer an intention to contract,[236] and in breaking, without legitimate reason, suddenly and unilaterally, advanced negotiations.[237] Expectation-based reliance can contribute to the finding of bad faith, in that 'bad faith consists in putting an end to the negotiations, in circumstances causing loss, after having induced a belief in the other negotiating party that a contract was going to be concluded'.[238] In this way, breaking off negotiations when the other party could

231 CA Pau 14 January 1969 (n. 145).

232 Cass com 22 April 1997, *Mabo c Iveco* (n. 82); Jacques Mestre, 'Note on Cass com 22 April 1997' RTDciv 1997, 651, 652. Also, Cass com 18 January 2011 (n. 114); CA Agen, 21 August 2002, JCP 2003 II 10162, note Lecourt.

233 Chauvel (n. 23) para. 9.

234 Cass com 7 April 1998 (n. 15). Also, Cass civ 1, 14 June 2000, CCC 2000, no. 157, note Leveneur.

235 Giliker (n. 43) p. 991.

236 e.g. *Manoukian* case (n. 22).

237 e.g. *Hydrotile machine* case (n. 15). Ghestin (n. 15) p. 538; Schmidt, 'La Sanction de la Faute Précontractuelle' (n. 23) p. 53.

238 CA Reims, 13 December 1989, Juris-Data no. 049 587, quoted by Chauvel (n. 23) para. 11.

reasonably expect the contract to be concluded, will be considered to be at variance with good faith.[239]

It can be seen that there is a connection between bad faith and reliance, which explains why authors who hold that *croyance/confiance légitime* or legitimate expectations is the true basis of liability for broken negotiations, still use the argument of good faith to construct their theories, or why authors who seem to support a good faith basis still make use of the notion of reliance. For instance, Schmidt-Szalewski links her criterion of *confiance légitime trompée*[240] with the violation of the rules of good faith in that precontractual fault is established by bad faith behaviour (which can be labelled as precontractual wrongful behaviour), which consists of any behaviour that deceives the other party's confidence, such as breaking off negotiations when the author of the break-off had led the other party to reasonably expect the contract to be concluded or had aroused in the other party the *confiance* in the future conclusion of the agreement.[241] Schmidt-Szalewski defines precontractual fault on the basis of good faith, stating that '[a] reasonable man's behaviour of reference would consist of loyal and good faith negotiating'.[242] Muir-Watt states that *confiance trompée* has emerged as the criterion and measure of the liability incurred for precontractual bad faith.[243] Terré, Simler and Lequette indicate that the duty of loyalty imposed by good faith in the formation of contracts, generally means that when a party gives rise to a relationship of *confiance* he must assume the consequences of deceiving it.[244] Aubry connects the notion of legitimate expectations with good faith in that the general duty of good faith takes in the precontractual period a specific character: it imposes the duty to not deceive the trust and the expectations that were raised by entering into the precontractual relationship.[245] Jourdain explains that the requirements of good faith increase with the *croyance légitime* of the negotiating parties in the conclusion of the contract which, in turn, increases as negotiations progress; therefore, the later in time the breaking-off takes place, the higher the risk of it constituting fault.[246]

---

239 Ewoud H. Hondius, 'General Report' in Ewoud H. Hondius (ed.), *Precontractual Liability: Reports to the XIIIth Congress International Academy of Comparative Law, Montreal, Canada, 18–24 August 1990* (Kluwer Law, 1991) p. 19, referring to the *Hydrotile machine* case (n. 15).

240 See text to (n. 125) above.

241 Schmidt, 'La Sanction de la Faute Précontractuelle' (n. 23) pp. 53, 57; *Négociation et Conclusion de Contrats* (n. 21) pp. 107–108, 111; 'L'évolution de la Responsabilité Précontractuelle en Droit Français' (n. 23) p. 148; 'La Période Précontractuelle en Droit Français' (n. 23) p. 550; 'France' in Hondius (n. 26) p. 150; 'France' in ICC (n. 26) p. 96.

242 'France' in Hondius (n. 26) p. 150; Schmidt (n. 21) p. 107.

243 Muir-Watt (n. 137) p. 57.

244 Terré, Simler and Lequette (n. 15) pp. 50, 201.

245 Aubry (n. 21) p. 333.

246 Jourdain (n. 23) p. 128.

A good faith basis of precontractual liability for breaking off negotiations is consistent with new articles 1104 and 1112 Cciv.[247] It is also consistent with most of the earlier reform projects.[248] However, neither the 2008 nor the 2009 *Projet de réforme du droit des contrats*, when regulating precontractual liability, referred to the notion of good faith,[249] although they both recognised good faith.[250] It is also important to highlight that, before the 2016 reform, not all French decisions on breaking off negotiations referred expressly to good (or bad) faith. For instance, in the *Eurolocatique c Banque franco-allemande* decision, the court found fault without referring to good faith but relying on the abuse of the right to break off negotiations.[251] The choice between the doctrines of good faith and abuse of rights may depend on whether the *Cour de cassation* seeks to control the matter (abuse of rights is a question of law) or to leave it to the sovereign power of assessment of the lower courts (good faith is a question of fact).[252] But it is also possible to consider that good faith was not the only principle influencing the courts' decisions in these cases.[253] As has been analysed,[254] the standard of good faith is not the only possible theoretical basis of liability for breaking off negotiations, as the required fault can also be founded on abuse of rights or under the notion of *croyance/confiance légitime*. In this way (and excluding the debatable basis of abuse of rights), the norm of behaviour imposed on negotiating parties can be interpreted in terms of a duty to negotiate in good faith or a duty not to breach a relationship of confidence and trust.[255]

Before the 2016 reform, the duty of good faith in the negotiation phase was often referred to but without much detail and, more frequently, the focus was directly on the type of blameworthy conduct, such as breaking off negotiations, without emphasising its assimilation with objective good faith.[256] Or simply the breach of a good faith duty became immersed in the notion of delictual fault.[257] After the 2016 reform came into force, it remains to be seen whether this approach will change, but it seems unlikely that it will considering that article 1112 codified the existing case law. It is suggested that the courts will have to refer to good faith, as they will have articles 1104 and 1112 Cciv as legal bases

---

247 See text to (nn. 210, 10) above.
248 See (nn. 13, 14, 212, 213) above.
249 art. 20 *2008 Projet de réforme* and art. 16 *2009 Projet de réforme* (n. 13).
250 See (n. 216) above.
251 Cass com 7 January 1997 (n. 97). Also, Cass com 22 February 1994 (n. 73).
252 Simon Whittaker and Reinhard Zimmermann, 'Coming to Terms with Good Faith' in Reinhard Zimmermann and Simon Whittaker (eds.), *Good Faith in European Contract Law* (CUP, 2000) p. 695; Muir-Watt, Sefton-Green and Reifegerste, case 13, in Zimmermann and Whittaker (n. 103) p. 394.
253 Giliker (n. 55) p. 130.
254 In this Ch. s. II 1 and 2 above.
255 Giliker (n. 55) p. 168.
256 Asúa (n. 140) p. 238.
257 Jourdain (n. 23) p. 128; see text to (n. 83) above.

for the imposition of precontractual liability, and from these articles it becomes clear that a fault will be committed if the commencement, continuation and breaking-off of negotiations are not conducted in good faith;[258] i.e. if there is a breach of the good faith requirement.[259] But because liability for breaking off negotiations remains delictual, it is probable that the focus of the courts will continue to be on finding precontractual fault, fault which has a reliance basis through the operation of the notion of *croyance/confiance légitime*. The standard of good faith, which now has an undeniable legal basis, can assist the reliance element in limiting precontractual freedom and in providing guidance for the determination of wrongful behaviour in the negotiation phase. However, the standard of good faith is not essential to the theoretical explanation of the imposition of precontractual liability[260] and can be subsumed by or merged with the reliance basis.[261]

III. CRITERIA FOR FINDING LIABILITY

In addition to the different theoretical bases analysed in section II above, there are certain objective circumstances that lead to the breaking-off which in each particular case can help in finding precontractual fault. Under the *croyance/confiance légitime* basis, when there are difficulties in assessing the existence and measure of the trust, these circumstances help determine the legitimacy of the trust or expectation.[262] At the same time, there are also several groups of reasons which can exclude liability. These are explored below.

1. OBJECTIVE CIRCUMSTANCES FOR THE FINDING OF FAULT (POSITIVE CRITERIA)

There are some objective circumstances, beyond the particularities of each case, which surround the breaking-off of negotiations that the courts look for in order to determine whether there has been a culpable breaking-off.[263] Fault is assessed with regard to the circumstances of the breaking-off.[264] From the case law,

258 Sefton-Green (n. 16) p. 60.
259 Kötz (n. 54) pp. 33, 36.
260 This is recognised by Ghestin (n. 15) p. 563.
261 This will be further explored in Ch. 6 s. III 3 below.
262 Sylviane Colombo, 'The Implications of Good Faith in Culpa in Contrahendo' (JSD thesis, Yale Law School, 1990) p. 105; Aubry (n. 21) p. 334; Danis-Fatôme (n. 84) p. 486.
263 Chauvel (n. 23) para. 10; Bernard Saintourens, 'Note on Cass com 11 July 2000' Bull Joly 2000 no. 288.
264 Deshayes and Maître, case 7, in Cartwright and Hesselink (n. 15) p. 199, citing the *Hydrotile machine* case (n. 15); Jourdain (n. 23) p. 128; Schmidt (n. 21) p. 112.

two objective elements emerge that play an important part in the finding of fault and, therefore, liability: the advanced stage of negotiations and the abruptness or suddenness of the break-off.[265] Some scholars add to these circumstances the quality of the parties, i.e. whether they are professionals or laymen.[266]

Regarding the advancement of negotiations, their duration will often be a significant element in finding a culpable breaking-off and, even more so, if the party that broke off had created a belief in the future conclusion of the negotiated contract or had left the other party to incur expenditure.[267] Psychologically, it is as if the obligation to conclude the contract becomes stronger and stronger with the passage of time, increasing the legitimate belief in a successful outcome.[268] Other criteria relevant to assess the advancement of the negotiations are the agreement on the majority of the essential elements of the contract and the climate of *confiance* and optimism existing between the negotiating parties.[269]

The length of the negotiations was relevant in finding fault for breaking off in the *Eurolocatique c Banque franco-allemande* decision, where the court found that the negotiations had taken place over a long period of time, and that the prolonged relationship between the parties had been voluntarily maintained in order to arrive at the final project of the negotiated contract.[270] The notion of a relationship between the negotiating parties, unlike German law, is not used to bring the precontractual stage closer to contract in order to impose contractual liability[271] but to establish the element of trust between negotiating parties (trust-dimension of reliance) which facilitates the finding of delictual liability. There is nothing absolute regarding the duration of negotiations, as they might have taken place over a short period of time, but be well advanced in terms of their subject-matter.[272] This was the situation in *Mabo c Iveco*, where the difference in agreement which remained between the parties was not large.[273]

The degree of advancement of the negotiations is particularly relevant in Schmidt-Szalewski's criterion of *confiance légitime trompée*.[274] Since the degree

---

265 Chauvel (n. 23) para. 10; Violet (n. 142); Lecourt (n. 142) p. 1830.

266 Danis-Fatôme (n. 84) p. 485; Aubry (n. 21) pp. 334–335; Schmidt: 'La Sanction de la Faute Précontractuelle' (n. 23) p. 54; *Négociation et Conclusion de Contrats* (n. 21) p. 110; 'L'évolution de la Responsabilité Précontractuelle en Droit Français' (n. 23) pp. 147–148; 'La Période Précontractuelle en Droit Français' (n. 23) p. 552.

267 Chauvel (n. 23) para. 11; e.g. CA Agen 21 August 2002 (n. 232); Cass com 11 July 2000 (n. 73); CA Paris 10 March 2000 (n. 15); Cass com 7 April 1998 (n. 15); CA Riom 10 June 1992 (n. 22); CA Rennes 29 April 1992 (n. 97); *Hydrotile machine* case (n. 15).

268 Chauvel (n. 23) para. 11.

269 Stoffel-Munck, 'Les Pourparlers' (n. 23) p. 3.

270 Cass com 7 January 1997 (n. 97).

271 See Ch. 3, text to (n. 24) above.

272 e.g. CA Agen 21 August 2002 (n. 232); Cass civ 1, 6 January 1998, Bull civ I no 7 (*Ossona c Al Esayi*).

273 Cass com 22 April 1997 (n. 82); Chauvel (n. 23) para. 12.

274 See this Ch. s. II 1 (b) above.

of *confiance* is greater as the negotiations are more advanced, negotiations where little progress has been made can be broken off at any moment without justification; but in advanced negotiations, as soon as one of the negotiating parties could reasonably believe that the contract would be concluded, the other party cannot break off without justification.[275]

Regarding the abruptness with which one of the parties broke off the negotiations, a number of judgments refer to this objective circumstance in order to establish fault.[276] However, in itself, the abruptness of the breaking-off is not an imperative autonomous requirement and very often it is not specially relied upon by the courts (and the same applies to the length of negotiations).[277] Finding fault is essentially a question of fact to which the advanced stage of the negotiations and the suddenness in terminating them will all be relevant factors.[278] Additional factors which indicate a relationship of confidence and trust during the negotiations and which, consequently, legitimise the expectation and justify liability are the intensity of the negotiations, signs of commitment given during the negotiations, work undertaken by the innocent party and the encouragement provided by the other negotiating party.[279]

A third objective element is the professional or non-professional quality of the negotiating parties. If a layman breaks off the negotiations with a professional, it will be difficult to find the layman at fault as the *confiance* created in the professional is normally very limited as the latter is expected to recognise the risks involved in the precontractual stage (*risque d'entreprise*).[280] In contrast, where the claimant is a layman suing a professional, the courts are more likely to find liability on the basis that the professional has abused the confidence placed in him due to his superior knowledge; the *confiance* created in the layman is considered to be greater than the ordinary *confiance*.[281]

Where both negotiating parties are professionals, it was rare for the breaking-off of negotiations to lead to liability, because the costs of unsuccessful negotiations are, in principle, considered to be part of the parties' general expenses, which they can incorporate into the price of contracts resulting from other successful negotiations.[282] A classic example of the reluctance to impose

---

275 Schmidt (n. 21) pp. 111–112; 'L'évolution de la Responsabilité Précontractuelle en Droit Français' (n. 23) p. 149; 'La Période Précontractuelle en Droit Français' (n. 23) pp. 550–551.

276 Chauvel (n. 23) para. 13; e.g. Cass com 22 April 1997 (n. 82); Cass com 7 January 1997 (n. 97); CA Rennes 29 April 1992 (n. 97); *Hydrotile machine* case (n. 15).

277 Chauvel (n. 23) para. 13; Danis-Fatôme (n. 84) p. 486.

278 Giliker (n. 55) p. 124; see text to (n. 60) above.

279 Giliker (n. 55) p. 168; Danis-Fatôme (n. 84) pp. 484–486; e.g. Cass com 7 April 1998 (n. 15).

280 Giliker (n. 55) p. 129; Schmidt (n. 21) p. 111; Schmidt, 'La Sanction de la Faute Précontractuelle' (n. 23) pp. 54–55; Aubry (n. 21) p. 335; e.g. Cass civ 12 April 1976 (n. 71).

281 Terré, Simler and Lequette (n. 15) p. 202; Giliker (n. 55) p. 129; Schmidt (n. 21) p. 110; Schmidt, 'La Sanction de la Faute Précontractuelle' (n. 23) p. 54.

282 Ghestin (n. 15) p. 529; Schmidt (n. 21) p. 106; *Ius Commune* (n. 15) p. 466; von Mehren (n. 131) para. 123.

liability between two commercial parties is a 1969 decision of the Court of Appeal of Pau, where the court held that preliminary work and provision of an estimate fell within the acceptable precontractual risks, and that, where two professionals were negotiating, only fault which was patent and beyond discussion (*faute patente, indiscutable*) could lead to the imposition of delictual liability.[283] Some interpreted this to mean that a higher degree of fault than ordinary was required and that fault should be assessed not in relation to the conduct of a *bon père de famille* but in relation to a *bon professionnel* of the same area of expertise.[284] However, in a commercial context, and particularly since the late nineties, it has been accepted that negotiations may give rise to relationships of trust and confidence, which, if abused, give rise to delictual liability.[285] Where negotiations have advanced beyond the ordinary risk stage, for example having taken place over a long period of time and having reached a particular level of intensity, the courts have imposed liability despite the commercial status of the parties.[286]

The French Commercial Code (Ccomm), in article L442-6, I, 5°, regulates the sudden breaking-off of established commercial relations (*rupture brutale des relations commerciales établies*) and imposes on the author of the break-off the obligation to compensate the damage caused. Considering that this norm applies in the case of precontractual relations[287] and that the sudden breaking-off of an established commercial relationship gives rise to liability of a delictual nature,[288] it could be argued that precontractual liability can arise in this particular scenario.

2. ABSENCE OF A LEGITIMATE REASON FOR BREAKING OFF (NEGATIVE CRITERION)

French courts are sensitive to the absence of any legitimate justification for the breaking-off of negotiations.[289] The breaking-off does not, as a matter of principle, have to be specially justified,[290] i.e. providing a reason when breaking off is not a requirement. However, the negative criterion of absence of a legitimate reason is an essential element of liability because the existence of a good reason

[283] CA Pau 14 January 1969 (n. 145); analysed by Giliker (n. 55) p. 129.

[284] e.g. Schmidt, 'L'évolution de la Responsabilité Précontractuelle en Droit Français' (n. 23) pp. 147–148; *Négociation et Conclusion de Contrats* (n. 21) p. 110; 'La Sanction de la Faute Précontractuelle' (n. 23) p. 54.

[285] Giliker (n. 43) p. 992; Kötz (n. 54) pp. 37–38; Ghestin (n. 15) pp. 529–530.

[286] Giliker (n. 55) p. 129; e.g. Cass com 11 July 2000 (n. 73); *Sandoz* case (n. 15); *Mabo c Iveco* (n. 82); *Eurolocatique c Banque franco-allemande* (n. 97).

[287] Danis-Fatôme (n. 84) p. 478; annotation no. 14 to art. L442-6 *Code de Commerce*, 111th ed., 2016, Dalloz.

[288] Annotation no. 20 to art. L442-6 Ccomm (n. 287).

[289] Chauvel (n. 23) para. 14.

[290] Chauvel (n.23) para. 19.

may remove liability.[291] In this way 'the legitimate reason serves as a justifying factor for the breaking-off'.[292]

Some judgments make express reference to the existence or absence of a 'legitimate reason' (*motif légitime*) for breaking off[293] and in others it can be implied that the court controls the reasons for the breaking-off, imposing liability where there is no legitimate reason.[294] The *Cour de cassation* seems to ask for such a reason in its more recent decisions.[295] If a reason is given, the court will have to determine whether it justifies the breaking-off of the negotiations.[296] In cases where the breaking-off is at a late stage, the courts might require a 'substantial justification'.[297] Chauvel, from a study of the case law, divides these legitimate reasons into three groups: the risk which remains regarding the conclusion of the contract, the blockage of negotiations, and a major modification of the proposals.[298] Ghestin points out that a reason is legitimate where it objectively relates to an element of the contract under negotiation and not to a situation that is particular to the party breaking off.[299]

The first group comprises situations where there is significant uncertainty as to whether the contract will be concluded and, as a result, each party must be conscious of the 'risk of non-conclusion'.[300] The negotiations might not have reached a level of development sufficient to give rise to an expectation of the future conclusion of the negotiated contract other than a 'premature or even chimerical hope'.[301] This is a manifestation of expectation-based reliance in that if the belief in the future conclusion of the contract is not reasonable, because there is still significant uncertainty as to its conclusion, there can be no liability.

The second group involves cases where negotiations were legitimately broken off as the inevitable result of a profound disagreement between

291 Chauvel (n. 23) para. 14; Terré, Simler and Lequette (n. 15) p. 202; Ghestin (n. 15) pp. 540–541; Deshayes and Maître, case 1, in Cartwright and Hesselink (n. 15) p. 29; Danis-Fatôme (n. 84) p. 487. Deshayes (n. 96) argues that the absence of a legitimate reason brings into play a presumption of fact of the existence of fault in the circumstances of the breaking-off. Aubry (n. 21) p. 336, holds the minority view that there could still be delictual liability even if there was a legitimate reason to break off.

292 Chauvel (n. 23) para. 14.

293 e.g. CA Agen 21 August 2002 (n. 232); Cass com 11 July 2000 (n. 73); *Sandoz* case (n. 15); Cass com 7 January 1997 (n. 97); Cass civ 3, 6 May 1996, no. 94-13745; *Hydrotile machine* case (n. 15).

294 e.g. Cass com 22 April 1997 (n. 82).

295 Deshayes and Maître, case 1, in Cartwright and Hesselink (n. 15) p. 29; e.g. Cass com, 21 February 2012, no. 11-10124; Cass com 18 January 2011 (n. 114); Cass com 13 October 2009 (n. 121); Cass com, 14 December 2004, no. 02-10157.

296 Deshayes and Maître, case 1, in Cartwright and Hesselink (n. 15) p. 29.

297 Editors' comparative observations to case 8, Cartwright and Hesselink (n. 15) p. 252.

298 Chauvel (n. 23) para. 15. Similarly, Violet (n. 142).

299 Ghestin (n. 15) 515. Similarly, Schmidt-Szalewski, 'Note on Cass com 7 April 1998' (n. 56). Chauvel disagrees, 'Note on Cass com 7 April 1998' (n. 56) para. 12.

300 Chauvel (n. 23) para. 16.

301 Chauvel (n. 23) para. 16.

the parties.[302] The third group includes cases where a party legitimately broke off the negotiations due to an essential modification of the negotiated terms,[303] or due to a major modification in the expectations of one of the parties.[304] An example is a significant and unpredictable increase in the cost of carrying out the work required by the other party.[305] This will also be the case in a situation where there is a considerable deterioration in the financial position of one party, leaving the other to fear the worst.[306] When the person of the other contracting party is a determining factor, it can even be argued that a mere 'loss of confidence' in the other party will be enough.[307] In a case where negotiations broke down after one party had publicly (and unfoundedly) accused the other of falsifying accounting documents and threatened criminal proceedings, the court found that such a loss of confidence (*perte de confiance*) was a legitimate reason for breaking off negotiations.[308] The trust-dimension of reliance is present in this type of legitimate reason: where the trust in the other party is lost, there is a good reason to break off. The test for an unexpected modification of the negotiated terms to be a legitimate reason for breaking off is that the modification must be of such a nature that, had the party breaking off known of it, he would not have entered the negotiations in the first place.[309]

According to the *confiance légitime trompée* basis of liability, the advancement of the negotiations influences the requirement to provide a (good) reason for breaking off,[310] in that the defendant is required to show a good reason for withdrawing from advanced negotiations,[311] whereas, where the negotiations are not very advanced, there is no such requirement and a negotiating party can withdraw without a good reason or without providing a reason at all.[312] If a climate of *confiance* has been created, the author of the break-off cannot escape liability without proving its justification.[313] For example, in the *Sandoz* case the *Cour de cassation* found that withdrawing from advanced negotiations, which had lasted for several years, due to internal considerations of the

---

302 Chauvel (n. 23) para. 17; Danis-Fatôme (n. 84) p. 487; e.g. Cass com, 18 December 1990, no. 89-15838.
303 Chauvel (n. 23) para. 18.
304 Deshayes and Maître, case 1, in Cartwright and Hesselink (n. 15) p. 29 fn. 29.
305 Cass civ 6 May 1996 (n. 293).
306 Chauvel (n. 23) para. 18, citing Cass com, 23 October 1990, no. 1215 Lexilaser.
307 Chauvel (n. 23) para. 18, citing CA Paris, 1 June 1995, no. 022850 Juris-Data.
308 CA Orléans, 19 October 2000, JCP 2001 no. 21, 2003.
309 Chauvel (n. 23) para. 18.
310 Schmidt (n. 21) pp. 111–112. Similarly, Ghestin (n. 15) pp. 515–516; Chauvel, 'Note on Cass com 7 April 1998' (n. 56) para. 6.
311 e.g. *Sandoz* case (n. 15); Ghestin (n. 15) p. 543.
312 e.g. Cass com, 12 January 1999, no. 96-14604; Cass civ 3, 18 December 2012, no. 10-30764; Cass civ 1, 20 December 2012, no. 11-27340. See text to (n. 275) above.
313 Danis-Fatôme (n. 84) p. 486.

pharmaceutical group which had nothing to do with the quality of the product, was not a legitimate reason for Sandoz's withdrawal.[314]

The courts accept that breaking off at an advanced stage may be necessary for financial reasons,[315] due to a change in circumstances,[316] due to the inability of the other party to meet certain technical requirements,[317] or simply because the parties cannot agree on a particular point.[318] Economic differences and the possibility to conclude another contract in more favourable conditions are other examples of justified reasons for breaking off and exclude their blameworthy character.[319] Thus, a better offer from a third party can be a sufficient good reason for breaking off.[320]

IV. BREAKING OFF NEGOTIATIONS FOR THE CONCLUSION OF A FORMAL CONTRACT AND LACK OF FORMALITY CASES

The same distinction that has been made in the German law chapter[321] must be made here in order to determine whether these case scenarios present any particularities in French law.

1. BREAKING OFF NEGOTIATIONS FOR THE CONCLUSION OF A FORMAL CONTRACT

Liability for breaking off negotiations for the conclusion of a formal contract (be it a solemn or a real contract)[322] does not seem to be a special case within the topic of precontractual liability in French law.[323]

This is possibly explained by the fact that the sale of land (which is the contract where this issue typically arises in German law) is not a formal contract. The contract of sale is consensual and the validity of a contract for the sale of

314 Cass com 7 April 1998 (n. 15).
315 e.g. Cass com, 4 April 1995, no. 93-13832; Cass com, 20 November 2007, no. 06-20332.
316 CA Orléans 19 October 2000 (n. 308).
317 Cass com, 7 March 2006, no. 04-17177.
318 Giliker (n. 55) p. 125; e.g. Cass civ 2, 13 January 2005, no. 03-15828.
319 Schmidt (n. 21) p. 112.
320 *Ius Commune* (n. 15) p. 465.
321 See Ch. 3 s. IV above.
322 New art. 1109 Cciv 'A contract is consensual where it is formed by the mere exchange of consents, in whatever way they may be expressed. A contract is solemn where its validity is subject to form prescribed by legislation. A contract is real where its formation is subject to the delivery of a thing'.
323 *Ius Commune* (n. 15) p. 466.

property is not subject to any particular formality requirement.[324] In France, in contrast to Germany,[325] Chile[326] and England,[327] an oral contract for the sale of land is valid and the buyer acquires title to the land without the need for any separate conveyance (articles 1196 and 1583 Cciv).[328] The proprietary effect (*effet translatif*)[329] of an oral sale of real estate applies only between the parties, because the buyer of land who wishes his title to be good against the world must have an authenticated instrument[330] in order to publish it in the land register.[331]

It appears that liability for breaking off negotiations for the conclusion of a sale of real estate presents no theoretical or practical differences from liability for breaking off negotiations for the conclusion of any other consensual contract. In *Monoprix*, a case of broken negotiations for the purchase of commercial premises, the *Cour de cassation* rejected the notion that an intention to cause harm to the other party was required.[332] However, as has been mentioned, a later judgment of the *Cour de cassation*, also in a case of broken negotiations for the sale of land, contradicted *Monoprix* and, in the absence of an intention to cause harm, appeared to require at least subjective bad faith in the course of negotiations.[333] In this case, where the defendant was not aware at the time of the negotiations that the land was not solely owned by him and where he would probably have discovered the real situation if he had looked for proof of his title to the property, his fault of negligence did not suffice to impose liability on him.[334] Still, this judgment remains isolated, and it is generally considered that precontractual fault in breaking off negotiations is not qualified (without excluding from this general conclusion contracts for the sale of land).[335] This has been reaffirmed by more recent case law dealing with liability for broken negotiations for the sale of land.[336]

With regard to breaking off negotiations for the conclusion of a solemn contract, there does not seem to be a special treatment of these cases in French law. For instance, in an early case about a promise to transfer a notary's office, where the transfer was a solemn act required to be in writing (article 6 of *loi*

---

324 Deshayes and Maître, case 11, in Cartwright and Hesselink (n. 15) p. 316.
325 See Ch. 3 s. IV 1 above.
326 See Ch. 5 s. IV 1 below.
327 See Ch. 7 s. I 1 below.
328 Kötz (n. 54) p. 83.
329 New art. 1196 Cciv.
330 New arts. 1369-1371 Cciv.
331 art. 4(1) Decree no. 55-22 of 4 January 1955; Konrad Zweigert and Hein Kötz, *Introduction to Comparative Law* (Tony Weir tr., 3rd rev. edn., Clarendon Press, 1998) p. 369.
332 Cass civ 3 October 1972 (n. 15); see text to (n. 67) above.
333 Cass civ 12 April 1976 (n. 71); see text following (n. 71) above.
334 Deshayes and Maître, case 3, in Cartwright and Hesselink (n. 15) p. 97.
335 See text to (nn. 85, 86) above.
336 e.g. Cass com, 9 November 2010, Bull civ IV no. 172; Cass civ 28 June 2006 (n. 93); Cass civ 13 January 2005 (n. 318); earlier, Cass civ 1, 19 January 1977, D 1977 p. 593, note Schmidt-Szalewski (*Humery c Epoux Gonzalès*).

23 June 1841), it was considered that the refusal to carry out the promise could give rise to delictual damages.[337]

2. LACK OF FORMALITY CASES

In French law, the contract of sale of land presents no difficulties as it is a consensual contract. If negotiating parties have orally reached agreement as to the sale, the agreement produces full effect between them from the moment it is reached and the buyer has to be considered as the owner of the property.[338] Following from article 1583 Cciv, which is applicable to any sale, the contract is enforceable and, consequently, there is no issue of delictual damage being suffered by the buyer.[339] If the seller contests the agreement, the buyer will have to present proof of it according to new articles 1359–1362 Cciv, and if the seller refuses to transfer the property, the buyer will have the contractual remedies of new article 1217 Cciv.[340]

But the question remains regarding formal contracts which have been agreed without complying with the required formality. It seems that in French law there is no distinct line of cases in this respect. Indeed, in a comparative study of good faith in different jurisdictions, including German and French law, reference is made to cases of inexplicable refusal to sign the definitive act, but no examples of French cases are provided.[341] Furthermore, in the same study it is said that the argument, which is often accepted in German law, that if the consequences of an act are important, the act may be considered to be illicit by virtue of good faith, does not feature in French law.[342]

Slightly altering the case scenario of an agreed sale of land, an example can be found in the case where an owner of land agrees to sell it to a buyer who has a certain time to give his answer, as this agreement is a unilateral promise of sale (*promesse unilatérale de vente*) of property, which is null if it is not recorded by an authenticated instrument or a signed instrument registered within ten days from the date of its acceptance by the beneficiary (article 1589-2 Cciv). Here, if the seller was aware of the formality requirement (or is a professional regarding sale of land) and knew that the buyer was ignorant of it, the seller might have an obligation to inform the buyer that the contract had to be registered to become fully valid, and if the seller deliberately keeps this information to himself,

---

337 CA Rennes 8 July 1929 (n. 110).

338 Deshayes and Maître, case 11, in Cartwright and Hesselink (n. 15) p. 316; see text to (n. 324) above.

339 Deshayes and Maître, case 11, in Cartwright and Hesselink (n. 15) p. 316.

340 A different issue is the enforceability of the contract against third parties: see text to (nn. 330, 331) above.

341 Jaluzot (n. 79) p. 364.

342 Jaluzot (n. 79) p. 89.

he would be liable under delict (new articles 1240 and 1241 Cciv). The solution would be the same where the seller misled the buyer about the formality requirement.[343] New article 1112-1 Cciv on the general duty of precontractual information may be applicable in such a case, leading to delictual compensation and, possibly, annulment of the contract. In theory, the judge could also decide that his judgment will serve as the act of sale, because the validity of the sale of real estate is not subject to a solemnity.[344]

Another example can be found in the oral promise of a gift of land which, according to article 931 Cciv, is void. If the promisor has allowed the promisee to live on the land and by his conduct has '*volontairement créé de faux espoirs dans l'esprit de celui-ci*' (voluntarily awakened false hopes in the other party),[345] he is guilty in delict and liable in damages under new articles 1240 and 1241 Cciv.[346] Contractual relief could be given to the promisee if the court finds that the contract is onerous and not gratuitous, as in such case no notarisation is necessary and the contract is perfectly valid.[347]

In conclusion, lack of formality cases do not represent an important problem in French law.[348] It does not give special treatment to cases where, due to the defendant's fraud or unintentional but careless conduct, an applicable formal requirement was not satisfied, and provides delictual relief for the economic loss caused to the claimant.[349] Expectation-based reliance is protected with delictual liability in the same manner as it is protected in the breaking-off of negotiations. Unlike German law, the principle of good faith is not used to provide for specific performance of an agreement which lacks the required legal formality. However, contractual relief for breach of a promise could be given in any case where a valid promise contract can be construed from the oral agreement.[350]

V. CONCLUSIONS

Although the 2016 reform established good faith as the legal basis of precontractual liability for breaking off negotiations, the other doctrinal bases

---

343 Case scenario and solutions proposed by Deshayes and Maître, case 11, in Cartwright and Hesselink (n. 15) p. 317. Asúa (n. 140) p. 240 reaches the same solution under the heading of invalidity of a contract and breach of a duty of information. Also Schmidt (n. 21) pp. 190, 192.

344 Malaurie, Aynès and Stoffel-Munck (n. 15) p. 317.

345 CA Aix-en-Provence, 11 January 1983, D 1985, 169 note Légier.

346 Kötz (n. 54) p. 85 fn. 48; Zweigert and Kötz (n. 331) p. 377.

347 Req, 14 April 1863, D 1863, 363.

348 Kötz (n. 54) p. 85; Zweigert and Kötz (n. 331) p. 377.

349 Arthur von Mehren, 'Formal Requirements' in *International Encyclopedia of Comparative Law*, vol. VII (JCB Mohr (Paul Siebeck) and Martinus Nijhoff Publishers, 1998) paras. 188, 192, 219.

350 Schmidt, 'La Période Précontractuelle en Droit Français' (n. 23) p. 557.

of this liability remain valid as they can be seen to emanate from good faith. Nevertheless, between the doctrine of abuse of rights and the criterion of legitimate belief or trust, only the latter embodies the essence of this liability and dominates the subject.[351] It corresponds to the notion of 'reliance' in both its dimensions (dimensions which interact between themselves in that trust-based reliance justifies expectation-based reliance) and as such it has been used by the courts to establish fault and impose liability for breaking off negotiations. Even though it appears that the French approach concentrates either on the wrongdoing of the defendant or on the reliance on the future conclusion of the contract by the claimant,[352] the reliance approach is the more suitable one for explaining the imposition of delictual liability where one party has induced a legitimate *croyance/confiance* in the other (be it a legitimate belief in the future conclusion of the contract or a trust between the parties). Good faith can assist the reliance basis in determining the precontractual blameworthy behaviour but, at least theoretically, it is not an essential element to explain the imposition of liability. Finally, French law, unlike German law, does not present a special treatment of broken negotiations for the conclusion of formal contracts and lack of formality cases.

351 Schmidt, 'La Sanction de la Faute Précontractuelle' (n. 23) p. 72.

352 Zimmermann and Whittaker (n. 103) p. 257, comparative observations to case 3.

CHAPTER 5

RELIANCE IN THE BREAKING-OFF OF NEGOTIATIONS IN CHILEAN LAW

The doctrine of precontractual liability entered into Chilean law and has become established via a process of mixed reception of ideas emanating from the French doctrine of *responsabilité précontractuelle* and the German doctrine of *culpa in contrahendo*.[1] This chapter will focus on the current state of precontractual liability for breaking off negotiations in Chilean law. Throughout the chapter it will be highlighted where Chilean law comes closer to German or to French law, but it will begin by referring to certain aspects of the doctrine of precontractual liability where it is clear that *la doctrina* and *la jurisprudencia* have taken elements from the German or from the French tradition and have sometimes combined these elements into a Chilean hybrid (section I). The chapter will continue with the analysis of the different theoretical bases that have been used to justify the imposition of precontractual liability for breaking off negotiations (section II), arguing in favour of the notion of *confianza*, which corresponds to the German notion of *Vertrauen* and the French notion of *croyance/confiance légitime* (II 1). The role that the principle of good faith (II 2) and the doctrine of abuse of rights (II 3) have played in providing a foundation for this liability will also be explored. The chapter will then look at the requirements of precontractual liability for breaking off negotiations that have been outlined by *la doctrina* and *la jurisprudencia* (section III). It will continue with the analysis of the particular scenarios of broken negotiations for the conclusion of a formal contract and lack of formality cases, as these seem to be the types of cases most frequently disputed before the courts (section IV). The chapter will argue that reliance, embodied in the notion of *confianza*, is the core element of precontractual liability for breaking off negotiations in Chilean law.

---

1 For the history of the reception process, see Ch. 2 s. I 2 (c).

I. AT THE CROSSROADS BETWEEN GERMAN AND FRENCH LAW

The doctrine of precontractual liability in Chilean law has continued to be mostly influenced by the developments of the doctrine in both German and French law. *La doctrina* and *la jurisprudencia*, when discussing precontractual liability for breaking off negotiations, frequently refer to legal scholars and judgments from these European jurisdictions. These references are sometimes made in order to reinforce the solutions reached by Chilean legal scholars[2] or to point out the correspondence between the doctrine of precontractual liability applied by Chilean judgments and the doctrine of precontractual liability applied by 'the superior courts of countries of greater legal tradition'.[3] What is more curious is that when *la doctrina* refer to foreign legal scholars in order to explain this type of liability in Chilean law, often citing German and French legal scholars[4] to a similar degree, they tend to combine their solutions to apply them to Chilean law. For instance, a prominent Chilean scholar, in the introduction to the section of his treatise on extra-contractual liability that deals with liability for precontractual wrongs, after referring to the importance of the protection of *confianza*, indicates that the following paragraphs especially follow a paper by the German author Stoll and then, when explaining cases that give rise to liability for breaking off negotiations, he cites a French book by Ghestin.[5]

In this section special attention will be paid to certain aspects of the doctrine of precontractual liability where German law and French law vary to some extent amongst themselves and where *la doctrina* and *la jurisprudencia*, although sometimes opting for the solution of one or the other, have also at times sought to combine elements taken from both European jurisdictions.

---

2 e.g. Marcelo Barrientos Zamorano, *Daños y Deberes en las Tratativas Preliminares de un Contrato* (2nd edn., Legal Publishing, 2010) pp. 49–51; CS, 13 December 2018, *Sociedad Comercial Timbres con Banco Itaú Chile, rol* 45.515-2017.

3 Ramón Domínguez Benavente, Ramón Domínguez Águila and Carmen Domínguez Hidalgo, 'Comentarios de Jurisprudencia 4' (1996) 200 Revista de Derecho Universidad de Concepción 192, commenting on Cass com 22 April 1997, D 1998 Jur 45, in relation to CA Concepción, 5 June 1996, *Forestal Bío-Bío SA con Madesal, rol* 1374-93 (ratified by CS 28 January 1999), unpublished, case note in Ramón Domínguez Benavente, Ramón Domínguez Águila and Carmen Domínguez Hidalgo, 'Comentarios de Jurisprudencia 1' (1996) 199 Revista de Derecho Universidad de Concepción 179.

4 References are also usually made to Spanish, Italian and Argentinean authors, who, in turn, are normally influenced by the German and French doctrines of precontractual liability.

5 Enrique Barros Bourie, *Tratado de Responsabilidad Extracontractual* (Editorial Jurídica de Chile, 2006) p. 1001 fn. 59, p. 1010 fn. 79.

1. LEGAL RECOGNITION AND NATURE OF THE LIABILITY

(a) Legal Recognition

The Chilean Civil Code, following the original French Civil Code of 1804, does not refer to the negotiations for a contract and does not deal with the formation process of a contract. The Chilean Commercial Code regulates the formation of consent of commercial contracts in general (articles 97–106 CComCh) and, after a long discussion in *la doctrina* and *la jurisprudencia*,[6] it was settled that these articles apply not only to commercial but also to civil contracts and not only to consensual civil contracts but also to real and solemn civil contracts.[7] Some articles of the CCivCh and of the CComCh have been interpreted as giving rise to different hypotheses of precontractual liability.[8] The Consumers' Rights Protection Law[9] has introduced other possible cases of precontractual liability.[10] However, Chilean law, like French law before the 2016 reform,[11] lacks a legal provision recognising precontractual liability for breaking off negotiations.

Some Chilean legal scholars have argued that the CCivCh should be reformed to introduce the express recognition of precontractual liability for breaking off negotiations.[12] One author, following article 1337 of the Italian Civil Code, has proposed a draft paragraph to be added to article 1545 of the CCivCh,[13] stating that '[t]he interested parties in preliminary negotiations aimed at the conclusion of a contract must act in good faith, and must compensate the other party for all losses if they act otherwise'.[14] Others, also following article 1337 of the Italian

6 Details in Hugo Rosende Álvarez, *Algunas Consideraciones sobre la Responsabilidad Precontractual* (Ediciones Universitarias de Valparaíso, 1979) ch. IV.

7 art. 1443 CCivCh ('The contract is real when, for it to be perfected, the delivery of the thing that is the object of the contract is necessary; it is solemn when it is subject to the observance of certain special formalities without which they produce no civil effect; and it is consensual when it is perfected by the sole agreement of the parties').

8 See Ch. 2, s. I 2 (c) above. After a reform in 2013 of the CComCh, art. 529 no. 1 can be considered to give rise to precontractual liability of the insurer for breach of information duties regarding concluded insurance contracts; Marcelo Barrientos, 'Nuevos Deberes Precontractuales de Información en los Certificados de Cobertura Provisorio, Definitivo y la Propuesta del Contrato de Seguro' (2015) 22 Revista de Derecho 65, pp. 85 ff.

9 *Ley 19.496 sobre Protección de los Derechos de los Consumidores* of 7 March 1997 (LPDC).

10 e.g. arts. 17E (compensation in case of nullity of certain clauses of an adhesion contract) and 17L (compensation where the consumer entered into a contract of financial services or products due to information provided by the supplier inducing mistake or false advertising) which also protect micro- and small businesses as consumers.

11 See Ch. 4, text to (n. 2) above.

12 e.g. Manuel Risueño, *De las Obligaciones Precontractuales* (Soc. Imp. y Lito. Universo, 1933) p. 141.

13 See text to (n. 167) below.

14 Álvaro Puelma Accorsi, 'Ponencia Principal' in Fundación Fernando Fueyo Laneri (ed.), *Estudios sobre Reformas al Código Civil y Código de Comercio: Título Preliminar, Teoría de la Imprevisión, Contratos Preparatorios* (Editorial Jurídica de Chile, 2000) p. 290.

Civil Code, have proposed a draft paragraph to be added at the beginning of article 1546 of the CCivCh,[15] stating that '[p]arties must conduct themselves according to good faith in the development of negotiations and in the formation of a contract'.[16] These are only academic proposals and, as yet, there is no bill before Congress contemplating such a reform of the Civil Code.

At a regional level, some Chilean legal scholars have been participating in an academic and non-binding harmonisation project on the Principles of Latin American Contract Law, PLACL (*Principios Latinoamericanos de Derecho de los Contratos*, PLDC),[17] which includes an article recognising precontractual liability for breaking off negotiations.[18]

(b) *Nature of the Liability*

The nature of precontractual liability in general has been much debated in Chilean law. Establishing its nature is extremely relevant as it determines the applicable regime of liability. The CCivCh establishes two general regimes of liability: contractual liability and delictual or extra-contractual liability.[19] There are considerable differences between these regimes.[20] Regarding liability for breaking off negotiations, its lack of express legal recognition makes the determination of its legal nature particularly difficult.

Legal scholars tend to distinguish between the different scenarios of precontractual liability in order to determine the nature of the liability. Therefore, it is considered that some particular cases are of a delictual nature while others

---

15 Text in s. II 2 below.

16 Rafael Gómez Balmaceda and Hugo Rosende Álvarez, 'Comentario Crítico' in Fundación Fernando Fueyo Laneri (ed.), *Estudios sobre Reformas al Código Civil y Código de Comercio: Título Preliminar, Teoría de la Imprevisión, Contratos Preparatorios* (Editorial Jurídica de Chile, 2000) p. 305.

17 Rodrigo Momberg and Stefan Vogenauer (eds.), *The Future of Contract Law in Latin America: The Principles of Latin American Contract Law* (Hart Publishing, 2017).

18 While art. 10 establishes that 'Freedom of negotiation. The parties are free to negotiate the contract and to withdraw from the negotiations at any time, in accordance with good faith', art. 11 recognises that 'Harm caused in the negotiation of contract. (1) Compensation must be provided for harm caused by withdrawing from negotiations in bad faith. (2) A party that initiates or continues negotiations when not able or not intending to reach an agreement is also required to provide this compensation. (3) In no event shall compensation be provided for the loss of expected benefits under a contract that is not concluded'; text of the PLACL in Spanish and in English, in their final version approved by the drafting committee in August 2017, in Rodrigo Momberg and Stefan Vogenauer, 'The Principles of Latin American Contract Law: Text, Translation, and Introduction' (2018) 23 Uniform Law Review 144, p. 153.

19 arts. 1545 ff. and arts. 2314 ff. CCivCh, respectively.

20 e.g. with regard to the burden of proof, extent of compensation, and prescription periods. For details, Barros Bourie (n. 5) §64; Pablo Rodríguez Grez, *Nuevas Tendencias de la Responsabilidad* (Abeledo Perrot, 2011) p. 181 ff.

are of a contractual nature or that, even if they are not truly of either nature, the legal regime of one or other type of liability is applicable depending on the particular case.[21] Which legal regime of liability is considered applicable often depends on which type of liability is considered to be the general regime of liability applicable to any case that does not have a typical contractual or delictual nature.[22]

In the case of liability for breaking off negotiations, the majority of *la doctrina* and *la jurisprudencia* consider that it is of a delictual nature or that the delictual regime of liability is applicable.[23] The rules on delictual liability (articles 2314–2334) are located in Title XXXV ('Of delicts and quasi-delicts') of Book IV ('Of Obligations in General and of Contracts') of the CCivCh. Two articles, in particular, establish a general principle of delictual liability, according to which all losses (including purely economic losses) caused to a person by the intent or negligence of another person can be compensated:

> Art 2314. He who has committed a delict or quasi-delict which has caused harm to another is under an obligation to indemnify; without prejudice to the punishment imposed by legislation for the delict or quasi-delict.
>
> Art 2329 [first paragraph]. As a general rule all damage that can be attributed to the malice or negligence of another person must be repaired by it.

---

21 e.g. Arturo Alessandri Rodríguez, *De la Responsabilidad Extracontractual en el Derecho Civil Chileno (Título 35 del Libro IV del Código Civil)* (Editorial Jurídica de Chile, 2005) p. 45; Arturo Alessandri, Manuel Somarriva and Antonio Vodanovic, *Tratado de las Obligaciones*, vol. 2 (2nd edn., Editorial Jurídica de Chile, 2004) pp. 362–363.

22 Some consider that the contractual regime of liability is the general one, while the delictual regime is exceptional (e.g. Alessandri Rodríguez (n. 21) p. 43). Others consider that it is, in principle, the other way around (e.g. Barros Bourie (n. 5) pp. 1068, 1071).

23 e.g. Rosende Álvarez (n. 6) p. 60; Domínguez Benavente, Domínguez Águila and Domínguez Hidalgo (n. 3) p. 182; Claudia Schmidt Hott and Solange Doyharçabal Casse, 'Chile' in Atilio Aníbal Alterini and Roberto López Cabana (eds.), *Enciclopedia de la Responsabilidad Civil*, vol. II (Abeledo Perrot, 1998) pp. 217, 235; Alessandri Rodríguez (n. 21) p. 45; Barrientos (n. 2) p. 117; Rosario Celedón and Patricia Silberman, *Responsabilidad Precontractual por Ruptura de Negociaciones Contractuales* (Editorial Jurídica de Chile, 2010) pp. 132–133; Iñigo de la Maza, 'El Retiro Unilateral como un Caso de Responsabilidad Precontractual' in Iñigo de la Maza (ed.), *Cuadernos de Análisis Jurídicos, Colección Derecho Privado III: Temas de Contratos* (Ediciones Universidad Diego Portales, 2006) pp. 131–133, 142; Iñigo de la Maza and Carlos Pizarro, *Responsabilidad Civil: Casos Prácticos* (5th edn., Abeledo Perrot, 2010) p. 56; Rodríguez Grez (n. 20) p. 199; Arturo Prado Puga, 'Sobre la Responsabilidad Civil Precontractual' (2015) 32 Revista Actualidad Jurídica 167, p. 172; CA Concepción 5 June 1996 (n. 3); CA Concepción, 30 June 1999, *Sociedad Ruz de la Barra con Comar S.A.*, unpublished, case note in Ramón Domínguez Benavente, Ramón Domínguez Águila and Carmen Domínguez Hidalgo, 'Comentarios de Jurisprudencia 3' (1998) 204 Revista de Derecho Universidad de Concepción 187; CS, 24 September 2010, *Sociedad Comercial e Inmobiliaria Beckna Limitada con Corporación Municipal de Ancud, rol* 4895-2008; CS, 29 December 2011, *Jiménez Mira con Armijo Cerda, rol* 1872-2010, replacement judgment (as opposed to the cassation judgment); CS 13 December 2018, *Sociedad Comercial Timbres con Banco Itaú Chile* (n. 2).

In establishing a general principle of delictual liability, Chilean law follows French law (and differs from German law),[24] which explains why the view that precontractual liability for breaking off negotiations is of a delictual nature is predominant in both Chilean and French law[25] and evidently differs from the contractual approach taken in German law.[26] Some Chilean scholars concede that there is a 'contractual likeness' in the relationship that the negotiations give rise to between negotiating parties, and consider that this liability, although delictual, is essentially dominated by the principles of contract law.[27] In some aspects, however, the Chilean law of delict is closer to the German law of delict. For instance, there is no vicarious liability; the fault of the employer is presumed when the fault of the employee is proved, but this presumption can be rebutted (although it is difficult to rebut in practice because of the exacting interpretation of the law applied by the courts) by proving that even acting with due diligence it would have been impossible to prevent the act that caused harm.[28]

In the majority view, in the absence of a contract (even a preliminary one), the malicious or culpable breaking-off of negotiations can give rise to a delict or quasi-delict if all the requirements of delictual liability are met ((i) a voluntary act by a capable person, (ii) carried out with intent or negligence, (iii) that caused another person to suffer harm).[29] The difference between a delict and a quasi-delict is that in the former there is an intention to cause harm (*dolo*) whereas in the latter the conduct is only negligent (*culpa*).[30] However, at least in theory, the consequences of both are the same according to the principle of the integral reparation of harm which compensates the victim for all the losses suffered, regardless of the seriousness of the illicit conduct.[31] It is commonly added by the supporters of this view that negotiations do not create any legal relationship between the negotiating parties and that since no legal or contractual obligation exists, only delictual liability is possible if indeed a delict or quasi-delict has been committed.[32]

---

24 arts. 2314 and 2329(1) CCivCh resemble new arts. 1240 and 1241 Cciv (see Ch.4, text to (n. 17) above); Barros Bourie (n. 5) pp. 19, 284, 286; Mauricio Tapia Rodríguez, *Código Civil 1855–2005: Evolución y Perspectivas* (Editorial Jurídica de Chile, 2005) p. 276.

25 For French law, see Ch. 4, text to (n. 15) above.

26 For German law, see Ch. 3, text to (n. 3) above.

27 Barros Bourie (n. 5) pp. 1004, 1008; see text to (n. 47) below.

28 arts. 2320 and 2322 CCivCh; Barros Bourie (n. 5) pp. 167, 168 fn. 265, 179, 183 fn. 311, 184; for German law see Ch. 3, text to (n. 28) above.

29 Barros Bourie (n. 5) pp. 61–62; Alessandri Rodríguez (n. 21) p. 95.

30 arts. 1437 and 2284 CCivCh. The distinction between delict and quasi-delict is not used in modern French law, John Bell, Sophie Boyron and Simon Whittaker, *Principles of French Law* (2nd edn., OUP, 2008) p. 294 fn. 1.

31 *La jurisprudencia* considers that this principle is recognised in art. 2329(1) CCivCh (text in p. 103 above); Barros Bourie (n. 5) pp. 37–38, 255.

32 Alessandri Rodríguez (n. 21) p. 45.

There are also some minority views. They are influenced, to some extent and in different ways, by the German doctrine of *culpa in contrahendo*. A Chilean author writing in the first half of the twentieth century, who was heavily influenced by Saleilles' doctrine of precontractual liability (who in turn was influenced by Jhering's doctrine of *culpa in contrahendo*), particularly by the idea that there is a tacit pact accessory to the main contract, the breach of which gives rise to contractual liability,[33] considered that precontractual liability for breaking off negotiations is of a contractual nature because there is a contractual fault in the violation of the *confianza* or *seguridad* that the contract will be entered into, that has been created by the party breaking off.[34]

A Supreme Court judge has expressed his view, as a minority (although he agreed with the majority as to the outcome of the case), that precontractual liability, while it shares with delictual liability the non-existence of a legal tie, fits more appropriately within contractual liability which, in his opinion, is the general regime of civil liability which should apply by default.[35]

Another minority view, which has more supporters, argues that the true nature of precontractual liability in general and in the particular case of breaking off negotiations is special and autonomous; that it is not truly a contractual or a delictual liability but constitutes a *tertium genus* or a special type of liability.[36] This approach is clearly inspired by German scholars.[37] This view argues that liability for breaking off negotiations is not contractual because no contract has been concluded and is not delictual because the party who breaks off is exercising his freedom to act and is not truly committing a delict or quasi-delict; it is a liability that is based on special reasons or simply a different type of liability.[38] It is argued that the nature of precontractual liability is of a special type. It presents some elements that are closer to contractual liability, such as the fact that negotiating parties are not strangers who only come into contact when an accident takes place (as is usual in delictual liability),

33 See Ch. 2 s. I 2 above.

34 Risueño (n. 12) pp. 70–73.

35 Judge Sergio Muñoz Gajardo in CS 29 December 2011 (n. 23).

36 e.g. Sara Eiler, *De la Formación del Consentimiento en los Contratos* (Editorial Nascimento, 1935) p. 71; Augusto Fuentes de la Sotta, 'La Responsabilidad por el Hecho de Otro en Materia Contractual' (Licenciado en Ciencias Jurídicas thesis, Universidad de Chile, 1938) p. 28; Isabel Zuloaga Ríos, *Teoría de la Responsabilidad Precontractual. Aplicaciones en la Formación del Consentimiento de los Contratos* (3rd edn., Legal Publishing, 2008) pp. 124–126; Pablo Vivanco Luengo, 'Aspectos Relevantes de la Responsabilidad Precontractual por Ruptura Injustificada de Negociaciones Precontractuales' (2008) 17 Revista de Derecho 139, p. 145.

37 See Ch. 3, text to (n. 8) above.

38 Eiler (n. 36) p. 71. Also, Antonio Vodanovic, *Manual de Derecho Civil: Parte Preliminar y General*, vol. II (4th edn., LexisNexis, 2006) pp. 67–68, but referring to liability for revocation of an offer (art. 100 CComCh).

but are familiar with each other because they have been involved in negotiations that have given rise to a special relationship between them. But it also presents some elements that are closer to delictual liability, such as the fact that no contract has been entered into (or if a contract has been entered into it has been declared null) and the general duty not to cause harm to another has been violated.[39] Nevertheless, in the absence of a legal recognition of liability for breaking off negotiations, the application of the delictual regime seems the only viable option.[40]

Although the courts adhere to the majority view,[41] some judgments,[42] while recognising that liability for broken negotiations is governed by the Civil Code's articles on delictual liability,[43] also base this liability on certain articles on formation of consent of the Commercial Code.[44] This is rather curious (and unnecessary) because the articles on delictual liability of the CCivCh are a sufficient legal basis to impose this liability and because these articles of the CComCh deal with a specific scenario of precontractual liability (revocation of an offer) which differs from that of broken negotiations. However, the mentioning of these articles of the CComCh by the courts can be understood if it is borne in mind that a leading scholar on precontractual liability has argued that the principles contained in the articles of the CComCh on formation of consent are the *derecho común*[45] regarding precontractual liability.[46]

2. A SPECIAL RELATIONSHIP WHICH GIVES RISE TO PRECONTRACTUAL DUTIES

The delictual nature of precontractual liability (influenced by French law) is not considered incompatible with the existence of a relationship that gives rise to special duties between the negotiating parties (influenced by German law).

According to Barros Bourie, although the nature of liability for breaking off negotiations is delictual and a feature of delictual liability is that no previous relationship exists between the persons involved as they are strangers, a previous relationship exists in this case: negotiations. Negotiations are entered into when there is a business contact (*contacto negocial*) and, consequently, a

---

39 Zuloaga Ríos (n. 36) pp. 124–125.
40 Zuloaga Ríos (n. 36) p. 140.
41 See (n. 23) above.
42 e.g. CS 24 September 2010 (n. 23).
43 arts. 2314 and 2329, text in p. 103 above.
44 arts. 99 and 100 CComCh (Ch. 2 n. 31).
45 The literal translation is 'common law' and the expression must be understood as the law applicable to any case of precontractual liability and not just to the specific situations regulated in the CComCh.
46 Rosende Álvarez (n. 6) p. 111.

business relationship (*relación negocial*) which is also a relationship of *confianza* and loyalty, originates. This relationship gives rise to reciprocal duties of loyalty and diligence.[47] Other scholars also consider that negotiations are a precontractual legal relationship (*relación jurídica precontractual*) which can be described as a relationship of *confianza* (*relación de confianza*).[48] Another indicates that the mere fact of being in social contact creates between negotiating parties a special legal relationship (*relación jurídica especial*) that gives rise to a reciprocal state of *confianza* that cannot be disappointed, and a reciprocal duty of loyalty and honesty originates that imposes positive and negative duties.[49]

The German influence in Chilean scholars in the use of notions such as 'precontractual relationship', a 'social' or 'business contact' and 'precontractual duties' is clear.[50] This influence is sometimes direct, in that German authors are cited to give strength to these ideas,[51] and sometimes indirect, through the reception of German legal thought by Spanish legal scholars who are cited by Chilean authors.[52]

In Chilean delictual law, the existence of a specific duty of care in relation to the victim is not necessary for liability to arise, because the violation of the general duty of care is enough.[53] However, in certain cases, such as in precontractual negotiations, the precontractual relationship between negotiating parties gives rise to specific duties of care that go beyond the general duty not to harm others, and contributes to determine their intensity.[54] The duties of care that arise during negotiations are mostly positive duties of conduct. These duties, unlike the general extra-contractual duties of care, are owed between parties who are not strangers because they are involved in the precontractual relationship. In the absence of a preliminary contract, these duties find their source in the law.[55]

47 Barros Bourie (n. 5) pp. 19 fn. 10, 118, 628, 979, 1004; see text to (n. 27) above. CA Arica, 17 August 2012, *Medina Cusi con ASOAGRO AG*, *rol* 179-2012 (ratified by CS 10 October 2012) recognised that during negotiations there is a *contacto negocial* which imposes duties of protection, loyalty and diligence. More recently, CS 13 December 2018, *Sociedad Comercial Timbres con Banco Itaú Chile* (n. 2) expressly refers to a relationship of *confianza* which gives rise to precontractual duties.

48 e.g. Barrientos, *Daños y Deberes en las Tratativas Preliminares de un Contrato* (n. 2) pp. 33, 49, 56; Cristián Boetsch Gillet, *La Buena Fe Contractual* (Ediciones Universidad Católica de Chile, 2015) p. 114.

49 Francisco Javier Saavedra Galleguillos, *Teoría del Consentimiento* (Editorial Jurídica ConoSur, 1994) pp. 265, 268.

50 Marcelo Barrientos Zamorano, 'Los Tratos Preliminares en la Relación Precontractual' (2008) 14 Revista de Derecho de la Empresa 9, p. 14.

51 e.g. Stoll is cited by Barros Bourie (n. 5) p. 1001; Larenz by Saavedra (n. 49) p. 265 and Boetsch (n. 48) p. 114.

52 e.g. Barrientos (n. 2) p. 116, citing Díez-Picazo, Roca Trías and Morales Moreno; Zuloaga Ríos (n. 36) p. 77, citing Díez-Picazo.

53 Barros Bourie (n. 5) pp. 20, 118.

54 Barros Bourie (n. 5) p. 118.

55 Ideas expressed by Barros Bourie (n. 5) pp. 131, 1003, 1069.

Although there are some specific laws that impose precontractual duties (particularly of information),[56] duties of care can always find their legal basis in the general articles of delictual liability.[57] However, precontractual duties are usually said to emanate from the principle of good faith and, consequently, they can also find their legal basis in article 1546 CCivCh.[58]

Precontractual duties are subject to different classifications. One classification, particularly reminiscent of the German doctrine of *culpa in contrahendo*, identifies the following: duties of protection or security, duties of loyalty, duties of information and duties to avoid the inefficiency of a legal act.[59] Other duties sometimes mentioned are: duties of secrecy, confidentiality or discretion, duties of custody and conservation, and the duty to warn about an essential mistake being made.[60]

The precontractual relationship that gives rise to these special duties is not binding in that it does not impose on negotiating parties an obligation to enter into the contract under negotiation (unless some form of binding preliminary agreement has been entered into). But the precontractual relationship and the duties that it gives rise to are binding in that they should be observed because if they are breached, precontractual liability may arise. It must be stressed that the notion of precontractual relationship and duties that emanate from it used by Chilean scholars does not correspond to the technical meaning that it has in German law.[61]

A particularity of Chilean law is that a number of legal scholars and judgments, when listing the requirements for precontractual liability to arise, indicate the need for consent, agreement or intention of the negotiating parties in entering the negotiations,[62] which suggests that some form of relationship exists between them. This requirement seems to stem from the reception of Saleilles' theory of precontractual liability by Chilean legal scholars at the beginning of the twentieth century.[63] Risueño stated that it is a requirement for precontractual liability to arise that both parties agreed to enter into negotiations and that if

---

56 e.g. LPDC (n. 10) above.

57 arts. 2314 and 2329(1) CCivCh. Similarly, de la Maza (n. 23) p. 142.

58 See this Ch. s. II 2 below.

59 Barros Bourie (n. 5) p. 1001.

60 Barrientos (n. 2) pp. 76, 100, 105.

61 For German law, see Ch. 3 s. I 1.

62 e.g. Eiler (n. 36) p. 72; Risueño (n. 12) p. 62; Mario Rossel, 'La Indemnización de Perjuicios en la Formación del Consentimiento y en el Contrato de Transporte Terrestre' (Licenciado en Ciencias Jurídicas y Sociales thesis, Universidad de Chile, 1966) p. 31; Rosende Álvarez (n. 6) pp. 59–60; Barrientos (n. 2) p. 49; *Forestal Bío-Bío* case (n. 3); CA Santiago, 13 September 2005, *Inmobiliaria e Inversiones Montecarlo S.A. con Fisco de Chile*, Westlaw Chile CL/JUR/1895/2005; CA Puerto Montt, 15 July 2008, *Sociedad Comercial e Inmobiliaria Beckna Limitada con Corporación Municipal de Ancud*, Legal Publishing no. 39449, ratified by CS 24 September 2010 (n. 23).

63 See Ch. 2, text to (nn. 15, 32) above. This is clear in de la Maza and Pizarro (n. 23) p. 51.

this agreement (which is not necessarily a contract but creates a security in the conclusion of the contract) was violated, it gave rise to contractual fault.[64] Similarly, Eiler listed as a requirement for liability to arise that there was a reciprocal agreement to negotiate, because if the party breaking off had not previously consented, he could not be liable for the expenses incurred or other losses suffered by the other party, as he had not deceived the *confianza* of the other party.[65]

More recent legal scholars and judgments have also listed the consent to negotiate as a requirement for liability to arise, arguing that this consent imposes on negotiating parties the obligation to act in accordance with commercial equity and good faith.[66] This argument is not convincing. Negotiating parties will be subject to the duty to negotiate in good faith from the mere fact of negotiating with each other.[67] An agreement to negotiate is not truly a requirement for precontractual liability for breaking off negotiations under Chilean law but is only a vestige of the influence of Saleilles' doctrine of precontractual liability in the initial reception of this doctrine into Chilean law.[68] There is no need to assimilate negotiations to a contractual relationship, as it is generally agreed that this liability is of a delictual nature.[69] In any case, if agreement or consent to negotiate is still required, this requirement is easily met in practice, as the mere fact of negotiating shows that there was consent in entering negotiations.

In conclusion, while the notion of a relationship of reliance that gives rise to precontractual duties between negotiating parties has an eminently German origin, some ideas taken from French legal scholars have also been incorporated by some Chilean authors and judgments in requiring consent or agreement to negotiate for precontractual liability to arise. This requirement seems incorrect or at least irrelevant in Chilean law, but it does contribute to the idea of the existence of a relationship between negotiating parties.

3. PRECONTRACTUAL FAULT

The requirements of delictual liability must be met for precontractual liability for breaking off negotiations to arise.[70] The focus is on the element of fault. As in French law (even after the 2016 reform), there is no specific definition of 'precontractual fault' and, consequently, it must be subsumed under the notion

64 Risueño (n. 12) pp. 62, 71–73, 142.
65 Eiler (n. 36) p. 72.
66 e.g. Rosende Álvarez (n. 6) pp. 59–60, 78; Barrientos (n. 2) p. 49; *Forestal Bío-Bío* case (n. 3).
67 See text following (n. 184) below.
68 See text to (n. 63) above.
69 See text to (n. 23) above.
70 See text to (n. 29) above.

of 'delictual fault'.[71] The wide notion of fault (*culpa*) involves both intentional (*dolo*) and non-intentional or negligent (*culpa* or *negligencia*) fault.[72] Because the paradigm case is of a negligent breaking-off of negotiations, the analysis will be restricted to non-intentional fault and references to 'fault' (*culpa*) should be understood as to negligence. In the determination of the notion of delictual fault, French but also German influences can be seen.

The CCivCh classifies fault into three species (*culpa grave*, *culpa leve* and *culpa levísima*) in article 44. Although it is generally thought that this classification of the different degrees of fault is only applicable in contract law,[73] other legal scholars consider that the definition of 'slight fault' (*culpa leve*) is the standard of conduct required in delict.[74] Article 44, in its third and fourth paragraphs, indicates:

> Slight fault, slight carelessness, light carelessness, is the lack of such diligence and care that men ordinarily employ in their own businesses. Fault or carelessness, without another description, means slight fault or carelessness. This type of fault is opposed to ordinary or medium diligence or care.
>
> He who must manage a business like a good father of a family is responsible for this type of fault.

Therefore, negligence is essentially the lack of due care according to a standard or model of conduct.[75] Due care is an objective notion in that the individual and subjective characteristics of a person are not taken into account but is determined according to a model of conduct. The imputation of fault is objective in that it is not a moral reproach to the author of the harm; the focus is not on the person but on his conduct. The assessment of the existence of fault is also objective in that the actual conduct of the author of the harm is compared to a general, flexible, abstract and objective standard of conduct that can be expected of a model type of person placed in the same circumstances. The pattern of conduct is that of the 'prudent man', the 'reasonable person', the 'diligent person', a 'person who is not particularly heroic but is respectful' or, using the language that comes from Roman law, that of a 'good father (or mother) of a family' (*buen padre (o madre) de familia*). Therefore, the standard of care is assessed on the basis of two paradigms that complement each other: a model type of person and the conduct that is rationally required. It is argued that the standard of *culpa leve*

---

71 For French law, see Ch. 4, text to (n. 26) above.

72 Barros Bourie (n. 5) pp. 62, 75–76.

73 Alessandri Rodríguez (n. 21) p. 44; Arturo Alessandri, Manuel Somarriva and Antonio Vodanovic, *Tratado de Derecho Civil: Partes Preliminar y General*, vol. II (7th edn., Editorial Jurídica de Chile, 2005) p. 161.

74 e.g. Barros Bourie (n. 5) p. 80.

75 This para. follows Barros Bourie (n. 5) pp. 28–29, 32, 37, 62, 72, 77–78, 80–81, 84–85, 119. Also Alessandri Rodríguez (n. 21) p. 127.

generally corresponds to the standards of care used in the French law of delict (model type of person) and in the German law of contract (socially required care).[76] Some consider that fault involves the breach of a duty of care and accept Planiol's definition of fault.[77] The duty of care will be established on the basis of an estimation of the conduct that in those circumstances a reasonable and diligent person would have had. The legislator can establish concrete duties of care but, in the absence of a specific legal text, their determination in the particular case corresponds to the judges using the standard of the diligent person.[78]

The notion of delictual fault relates to the notions of reliance (*confianza*) and legitimate expectations (*expectativas legítimas*) which are suggested to be the true theoretical basis of precontractual liability for breaking off negotiations.[79] The objective notion of fault strengthens reliance because it looks to the reasonable expectations that can be had in relation to the conduct of others, and in the construction of these expectations no regard can be had to the subjective characteristics of each person.[80] Fault liability is based on the disregard of the legitimate expectation of the victim not to suffer wrongful harm due to the conduct of others.[81]

Legal scholars do not place great emphasis in determining where the fault is placed in cases of liability for breaking off negotiations; that is, if in the conduct during negotiations or if in the breaking-off itself. Rosende Álvarez considered that it is not the actual breaking-off but the culpable conduct during negotiations that gives rise to liability.[82] In the more recent *doctrina* mention is usually made of two elements: (i) breaking off without a justified reason, (ii) after negligently or intentionally inducing and then disappointing a legitimate *confianza* in the other party.[83] Some judgments consider that the breaking-off itself is abusive or arbitrary and, hence, culpable, but to reach this conclusion they also take into account the conduct of the parties during the negotiations.[84] The Supreme Court has stated that the precontractual wrong is not found in the refusal to contract but in having negotiated in bad faith or with grave disregard of the interests of the other party and that, consequently, the loss is caused by having placed *confianza* in the diligence and good faith of the other party.[85]

---

76 Barros Bourie (n. 5) pp. 81 fn. 17, 82 fn. 21.

77 See Ch. 4, text to (n. 31) above; e.g. Barros Bourie (n. 5) p. 95. Alessandri Rodríguez (n. 21) p. 125, rejects Planiol's definition of fault.

78 Barros Bourie (n. 5) pp. 28, 94–95, 97, 105–106.

79 See this Ch. s. II 1 below.

80 Barros Bourie (n. 5) pp. 79, 89.

81 Barros Bourie (n. 5) pp. 81, 106.

82 Rosende Álvarez (n. 6) p. 75.

83 e.g. Celedón and Silberman (n. 23) p. 136; Barrientos (n. 2) p. 58.

84 e.g. *Forestal Bío-Bío* case (n. 3) *considerando* (ground of ruling) 5; CS, 12 April 2012, *Urrea Fuentes con Corpbanca*, *rol* 218-2011, replacement judgment *considerando* 3.

85 *Jiménez Mira* case (n. 23) *considerando* 8, citing Barros Bourie (n. 5) p. 1007.

In the same judgment the two elements previously mentioned were considered as requirements for precontractual liability to arise.[86] Therefore, it seems that fault at both levels is required.

As to the proof of fault in cases of liability for breaking off negotiations, the general principle applies which is that delictual fault has to be proven by the claimant.[87] The claimant must prove the act or omission of the defendant and all the circumstances that will allow the judge to rule on the diligence or negligence of the defendant.[88] It is debated whether article 2329 CCivCh establishes a presumption of fault for one's own act. However, even if it is recognised that such a presumption exists, it is highly unlikely that it could be applicable in cases of liability for breaking off negotiations, as it refers to situations of particularly dangerous activities or where the circumstances indicate *prima facie* that the harm has been caused by negligence.[89]

Finally, *la doctrina* is unanimous in considering that the characterisation of the act or omission as negligent, i.e. determining whether the defendant breached a duty of care, is a question of law (*cuestión de derecho*) and is, therefore, subject to the *recurso de casación en el fondo* before the Supreme Court.[90] The current position of the Supreme Court is not clear, but it frequently evaluates the facts of the case in order to characterise the conduct as culpable.[91]

II. THEORETICAL BASES OF PRECONTRACTUAL LIABILITY FOR BREAKING OFF NEGOTIATIONS

The doctrinal basis of this liability is still subject to discussion among Chilean legal scholars and has also varied in the judgments of the courts. It is frequent that legal scholars and judgments combine different bases in order to justify the imposition of this liability. Thus, it is not surprising to find references to delictual fault, *confianza*, breach of good faith and abuse of rights in the reasoning of a single legal scholar or judgment.[92] Three main doctrinal bases have been put forward: legitimate *confianza*, breach of good faith (or bad faith) and abuse of rights. These main bases sometimes encompass other arguments

---

86 *Jiménez Mira* case (n. 23) *considerando* 7.

87 Application of art. 1698(1) CCivCh.

88 Barros Bourie (n. 5) p. 140.

89 Barros Bourie (n. 5) p. 151.

90 See (n. 174) below; e.g. Barros Bourie (n. 5) p. 145; Alessandri Rodríguez (n. 21) pp. 149–151, citing French legal scholars.

91 Alessandri Rodríguez (n. 21) pp. 151–152; Barros Bourie (n. 5) p. 146 fn. 205.

92 e.g. in Barros Bourie (n. 5) pp. 1008–1012; *Forestal Bío-Bío* case (n. 3); *Ruz de la Barra* case (n. 23); CA Talca, 8 November 1999, *Luna Espinoza con Bobadilla Valenzuela*, quashed by CS, 22 November 2001, *rol* 2217-2000, Gaceta Jurídica 2001 no. 257 pp. 56–74; *Jiménez Mira* case (n. 23).

and are frequently combined. This section will argue that the appropriate basis to explain the rationale of precontractual liability for breaking off negotiations is 'reliance' expressed in the notion of legitimate *confianza*. Good faith and abuse of rights will also be analysed and particular emphasis will be placed on how they interact with *confianza* and whether *confianza* on its own is sufficient to justify this liability.

1. *CONFIANZA LEGÍTIMA*

In the initial reception of the doctrine of precontractual liability into Chilean law it was seen that the notion of *confianza* was used in order to explain its rationale.[93] In the current state of precontractual liability for breaking off negotiations in Chilean law, although reference is still made to other doctrinal arguments, the use of the notion of *confianza* has been increasing in the more recent *doctrina* and in judgments.

(a) Confianza *in* La Doctrina *and* La Jurisprudencia

Many renowned contemporary legal scholars and recent judgments refer to *confianza*, if not as the sole foundation of precontractual liability for breaking off negotiations, then at least as part of the argument for the imposition of this liability, usually combining it with other legal and doctrinal bases.

For instance, Barros Bourie, who holds that some cases of liability for breaking off negotiations can be understood as applications of the doctrine of abuse of rights[94] and who also holds that bad faith gives rise to this liability,[95] at the same time argues that the protection of *confianza* gives rise to certain hypotheses of liability when one party has created or nourished in the other party the *confianza* that the contract will certainly be entered into.[96] The protected legal interest is *confianza* and it is the abuse of this *confianza* that founds this liability.[97]

De la Maza considers that the determining factor in order to characterise the precontractual period and, hence, solve the problem of accountability is the position of the parties. He argues that the pendulum of precontractual liability oscillates between two extremes: the self-interest and the *confianza* of the negotiating parties and that both should be protected in a balanced manner. The duty of conduct in the precontractual phase only requires a party not to disappoint the reasonable *confianza* of the other party. The disappointment of

---

93 See Ch. 2 s. I 2 (c).
94 See this Ch. s. II 3 below.
95 See text to (n. 208) below.
96 Barros Bourie (n. 5) p. 1009.
97 Barros Bourie (n. 5) p. 1010.

the *confianza* that is subject to protection constitutes the civil wrong, which can be denominated, depending on the circumstances, as fault (intentional or non-intentional), violation of good faith, breach of a duty to act properly or abuse of rights; and beyond the name, the determinant factor in the assessment of the wrong is to consider the nature of negotiations which is determined by the position of the parties.[98]

Barrientos enumerates as the first requirement of precontractual liability for breaking off negotiations the creation of a reasonable *confianza* in the conclusion of the negotiated contract.[99] Celedón and Silberman also refer to a *confianza* in the conclusion of the negotiated contract as an element that, alongside the absence of a justified reason, shapes the conduct of breaking off negotiations as a civil wrong.[100]

A relevant judgment which refers to *confianza* is that of the Court of Appeal of Concepción of 5 June 1996, ratified by the Supreme Court.[101] This is one of the most important Chilean judgments regarding precontractual liability, as it is the first to award damages to the claimant for the unilateral breaking-off of negotiations by the other party. Two groups of companies negotiated for over a year for the sale of plots of land for forest use of a value of millions of US dollars. They had exchanged the documents of title of the properties for their study, had studied them, made observations on them, had drafted and revised drafts of the promise of sale contract and of a mandate contract and had even set a date for the signing of the promise of sale contract. However, on that date the sellers communicated to the buyers that they were withdrawing from the negotiations because they had just sold the plots to a third party who had paid them a higher price than the price which had been agreed to be included in the promise of sale. In Chilean law, a promise to conclude a contract is valid as a preliminary contract if perfected with the legal formality of being in writing and sets a date or condition for the perfection of the promised contract and contains the essential elements of such contract, which in turn must not be a contract considered unenforceable by the law (article 1554 CCivCh).[102]

This judgment begins by stating that the claim is based on the precontractual liability of the defendant and provides different definitions of this liability from

---

98 de la Maza (n. 23) pp. 134, 135 fn. 11, 147.

99 Barrientos (n. 2) p. 51.

100 Celedón and Silberman (n. 23) p. 136. Similarly, Francisco Segura Riveiro, 'El Interés Indemnizable en las Hipótesis de Responsabilidad Precontractual' in Juan Andrés Varas Braun and others (eds.), *Estudios de Derecho Civil: Jornadas Nacionales de Derecho Civil 2005–2009*, vol. III (Abeledo Perrot, 2011) p. 106.

101 *Forestal Bío-Bío* case (n. 3).

102 A promise contract is solemn (see legal definition in (n. 7) above), preliminary, and usually bilateral in that both parties are obliged to enter into the promised contract; the promised contract can be any type of enforceable contract but the most common is the sale of real estate, René Abeliuk Manasevich, *Contrato de Promesa, de Opción y Otros Acuerdos Previos* (3rd edn., Abeledo Perrot, 2012) pp. 10, 21 ff.

Chilean and foreign authors.[103] It quotes a definition by a Spanish author who indicates that precontractual liability is 'that which is incurred in by someone who (…) unjustifiably breaks off the preliminary negotiations, breaching duties of loyalty and *confianza* of which the other party was worthy'.[104] It then quotes a Chilean author in order to establish that '(…) by the mere fact that persons enter into a relation with the purpose to negotiate the conclusion of a contract, a connection between them is established which creates a state of reciprocal *confianza* which must not be disappointed'.[105]

A scholar commenting on this case indicates that it demonstrates that, normally, negotiations imply collaboration between the negotiating parties which is only possible if they can trust (*confiar*) each other, even if to a minimal extent. Here, the parties collaborated in the negotiation and such collaboration was justified by the *confianza* in the other party. In his opinion, from the moment the parties agreed on the terms of the draft promise contract, the prospective buyers could legitimately rely (*confiar*) on its conclusion.[106]

A more recent judgment is of paramount importance because it is the first where the Supreme Court itself granted damages for precontractual liability for the breaking-off of negotiations based on the notion of *confianza* in connection with good faith.[107] The claimant and the defendant negotiated for the sale of a supermarket. Due to a technical impossibility to conclude the sale, the negotiating parties agreed to enter into a promise of sale contract regarding the property. They had agreed on the sale price but were still in disagreement as to the payment of a balance of the price and as to the content of a penalty clause. They had agreed to sign the promise contract in a notary's office but the defendant did not attend and later indicated that he did not want to sign because it was not convenient to do so. The judgment considered that the negotiations had created a scenario of *confianza* in the claimant that the contract of promise of sale would be concluded.[108]

Another Supreme Court judgment[109] also granted damages for precontractual liability, although the judgment is not entirely clear as to the specific ground on which it based the liability (whether breaking off negotiations, revoking an offer, revoking an acceptance or breaching a pre-agreement).[110] The client of a bank

---

103 It is common for the courts to cite relevant Chilean authors and sometimes foreign authors as part of the grounds of ruling of their judgments.

104 Ricardo de Ángel Yagüez, *Tratado de Responsabilidad Civil* (1993), in *Forestal Bío-Bío* (n. 3) *considerando* 1.

105 Saavedra (n. 49), in *Forestal Bío-Bío* (n. 3) *considerando* 4.

106 de la Maza (n. 23) pp. 136–137, 152.

107 CS 29 December 2011, *Jiménez Mira* (n. 23); see text to (n. 191) below.

108 CS 29 December 2011 (n. 23) *considerando* 9; see text to (n. 85) above.

109 CS 12 April 2012, *Urrea con Corpbanca* (n. 84).

110 The cassation judgment, reproduced in the replacement judgment (n. 84), held that arts. 100, 102, 105 CComCh had been breached by the CA, which would suggest that the liability is founded on the revocation of an offer.

applied to the bank to obtain a mortgage loan to buy a house. After a short time, the bank informed him via email that the mortgage had been approved in its entirety and that an additional loan to make repairs to the property had also been approved. This was also communicated by the bank to the construction company who owned the property, with the bank requiring from that company legal and technical information about the property so that the bank could study it. The bank was told by the owner that because the mortgage loan had been approved, the owner would sign a promise contract with the bank's client regarding the sale of the property and the owner asked the bank to confirm the amount of the loan and its duration, which the bank did. Under the conviction that the mortgage loan was approved, the client concluded the promise contract with the construction company and the latter physically delivered the property to the client, who proceeded to use the money from the additional loan to do works on the property. Ten months later, the bank communicated to its client that it would not approve the mortgage loan due to its financial burden. This led the construction company to ask the client to return the house and to pay an amount as rent for the period of time he had occupied it. Although the Supreme Court did not use the word *confianza*, this judgment has been interpreted as reaffirming the current line of case law established in *Jiménez Mira*[111] regarding precontractual liability for breaking off negotiations based on the protection of *confianza*.[112]

(b) *The Meaning and Dimensions of* Confianza

It is suggested that *confianza* is the broad equivalent of the German notion of *Vertrauen* and the French notion of *croyance/confiance légitime*, all of which can ultimately be translated as 'reliance'.[113]

For instance, a Chilean scholar has indicated that on the notion of *confianza*, the French author Ghestin should be consulted, seeming to imply that the concept of reasonable *confianza* directly corresponds to that of *confiance légitime*.[114] There are powerful reasons to believe that *la doctrina* translate 'reliance' as *confianza*. For example, when explaining Jhering's idea of the negative interest, which is also referred to by English speaking authors as the reliance interest,[115] Chilean authors refer to the *interés negativo* or

111 CS 29 December 2011 (n. 23).

112 Marcelo Barrientos, 'Culpa *In Contrahendo* en Mutuo Hipotecario' (2012) 39 Revista Chilena de Derecho 829, pp. 839, 842 fn. 32. This trend has been confirmed in CS 13 December 2018, *Sociedad Comercial Timbres con Banco Itaú Chile* (n. 2).

113 See Ch. 3 text following (n. 11) and Ch. 4 text to (n. 22) above.

114 de la Maza (n. 23) p. 135 fn. 11, citing Ghestin.

115 See Ch. 6, text to (n. 181) below.

interés de confianza.[116] Also, when explaining the reliance interest as understood in common law countries,[117] the translation used is *interés de confianza*.[118] And when discussing the extent of damages for precontractual liability, reliance losses[119] are referred to as *gastos de confianza*[120] or *daños de la confianza*.[121] But beyond the literal translation of the word 'reliance' into *confianza*, is the use of *confianza* in the same way as authors writing in English use 'reliance' when discussing precontractual liability for breaking off negotiations.

Chilean legal scholars use the language of *confianza* in a loose sense which can cover both the trust-dimension and the expectation-dimension of reliance. It is frequent for *confianza* to be used in the latter dimension; i.e. as a reasonable or legitimate *confianza* that the contract would be concluded that was created in one party by the conduct of the other party.[122] A reply to the question 'what is precontractual *confianza*?' is that there is no legal definition of it and that it is an undetermined concept which allows different degrees of interpretation, but that '(...) a duty of *confianza in contrahendo* relates to the conviction that the conduct of one party reasonably generates in the other; that is to say, the certainty in the fulfilment of a determined legal act'.[123]

Some scholars believe that the *confianza* created or nourished by one party in the other relates to the fact that the contract will certainly or surely be entered into.[124] This requirement would resemble that of German law.[125] The better view is that this is not a requirement in Chilean law. It is sufficient that there is a high degree of *confianza* regarding the level of expectation that the negotiated contract will be entered into, but it is not necessary to reach the extreme of expecting that the contract will undoubtedly be entered into. A judgment of the Supreme Court would support this view because, while it cites Barros Bourie in

116 e.g. Celedón and Silberman (n. 23) p. 90; also Spanish authors Clara Asúa González and José Javier Hualde Sánchez, 'Codificación de la *Culpa in Contrahendo* en el Derecho Alemán' in Antonio Cabanillas Sánchez and others (eds.), *Estudios Jurídicos en Homenaje al Profesor Luis Díez-Picazo*, vol. II (Thomson Civitas, 2003) p. 1429.

117 See Ch. 6, text to (n. 175) below.

118 e.g. Celedón and Silberman (n. 23) p. 98 fn. 162.

119 See Ch. 6, text to (n. 178) below.

120 de la Maza (n. 23) p. 146 fn. 38.

121 Barrientos (n. 112) p. 842.

122 e.g. Barros Bourie (n. 5) p. 1009; Barrientos (n. 112) p. 839, commenting on CS 12 April 2012 (n. 84); Barrientos (n. 2) p. 51; de la Maza (n. 23) p. 151; Celedón and Silberman (n. 23) p. 148; Risueño (n. 12) p. 60.

123 Barrientos (n. 2) pp. 55–56.

124 e.g. Barros Bourie (n. 5) p. 1009; Celedón and Silberman (n. 23) p. 140.

125 See Ch. 3, text to (n. 97) above.

several aspects, it does not expressly require that the *confianza* lie on the certain conclusion of the contract.[126] In some cases the *confianza* might reach the point of having the conviction that the contract has been concluded.[127]

Sometimes *confianza* is used in its trust-dimension (even by the same legal scholars that refer to it in its expectation-dimension) as relying on the conduct of the other party or on a standard of conduct expected from the other party. This dimension relates to trusting that the other party will conduct itself according to the standard of good faith or in an honourable manner.[128] One author refers to the iniquitous disappointment of the *confianza* in another person's honour, pointing out that negotiations consist of a process of laying the foundations of 'reciprocal conducts of *confianza*' between the negotiating parties.[129] Another emphasises that collaboration between negotiating parties is only possible if they can trust that the other will not engage in conduct which is not acceptable.[130] The trust-dimension of *confianza* can also be applied to a very close and personal level of trust through the use of the notion of 'interpersonal *confianza*', which refers to the family or friendship ties between negotiating parties or parties who frequently contract with each other.[131]

The Supreme Court has used the notion of *confianza* in a manner that encompasses both its dimensions. In the pivotal judgment of *Jiménez Mira*, the court referred to the creation in the other party of a *confianza* that the contract would be concluded and listed the creation of a reasonable *confianza* in the conclusion or perfection of the planned contract as the first element of precontractual liability.[132] This corresponds to the expectation-dimension of reliance. It also indicated that the damage is caused by the effects that follow from the *confianza* placed on the diligence and good faith of the other party.[133] This corresponds to the trust-dimension of reliance.

In the landmark judgment of *Forestal Bío-Bío*,[134] both dimensions of reliance can be found in the way that the court reasoned on the basis of *confianza*. Citing foreign and Chilean legal scholars, it referred to the breach of duties of loyalty and *confianza* of which the other party was worthy and to a state of reciprocal *confianza* that must not be disappointed (which corresponds to the trust-dimension), and also referred to the legitimate expectations

---

126 CS 29 December 2011 (n. 23) *considerando* 7.
127 Barros Bourie (n. 5) p. 638. This often occurs in lack of formality cases; see this Ch. s. IV 2 below.
128 Barros Bourie (n. 5) p. 1007.
129 Barrientos (n. 2) pp. 55–56, 59, 64; Barrientos (n. 112) p. 839.
130 de la Maza (n. 23) pp. 136, 147.
131 de la Maza (n. 23) p. 137 fn. 16.
132 CS 29 December 2011 (n. 23) *considerandos* 3, 7, 8, citing Barros Bourie and Barrientos.
133 CS 29 December 2011 (n. 23) *considerando* 8, citing Barros Bourie.
134 CA Concepción 5 June 1996 (n. 3).

(*legítimas esperanzas*) that the contract would be concluded (which corresponds to the expectation-dimension).[135] The expectation-dimension appears to be recognised in another judgment of the Court of Appeal of Concepción which referred to the justified expectation (*fundada esperanza*) that the contract would be entered into[136] and in an earlier judgment of the Court of Appeal of Santiago.[137]

(*c*) Confianza *and* Expectativa

The notions of *confianza* and expectation (*expectativa*) are linked within the notion of precontractual fault[138] and are also connected in the expectation-dimension of *confianza*.[139]

Some legal scholars, in order to explain the imposition of precontractual liability for breaking off negotiations, refer to the idea of acting in a manner which is inconsistent with the expectations generated in the other party in relation to the so-called 'doctrine of one's own act' (*doctrina de los actos propios, venire contra factum proprium*). The objection to the conduct of the person that breaks off is based on the fact that it is contrary to good faith to act in a manner which is inconsistent with the *confianza* generated in another by one's previous conduct. Therefore, by imposing liability on the party that has conducted himself in a way which is inconsistent with the sure expectations to which his own conduct had given rise, the disappointment of the *confianza* that he had created in the other party is protected.[140]

Other scholars connect the doctrine of one's own act with the doctrine of appearance regarding liability for breaking off negotiations. Thus, it is argued that the general rule is that each party must assume the risk that the other might break off, unless the party breaking off had created a different appearance in terms that the other party could reasonably rely on his intention to enter into the contract. What characterises the conduct of the withdrawing party is that it contradicts his previous acts, disappointing the reasonable expectations that he himself had created.[141]

It is suggested that the doctrine of appearance is not an appropriate basis to explain liability for breaking off negotiations because the proper effect of this doctrine is to subject the party who created the appearance to it, allowing

---

135 CA Concepción 5 June 1996 (n. 3) *considerandos* 1, 4, 5; see text to (nn. 104, 105) above.

136 CA Concepción 30 June 1999, *Sociedad Ruz de la Barra con Comar* (n. 23).

137 CA Santiago 25 August 1948 *Caja de Crédito Popular con Schiavetti viuda de Maino*, RDyJ, T. 46, 1949, Second Part, Second Section; see Ch. 2, text following (n. 37) above.

138 See this Ch. s. I 3 above.

139 See this Ch. s. II 1 (b) above.

140 Celedón and Silberman (n. 23) p. 122, explaining ideas by Barros Bourie (n. 5).

141 de la Maza (n. 23) pp. 147, 151–152.

the other party to rely on such an appearance even if it does not correspond to reality.[142] If applied to a case of broken negotiations, the effect of this doctrine would at least give rise to expectation damages, whereas the proper remedy for precontractual liability is reliance damages.[143] It also seems that the doctrine of one's own act is not the true basis of this liability because, according to this doctrine, the previous conduct of the party who then behaves in a contradictory manner must reveal a determined legal position,[144] and this is not the case in many situations of liability for breaking off negotiations because the legal position of the party breaking off (as to its intention to enter into a contract) is still undetermined.

(d) *Creation of* Confianza *and Legitimacy of the* Confianza

One side of reliance is that the *confianza* in the future conclusion of the negotiated contract must have been created or at least nourished by the conduct of the party breaking off. The other side is that this *confianza* which is held by the other party must be legitimate or reasonable.

Within the conduct of the party breaking off that creates or nourishes *confianza* in the other party, different and unlimited variables are possible. It is impossible to list all the forms of conduct that may create this *confianza* as it is a question that inevitably depends on the case.[145] For example, the following have been mentioned: an express statement that the contract will be concluded or that the negotiations will be successful; a proposal to carry out certain acts that suppose that the contract will be concluded; a request to put an end to a current activity in view of the conclusion of the negotiated contract; a request or an authorisation to carry out repairs, construction, or generally to incur expenses.[146] In *Forestal Bío-Bío*, it was established as a fact of the case that the defendants had communicated to the claimants that since the beginning of the negotiations they had been driven by a spirit of *confianza* and seriousness and that they felt morally committed to them.[147] In *Urrea con Corpbanca*, the bank had sent an email to the claimant stating that the mortgage loan had been approved.[148]

The sole creation or nourishment of reliance is not sufficient because this *confianza* must be legitimate, reasonable, well founded or justified (these words

---

142 Jorge López Santa María and Fabián Elorriaga De Bonis, *Los Contratos: Parte General* (6th edn., Legal Publishing Chile, 2017) p. 456 fn. 766.
143 See Ch. 6 s. IV 1 (a) below.
144 López Santa María and Elorriaga De Bonis (n. 142) p. 454.
145 Similarly, de la Maza (n. 23) p. 151.
146 Barros Bourie (n. 5) p. 1011.
147 CA Concepción 5 June 1996 (n. 3) *considerando* 9.
148 CS 12 April 2012 (n. 84); see text following (n. 110) above.

are used interchangeably).[149] The legitimacy of *confianza* must be found through objective elements present in the circumstances of the case; that is, the assessment of its legitimacy is objective.[150] The standard is whether an average person placed in similar circumstances would be led to expect the conclusion of the contract due to the other party's conduct.[151] The length, seriousness and advancement of the negotiations are often referred to.[152] It has been indicated that a 'state of *confianza* worthy of legal protection' is created only when the negotiations have reached a significant state of advancement and development which would have foreseeably allowed any of the negotiating parties to suppose that not only was there a relationship of *confianza* between them but also that this relationship led them to rationally estimate as possible the conclusion of the future contract.[153] In *Jiménez Mira*, it was held that because the negotiations were quite advanced, the claimant could trust that the promise of sale contract would be concluded, proof of which was the fact that the parties had made an inventory of the merchandise, the claimant had requested an audit as to the profit projection and, especially, that they had agreed to sign the contract in a notary's office but the defendant did not attend.[154] In *Forestal Bío-Bío*, the court stated that when negotiations advance more than usual, they give rise to legitimate expectations in one party that the contract will take place (the parties had also agreed to sign the promise of sale contract at a notary's office with the claimants attending but not the defendants).[155]

Some authors[156] indicate that agreement on all essential aspects of the negotiated contract is necessary for liability for breaking off negotiations to arise. This view should be rejected. Some level of agreement is necessary to show that the negotiations were reasonably advanced[157] but it is not required that all the essential elements have been agreed because if this was the case, and the negotiated contract is a consensual one,[158] the contract would be concluded and any refusal to continue with its performance would constitute contractual liability.

The conduct of both negotiating parties during the negotiations is relevant to determine the legitimacy of *confianza*.[159] One author, going further, has argued

149 e.g. de la Maza (n. 23) p. 151; Barrientos (n. 2) pp. 51, 62–63, 116; Barrientos (n. 112) p. 839.
150 Barrientos (n. 2) p. 55.
151 Barrientos (n. 50) pp. 31–32.
152 Barros Bourie (n. 5) p. 1012.
153 Barrientos (n. 2) p. 56.
154 CS 29 December 2011 (n. 23) *considerando* 9; see text to (n. 108) above.
155 CA Concepción 5 June 1996 (n. 3) *considerandos* 5, 9.
156 e.g. Barros Bourie (n. 5) p. 1010.
157 e.g. Barrientos (n. 2) p. 61.
158 See (n. 7) above.
159 René Abeliuk Manasevich, *Las Obligaciones*, vol. II (6th edn., Legal Publishing, 2014) pp. 1073 fn. 1199.

that regarding the conduct of the party who remains, as opposed to the party who withdraws, the judge must consider whether the appearance created by the latter was sufficiently intense to justify the former's *confianza*, and that it will be when it has an unequivocal character; i.e. when it reveals beyond reasonable doubt an intention to conclude the contract.[160] It seems that the better view is that, while in some cases an appearance of an undoubted intention to contract may be present,[161] the requirement for the legitimacy of *confianza* is less extreme and can be formulated in terms of what can reasonably be expected.[162]

Finally, the level of experience or professional status of the negotiating parties is also sometimes mentioned[163] in that when one party is acting as an expert, professional or specialist, the *confianza* of the other party on its conduct is correspondingly higher.[164]

(e) *Conclusions*

Although the notion of *confianza* appears entangled with other legal and theoretical bases of precontractual liability for breaking off negotiations, it is the true basis of this liability; it corresponds with the notion of reliance, and is used in much the same way as the notions of *Vertrauen* and *croyance/confiance légitime* are used in German and French law. *Confianza* reflects both dimensions of reliance: it is used to refer to a belief or expectation that a contract will be concluded, or that negotiations will be successful, or at least that negotiations will be carried out; and it is used in the sense of relying on the conduct of the other party, or on a standard of conduct expected from the other party, or trusting the other party's behaviour or morality. Sometimes application of both dimensions is made in a legal writing or judgment and sometimes application of only one dimension is made (typically the expectation-dimension). Consequently, *confianza* is inextricably linked to the notion of expectation.

2. GOOD FAITH

Good faith or the breach of good faith duties, in combination with other arguments, is frequently advocated by Chilean legal scholars and judgments to explain the imposition of liability for breaking off negotiations. This doctrinal basis does not exclude other legal or doctrinal bases and, in practice, it is always

---

160 de la Maza (n. 23) pp. 147, 151–152.
161 e.g. in lack of formality cases; see this Ch. s. IV 2 below.
162 Similarly, Barrientos (n. 2) pp. 62, 117.
163 e.g. *Urrea con Corpbanca* (n. 84) cassation judgment *considerando* 7.
164 Barros Bourie (n. 5) p. 89.

found combined with other foundations, particularly with delictual fault and *confianza*. It will be argued that although good faith can be a useful tool to determine the objectionable conduct, in practice it often gets confused with delictual fault and loses its autonomy.

The CCivCh only recognises that contracts must be performed in good faith, omitting any reference to their being negotiated or even concluded in good faith. Article 1546, located in Title XII 'Of the Effects of Obligations' of Book IV states that '[c]ontracts must be performed in good faith and, consequently, bind not only to what is expressed in them, but to all things that precisely emanate from the nature of the obligation, or that by law or custom belong to it'. The first line of article 1546 states the same as the third paragraph of old article 1134 of the *Code civil* (before the 2016 reform)[165] because, historically, the drafting of the former was taken from the latter.[166] Andrés Bello divided into two the content of old article 1134 Cciv, leaving in article 1545 of the CCivCh the principle of the binding force of contracts and in article 1546 of the CCivCh the principle of good faith.[167]

Despite the fact that article 1546 CCivCh does not expressly refer to the precontractual period, Chilean legal scholars, following the historical arguments given by French legal scholars as to the reason for the final drafting of article 1134(3) Cciv,[168] agree that article 1546 CCivCh contains the general principle of good faith which extends to all the phases in the life of a contract, including the precontractual period.[169] Barros Bourie argues that article 1546 CCivCh is analogous to §242 BGB,[170] which is also interpreted to contain the general principle of good faith in German law.[171] *La jurisprudencia* has recognised that the principle of good faith (contained in article 1546) applies during the negotiations for a contract.[172]

165 For French law, see Ch. 4 s. II 3 above.

166 Ramón Domínguez Águila, 'Comentarios de Jurisprudencia 1' (2005) 217–218 Revista de Derecho Universidad de Concepción 305, p. 309; Fernando Fueyo Laneri, *Instituciones de Derecho Civil Moderno* (Editorial Jurídica de Chile, 1990) p. 152.

167 Domínguez Águila (n. 166) p. 309.

168 See Ch. 4, text to (n. 200) above.

169 e.g. Domínguez Águila (n. 166) p. 309; López Santa María and Elorriaga De Bonis (n. 142) p. 439 fn. 733; René Ramos, *De la Responsabilidad Extracontractual* (4th edn., Legal Publishing, 2008) p. 11; Boetsch (n. 48) p. 113.

170 Barros Bourie (n. 5) p. 630 fn. 50.

171 For German law, see Ch. 3, text to (n. 143) above.

172 e.g. CS, 24 March 2016, *Pinochet con Luz Agro S.A.*, *rol* 2786-2015, Westlaw Online CL/JUR/1963/2016; CS, 26 August 2015, *Wilibaldo Moreno Loyola con Banco Santander Chile S.A.*, *rol* 26847-2014, Westlaw Online CL/JUR/4847/2015; CS 12 April 2012, *Urrea con Corpbanca* (n. 84) cassation judgment *considerando* 11; CS 29 December 2011, *Jiménez Mira con Armijo Cerda* (n. 23) *considerando* 4; CA Santiago, 29 November 2007, *Glide Diversiones Limitada con Compañía de Inversiones y Desarrollo Sur S.A.*, reaffirmed by CS, 19 May 2008, Legal Publishing no. 39372; CS, 11 June 2007, *Video Show System S.A. con Metrópolis Intercom S.A.*, *rol* 2049-2005 (in the minority vote); CS, 31 October 2006, *Banco Español de*

However, the fact that article 1546 CCivCh does not expressly refer to the precontractual period poses a problem for providing a legal basis for the imposition of precontractual liability.[173] The problem lies in the possibility to file a *recurso de casación en el fondo*[174] because the Supreme Court, in a 2004 judgment, took the position that this motion can only be granted where there is an infraction of a 'law' in the technical sense of article 1 CCivCh and the breach of a general principle of law, like good faith, cannot be assimilated to the infraction of a legal precept.[175] The court, rejecting such a motion, took a literal interpretation of article 1546 considering that its sphere of application is restricted to the performance of contracts and, consequently, only deals with matters of contractual liability.[176] Legal scholars have strongly opposed the position taken by the Supreme Court in this judgment[177] and, taking it into account, some have argued that precontractual liability (for breach of precontractual duties) is legally based on the articles on delictual liability (2314 ff. CCivCh).[178] Others have argued for the need to reform article 1546.[179] It appears that the position taken by the Supreme Court in this judgment, restricting the sphere of application of article 1546 to the performance of contracts, is an isolated one, considering that more recent judgments recognise that article 1546 also applies to the precontractual period.[180] But the difficulty of reaching the Supreme Court via a *recurso de casación en el fondo* based solely on the infraction of article 1546 applied to the precontractual period, remains. It is, therefore, advisable, in a case of liability for broken negotiations, to base this motion on the articles of the CCivCh on delictual liability.

La doctrina and *la jurisprudencia* usually distinguish between two notions of good faith: subjective and objective.[181] The objective notion of good faith,

Crédito S.A. con Auca Forestal S.A., rol 3507-2003; CS, 31 May 2006, *Irribarra Varela con Inacap, rol* 1778-2006; CA Concepción 5 June 1996, *Forestal Bío-Bío S.A. con Madesal* (n. 3) *considerando* 4.

173 Patricio-Ignacio Carvajal, 'Prólogo' in Barrientos (n. 2) p. xi.

174 Motion that allows a case to go up to the Supreme Court based on the infraction of a law (art. 767 Civil Procedure Code).

175 CS, 12 July 2004, *Empresa de Telecomunicaciones Asintec S.A. con Club Hípico de Concepción S.A., rol* 2622-2000, RDyJ, 2004, Second Part, First Section, pp. 175–178.

176 CS 12 July 2004 (n. 175) *considerando* 9.

177 e.g. Domínguez Águila (n. 166) p. 308. Also, Cristóbal Eyzaguirre and Javier Rodríguez, 'Expansión y Límites de la Buena Fe Objetiva – A Propósito del "Proyecto de Principios Latinoamericanos de Derecho de los Contratos"' (2013) 21 Revista Chilena de Derecho Privado 137, pp. 207–208.

178 e.g. Barrientos (n. 2) p. 58.

179 See this Ch. text to (n. 15) above.

180 See cases cited in (n. 172) above.

181 e.g. López Santa María and Elorriaga De Bonis (n. 142) p. 431 ff.; Alessandri, Somarriva and Vodanovic, *Tratado de Derecho Civil* (n. 73) p. 242; CS 11 June 2007, *Video Show System con Metrópolis Intercom* (n. 172).

contained in article 1546 CCivCh, is a possible doctrinal basis of liability for breaking off negotiations. The standard of good faith in the negotiation period requires that negotiating parties conduct negotiations in a loyal and honest manner, notwithstanding the freedom they have to try to obtain advantages.[182] In *Forestal Bío-Bío*, it was stated that, for the development of healthy negotiations, a just balance must be sought between two basic principles: freedom of withdrawal and the protection of the negotiating parties' assets. The solution must conform to equity which points to the existence of a liability that has good faith as its basis, which translates into an honest, loyal and true conduct, in accordance with the required collaboration.[183]

It must be recalled that some authors and judgments consider that consent to negotiate gives rise to the duty to negotiate in good faith.[184] It seems an unnecessary complication to subject the birth of good faith in the negotiation period to the consent of the parties, when considering that the sole fact that they begin to negotiate subjects them to the general principle of good faith contained in article 1546 CCivCh.

The good faith standard of conduct imposes a series of precontractual duties on negotiating parties, such as duties of loyalty, information, diligence, honesty, collaboration, discretion and confidentiality.[185] The duty of loyalty is particularly relevant[186] as it requires that negotiations be carried out in good faith, i.e. with the effective purpose to enter into a contract, and it also involves duties of care in putting an end to negotiations when reliance has been created in the other party that the contract will be concluded. The duty to negotiate in good faith requires that a purely strategic game, where each party seeks its own interest, is subjected to the limits imposed by minimum duties of loyalty that can be expected from an honest party. These duties cannot be precisely defined in advance because good faith is an open standard that can only be applied taking into account the circumstances of the case, particularly the relationship between the negotiating parties that arises with the negotiations. Good faith duties are more intense when negotiating parties have fewer real possibilities of protecting their own interests during the negotiations, so that they have to place a greater amount of *confianza* in the other party.[187]

182 Rosende Álvarez (n. 6) p. 74.

183 CA Concepción 5 June 1996 (n. 3) *considerando* 5. Similarly, CA Concepción 30 June 1999 (n. 23).

184 See text to (n. 66) above.

185 e.g, Barrientos (n. 2) pp. 52, 54; Barros Bourie (n. 5) p. 1005; Boetsch (n. 48) pp. 115–118; Ramón Domínguez Águila, *Teoría General del Negocio Jurídico* (2nd edn., Editorial Jurídica de Chile, 2013) pp. 56 ff.

186 The following corresponds to Barros Bourie (n. 5) p. 1001, cited in the *Jiménez Mira* judgment (n. 23) *considerando* 3.

187 Barros Bourie (n. 5) p. 1026.

In Chilean law, good faith on its own is not a sufficient legal basis of liability for breaking off negotiations.[188] Therefore, it is usually accompanied by the notion of delictual fault.[189] In *Forestal Bío-Bío*, it was stated that the violation of good faith conduct amounts to committing a wrongful act which causes harm under articles 2284 and 2314 CCivCh.[190] In *Jiménez Mira*, it was concluded that the defendant had acted in bad faith because his refusal to enter into the promise contract was untimely and without a legitimate justification (which amounted to negligent conduct), and articles 1546 and 2314 ff. CCivCh were cited as the legal basis for the imposition of liability.[191] Consequently, it is said that good faith and the principle of fault are the basis of this liability.[192] The problem is that it is not always clear where the fault lies: whether in the breach of the duty to negotiate in good faith[193] or in the breaking-off itself.[194]

Good faith presents a 'strong analogy' with fault in that it is an open standard that needs to be concretised.[195] Regarding fault, the concrete duty of care that emanates from the abstract standard of care can only be determined in relation to the circumstances of the case,[196] and the same can be said about precontractual duties of good faith.[197] Ultimately, delictual duties of care and precontractual duties of good faith emanate from the law[198] and the specific legal norms seem to be articles 2314 and 2329 CCivCh, considering that it is debatable whether article 1546 CCivCh can provide a solid legal basis for precontractual good faith.[199] In practice, the notions of fault and good faith (or breach of it) can become confused.[200] Thus, it is said that precontractual liability finds its basis in the breach of a general duty of conduct because the breach of precontractual good faith constitutes a breach of the general principle not to harm others.[201]

---

188 See text to (n. 173) above.

189 An exception is CS 12 April 2012, *Urrea con Corpbanca* (n. 84) cassation judgment *considerandos* 13–14, where the court stated that good faith was the basis of precontractual liability and then ruled that the arts. of the CComCh on revocation of an offer had been breached, without mentioning art. 1546 (on good faith) or arts. 2314 ff. (on delictual liability) CCivCh; see (n. 110) above. Also, CA Talca 8 November 1999, quashed (for other reasons) by CS 22 November 2001 (n. 92), which stated that good faith was the basis of precontractual liability and then ruled on the legal basis of arts. 97 and 100 CComCh.

190 CA Concepción 5 June 1996 (n. 3) *considerandos* 4–5.

191 CS 29 December 2011 (n. 23) *considerando* 9 and ruling. In similar terms, CS 13 December 2018, *Sociedad Comercial Timbres con Banco Itaú Chile* (n. 2).

192 Domínguez Benavente, Domínguez Águila and Domínguez Hidalgo, 'Comentarios de Jurisprudencia 1' (n. 3) pp. 182–183.

193 e.g. Rosende Álvarez (n. 6) p. 74.

194 See text to (n. 84) above.

195 Barros Bourie (n. 5) p. 1001.

196 Barros Bourie (n. 5) p. 86.

197 See p. 125 above.

198 Barros Bourie (n. 5) p. 95; Barrientos (n. 2) p. 118.

199 See text to (n. 188) above.

200 Boetsch (n. 48) pp. 143–145 highlights the differences between fault and bad faith.

201 Barrientos (n. 2) p. 118.

Therefore, it is pertinent to ask whether a reference to good faith or breach of good faith adds anything. It seems that it does not add much. It allows the reasoning of the judgments to be framed on more specific duties (such as loyalty, honesty and information) than the general duty of care, but because they are all ultimately legally based on the articles on delictual liability, it appears that precontractual duties of good faith are more detailed duties of care. It has been argued that the debate about the need to impose positive duties of conduct based on good faith on negotiating parties who are not yet contractually bound is unnecessary because fault is enough to protect their interests.[202] However, this argument must be tempered in that it is still possible for good faith to play a role in identifying typical conduct during the negotiations and their termination that can constitute fault, depending on the circumstances of the case.

Good faith on its own is usually considered not to be a sufficient doctrinal basis of liability for breaking off negotiations. It often appears accompanied by the notion of *confianza*. It is said that precontractual good faith justifies *confianza* because it is an essential requirement for the conduct of negotiations.[203] Consequently, in order to violate the duty to negotiate in good faith, the reasonable expectations or the protection-worthy *confianza* of the other party must have been disappointed.[204] It is argued that in the conflict between freedom and *confianza*, good faith requires the most basic respect from the other party and that even in legal systems which explicitly recognise precontractual duties which protect the *confianza* created in the other negotiating party, it is assumed that this cannot be a road for the birth of obligations without consent nor for the introduction of unforeseeable risks by the fact of initiating negotiations.[205] In the conflict between the principle that without will there is no obligation and the principle of *confianza*, duties of collaboration based on good faith during negotiations (particularly duties of loyalty and discretion) have been recognised in order to mitigate the principle of *caveat emptor*, duties which allow for the protection of the *confianza* that one party has a right to place on the other, without imposing a duty to contract.[206] The *confianza* which must be protected, beyond which is the 'reign of *caveat emptor*', is that negotiating parties can assume that certain forms of conduct are not acceptable and can trust that the other party will not engage in them, despite the fact that negotiations have an adversarial nature and persons who enter into them must do so knowing that the other party is there to obtain as great an advantage as possible.[207]

---

202 Celedón and Silberman (n. 23) p. 148. Barrientos (n. 50) p. 36 and Boetsch (n. 48) p. 119 are of the contrary opinion.

203 Barrientos (n. 50) p. 32.

204 de la Maza (n. 23) p. 147.

205 Barros Bourie (n. 5) p. 1002, cited in *Jiménez Mira* (n. 23) *considerando* 5.

206 Barros Bourie (n. 5) p. 1005.

207 de la Maza (n. 23) p. 147.

Barros Bourie, who holds a restrictive view of liability for breaking off negotiations, states that in the precontractual sphere the duty of care is most clearly expressed in the negative form of bad faith, which includes both deceit and the complete disregard of the *confianza* that has been created.[208] Barrientos, who holds a broader view of this liability, considers that bad faith consists of initiating negotiations without a serious intention to contract, prolonging them without intending to contract, or unilaterally breaking them off without a justified reason,[209] and that the intentional infringement of the *confianza* that has been created and which causes economic loss, also supposes disregard of good faith.[210]

In conclusion, good faith, on its own, does not constitute a sufficient legal or doctrinal basis to explain liability for breaking off negotiations in Chilean law and has been frequently linked to the concept of *confianza* in order to shape the wrongful act which will give rise to delictual liability.

3. ABUSE OF RIGHTS

This doctrine has also been received by *la doctrina* and *la jurisprudencia* despite it not being expressly regulated in Chilean law.[211] Some legal scholars[212] and judgments[213] have used this doctrine, which has found a legal basis in the articles on delictual liability (2314 ff. CCivCh), to explain precontractual liability for breaking off negotiations. It will be argued that the doctrine of abuse of rights does not adequately explain the essence of this liability, at the core of which is not the abuse of a right.

The doctrine of abuse of rights[214] has been understood as a corrective to the excessive or abnormal exercise of a right, in both a subjective (unequivocal intention to harm) and objective (assessment of the circumstances surrounding the exercise of a right according to minimum standards of sociability and loyalty) sense. The doctrine is exceptional in that it only applies in cases where

208 Barros Bourie (n. 5) p. 1002, cited in *Jiménez Mira* (n. 23) *considerando* 5.

209 Barrientos (n. 2) p. 51, cited in *Jiménez Mira* (n. 23) *considerando* 5.

210 Barrientos (n. 2) p. 55.

211 Enrique Barros Bourie, 'Límites de los Derechos Subjetivos Privados. Introducción a la Doctrina del Abuso de Derecho' (1999) 7 Revista Derecho y Humanidades 11.

212 e.g. Barros Bourie, *Responsabilidad Extracontractual* (n. 5) pp. 632, 1008 ff.; Domínguez Benavente, Domínguez Águila and Domínguez Hidalgo, 'Comentarios de Jurisprudencia 1' (n. 3) p. 181; Domínguez Benavente, Domínguez Águila and Domínguez Hidalgo, 'Comentarios de Jurisprudencia 3' (n. 23) p. 187.

213 e.g. CA Concepción 30 June 1999, *Sociedad Ruz de la Barra con Comar* (n. 23); CA Talca 8 November 1999, quashed by CS 22 November 2001, *Luna con Bobadilla* (n. 92).

214 This para. and the next two paras. follow Barros Bourie, *Responsabilidad Extracontractual* (n. 5) pp. 626–629, 637–638, 1008–1012.

the conduct of the holder of a right defies minimum standards of conduct, which are expressed in the general clauses of good customs (*buenas costumbres*, articles 1461 and 1467 CCivCh) and good faith (*buena fe*, article 1546 CCivCh).

The objective standard of good faith, in particular, limits the exercise of a right. Thus, the abuse of a right is associated to acting in a manner contrary to good faith. However, due to the indetermination of the general clauses on which it is based, the doctrine of abuse of rights is concretised in some typical groups of cases and one group is formed by cases of conduct contrary to one's own act (*venire contra factum proprium*).[215] The doctrine of one's own act is a typical application of the principle of good faith as a limit to the exercise of rights, protecting the notion of a justified *confianza*. In this way, the exercise of a right is contrary to good faith and, hence, abusive, when it does not correspond to the certain expectations that the holder of a right had generated in another person with its own conduct. Some cases of precontractual liability for breaking off negotiations can be understood as applications of the doctrine of abuse of rights for acting in a manner contrary to one's own acts. Such is the case when during the negotiations one party has created in the other the conviction that the contract will surely be entered into and the latter has acted accordingly to this expectation.

Negotiations embody a special type of relationship where good faith gives rise to duties between negotiating parties that limit the right to put an end to these negotiations. The abuse of this right is manifested in abusive conduct that shows a serious disregard of the reliance (*confianza*) that has been created by one negotiating party in the other as to the future conclusion of the negotiated contract. For liability to arise, it is necessary that the disloyal conduct of the right holder is *culpable* (intentional or negligent) and this will be the case where it has seriously breached the reciprocal duties of respect owed between negotiating parties, abusing the *confianza* that it has created or encouraged in the other party.

The theory of abuse of rights is not helpful in explaining the rationale of liability for breaking off negotiations in Chilean law. The arguments for rejecting this theoretical basis are very much the same as those mentioned in French law.[216] Particularly, the terminology of abuse of rights is not appropriate here as there is no legal 'right' to put an end to negotiations but rather a freedom (that flows from the general principle of freedom of contract) to not enter into a contract and, consequently, to put an end to negotiations.[217] But, more importantly, the doctrine of abuse of rights, as it currently stands (unrecognised by Chilean legislation and underdeveloped by Chilean legal scholars and judgments), lacks

215 See text to (n. 140) above.
216 See Ch. 4, text following (n. 185).
217 Similarly, Barrientos (n. 2) p. 55 fn. 105; Celedón and Silberman (n. 23) p. 121.

the independence and precise contours that it would require to constitute a useful theoretical basis of precontractual liability, appearing subsumed within delictual liability and entangled with notions of good faith and *confianza*.

III. THE REQUIREMENTS OF PRECONTRACUTAL LIABILITY FOR BREAKING OFF NEGOTIATIONS

1. DIFFERENT REQUIREMENTS

Legal scholars and judgments have listed different requirements for this liability to arise. Some of these requirements have already been rejected or questioned, particularly: consent to negotiate,[218] that all essential elements of the contract have been agreed,[219] and breach of a precontractual duty of good faith.[220] Therefore, this section will focus on the requirements that undoubtedly must be met.

In *Jiménez Mira*, the Supreme Court listed the following requirements: (i) the creation of a reasonable *confianza* in the conclusion or perfection of the contract under negotiation; (ii) the unjustified and untimely character of the break-off of the negotiations; (iii) harm caused to the assets of one of the parties; and (iv) a causal relationship between the harm suffered by one party and the *confianza* that was encouraged and then disappointed by the other party.[221] The first requirement has already been analysed above[222] and the third and fourth requirements are referred to in Chapter 6.[223] Therefore, the following subsections will focus on the second requirement, dividing it into two correlated components.

2. THE REASON FOR BREAKING OFF

The party who breaks off the negotiations must justify his actions, providing a reason for doing so. If the reason for breaking off is a 'good' reason, his withdrawal is justified, this requirement for liability to arise will fail and, consequently, he will not be liable.

---

218 See text to (n. 68) above.

219 See text following (n. 156) above.

220 See text following (n. 201) above.

221 CS 29 December 2011 (n. 23) *considerando* 7, citing Barrientos (n. 2) p. 51. These requirements are again listed in CS 13 December 2018, *Sociedad Comercial Timbres con Banco Itaú Chile* (n. 2).

222 In this Ch. s II 1.

223 See Ch. 6 s. IV 1 (a) below.

A good reason can be described as legitimate, reasonable or plausible and the following have been given as examples: a better offer from a third party,[224] a more detailed study of the business that leads to the conclusion that the contract is not convenient, an illness that affects the benefit of entering into the contract, changes in market conditions,[225] the impossibility to reach agreement on some aspect of the contract, the blameless loss of a right which is necessary to conclude the contract,[226] and reaching the conviction that it will not be possible to provide the service that had been offered.[227]

The reason for breaking off is connected with the notions of good faith and *confianza*. If the party breaking off had a good reason to do so then he acted according to good faith and cannot be liable,[228] and, on the contrary, the lack of a reason or a reason without merit implies the lack of good faith.[229] In order to assess whether the reason to break off is justified, the degree of reasonable *confianza* that has been created in the victim of the break-off must be taken into consideration, because if no *confianza* has yet arisen, then the reason for breaking off cannot be unjust and no liability can ensue.[230]

3. THE ARBITRARINESS OF THE BREAKING-OFF

The reason for breaking off is intimately related with the characterisation of the breaking-off. Therefore, when the reason for breaking off is 'bad', i.e. when it lacks any plausible basis or is unreasonable or illegitimate, then the break-off itself is considered unjust, arbitrary or abusive.[231] However, it is not only the reason for breaking off that is relevant for characterising the breaking-off as arbitrary, because certain objective circumstances present in the case must also be taken into account.[232]

Typical circumstances are the length and degree of advancement of the negotiations, the conduct of the parties and the statements made by them.[233] The fact that the break-off was untimely, unexpected, sudden or without notice

224 Domínguez Águila (n. 185) pp. 59–60.
225 Barros Bourie, *Responsabilidad Extracontractual* (n. 5) p. 1011.
226 de la Maza (n. 23) p. 150.
227 CA Concepción, 29 June 2000, *rol* 781-1999, *considerando* 21, reaffirmed by CS 12 July 2004, *Asintec con Club Hípico* (n. 175).
228 CA Concepción 29 June 2000 (n. 227), *considerando* 21, reaffirmed by CS 12 July 2004, *Asintec con Club Hípico* (n. 175).
229 *Urrea con Corpbanca* (n. 84) cassation judgment *considerando* 11; *Jiménez Mira* (n. 23) *considerando* 9; see text to (n. 191) above.
230 Barrientos (n. 2) p. 116; Celedón and Silberman (n. 23) p. 50 fn. 69.
231 Barros Bourie, *Responsabilidad Extracontractual* (n. 5) p. 1011 fn. 81–82, citing German and French case law; Barrientos (n. 2) pp. 61–62; Domínguez Águila (n. 185) p. 59.
232 Segura (n. 100) p. 107; Domínguez Águila (n. 185) p. 60.
233 See this Ch. s. II 1 (d) above.

is often mentioned.[234] In *Forestal Bío-Bío*, it was emphasised that the defendants had not given the claimants any notice of their intention to withdraw.[235] In *Urrea con Corpbanca*, the Supreme Court focused on the conduct of the bank, particularly on the fact that it allowed a considerable amount of time to go by between informing its client that the mortgage loan had been approved and then informing him that the loan had finally not been approved.[236] In a recent case, it was held that the withdrawal was justified and timely because after several years of negotiations the parties had been unable to agree on essentials elements of the contract under negotiation.[237]

In order to assess whether the reason for breaking off was justified or not, objective criteria that may be applied in similar cases must be used.[238] Therefore, the view expressed in some judgments of the higher courts that determining whether the breaking-off was unjust or unjustified is subjective,[239] should not be followed.

IV. BREAKING OFF NEGOTIATIONS FOR THE CONCLUSION OF A FORMAL CONTRACT AND LACK OF FORMALITY CASES

The same distinction that has been made in the German law and in the French law chapters[240] must be made in Chilean law in order to explore whether these case scenarios present any particularities and whether the notion of *confianza* is present.

1. BREAKING OFF NEGOTIATIONS FOR THE CONCLUSION OF A FORMAL CONTRACT

The principle of consensualism is one of the pillars of the Chilean law of contract.[241] However, different types of formalities are recognised by the law

234 Segura (n. 100) p. 106.
235 CA Concepción 5 June 1996 (n. 3) *considerando* 14.
236 CS 12 April 2012 (n. 84) replacement judgment *considerando* 3.
237 CA Santiago, 10 October 2014, *Frutícola El Aromo S.A. con Camposano Ibarra, rol* 579-2014, *considerando* 6, ratified by CS, 5 March 2015, *rol* 30469-2014.
238 Barrientos (n. 2) p. 116.
239 e.g. *Urrea con Corpbanca* (n. 84) replacement judgment *considerando* 3; *Frutícola El Aromo con Camposano* (n. 237).
240 See Ch. 3 s. IV and Ch. 4 s. IV.
241 CS 12 April 2012 (n. 84) cassation judgment *considerando* 5; Arturo Alessandri Rodríguez, *De los Contratos* (reprint 1993 1st edn., Editorial Jurídica de Chile, 2004) p. 32.

and among them are 'solemnities'.[242] These are formalities without which a legal act cannot exist.[243] The CCivCh defines solemn contracts in article 1443.[244] A typical example of a solemn contract is the sale of real estate. The solemnity that must be fulfilled for this contract to exist is that it is issued by public deed before a public notary.[245]

The traditional view in *la doctrina*[246] was that in solemn contracts (and in real contracts)[247] consent was only formed with the fulfilment of the solemnity (or with the delivery of the thing) and that the only liability that could arise in the stage of formation of consent of these contracts was contractual liability for breach of a promise contract (which in itself is a solemn contract).[248] Therefore, this view rejected the possibility of precontractual liability for breaking off negotiations for the conclusion of these types of contracts. This view also rejected the possibility that the liability for revocation of an offer established in the CComCh,[249] could apply to these contracts because it considered that the rules on formation of consent established in the CComCh applied only to consensual contracts. In a 1948 judgment the Court of Appeal of Santiago embraced this traditional view.[250]

However, the modern view in *la doctrina* is that in solemn contracts (as well as in real contracts), consent is necessary but it is not sufficient for the contract to exist; i.e. consent may be formed (agreement may be reached), but the contract will only exist when the solemnity is fulfilled (or the thing is delivered).[251] Therefore, it is perfectly possible that precontractual liability for breaking off negotiations for the conclusion of a solemn or a real contract may arise, and the rules of the CComCh on formation of consent (including liability for revocation of an offer) are also applicable to these contracts.[252] When consent has already been formed but one party refuses to fulfil the solemnity, it is a lack of

---

242 López Santa María and Elorriaga De Bonis (n. 142) pp. 260 ff.

243 Alessandri Rodríguez (n. 241) p. 32.

244 See (n. 7) above.

245 art. 1801(1)(2) CCivCh.

246 Explained by Rosende Álvarez (n. 6) p. 102; Hugo Rosende, 'La Responsabilidad Precontractual en la Formación del Consentimiento en los Contratos Reales y Solemnes' in Fundación Fueyo (ed.), *Instituciones Modernas de Derecho Civil: Homenaje al Profesor Fernando Fueyo Laneri* (Editorial Jurídica ConoSur, 1996) pp. 341–342.

247 See (n. 7) above.

248 See (n. 102) above.

249 See Ch. 2 (n. 31) above.

250 *Caja de Crédito Popular con Schiavetti* (n. 137).

251 e.g. Luis Claro Solar, *Explicaciones de Derecho Civil Chileno y Comparado*, vol. XI De las Obligaciones II (Editorial Jurídica de Chile, 1992) pp. 57, 113; Eiler (n. 36) pp. 152–153; Rosende Álvarez (n. 6) p. 111; Avelino León Hurtado, *La Voluntad y la Capacidad en los Actos Jurídicos* (4th edn., Editorial Jurídica de Chile, 1991) p. 53; Carlos Ducci, *Derecho Civil: Parte General* (4th edn., Editorial Jurídica de Chile, 2005) p. 252.

252 Rosende Álvarez (n. 6) pp. 113, 114.

formality case.[253] But when consent has not yet been formed and one party breaks off the negotiations, it is a case of breaking off negotiations for the conclusion of a formal contract.

Such a case was *Forestal Bío-Bío*, where the Court of Appeal of Concepción explained the traditional and the modern views,[254] and favoured the latter, awarding delictual damages for the breaking-off of negotiations for the sale of real estate, based on the notions of *confianza* and good faith.[255] This case could be analysed as one of lack of formality because the parties had agreed to conclude a promise of sale contract and the defendants refused to fulfil its solemnity and broke off the negotiations. But because the ultimate aim of the negotiations was the conclusion of the final contract of sale and consent had not been reached regarding this contract, it seems more appropriate to categorise it as a case of broken negotiations for the conclusion of a solemn contract.

A similar case is *Jiménez Mira*,[256] where the parties had agreed to conclude a promise of sale contract and the defendant refused to fulfil its solemnity (they had not yet reached agreement on all aspects of the sale contract).[257] The Supreme Court invalidated of its own initiative for defect of form the Court of Appeal's judgment which had confirmed the first instance judgment which, in turn, had argued on the basis of the traditional view in order to reject the claim.[258] The Supreme Court implicitly embraced the modern view declaring that the claim was based on precontractual liability and awarded damages for the defendant's unilateral breaking-off of negotiations, on the basis of *confianza* and good faith.[259]

In another relevant case the Supreme Court held that consent to conclude a promise contract of sale of real estate had been reached but consent to conclude the final sale contract had not, and that this consideration alone was enough to reject the principal claim of contractual performance.[260] Regarding the alternative claim of damages for the defendant's untimely withdrawal from the negotiations, the court concluded that it failed due to lack of proof of the losses suffered.[261] The court offered no other objection for this claim to succeed,

---

253 See this s. IV sub-s. 2 below.

254 CA Concepción 5 June 1996 (n. 3) *considerandos* 2–5.

255 See text following (n. 101) above, and text to (n. 183) above.

256 CS 29 December 2011 (n. 23).

257 See facts of the case in text following (n. 107) above. Lilian San Martín, 'Responsabilidad Precontractual por Ruptura Injustificada de Negociaciones: "*Jiménez Mira, David Alejandro con Armijo Cerda, Antonio de los Ángeles" Corte Suprema, Rol 1872/2010*' (2013) 40 Revista Chilena de Derecho 317, analyses it as a lack of formality case.

258 2nd JLC San Antonio, 28 October 2009, *rol* no. 26108-2007, confirmed by CA Valparaíso, 5 January 2010, *rol* no. 2247-2009.

259 See text to (n. 107) above.

260 CS, 31 August 2012, *Territoria S.A. con Inmobiliaria Leja Limitada*, *rol* 3647-2012.

261 CS 31 August 2012 (n. 260) replacement judgment *considerando* 13.

which suggests that it embraced the modern view that an award of damages for breaking off negotiations for the conclusion of a solemn contract is possible if the requirements of this liability are met and proved. This is further supported by a recent case where the claim for delictual damages failed because the court considered that the claimant did not prove that the defendants had culpably breached the duty of good faith in their withdrawal from the negotiations, although it recognised that the parties had created between them a *confianza* that the sale contract would be concluded.[262]

It can be concluded that *la doctrina* and *la jurisprudencia* have embraced the modern view on the formation of consent in solemn contracts, and that precontractual liability for breaking off negotiations for the conclusion of a solemn contract can arise much in the same way that it can regarding consensual contracts, with *confianza* as one of its bases. Objections to this liability of the sort that have been adduced in German law[263] do not seem to be present in Chilean law.

2. LACK OF FORMALITY CASES

It appears that most cases that have come before the courts belong to this category.[264] The factual situation generally is that negotiating parties have agreed on all the elements of a sale contract of real estate, but one of the parties then refuses to fulfil the solemnity (the signing of the public deed in a notary's office).[265]

Such a case was *Caja de Crédito Popular*,[266] where the parties had orally agreed to the sale of a property but, pending the fulfilment of the solemnity, the defendants refused to carry it out. The claimant sued for damages for revocation of an offer based on article 100 CComCh and, in the alternative, for damages for delictual liability for refusing to fulfil the solemnity to perfect the contract. The alleged loss was the fees paid to an architect and an engineer for the planning of the building that was to be built on the site and the increase in construction costs. The judgment expressly identified the situation regulated by article 100 CComCh as a case of precontractual liability and defined this liability on the basis of *confianza*[267] but, embracing the traditional view, held

262 CS 5 March 2015 *considerando* 4, *Frutícola El Aromo con Camposano* (n. 237); see text to (n. 237) above.
263 For German law, see Ch. 3, text to (nn. 184, 185) above.
264 Barros Bourie, *Responsabilidad Extracontractual* (n. 5) p. 1013, analyses these cases as precontractual liability for null contracts.
265 See text to (n. 245) above.
266 CA Santiago 25 August 1948 (n. 137).
267 See the definition in Ch. 2, text following (n. 37) above.

that this article was not applicable in this case as this was a civil contract. Regarding the claim for delictual liability, the judgment held that no delict had been committed as it considered that the refusal to perfect the contract was 'perfectly legitimate',[268] being a mere consequence of the legitimate exercise of the right not to persevere in the negotiations, a right which was exercised within the rule of good faith. This judgment has been criticised for holding that the refusal to sign a public deed of sale, after all the elements of the contract were agreed, is a licit act.[269]

Although legal scholars generally agree that these cases give rise to liability, there are two distinct views as to the legal regime which is applicable. On the one hand, Rosende Álvarez argues that the contractual regime is applicable. He explains that where consent is formed but the solemnity is not yet fulfilled, the contract does not exist, but there is a quasi-contractual[270] relationship that gives rise to precontractual liability in case of withdrawal (which imposes an obligation to compensate the losses caused). This liability emanates from the articles of the CComCh on formation of consent because they are applicable to solemn (and real) contracts.[271] An agreement on all the elements of a solemn contract before the fulfilment of the solemnity is a *cierre de negocios* (a non-regulated type of pre-contract) which leads to the application of the rules of contractual liability.[272] On the other hand, Ducci argues that the refusal to perfect a contract where consent has been formed is an act of bad faith which violates the other party's *confianza* on the word of the refusing party, and that this constitutes an illicit act which leads to the application of the delictual regime of liability.[273]

Lack of formality cases have often failed before the courts. It appears that in most cases this is because the claims have been wrongly framed in terms of contractual liability. *Luna con Bobadilla*[274] is a case which, under the modern view, should have succeeded if the claim had been made on the basis of delictual liability. The negotiating parties (two individuals) orally agreed on all the elements of the sale of a property and the 'buyer' paid the price and the 'seller' delivered the property. Both parties knew that a public deed had to be signed

[268] CA Santiago 25 August 1948 (n. 137) *considerando* 13.

[269] León Hurtado (n. 251) pp. 58–59.

[270] *Cuasicontratos* are one of the sources of obligations according to arts. 1437 and 2284 CCivCh.

[271] See text to (nn. 45, 46) above.

[272] Rosende Álvarez, *Algunas Consideraciones sobre la Responsabilidad Precontractual* (n. 6) pp. 106, 111; Rosende, 'La Responsabilidad Precontractual en la Formación del Consentimiento' (n. 246) p. 341. Similarly, Hernán Corral, *Lecciones de Responsabilidad Civil Extracontractual* (2nd edn., Legal Publishing, 2013) p. 39.

[273] Ducci (n. 251) p. 255. Similarly, de la Maza and Pizarro (n. 23) pp. 57–58; Corral (n. 272) p. 39 (in cases where the agreement does not constitute a valid non-regulated contract).

[274] CS 22 November 2001 (n. 92).

before a notary but they postponed its signing until the seller could obtain a clear title of the property. When this happened the seller refused to sign the public deed alleging that there were differences in the boundaries that had been agreed. In the meantime, the buyer had done work on the land and had incurred significant expenses. The claimant buyer asked the court to declare that the defendant had to sign the public deed of sale and pay him damages. Declaring that the seller was obliged to sign the public deed was clearly inadmissible because no promise contract had been concluded.[275] However, the first instance court and the Court of Appeal awarded damages, but on different grounds: the first instance judgment based them on the delictual liability of the defendant and the Court of Appeal on the precontractual liability of the defendant (without determining whether the damages were contractual or delictual).[276]

The Supreme Court held that the claimant's action was based on article 1489 CCivCh which establishes the right to sue for the resolution or specific performance of the contract, and damages, in case of a contractual breach. Thus, it invalidated of its own initiative the Court of Appeal's judgment and, in its replacement judgment, held that because the contract of sale had not been perfected and the existence of a promise of sale contract had not been proved, it was impossible to ask for contractual performance, and that because the compensation sought was for contractual breach it was also inadmissible. Therefore, it rejected the claim in all its parts.[277] In *Territoria*,[278] the Supreme Court pointed out that its judgment in *Luna con Bobadilla* followed the traditional doctrine on the formation of contractual consent.

Another case that failed is *Jorge Sepúlveda Rey con Banco del Desarrollo S.A.*,[279] where consent regarding the purchase of a property by a farmer from a bank had been reached. The farmer was already in possession of the property, to the knowledge of the bank, because the farmer had paid an amount to the previous owner so that she could pay the bank the money that she owed and sell the property directly to him. But the previous owner did not pay the bank and the bank foreclosed the mortgage. The farmer asked the bank several times to conclude with him a promise of sale contract, but the bank said that it was not necessary and that the final sale contract would be concluded as soon as the farmer demonstrated that he had the funds to pay the initial instalment of

---

275 If a valid promise contract had been concluded and it had been breached, the remedy of specific performance (*ejecución forzada en naturaleza*) would have been available based on art. 1553 CCivCh; Abeliuk Manasevich (n. 102) pp. 135–136, 155–156.

276 1st JLC Talca 31 March 1997, quashed by CA Talca 8 November 1999 (n. 92). The CA Talca expressly embraced the ideas formulated by Rosende: see text to (n. 272) above.

277 CS 22 November 2001 (n. 92).

278 CS 31 August 2012 (n. 260) replacement judgment *considerando* 10.

279 CS, 10 October 2006, *rol* 486-2004, Legal Publishing no. 35392.

the price. The farmer claimed he did this by giving a promissory note for the required amount to a public notary and also by paying an amount required by the bank to cover expenses. The bank sent to the same public notary a draft of the sale contract and when the farmer went to sign it (about a month later) he found out that the bank had sold the property to another person who was, at that very same time, signing the public deed of sale. The farmer sued for contractual damages for the bank's breach of a preparatory sale contract.

The first instance judgment rejected the claim for lack of proof.[280] The Court of Appeal,[281] embracing the traditional approach, held that the claimant had not shown that he had a true will to formalise his consent with the bank because, regarding real estate, binding agreements are governed by the rules of promise contracts established in article 1554 CCivCh, the requirements of which had not been met. It also held that the claimant had been reluctant to sign the public deed of sale. The Supreme Court, in the majority, agreed with the Court of Appeal in that the claimant never had a firm will to formalise its consent by signing the public deed of sale and concluded that no agreement that gave rise to obligations existed and that, consequently, no breach which gave rise to damages was possible.[282] The minority opinion was that contractual damages for breach of a preparatory contract different from a promise contract (*cierre de negocios*) should have been granted.[283]

Another example of a case that failed is *Sepúlveda González con Lacoste Morgado*.[284] The parties negotiated for the sale of a property. According to the claimant, they orally agreed that they would conclude the sale contract at a later date. The claimant made improvements to the property and went to live there because it was agreed that the claimant would occupy the property under a lease pending the sale contract being concluded. The claimant asserted that he sent to the defendant a draft of a promise of sale contract several times, but they did not sign it and, after a few months, the defendant told the claimant that she would only sell to him at a much higher price and that the rent for the lease was also a much higher amount than they had agreed. Consequently, the claimant vacated the property but owing the rent. The claimant sued for damages for 'precontractual breaches' relating to an 'agreement of sale'. The Supreme Court reaffirmed the Court of Appeal's judgment, which embraced the traditional view,[285] and held that the claim failed because no written or oral promise of sale contract existed and it had not been proved that the parties had reached the

280 22nd JLC Santiago, 31 August 2000, *rol* 1804-1995.
281 CA Santiago, 27 November 2003, *rol* 7900-2000.
282 CS 10 October 2006 (n. 279) *considerando* 8.
283 Judge Sergio Muñoz Gajardo (n. 279), who appears to be following Rosende's argument: see text to (n. 272) above.
284 CS, 22 September 2011, *rol* 4170-2010.
285 CA San Miguel, 7 April 2010, *rol* 17-2010.

agreement alleged by the claimant. It also held that it had not been claimed or proved that the negotiations were broken off in an untimely manner, but simply that the negotiations did not succeed. Finally, it held that article 2329 CCivCh had not been breached because this article had nothing to do with the claim, as the claim was for alleged breaches of precontractual agreements and not for the deceitful or negligent conduct of the defendant.[286]

In *Territoria*,[287] the Supreme Court stated that due to its function to guide in legal matters, it would consider the hypothetical situation that consent to conclude the sale contract had been formed. It explained the traditional and the modern views on the formation of contractual consent[288] and concluded that even under the modern view the claim of contractual enforcement had to fail. The appropriate remedy where a contract of sale of real estate has not been perfected due to the refusal of one of the parties to fulfil the solemnity, even though consent to conclude the contract has been reached, is an award of damages for precontractual liability (governed by the rules of delictual liability); not specific performance of a contract that has not been perfected. This is the case even if it is accepted (as the claimant argued) that an agreement to conclude a sale contract constitutes a valid unnamed contract (*contrato innominado*). Therefore, the court appears to recognise that if the claim had been for delictual damages for the defendant's refusal to fulfil the solemnity of the sale contract, the claim might have succeeded if sufficient evidence of the losses suffered had been provided.[289]

This has been confirmed by a recent judgment of the Supreme Court[290] in a case where the negotiating parties had reached agreement to conclude a sale contract of a flat but then the defendant 'buyer' refused to sign the public deed of sale. According to the claimant 'seller', a preparatory contract which gave rise to an obligation to enter into the sale contract, but which was different from a promise contract, had been entered into, and he sued for the resolution of this contract and damages for breach of contract. The court rejected the claim holding that the only contract which can give rise to the obligation to enter into another contract is a promise contract. However, it expressly recognised that precontractual losses may be compensated under the rules of delictual liability, but that this claim had not been made.[291] Furthermore, damages for

286 CS 22 September 2011 (n. 284) *considerandos* 10, 12–13.

287 CS 31 August 2012 (n. 260) replacement judgment *considerandos* 4–12.

288 For details on these views see this Ch. s. IV 1 above.

289 See text to (n. 261) above.

290 CS, 23 September 2015, *Lange Haensgen con Ibáñez Santa María*, *rol* 1077-15.

291 CS 23 September 2015 (n. 290) *considerando* 8. In a similar case, *Sociedad Comercial Timbres con Banco Itaú Chile* (n. 2), the claimant sued for delictual damages and these were granted by the CA Talca, 16 October 2017, *rol* 4522-2016, and confirmed by the CS, 13 December 2018 (n. 2), but in both judgments the superior courts treated it as a case of liability for breaking off negotiations rather than as a lack of formality case.

precontractual liability were granted in *Urrea con Corpbanca*,[292] which could be categorised as a lack of formality case or as akin to this category, in that consent to conclude a mortgage loan was formed (a loan is a real contract),[293] but the mortgage loan was not concluded because the money was not given by the bank.[294]

The reason why many lack of formality cases have failed is because the claims have been made on a contractual basis. The motivation to sue under contract (either a preliminary contract or the final contract) is presumably because contractual liability gives rise to remedies that delictual liability does not.[295] Suing under contract presents considerable obstacles because promise contracts are preparatory solemn contracts subject to strict requirements[296] and although other preparatory consensual contracts are possible,[297] they cannot impose the obligation to conclude another contract, because this is the realm of promise contracts and its requirements must not be undermined.[298] Therefore, the better view, which finds support in *Territoria* and in *Lange con Ibáñez*,[299] is that the claim should be made for delictual damages for precontractual liability for the refusal to perfect the solemnity.

V. CONCLUSIONS

Within the process of reception of the doctrine of precontractual liability into Chilean law, influences from French and German law have been especially relevant in order to shape this doctrine within the particularities of the Chilean legal system. Regarding precontractual liability for breaking off negotiations, the different theoretical bases that have been put forward, which correspond to those mentioned in German and French law, are usually presented as complementing each other. Good faith, which is frequently mentioned by *la doctrina* and *la jurisprudencia*, is usually applied via the notion of *confianza*

---

292 CS 12 April 2012 (n. 84); see text to (n. 110) above.

293 For the definition of real contracts see (n. 7) above.

294 In a similar case the claim for damages for breach of a loan contract was rejected and it was held that the claim should have been for delictual damages, CA Rancagua, 16 September 2014, *Mendoza Lara con Banco Santander Banefe*, ratified by CS, 4 June 2015, *rol* 27186-2014.

295 See Ch. 6, s. IV 1 (a) below.

296 See text to (n. 102) above.

297 e.g. agreements granting pre-emptive rights, lock-out agreements, lock-in agreements, agreements that organise the negotiations (mentioned in the *Lange con Ibáñez* case (n. 290) *considerando* 8).

298 *Lange con Ibáñez* (n. 290) *considerando* 8.

299 See text to (nn. 289, 291) above.

in both its dimensions. *Confianza* is a notion analogous to those used in German and in French law to refer to 'reliance' and is the better suited for explaining the rationale of this liability, which finds its legal basis in the general principle of delictual liability. The same is true in cases of broken negotiations for the conclusion of a formal contract and in lack of formality cases, which do not present the special treatment that they have in German law.

CHAPTER 6

RELIANCE AS THE CORE ELEMENT OF PRECONTRACTUAL LIABILITY FOR BREAKING OFF NEGOTIATIONS

Following on from the study of reliance in the breaking-off of negotiations in each selected jurisdiction, this chapter brings together the findings of the three previous chapters and argues that reliance is the core notion of precontractual liability for breaking off negotiations. The chapter will first make a comparative analysis of the general characteristics of this liability in the selected jurisdictions (section I). Particular attention will be paid to the much-debated issue of the nature of this liability, that it is a fault-based liability, and the presence of other requirements shared by the selected jurisdictions. The chapter will then focus on the comparative analysis of the two more prominent bases of liability for breaking off negotiations in the selected jurisdictions: reliance and good faith. It will first examine, from a comparative perspective, the reliance basis, looking at its meaning, manifestations, genesis and justification, and showing that it is the core element that explains the imposition of this liability (section II). It will then address the role of good faith in the breaking-off of negotiations, focusing on determining whether it is an essential factor in the configuration of this liability or whether it could potentially be replaced or displaced by the reliance element (section III). The chapter will conclude with a comparative analysis of the remedies that the reliance-based approach gives rise to in the selected jurisdictions and also in certain harmonising instruments (section IV).

I. GENERAL CHARACTERISTICS OF PRECONTRACTUAL LIABILITY FOR BREAKING OFF NEGOTIATIONS IN THE SELECTED JURISDICTIONS

From the previous chapters it is clear that the German doctrine of *culpa in contrahendo* and the French doctrine of precontractual liability have some marked differences. It has also been shown that in receiving these doctrines, Chilean law has taken some elements from each of these jurisdictions and has developed them in light of the particularities of its legal system. Nevertheless, and despite the differences, the selected jurisdictions have many commonalities and provide for a similar protection in the breaking-off of negotiations. Indeed, it has been stated that the new articles 1112 and following of the *Code civil*, structurally and conceptually, are not dissimilar to §§241(2) and 311(2) BGB, which codified the doctrine of *culpa in contrahendo*.[1] A summary of the general characteristics of this liability in the selected jurisdictions is presented below.

1. NATURE OF THE LIABILITY

At a doctrinal level, the nature of precontractual liability is one of the most debated issues. In cases of broken negotiations, the lack of a contract and the fact that the parties are not strangers (as they have been engaged in negotiations) pose serious difficulties for the classification of this liability as belonging within or outside the realm of contract.[2] Therefore, it is not surprising that a primary difference between the selected jurisdictions in their treatment of liability for breaking off negotiations is found in the nature of this liability and in its applicable legal regime.

In Germany, starting from Jhering's doctrine of *culpa in contrahendo* and due to the particularities of its law of delict, it has long been held that the contractual regime applies to precontractual liability and this was reaffirmed by the 2001 reform.[3] But it is also accepted that *culpa in contrahendo*, in its nature, is a *sui generis* concept, 'floating freely between contract and tort'.[4] In France, by contrast, the delictual nature of precontractual liability and the applicability of the delictual regime are undisputed.[5] In Chile, while the courts follow the French approach as to the delictual nature of this liability and the applicability of the delictual regime, some authors have voiced a preference for a third category of liability, following the German 'third way' (*dritte Spur*) language.[6]

Despite the fact that the leading civil law jurisdictions take polar positions regarding the nature of precontractual liability, this divergence does not affect their ability to reach similar levels of protection (in contract or in delict). Indeed, in spite of the 'contractual' or 'delictual' label, the requirements and remedies of this liability are very similar.[7]

---

1 Birke Häcker, '*La Troisième Jeunesse du Code Civil*: A German Lawyer Looks at the Reform of French Contract Law' in John Cartwright and Simon Whittaker (eds.), *The Code Napoléon Rewritten: French Contract Law after the 2016 Reforms* (Hart Publishing, 2017) p. 397.

2 Ingeborg Schwenzer, Pascal Hachem and Christopher Kee, *Global Sales and Contract Law* (OUP, 2012) pp. 275, 283.

3 See Ch. 2 s. I 2 (a) and Ch. 3, text to (n. 3) above.

4 Basil Markesinis, Hannes Unberath and Angus Johnston, *The German Law of Contract: A Comparative Treatise* (2nd edn., Hart, 2006) p. 92.

5 See Ch. 4, text to (n. 15) above.

6 See Ch. 5, text to (nn. 23, 36) above.

7 For details, see this Ch. ss. II and IV below.

2. A FAULT-BASED LIABILITY

In the selected jurisdictions precontractual liability emanates from the principle of *neminem laedere*[8] and precontractual fault is required for liability for breaking off negotiations to arise.[9] In all of them precontractual fault is not qualified, in that negligence suffices,[10] and the assessment of negligence is abstract and objective.[11] However, some differences can be identified.

First, there is an evident difference in the nature of precontractual fault which results from the divergence as to the nature of this liability.[12] In France and Chile precontractual fault is considered to be of a delictual nature, while in Germany it is contractual.[13] This difference does not, however, affect the basic notion of fault as breach of a duty or a general standard.[14] Nevertheless, the divergence does have some practical impact, for instance, with regard to the burden of proof: in Germany, because precontractual fault is considered to be contractual, it is presumed, whereas in France and Chile, because it is considered to be delictual (and does not fall within special presumptions of fault), it has to be proved.[15]

Secondly, there is a theoretical distinction as to the place of precontractual fault. In German law, fault can be found at two levels: in the creation of the expectation of the future conclusion of the negotiated contract, and in the breaking-off; and the fault requirement is normally established by a combination of both.[16] In French law, precontractual fault lies in the circumstances of the breaking-off and not in the breaking-off itself.[17] In Chilean law, although little emphasis has been placed on this distinction, it seems that fault at both levels is required.[18] Despite this theoretical difference, the results obtained in practice are much the same because in German and Chilean law fault is normally found in a combination of the levels, and in French law fault is normally found in a combination of the conduct of the party breaking off during the negotiations and additional objective circumstances (such as the abruptness of the breaking-off).

---

8 Markesinis, Unberath and Johnston (n. 4) p. 312; John Bell, Sophie Boyron and Simon Whittaker, *Principles of French Law* (2nd edn., OUP, 2008) p. 367; Marcelo Barrientos Zamorano, *Daños y Deberes en las Tratativas Preliminares de un Contrato* (2nd edn., Legal Publishing, 2010) p. 58.

9 See Ch. 3, text to (n. 56), Ch. 4, text to (n. 24), Ch. 5, text to (n. 71) above.

10 See Ch. 3, text to (n. 59), Ch. 4, text to (n. 86), Ch. 5, text to (n. 72) above.

11 See Ch. 3, text to (n. 59), Ch. 4, text to (n. 45), Ch. 5, p. 110 above.

12 See this Ch. sub-s. 1 above.

13 See Ch. 3, text to (n. 59), Ch. 4, text to (n. 26), Ch. 5, text to (n. 71) above.

14 See Ch. 3, text to (n. 59), Ch. 4, text to (n. 54), Ch. 5, text to (n. 78) above.

15 See Ch. 3, text to (n. 31), Ch. 4, text to (n. 21), Ch. 5, text to (n. 87) above.

16 See Ch. 3, text to (n. 93) and, generally, Ch. 3 s. II I (b) above.

17 See Ch. 4, text to (n. 99) above.

18 See Ch. 5, text following (n. 86) above.

Therefore, there is a functional convergence between the selected jurisdictions regarding the fault requirement in cases of breaking off negotiations, despite the fact that they have some theoretical differences which may have some impact in practice.

3. FURTHER REQUIREMENTS OF LIABILITY

The fault requirement has been analysed in sub-section 2 above and the reliance requirement and the notion of good faith are analysed in sections II and III below. Here, mention will be made of other requirements that, to some degree, are present in all the selected jurisdictions.

(a) Existence of a Precontractual Relationship

An initial distinction must be made between the notions of 'negotiations' and 'precontractual relationship'. It has been seen that 'negotiations' refers both to a time period and to the relationship that forms between negotiating parties.[19] In the latter sense, the interaction and connection between the negotiating parties can be termed as a 'precontractual relationship' in order to highlight the fact that they are not strangers (as would normally be the case in a purely delictual scenario), and that they are connected to some extent, although not yet bound by an obligation to enter into a contract. In this broad sense, all the selected jurisdictions consider negotiations as a precontractual relationship. However, the notion of 'precontractual relationship' has a much more technical meaning in German law, as the commencement of negotiations gives rise to an obligation which imposes duties on the negotiating parties.[20] Under this narrow sense, a precontractual relationship is required in German law, is not required in French law, and is sometimes incorrectly required in Chilean law.

In German law, the notion of 'precontractual relationship' acquires its true relevance as the source of the precontractual duties of the negotiating parties. Thus, determining the beginning of the negotiation period is particularly relevant for German law,[21] as the beginning of negotiations involves the beginning of the precontractual relationship from which protective duties arise for the negotiating parties.[22] This precontractual relationship is contract-like,

---

19 See Preface s. I above.

20 See Ch. 3, text following (n. 37) above.

21 On the notions of 'social contact' and 'business contact', Clara Asúa González and José Javier Hualde Sánchez, 'Codificación de la *Culpa in Contrahendo* en el Derecho Alemán' in Antonio Cabanillas Sánchez and others (eds.), *Estudios Jurídicos en Homenaje al Profesor Luis Díez-Picazo*, vol. II (Thomson Civitas, 2003) pp. 1421–1424.

22 See Ch. 3, text to (nn. 12, 13) above.

which brings the precontractual phase closer to the contractual domain in order to apply the contractual regime due to the shortcomings of the law of delict.[23]

In France and Chile the situation is much different. Their laws of delict allow for compensation of pure economic loss, they have general principles of delictual liability, and it is generally accepted that precontractual liability is subject to the delictual regime.[24] Consequently, there is no need to resort to a contract-like precontractual relationship in order to justify the imposition of precontractual liability. However, in both jurisdictions the notion of a precontractual relationship in the broad sense is perfectly acceptable and reference is sometimes made to a relationship of trust between the negotiating parties.[25] Some Chilean authors and judgments require an agreement to enter into negotiations for liability to arise, which suggests the need for a contract-like relationship between the negotiating parties. It has been argued that this is incorrect or at least irrelevant as it will be satisfied by the mere fact of the existence of negotiations.[26]

Therefore, in all the selected jurisdictions it is evidently a requirement of precontractual liability for breaking off negotiations that the parties have entered into negotiations, but care must be taken when characterising these negotiations as a precontractual relationship. The 'precontractual relationship' understood as a relationship of obligation from which duties emanate (the breach of which allows the imposition of contractual liability) only truly makes sense in German law, due to the need to have a 'contractual likeness' in the negotiations, but not in jurisdictions such as French and Chilean law where the delictual regime is applied to liability for breaking off negotiations. In the latter jurisdictions negotiations can be described as a precontractual relationship (of reliance) in the broad sense but not in the contract-like sense of German law. However, the fact remains that in French and Chilean law reference is also made to precontractual duties. If they do not emanate from a contract-like precontractual relationship, it must be determined from where they originate. This leads to the next requirement.

(b) Breach of Precontractual Duties

Although the language of violation of precontractual duties is common to all the selected jurisdictions, they use it with different degrees of clarity and relevance, with German law being the clearest as to why the breach of precontractual duties is needed in order to impose *culpa in contrahendo* liability, and with French and Chilean law being far less clear as to the utility of framing liability for

---

23 See Ch. 3, text to (nn. 24, 25) above.

24 See Ch. 4, text to (n. 15) and text following (n. 16), Ch. 5, text to (n. 23) and text following (n. 23), this Ch., text following (n. 195) and text to (n. 218).

25 See Ch. 4 s. II 1 (b) and Ch. 5 s. I 2 above.

26 See Ch. 5 s. I 2 above.

breaking off negotiations in terms of breach of precontractual duties. It must be recognised that although it is regularly said that negotiating parties are subject to precontractual duties, there is a difficulty in determining where these duties emanate from in this 'grey area'[27] where negotiators are no longer strangers but are also not parties to a contract.

In German law it is clear that precontractual duties emanate from the precontractual relationship of trust and, after the 2001 reform, these duties also have a legal basis in §241(2) BGB.[28] The reason for framing *culpa in contrahendo* for breaking off negotiations in terms of breach of protective duties emanating from a contract-like precontractual relationship is evident due to the need to apply the contractual regime of liability. In French and Chilean law, where the delictual regime applies to liability for breaking off negotiations, it is not clear why the rationalisation of this liability should be done in terms of breach of precontractual duties.

In French law, the notion of breach of a duty is found in the definition of fault (although not all agree on such a definition)[29] and in the breach of duties emanating from the principle of good faith which gives rise to precontractual liability.[30] In Chile, reference to the breach of duties emanating from good faith is also sometimes made in the analysis of liability for breaking off negotiations.[31] The relevance and necessity of these duties emanating from good faith as a basis of precontractual liability is analysed in this chapter in section III 3 below.

(c) *Bad Reason for Breaking Off*

Reference to an unjustified reason for breaking off or, on the contrary, to a legitimate reason for breaking off is made in all the selected jurisdictions, but with varying degrees of significance.

The lack of a good reason for breaking off is a requirement of liability for breaking off negotiations in German law.[32] Indeed, fault at the level of the breaking-off is found in breaking off without a good reason.[33] Chilean authors and judgments seem to follow German law in this respect, mentioning the lack of a justified reason for breaking off as a requirement of precontractual liability.[34] In French law, breaking off without a justified reason is not formulated in terms of a requirement of precontractual liability, but the same result is reached by

27 Schwenzer, Hachem and Kee (n. 2) p. 275.
28 See Ch. 3, text to (nn. 35, 36) above.
29 See Ch. 4 s. I 1 above.
30 See Ch. 4, text to (nn. 217, 218) above.
31 See Ch. 5 s. II 2 above.
32 See Ch. 3 s. II 2 above.
33 See Ch. 3, text following (n. 94) above.
34 See Ch. 5 s. III 2 above.

recognising that a legitimate reason that justifies the breaking-off excludes liability (i.e. there is liability in the absence of a legitimate reason).[35]

Although this slightly different approach to the reason for breaking off in German and French law could have some impact on the burden of proof, it is suggested that the outcome will normally be the same. In German law, because the contractual regime applies, fault is presumed and, therefore, the defendant would have to prove a good reason for breaking off to destroy the presumption. In French law, because the delictual regime applies, fault must be proved and the claimant should have to prove that the defendant broke off without a legitimate reason, but because the reason for breaking off is not framed as a requirement but rather as an exemption from liability, it will fall to the defendant to prove a good reason for breaking off. Chilean law seems to be the odd one out, because since the delictual regime applies and fault must be proved, and the lack of a legitimate reason for breaking off is considered a requirement for liability to arise, the claimant would have to show that the defendant did not have a good reason for breaking off.

(d) The Presence of Certain Objective Circumstances

In all the selected jurisdictions use is made of certain objective circumstances in order to justify the reasonableness or legitimacy of the reliance or expectations of the other party (Germany and Chile)[36] or to find the fault of the party breaking off (France).[37] In French law, because the reliance element is found within the configuration of precontractual fault, the result is that these circumstances also serve to justify the reasonableness or legitimacy of the other party's reliance. These objective circumstances are analysed in this chapter section II 2 (b) below.

II. RELIANCE AS THE KEY FEATURE

It has been shown that in German, French and Chilean law the notion of reliance, embodied, respectively, in the concepts of *Vertrauen*, *confiance/croyance légitime* and *confianza*, is a core requirement of precontractual liability for breaking off negotiations and it has been argued that it is the appropriate theoretical basis of this liability.[38] It has been seen that other doctrinal bases which have been put forward are not suitable for explaining the rationale (doctrine of abuse of rights in French and Chilean law)[39] or the consequences

---

35 See Ch. 4 s. III 2 above.
36 See Ch. 3 s. II 1 (d) and Ch. 5, text to (n. 150) above.
37 See Ch. 4, text to (n. 263) above.
38 In s. V of Chs. 3, 4, 5.
39 See Ch. 4 s. II 2 and Ch. 5 s. II 3 above.

(prohibition of *venire contra factum proprium* in German law and theory of appearance in French law)[40] of this liability and have thus been rejected. Therefore, this section and the next will focus on the remaining bases that have been suggested: reliance and good faith, advocating in favour of the former while recognising the role of the latter.

1. UNDERSTANDING RELIANCE

(a) *The Notion and Dimensions of Reliance*

The language of 'reliance' present in the selected jurisdictions is difficult to define, as it is used quite loosely to encompass notions of trust, confidence, expectation and belief. It is used 'in different contexts and in different senses'[41] within the topic of precontractual liability and this contributes to the difficulty in determining the content and boundaries of reliance. This book has identified in all the selected jurisdictions two dimensions of reliance and has proposed to refer to them as 'trust-based reliance' and 'expectation-based reliance'. Although the ideas evoked by each of these dimensions can be seen in the case law and in the writings of legal scholars in the selected jurisdictions, and in comparative studies,[42] often it is not easy to distinguish them as they are intertwined, with the focus oscillating from one to the other. In order to truly understand what is meant by reliance in the breaking-off of negotiations and to provide a structure that can organise the ideas behind the notions of *Vertrauen*, *confiance/croyance légitime* and *confianza*, it is necessary to analyse the content of these dimensions and the interaction between them.

In the trust dimension of reliance, 'trust' refers to the confidence that negotiators place in each other when negotiating a contract. This should be understood from an objective perspective, in that they trust that each will observe certain expected standards of conduct. It is difficult to define this trust dimension in the abstract as it is a flexible notion that acquires a more tangible meaning in the particular case. The trust or confidence in the other party's conduct or person can be induced or nourished by the other party and can also arise due to the circumstances surrounding the negotiations.[43]

In German law, the trust dimension of reliance is embodied in the precontractual relationship (defined as a relationship of mutual trust and confidence) and the

40 See Ch. 3, text following (n. 176) and Ch. 4, text to (n. 157) above.
41 John Cartwright and Martijn Hesselink (eds.), *Precontractual Liability in European Private Law* (CUP, 2008) p. 454.
42 e.g. in Cartwright and Hesselink (n. 41) p. 455.
43 See this Ch. sub-s. 2 below.

duties emanating from it.[44] A specific application of trust-based reliance is found in §311(3) second sentence BGB which refers to a particularly high degree of reliance induced in respect of his own person by a person who is not intended to be party to the contract.[45] While possible English translations of the wording of this provision can be 'nourishing the trust of the other party' or 'inducing special trustworthiness', these translations seem to point towards ethical duties, whereas the notion that the courts apply in these cases involving the liability of intermediaries is closer to the 'reasonable reliance' of English negligence cases.[46] Defining the 'normal' standard of trust or reliance and, consequently, the 'special' reliance in these cases has not caused major problems in practice.[47]

In French and Chilean law, the notion of a precontractual relationship in the broad sense embodies the trust dimension of reliance.[48] This relationship of trust and confidence between the negotiating parties reaffirms the idea that they are not strangers and are subject to certain standards of conduct. The notions of *confiance légitime* and *confianza* are wide enough to encompass trust-based reliance.[49]

The second dimension of reliance is 'expectation-oriented'. Here, the focus is on a specific expectation of the future conclusion of the negotiated contract. Before analysing this dimension, it is necessary to establish the relationship between the two dimensions of reliance. The expectation dimension is a specific manifestation of the trust dimension, in that the expectation of the future conclusion of the contract presupposes the existence of trust between the negotiating parties.[50] Therefore, expectation-based reliance emanates from trust-based reliance as a particular manifestation of it. Because the trust dimension is of a more general nature, it can operate in different scenarios of precontractual liability, whereas the expectation dimension is specific to cases of broken negotiations. Thus, it can be understood that in the selected jurisdictions, while mention of what is essentially trust-based reliance is sometimes made in breaking off cases, the key requirement for this liability to arise is expectation-based reliance.[51] Consequently, the emphasis in this sub-section and the next is on the expectation dimension of reliance, unless otherwise indicated.

---

44 See Ch. 3, text following (n. 20) above.

45 Peter Jung, 'La Protection de la Confiance en Droit Allemand des Contrats' in Bénédicte Fauvarque-Cosson and Peter Jung (eds.), *La Confiance: 11èmes Journées Bilatérales Franco-allemandes, Paris, 22 et 23 Novembre 2012* (Société de Législation Comparée, 2013) p. 37.

46 Markesinis, Unberath and Johnston (n. 4) p. 104; see Ch. 7, text to (n. 289) below.

47 Markesinis, Unberath and Johnston (n. 4) p. 105.

48 See text to (n. 25) above.

49 See Ch. 4 s. II 1 (b) and Ch. 5 s. II 1 (b) above.

50 Hélène Aubry, *L'influence du Droit Communautaire sur le Droit Français des Contrats* (PUAM, 2002) p. 251, indicates that the existence of an expectation presupposes an act of faith, in that there can be no hope without trust.

51 See Ch. 3 text to (nn. 118, 119), Ch. 4 s. II 1 (f) and Ch. 5 s. II 1 (e) above.

In this dimension, 'reliance' is 'inextricably linked'[52] to the 'expectation' of the future conclusion of the negotiated contract, created in one party by the conduct of the other party during the negotiations. Although the notion of 'expectation' can be thought to have a subjective element, often referred to as a hope or belief in the future conclusion of the contract,[53] it should be objectively understood as a legitimate or reasonable expectation that arises in the other party from certain conduct of the party who breaks off, and should be objectively assessed in terms of whether a reasonable person in similar circumstances would be justified to expect the future conclusion of the contract.[54] Therefore, it is preferable to express this dimension of reliance as an 'expectation' in the success of the negotiations, rather than as a 'hope' or 'belief' in such success, as the latter notions seem too subjective, being linked to personal desires or feelings, and could also be confused with a subjective notion of good faith.[55] It is also preferable to speak of giving rise to an 'expectation' rather than giving rise to a 'mistaken belief' or not informing of or correcting a 'mistaken belief', because situations of mistaken beliefs usually relate to other cases of precontractual liability (regarding null or even valid contracts).

This is a 'precontractual expectation' of the future conclusion of the contract under negotiation. It is not an expectation of the actual conclusion of such contract,[56] nor is it a contractual expectation of the fulfilment of a contractual obligation. Because the final terms of the contract under negotiation are generally still not entirely agreed on and because there is no obligation to actually conclude the contract, it is clear that this precontractual expectation is 'weaker'[57] than a contractual expectation. But, this does not mean that the precontractual expectation is not worthy of protection, and the selected jurisdictions, as many others do, provide for its protection through the doctrine of *culpa in contrahendo* or precontractual liability.[58] However, they place stringent requirements for this liability to arise and restrict the protection only to reasonable or legitimate expectations.[59] German law seems to require more than the other selected

52 Cartwright and Hesselink (n. 41) p. 455.

53 See Ch. 3 s. II 1 (c), Ch. 4 s. II 1 (a) and Ch. 5 s. II 1 (e) above. Aubry (n. 50) p. 251, states that an 'expectation' (*attente*) is a psychological notion that falls within the perceptions of the individual.

54 Similarly, Vladimir Monsalve Caballero, 'El Comportamiento del Contratante como Determinante para la Calificación de la Ruptura Injustificada de las Negociaciones: Visión desde el Derecho Europeo' (2009) 119 Vniversitas 251, p. 273.

55 See this Ch. s. III 1 below.

56 In some lack of formality cases in German law, the aggrieved party actually believed that the contract had been validly concluded, see Ch. 3, text to (n. 225) above.

57 Cartwright and Hesselink (n. 41) p. 454.

58 Cartwright and Hesselink's comparative observations to cases 1 and 7 (n. 41) pp. 60–63, 229–232.

59 See this Ch. sub-s. 2 (b) below.

jurisdictions, in that the expectation should normally be that the contract will certainly be concluded.[60]

(b) The Essence of Reliance

At the core of expectation-based reliance, which is the basis of precontractual liability for breaking off negotiations, is the protection of a legitimate expectation that has been disappointed.

The creation and subsequent disappointment of this expectation (on which the claimant legitimately relied) by the conduct of the defendant is the reason that makes him liable. Thus, it is generally recognised that it is not the breaking-off itself that gives rise to liability, but the conduct of the defendant in giving rise to an expectation of the future conclusion of the negotiated contract and then disappointing it by refusing to continue with the negotiations or breaking them off entirely.[61] This approach is wholly consistent with the principle of freedom of contract which reigns in the selected jurisdictions: liability does not arise for failing to enter into a contract, as there is no obligation to enter into one,[62] but for culpably creating a legitimate expectation and then disappointing it without good reason.

Because the selected jurisdictions have fault-based doctrines of precontractual liability,[63] the fault requirement must interact with expectation-based reliance. In this interaction, the notions of fault and reliance function together but without being interdependent. Consequently, fault is found in the wrongful (negligent and intentional conduct) creation and subsequent disappointment of an expectation on which the other party legitimately relied.

2. GENERATING RELIANCE AND LEGITIMATELY RELYING

In the selected jurisdictions, liability for breaking off negotiations will only arise when its requirements are met and expectation-based reliance is a core requirement. Therefore, it is necessary to establish what creates in the claimant the expectation that the negotiated contract will be concluded in order to then determine when the claimant may legitimately rely on this expectation.

(a) The Creation of Reliance

In general terms, it is the conduct of the defendant that triggers the claimant's reliance on the expectation of the future conclusion of the negotiated contract.

---

60 See Ch. 3, text to (n. 97) above.

61 See Ch. 3, text to (n. 93), Ch. 4, text to (n. 100), Ch. 5, text to (n. 83) above.

62 See Ch. 2 s. II above.

63 For details, see this Ch. s. I 2 above.

This is the 'starting point' for the protection of this expectation.[64] The word 'conduct' is being used in a wide sense. It can encompass different forms of actions,[65] which can range from express to implied declarations or behaviour, such as making promises, statements or assurances about the likely success of the negotiations and future conclusion of the contract,[66] or adopting certain attitudes towards the other party or regarding the other party (even before other people) that indicate the ultimate success of the negotiations.[67] It can also include inaction or omissions,[68] such as a failing to warn, inform or explain to the other party that it had not yet decided whether it would enter into the contract or had changed its mind about concluding the contract when knowing that the other party had already acted in reliance on its future conclusion,[69] or failing to inform the other party that it had already concluded the contract with a third party.[70]

---

64 Florian Faust and Volker Wiese, 'Protecting Legitimate Expectations The German Perspective' in Bénédicte Fauvarque-Cosson (ed.), *La Confiance Légitime et L'Estoppel*, vol. 4 (Societé de Législation Comparée, 2007) p. 135.

65 Clara Asúa González, *La Culpa in Contrahendo: Tratamiento en el Derecho Alemán y Presencia en Otros Ordenamientos* (Universidad del País Vasco, 1989) p. 156, regarding German law, understands that it is a positive conduct which makes the other party trust in the future conclusion of the contract.

66 e.g. in Germany, BGH, 12 June 1975, NJW 1975, 1774 ('making a promise', 'by the manner of his negotiations', 'by his conduct'); in France, Cass com, 15 October 2002, no. 00-13738 ('maintaining his [the other party's] confidence by the statement and reminder of their ambitious common prospects, by its orders and significant cash advances'); CA Rennes, 8 July 1929, DH 1929 p. 548 ('having dangled in the eyes of the other party the expectation of an agreement'); CA Dijon, 15 February 1893, Sirey 1894, 2, 144 ('assurances'); in Chile, CS, 12 April 2012, *Urrea Fuentes con Corpbanca, rol* 218-2011 (statement that the loan had been approved); CS, 29 December 2011, *Jiménez Mira con Armijo Cerda, rol* 1872-2010 (agreement to conclude a promise contract).

67 e.g. in Germany, BGH 22 February 1989, NJW-RR 1989, 627 ('the defendant had encouraged the plaintiff to take measures that would only be of use if a contract should arise'); in France, Cass com, 11 July 2000, Bull Joly 2000 no. 288, note Saintourens, PA 2001 no. 57 p. 19, note Dagorne-Labbé ('did not hesitate to present [the other party] as his associate'); CA Paris, 10 March 2000, JCP 2001 II 10470, note Violet (letting the other party believe it had agreed and letting the work advance); in Chile, CA Talca, 8 November 1999, *Luna Espinoza con Bobadilla Valenzuela*, quashed by CS, 22 November 2001, *rol* 2217-2000, Gaceta Jurídica 2001 no. 257 (the parties had performed the contract).

68 Horatia Muir-Watt, 'Les Pourparlers: De la Confiance Trompée à la Relation de Confiance' in Pauline Rémy-Corlay and Dominique Fenouillet (eds.), *Les Concepts Contractuels Français à L'heure des Principes du Droit Européen des Contrats* (Dalloz, 2003) p. 58.

69 e.g. in Germany, BGH, 29 March 1996, NJW 1996, 1884 ('statement of final preparedness to contract', 'prior conduct', 'knowledge of the claimant's current works'); BGH, 20 June 1952, BGHZ 6, 330 ('the defendant's statements and behaviour'); in France, Cass com, 20 March 1972, Bull civ IV no. 93, JCP 1973 II 17543, note Schmidt (*Gerteis c Vilbert-Lourmat*) (*The Hydrotile machine*) ('that company had already, to the other's knowledge, incurred considerable expense', 'intentionally kept that company in a state of protracted uncertainty'); in Chile, CA Concepción, 5 June 1996, *Forestal Bío-Bío SA con Madesal, rol* 1374-93 (ratified by CS 28 January 1999) ('the defendants did not give any notice to the claimant of their intention to withdraw').

70 In France, Cass com, 26 November 2003, Bull civ IV no. 186, JCP éd E 2004, 738, note Stoffel-Munck (*Manoukian c X et Les Complices*) ('letting [the claimant] think', 'negotiations which they had never given the impression of abandoning').

The defendant, through his conduct, creates or awakens in the claimant the expectation of the future conclusion of the contract which induces the claimant to rely on this expectation.[71] However, it is also possible that the expectation arose in the claimant due to reasons other than the conduct of the defendant. In these cases, the defendant may still be liable if he encouraged the claimant's reliance on such an expectation. In other words, the claimant's reliance on the expectation of the success of the negotiations must be directly caused by the defendant's conduct; it must be a consequence of the defendant's conduct.

A question which arises is whether it is a requirement for the defendant to know that this expectation has arisen in the claimant and that the latter has acted in reliance upon it. Some cases mention the defendant's knowledge of the other party's expenditure, work or, in general, detrimental actions taken in reliance on the expectation of the future conclusion of the contract.[72] The defendant's knowledge evidently supports finding him liable, but it cannot be said that it is a general requirement for the imposition of liability to show that the defendant knew of the claimant's reliance.[73] If the defendant knows that the other party has acted or will likely act in reliance, it can be argued that the defendant has a duty to inform or warn the claimant that it does not intend to continue with the negotiations.[74]

Knowledge of other aspects of the negotiations can also be relevant. For instance, creating or inducing the expectation of the future conclusion of the contract when knowing that the contact cannot or will not be concluded (for example because a requirement is lacking, there is an obstacle, or there is no intention to finally conclude the contract), normally amounts to fraud, deceit, intention to harm or bad faith on the part of the defendant.[75] The knowledge of one or both parties as to the existence and fulfilment of formality requirements has particular relevance in breaking off negotiations for the conclusion of formal contracts cases and lack of formality cases in German law.[76] And the claimant's knowledge of the state of the negotiations is relevant for assessing the reasonableness of his reliance.[77]

Although the language of 'risk' is not very common in the selected jurisdictions in the analysis of precontractual liability for breaking off negotiations, it is possible to formulate it under this perspective, stating that the economic risk of the failure of the negotiations which, in principle, belongs to each negotiating party, shifts when the claimant is entitled to rely on the expectation of the future

---

71 See Ch. 3, text to (n. 104), Ch. 4, text to (n. 109) and Ch. 5, text following (n. 145) above.
72 e.g. see (nn. 67, 69) above.
73 See Ch. 3, text to (n. 111), Ch. 4, text to (n. 230), Ch. 5, text to (n. 146) above.
74 See Ch. 3, text to (n. 136), Ch. 4, text to (n. 224) and Ch. 5, text to (n. 185) above.
75 See Preface, text to (n. 7) and this Ch., text to (nn. 123, 124).
76 See Ch. 3, text to (nn. 184, 219) above.
77 See in this sub-s., letter (b) below.

conclusion of the contract, created or encouraged by the defendant.[78] At what moment this takes place is analysed below.

(b) *Reasonableness/Legitimacy of Reliance*

The creation or inducement of the claimant's expectation regarding the future conclusion of the contract by the conduct of the defendant is only one side of the reliance element. The other side, now from the claimant's perspective, is that this expectation and the claimant's actions based on it must be reasonable or legitimate. The notions of 'reasonable' and 'legitimate' are close in meaning but are not exactly the same.[79] However, as they are normally used interchangeably in the selected jurisdictions, this approach will be followed. It is not enough for liability to arise for the claimant to assert that he expected that the contract would be concluded and consequently acted in reliance on such an expectation. Liability will only arise when such an expectation and the reliance placed on it are reasonable or legitimate.[80]

The negotiation process involves a period of uncertainty where the negotiators simply do not know whether the negotiations will succeed or fail; each will have their own views, beliefs and expectations as to the likely outcome of the negotiations. Therefore, in principle, relief will not be given to a party who claims that it relied on the success of the negotiations simply because it believed or hoped that that would be the case. In other words, a 'plain' expectation is not enough, only a 'legitimate' or 'reasonable' expectation will be protected. While 'legitimate' can be easily understood as that which is in accordance with the law, there are difficulties in defining in the abstract what must be understood as a 'legitimate expectation'. It has been rightly described as a general standard or 'framework concept' (*notion-cadre*) which must be positively and negatively defined by the case law.[81] The same can be said in relation to the notion of a 'reasonable' (i.e. that which is in accordance with reason or sound judgement) expectation.

The justification for the legitimacy or reasonableness of the claimant's expectation-based reliance will be found in the conduct of the defendant (who created, encouraged or induced it),[82] but also in the claimant's own conduct in relying on the expectation, and in the presence of objective circumstances surrounding the negotiations. All these elements will allow the court to assess whether, in the particular case, it was reasonable or legitimate for the claimant

---

78 Cartwright and Hesselink (n. 41) p. 456.
79 Aubry (n. 50) p. 255 fn. 889.
80 Cartwright and Hesselink (n. 41) pp. 455–456.
81 Aubry (n. 50) pp. 250, 258.
82 See in this sub-s., letter (a) above.

to rely on an expectation of the future conclusion of the contract under negotiation.

In the selected jurisdictions, the courts and legal scholars recognise that the presence of certain objective circumstances surrounding the negotiations and their breaking-off can serve to found the reasonableness or legitimacy of the claimant's reliance.[83] Although much the same circumstances are present in these jurisdictions, there are variances as to the degree of relevance attributed to them and the degree of intensity required of them.[84] Some of these circumstances are directly connected with the conduct of one or both parties during the negotiations, while others are more 'external' to the negotiation process. Examples of external circumstances that accentuate the trust in the other party are previous contractual relations, the negotiating parties' professions, advertising done by one of the parties, and each of the parties' reputation as a businessman or as an individual.[85] Trust-based reliance will be particularly influenced by these external factors, while expectation-based reliance will be particularly influenced by the actual conduct of the parties during the specific negotiations taking place.

The length of the negotiations is a relevant circumstance to take into account, although it is not decisive because breaking off negotiations that have not lasted a long time can potentially give rise to liability.[86] The degree of advancement of the negotiations is more significant; the more advanced they are, the higher the degree of trust that has developed between the negotiating parties and the more reasonable it is for the claimant to rely on the future conclusion of the contract.[87] The level of agreement reached on the terms of the negotiated contract can evidence the degree of advancement of the negotiations, although in all the selected jurisdictions agreement on all essential elements of the negotiated contract is not required for liability for breaking off negotiations to arise.[88] Knowledge that the other party has incurred expenses relying on the expectation of the future conclusion of the negotiated contract is also a relevant but not decisive circumstance.[89]

Another important circumstance, particularly in French law, is the status of the parties: whether one or both are professionals. It is generally considered that it is more difficult for a professional to claim legitimate reliance when dealing

---

83 Some of these are listed in Vladimir Monsalve Caballero, 'La Ruptura Injustificada de los Tratos Preliminares' (Doctoral Thesis, Universidad de Salamanca, 2008) pp. 268 ff.

84 Cartwright and Hesselink (n. 41) pp. 477–478.

85 Monsalve Caballero (n. 83) pp. 254 ff.

86 See Ch. 3, text to (n. 106), Ch. 4, text to (n. 272), Ch. 5, text to (n. 152) above.

87 See Ch. 3, text to (n. 105), Ch. 4, text to (n. 274), Ch. 5, text to (n. 153) above.

88 e.g. in Germany, BGH, 10 July 1970, NJW 1970, 1840, *The letter* case; in France, Cass com, 22 April 1997, D 1998 Jur 45, note Chauvel (*Mabo & Co c Iveco France & Co*); in Chile, Ch. 5, text following (n. 157) above.

89 See text to (nn. 72, 73) above.

with a non-professional than in the reverse situation, and liability arising between professionals used to be the exception.[90] Reference to a similar criterion of the commercial experience of the parties can be seen in lack of formality cases in German law.[91] The experience or professional status of the negotiating parties is also sometimes mentioned in Chilean law.[92] Other circumstances which are sometimes mentioned are the climate of trust between the negotiating parties, the suddenness or abruptness of the breaking-off, and signs of commitment given during the negotiations.[93]

Consequently, where there is nothing in the conduct of the defendant that could lead the other party to legitimately expect the future conclusion of the contract (particularly if the defendant expressly manifested its doubts or unwillingness to commit),[94] or where the circumstances surrounding the negotiations do not support the reasonableness of the claimant's reliance (for instance, if there are many issues still pending agreement, obstacles to conclude the contract exist, parallel negotiations with third parties are taking place to the claimant's knowledge), the claimant's expectation-based reliance will not be legitimate or reasonable and liability will not arise for the defendant.

To conclude this section, it must be stressed that although the analytical distinction between the two dimensions of reliance proposed by this book is not always easy to recognise in practice, it is very relevant. It allows us to distinguish between the specific requirement that explains the imposition of liability for breaking off negotiations and that is at the heart of this liability (expectation-based reliance) from the more generic and distant element (trust-based reliance) that serves to provide a justification for the existence of the first.

III. THE ROLE OF GOOD FAITH

In the selected jurisdictions the notion of good faith (*Treu und Glauben* in German law, *bonne foi* or *mauvaise foi* in French law and *buena fe* or *mala fe* in Chilean law) is frequently mentioned as a basis of liability for breaking off negotiations. This section will first refer to the meaning of good faith and will then look at the theoretical relationship that good faith and reliance have when applied to this liability. It will conclude with an assessment as to whether good faith is an essential element in the configuration of this liability or whether its role is more auxiliary as a helpful (but not indispensable) tool for its development.

---

90 See Ch. 4, text following (n. 279) above.

91 See Ch. 3, text to (n. 231) above.

92 See Ch. 5, text to (n. 163) above.

93 See Ch. 3, text to (n. 115), Ch. 4, text to (nn. 269, 276, 279), Ch. 5, text to (n. 234) above.

94 e.g. CA Paris, 13 December 1984, RTDciv 1986, 97, note Mestre (*Société Sofracima c Isabelle Adjani*).

Good faith is a vast topic in all the selected jurisdictions with far-reaching impact in different areas of each legal system.[95] Because the interest of this book in good faith only relates to its role in justifying liability for breaking off negotiations, the discussion that follows is not meant to be a study on good faith in general but only in its application to this liability.

1. THE NOTION AND DIMENSIONS OF GOOD FAITH

Although good faith is a concept which is difficult if not impossible to define in the abstract,[96] it can be given a concrete content in different types of situations. However, some initial clarifications must be made before attempting to establish its meaning regarding liability for breaking off negotiations.

First, there are differences in the terminology for conceptually characterising good faith, for instance, as a (general) principle, a general clause, a rule, a norm, a standard. It has been correctly argued that these differences in theoretical conception are not very relevant.[97] Indeed, the terminology is often not used consistently within and among the legal systems and, to some extent, all these terms can be used interchangeably in a legal system that has a general recognition of good faith. In the selected jurisdictions good faith is viewed as a general principle of contract law that governs all the stages of a contract (including its negotiation and formation), despite the fact that in most of them the legal recognition of good faith is expressed in limited terms.[98] The legal norms that codify good faith have a distinctive feature in that they do not establish the facts to which they apply nor the effects that they produce.[99] The content of these general or 'open' norms or clauses must be established by the courts through a

---

95 For an analysis of good faith in the contract law of the selected jurisdictions, see Werner F. Ebke and Bettina M. Steinhauer, 'The Doctrine of Good Faith in German Contract Law' in Jack Beatson and Daniel Friedmann (eds.), *Good Faith and Fault in Contract Law* (Clarendon Press, 1995); Patrice Jourdain, 'Rapport Français' in Association Henri Capitant (ed.), *La Bonne Foi: (Journées Louisianaises) Tome XLIII 1992* (Litec, 1994); Jorge López Santa María and Fabián Elorriaga De Bonis, *Los Contratos: Parte General* (6th edn., Legal Publishing Chile, 2017).

96 Stefan Vogenauer, '"General Principles" of Contract Law in Transnational Instruments' in Louise Gullifer and Stefan Vogenuaer (eds.), *English and European Perspectives on Contract and Commercial Law: Essays in Honour of Hugh Beale* (Hart Publishing, 2014) p. 313.

97 Martijn W. Hesselink, 'The Concept of Good Faith' in Arthur S. Hartkamp and others (eds.), *Towards a European Civil Code* (4th edn., Kluwer Law International, 2011) pp. 622–623.

98 §242 BGB (Ch. 3, (n. 144)) and art. 1546 CCivCh (Ch. 5, text to (n. 165)) above. This used to be the case in France before the 2016 reform, which introduced new art. 1104 Cciv (Ch. 4, text to (n. 210) above).

99 Hesselink (n. 97) p. 622, thus, argues that they are not properly rules. New art. 1112 Cciv (Ch. 4, text to (n. 10) above) would be an exception.

process of 'concretisation' which is highly dependent on the circumstances of the case.[100]

The selected jurisdictions have a similar process of concretisation in that it involves an objective materialisation of the abstract principle of good faith in the concrete case; the courts are not allowed to act arbitrarily and cannot rule based on personal or subjective beliefs or opinions. The process, however, is not identical: in Germany the approach is more inductive, whereas in France (and Chile) it is more deductive.[101] In Germany, the courts have developed the law through the use of the general clause of good faith,[102] and legal scholars have developed methods for analysing the decisions of the courts in a rational and objective manner, distinguishing the functions of good faith, identifying certain typical circumstances and establishing groups of cases where good faith has been applied (*Fallgruppen*),[103] and one of these groups is formed by *culpa in contrahendo* cases. In France and Chile, the use of good faith as a tool to develop the law has been much more recent and more restricted than in Germany,[104] but legal scholars have deduced from the general principle of good faith different duties that emanate from it, and have identified concrete manifestations of good faith, such as cases of precontractual liability, building a system into which the decisions of the courts are later inserted.[105]

Secondly, a primary distinction must be made between two dimensions of good faith: objective and subjective.[106] Objective good faith refers to a standard of conduct that is required or expected from an individual, it 'evokes ideas of rectitude, correction and loyalty'.[107] It is a rule of behaviour that gives rise to

---

100 Hesselink (n. 97) pp. 623–624; Béatrice Jaluzot, *La Bonne Foi dans les Contrats: Étude Comparative des Droit Français, Allemand et Japonais* (Dalloz, 2001) pp. 488 ff.

101 Hesselink (n. 97) p. 624.

102 Simon Whittaker and Reinhard Zimmermann, 'Good Faith in European Contract Law: Surveying the Legal Landscape' in Reinhard Zimmermann and Simon Whittaker, *Good Faith in European Contract Law* (CUP, 2000) pp. 22 ff.

103 Hesselink (n. 97) p. 623; Whittaker and Zimmermann (n. 102) p. 23.

104 For France, Whittaker and Zimmermann (n. 102) pp. 34 ff.; for Chile, López Santa María and Elorriaga De Bonis (n. 95) pp. 445.

105 Hesselink (n. 97) p. 624; López Santa María and Elorriaga De Bonis (n. 95) pp. 438 ff.; Enrique Barros Bourie, *Tratado de Responsabilidad Extracontractual* (Editorial Jurídica de Chile, 2006) p. 1001.

106 Some argue for a unitary notion of good faith, e.g. Daniel Peñailillo Arévalo, *Obligaciones: Teoría General y Clasificaciones, La Resolución por Incumplimiento* (Editorial Jurídica de Chile, 2003) p. 52; Francisco Javier Saavedra, 'El Principio General de la Buena Fe' in Fundación Fueyo (ed.), *Instituciones Modernas de Derecho Civil: Homenaje al Profesor Fernando Fueyo Laneri* (Editorial Jurídica ConoSur, 1996) p. 366. For a law-and-economics analysis considering subjective good faith as justifiable ignorance and objective good faith as not taking advantage, and viewing the arbitrary breaking-off of lengthy negotiations as an example of *ex-ante* opportunism, Ejan Mackaay, 'Good Faith in Civil Law Systems: A Legal-Economic Analysis' (2012) 18 Revista Chilena de Derecho Privado 149, pp. 164–165; Ejan Mackaay, 'Good Faith in Civil Law Systems: A Legal-Economic Analysis' (2011) 74 Cirano-Scientific Series 1.

107 López Santa María and Elorriaga De Bonis (n. 95) p. 430.

objective standards, requiring parties to behave according to the requirements of good faith and fair dealing.[108] Subjective good faith refers to a psychological state of mind of not knowing of a certain fact or believing to be acting correctly or in accordance with the law (even if this is not the case).[109] While subjective good faith is very relevant in other areas of the law, it is objective good faith which is primarily relevant for contract law.[110] The good faith norms codified in the selected jurisdictions refer to objective good faith: to an objective standard of conduct that is required of contracting parties.[111] Given that these norms also apply to the precontractual stage, this objective standard of conduct is also required of negotiating parties.[112]

Contractual (and precontractual) good faith can be considered to be a moral standard,[113] but it corresponds to a 'morality of duty' as opposed to a 'morality of aspiration';[114] the objective of a morality of duty being 'not to make of a person a saint or hero, but a citizen who fulfils the basic requirements of social life'.[115] Good faith is a normative concept that contains a generic reference to normative ideas spontaneously shared in society about what is right.[116] Objective good faith is a flexible legal rule or a standard: instead of providing a rigid solution, it allows for a flexible parameter that must be concretised in each case by the judgement, prudence and wisdom of the judge; therefore, it can take an empirically variable content but has a basic and fixed unity of meaning that must be obeyed by the judge.[117]

Precontractual good faith is a standard of conduct which requires negotiating parties to act in accordance with good faith. Different legal systems vary between requiring the promotion of good faith conduct or only the avoidance of bad faith conduct.[118] German and Chilean law seem closer to the first model, while

---

108 Matthias E. Storme, 'Good Faith and Contents of Contracts in European Private Law' in Santiago Espiau Espiau and Antoni Vaquer Aloy (eds.), *Bases de un Derecho Contractual Europeo* (Tirant Lo Blanch, 2003) p. 20.

109 Hesselink (n. 97) p. 619; López Santa María and Elorriaga De Bonis (n. 95) p. 431; Jourdain (n. 95) p. 121.

110 Hesselink (n. 97) p. 619; López Santa María and Elorriaga De Bonis (n. 95) p. 434.

111 Hesselink (n. 97) pp. 619–620.

112 See Ch. 3, text to (n. 147), Ch. 4, text to (nn. 210, 211), Ch. 5, text to (n. 182) above.

113 Hesselink (n. 97) p. 621; Jourdain (n. 95) p. 121; Fernando Fueyo Laneri, *Instituciones de Derecho Civil Moderno* (Editorial Jurídica de Chile, 1990) p. 146.

114 López Santa María and Elorriaga De Bonis (n. 95) p. 437.

115 Enrique Barros, 'Derecho y Moral: Consideraciones A Propósito de la Teoría de los Delitos Económicos' (1983) 10 Estudios Públicos 1, p. 13, developing on the notions formulated by Lon Fuller, *The Morality of Law* (Rev. edn., Yale University Press, 1969) pp. 5 ff.

116 Barros Bourie, *Responsabilidad Extracontractual* (n. 105) pp. 629–630.

117 López Santa María and Elorriaga De Bonis (n. 95) p. 435.

118 Sjef van Erp, 'A European "Culpa in Contrahendo" Doctrine? Towards a Model of Contract as a Legal Relationship and Situation-Specific Duties to Inform' in Santiago Espiau Espiau and Antoni Vaquer Aloy (eds.), *Bases de un Derecho Contractual Europeo* (Tirant Lo Blanch, 2003) p. 74.

French law seems closer to the second (although this could change with the 2016 reform).[119] Nevertheless, in cases of liability for breaking off negotiations they are able to reach a similar degree of protection.[120] A further clarification must be made as to what is meant by 'bad faith'.[121] This terminology presents the difficulty of having a subjective and an objective sense. Subjectively, bad faith is understood as dishonesty in mind or intention to harm.[122] Subjective bad faith is present in some precontractual liability cases, particularly those of 'sham negotiations'.[123] It can also be understood as 'the opposite of good faith in the subjective meaning, indicating knowledge of what is not to be done and equally is done'.[124] Objective bad faith refers to acting in a manner contrary to good faith or not acting in good faith. For instance, one negotiating party should not make the other party's position worse by behaving in an unreasonable way or without any legitimate interest.[125] The objective meaning of precontractual bad faith is the relevant one in the paradigm case.

Consequently, the notion which needs to be given concrete meaning in the breaking-off of negotiations is 'objective precontractual good faith (or bad faith)'. The standard of conduct required of precontractual parties is to behave honestly, correctly and loyally; to have regard for the other party's interests, which does not mean denying or forgoing one's own interests.[126] Legal scholars have identified and classified and courts have applied different precontractual duties that are seen to emanate from the principle of good faith.[127] These precontractual duties have been linked to different subgroups of precontractual liability: duties of information or disclosure are linked to cases of precontractual liability where a (valid or invalid) contract was concluded, duties of confidentiality to precontractual liability for disclosure or misuse of confidential information, and duties of loyalty and not to behave inconsistently to precontractual liability for breaking off negotiations.[128] With regard to duties of loyalty and to not

---

119 See Ch. 3, text to (n. 147), Ch. 4, text to (n. 238), Ch. 5, text to (n. 182) above.

120 For details, see this Ch. s. IV 1 (a) below.

121 In France, see Ch. 4, text following (n. 78) above. For a discussion of 'bad faith' in negotiations in the PICC, Isabel Zuloaga Ríos, 'Article 2.1.15' in Stefan Vogenauer (ed.), *Commentary on the UNIDROIT Principles of International Commercial Contracts (PICC)* (2nd edn., OUP, 2015) pp. 351–354.

122 Storme (n. 108) p. 20; Simon Whittaker and Reinhard Zimmermann, 'Coming to Terms with Good Faith' in Zimmermann and Whittaker (n. 102) p. 691.

123 See Preface, text to (n. 7) above.

124 Carlo Castronovo, 'Precontractual Liability' in José Lebre de Freitas and others (eds.), *Estudos em Homenagem ao Professor Doutor Carlos Ferreira de Almeida*, vol. II (Almedina, 2011) p. 233 fn. 24.

125 Whittaker and Zimmermann (n. 122) pp. 692–693; e.g. case 3 in Zimmermann and Whittaker (n. 102).

126 Whittaker and Zimmermann (n. 102) pp. 31, 38.

127 See Ch. 3, text to (n. 146), Ch. 4, text to (n. 218), Ch. 5, text to (n. 185) above.

128 See Ch. 3, text to (n. 42), Ch. 4, text to (n. 225) and Ch. 5, text following (n. 186) above.

behave inconsistently, it is required that parties do not conduct themselves in a manner that creates legitimate expectations in the other party only for them to subsequently disappoint these expectations in an unjust manner.[129]

Precontractual duties have served the function of supplying an abstract standard of conduct with concrete content in the different scenarios of precontractual liability, particularly, in the breaking-off of negotiations. The courts are thus able to objectively determine what type of conduct is contrary to that expected in the negotiation process in the concrete case, taking into account equity, usages and practices, and the requirements of society in general according to the model of a reasonable man.[130]

2. THE RELATIONSHIP BETWEEN GOOD FAITH AND RELIANCE

In the selected jurisdictions it was seen that even if good faith is considered to be the basis of precontractual liability for breaking off negotiations, the notion of reliance is still present and, conversely, that even if reliance is considered to be the basis of this liability, the notion of good faith is still present.[131] At least two relevant questions arise with regard to the relationship between good faith and reliance: how is this relationship structured? And can it be severed? The first question will be analysed here and the second in sub-section 3 below.

On the one hand, those who consider that good faith is the doctrinal basis of liability for breaking off negotiations recognise that reliance is a relevant element for establishing this liability.[132] Therefore, it can be understood that cases of precontractual liability are analysed as cases of conduct contrary to good faith, where the expectation-based reliance induced by one party in the other is a relevant element for establishing the breach of a good faith duty and the ensuing liability for broken negotiations.[133] On the other hand, those who consider that reliance is the doctrinal basis of this liability also generally recognise that it is linked (even if only historically)[134] with the notion of good faith.[135] In this way, it can be understood that expectation-based reliance is seen

---

129 See Ch. 3, text to (n. 154), Ch. 4, text to (n. 227) and Ch. 5, text following (n. 186) above.

130 On the abstract assessment of objective good faith, as opposed to the concrete assessment of subjective good faith, López Santa María and Elorriaga De Bonis (n. 95) pp. 435–436. Also, Jourdain (n. 95) p. 121.

131 See Ch. 3, text following (n. 149), Ch. 4, text following (n. 239), Ch. 5, text to and text following (n. 203) above.

132 See references in (n. 131) above.

133 e.g. the approach taken in Hugh Beale and others, *Ius Commune Casebooks for the Common Law of Europe: Cases, Materials and Text on Contract Law* (3rd edn., Hart, 2019) pp. 427 ff.

134 Particularly in Germany, see Ch. 3, text to (n. 166) above.

135 See Ch. 4, text following (n. 239) and Ch. 5 s. II 1 (c) above.

as a particular manifestation of good faith, and that some see in bad faith conduct the fulfilment of the fault requirement of which reliance is part.[136]

At a more general level, in relation to the whole 'life' of the contract (including its negotiation and formation), the notions of good faith, reliance, trust and expectation are frequently seen as being connected,[137] with the border between these notions sometimes becoming blurred in the writings of legal scholars.[138] Thus, it is stated that good faith is the basis of the trust that should inspire the conduct between contracting parties,[139] that good faith establishes the protection of a certain degree of reliance in the conclusion of a valid and effective contract,[140] that good faith implies and includes the protection of reasonable reliance,[141] that acting in bad faith frustrates the justified expectations of another,[142] and that good faith, in the exercise of discretionary contractual powers, manifests itself in the trust that one party places on the other and the loyalty that the latter should show to the former.[143]

This book argues that in jurisdictions that acknowledge a general principle of good faith applying to the precontractual stage, such as the selected jurisdictions, expectation-based reliance can be considered to emanate from objective good faith, as a particular manifestation of it, because in these jurisdictions the notions of objective good faith and trust-based reliance are superimposed to such an extent that they become merged. Therefore, the relationship between good faith and reliance is twofold: on the one hand, there is a genus-to-species relationship between objective good faith and expectation-based reliance and, on the other hand, there is a fusion at the genus level between objective good faith and trust-based reliance. Thus, a negotiating party's reliance on an expectation of the future conclusion of the negotiated contract is a particular manifestation of the reliance and trust required to exist between negotiating parties, i.e. of the good faith standard of conduct.

---

136 See Ch. 4, text to (n. 241), Ch. 5, text to (n. 204) above.

137 e.g. Ana Quiñones Escámez, 'Buena Fe y Lealtad Contractual' in Sixto Sánchez Lorenzo (ed.), *Derecho Contractual Comparado: Una Perspectiva Europea y Transnacional* (Thomson Reuters, 2009) p. 356; Barros, 'Derecho y Moral' (n. 115) p. 21.

138 e.g. Monsalve Caballero (n. 54) pp. 259, 270.

139 Monsalve Caballero (n. 54) p. 258.

140 Dário Moura Vicente, *Da Responsabilidade Pré-Contratual em Direito Internacional Privado* (Almedina, 2001) p. 349.

141 Whittaker and Zimmermann (n. 102) p. 31; Vladimir Monsalve Caballero, 'La Buena Fe como Fundamento de los Deberes Precontractuales de Conducta: Una Doctrina Europea en Construcción' (2008) 30 Revista de Derecho 30, p. 42.

142 Robert Summers, '"Good Faith" in General Contract Law and the Sales Provisions of the Uniform Commercial Code' (1968) 54 Virginia Law Review 195, p. 263.

143 Javier Humberto Facco, '*Good Faith* en el Ejercicio de Poderes Contractuales Discrecionales (¿Un Punto de Contacto entre *Common Law* y *Civil Law*?)' (2012) 22 Revista de Derecho Privado 149, p. 157.

Nevertheless, some questions remain. Regarding jurisdictions that do not recognise a general principle of good faith, such as English law, can trust-based and expectation-based reliance exist and, if so, where do they emanate from? This will be analysed in Chapter 7 section III 1 below. Regarding jurisdictions that do recognise a general principle of good faith, such as the selected jurisdictions, can the relationship between good faith and reliance in the breaking-off of negotiations be severed? This will be analysed below.

3. THE NEED FOR GOOD FAITH

The notion of good faith is generally thought to be intimately related to the doctrine of precontractual liability,[144] but it can be questioned whether good faith is truly an essential element of precontractual liability for breaking off negotiations, or whether this liability can be understood without resorting to good faith. This book argues for the latter conclusion.

Although the analysis of liability for breaking off negotiations has traditionally been framed in terms of good faith, the reality is that precontractual liability today functions very much independently from good faith.[145] In Germany, the doctrine of *culpa in contrahendo* has gained not only doctrinal but also legal independence from good faith, and in Chile precontractual liability has been inserted into another legal basis (delictual liability) while retaining some degree of doctrinal independence from good faith.[146] In France, with the 2016 reform, the new legal basis of this liability (article 1112 Cciv) establishes that the requirements of good faith must be satisfied, but, at the same time, maintains the fault requirement, and it has been suggested that it is likely that the courts will continue to focus on the configuration of fault (where the reliance element is found).[147] Thus, in the selected jurisdictions, good faith is in the background[148] because they accept a general principle of good faith that potentially serves as a 'blanket' that covers the doctrine of precontractual liability,[149] but the latter, in its actual implementation and functioning, is very much independent from the former.

---

144 Whittaker and Zimmermann (n. 122) pp. 675–676.

145 Hesselink (n. 97) p. 647.

146 See Ch. 3, text to (n. 165) and Ch. 5, text following (n. 210) above.

147 See Ch. 4, text following (n. 259) above.

148 van Erp (n. 118) p. 72.

149 E. Allan Farnsworth, 'Duties of Good Faith and Fair Dealing under the UNIDROIT Principles, Relevant International Conventions, and National Laws' (1995) 3 Tulane Journal of International and Comparative Law 47, p. 60, observes the 'unsettling tendency to use the doctrine of good faith as a cloak with which to envelop other doctrines'.

This phenomenon is clearest in Germany, where the relationship between good faith and the doctrine of *culpa in contrahendo* is essentially historical.[150] The general good faith clause (§242 BGB) served the function of supplementation of duties[151] in the precontractual stage, defining the precontractual duties whose breach is remedied by *culpa in contrahendo*. However, this function of good faith in relation to *cic* is no longer needed. Since the 2001 reform, precontractual duties have their own legal basis in §241(2) and §311(2)(3) BGB[152] and any development of these duties by the courts can be made on the basis of these paragraphs. Even before the reform, courts normally based the doctrine of *culpa in contrahendo* and precontractual duties on §276 rather than on §242 BGB.[153] It is true that good faith can be used to provide additional support to any new development that the doctrine of *culpa in contrahendo* might have in the future, but it is clear that this role is only auxiliary and in no way essential to the establishment of precontractual liability for breaking off negotiations.

In France, the relationship between good faith and precontractual liability can also be traced to its historical origins.[154] It has been seen that good faith is not always present in the analysis of liability for broken negotiations (with the caveat that good faith has acquired express legal recognition with the 2016 reform), and that the good faith basis of this liability competes with other doctrinal bases.[155] Even if the good faith analysis is accepted (on its own or coexisting with any of the other bases) it is necessary to assess the role that it plays in the configuration of this liability. An initial difficulty is found in the fact that the principle of good faith (now expressly recognised in article 1104 Cciv) is contractual and it is undisputed that this liability is delictual.[156] Before the 2016 reform it seems that this did not give rise to concern as it was accepted that good faith can operate in a non-contractual scenario with the law of delict condemning a failure to act in good faith.[157] This view will most likely remain unaltered.

A more significant difficulty is whether there is any actual difference between an analysis of precontractual liability phrased in terms of breach of good faith or in terms of delictual fault. It is suggested that a breach of good faith analysis in the precontractual period is redundant as breaches of good faith (or bad faith) are absorbed by or confused with delictual fault.[158] Before the 2016 reform,

150 See (n. 134) above; Mackaay (2012) (n. 106) pp. 159, 171.
151 Hesselink (n. 97) pp. 624 ff., 638 ff.
152 See Ch. 3, text to (n. 35) above.
153 See Ch. 3, text to (n. 162) above.
154 See Ch. 2, text to (n. 15) above.
155 See Ch. 4, text following (n. 250) above.
156 See Ch. 4, text to (nn. 15, 210) above.
157 Whittaker and Zimmermann (n. 122) p. 684; Jaluzot (n. 100) pp. 361, 540, argued, however, that the rule of good faith should be limited to its domain of origin: contracts.
158 See Ch. 4, text to (n.257) above; similarly, Jaluzot (n. 100) p. 540.

it was recognised that the presence of a general principle of delictual liability which applies to faults committed during the negotiation period rendered the intervention of good faith 'partially superfluous'.[159] It was also found that even if the courts noted a violation of good faith, it was generally sanctioned under another legal basis, such as abuse of rights, which made the existence of good faith very vague because it depended on other institutions of contract law.[160] With the 2016 reform now in force, unless there is a radical shift in the case law, it is likely that the situation will remain unchanged, i.e. that doctrinally the notion of good faith plays a role in the precontractual stage, particularly in defining the precontractual duties that govern the conduct of negotiating parties,[161] while in practice the analysis is centred on finding delictual fault which absorbs breaches of good faith.[162]

In Chile,[163] the situation is similar to that in France before the 2016 reform. The good faith basis is only one among others that have been argued to be the doctrinal basis of precontractual liability for breaking off negotiations. The article on good faith in the CCivCh refers to contractual good faith, while this type of liability is considered to be of a delictual nature or at least that the delictual regime applies to it. However, it is also accepted that good faith is a general principle of law that can apply outside of contract and the importance of good faith as the legal basis for the construction of precontractual duties is traditionally highlighted. Nevertheless, the analysis of the courts usually centres on the establishment of fault and the breach of good faith is generally mentioned to reinforce the finding of liability.

Consequently, in all the selected jurisdictions the argument can be made that good faith is not needed as a basis for the imposition of precontractual liability for breaking off negotiations, mainly because it is no longer performing its supplementing function. This function has already been performed by good faith in relation to precontractual liability and, today, the latter has evolved to achieve a certain degree of legal and doctrinal independence from the former. Legal independence has been complete in Germany since the 2001 reform. In Chile, there is legal independence in that the legal basis used for the imposition of liability for breaking off negotiations has been the articles on delictual liability rather than the article on contractual good faith. In France, with the 2016 reform, there is no legal independence as new articles 1112 and 1104 Cciv expressly subject negotiations to the requirements of good faith. Regarding doctrinal independence, it is clearest in Germany where it is accepted that *culpa in contrahendo* for breaking off negotiations is a reliance-based liability. In France

159 Jaluzot (n. 100) p. 361.
160 Jaluzot (n. 100) p. 372.
161 See Ch. 4, text to (n. 218), and this Ch., text to (n. 167).
162 See Ch. 4, text following (n. 259) above.
163 For details, see Ch. 5 s. II 2 above.

and Chile, although good faith is traditionally mentioned as the basis of this liability, the reliance approach is also present and seems to be gaining ground.

The same conclusion can be reached in terms of the requirements that must be met for a solution to be considered to be an application of the good faith principle.[164] While the first requirement (to positively conform to the open norm) is met by the doctrine of precontractual liability in the selected jurisdictions, the second requirement (to not already follow from another firmly established norm) is not. Therefore, even though precontractual liability can be traced back to good faith, good faith is not truly necessary to justify this liability as more specific legal bases are found in the paragraphs on *culpa in contrahendo* (in Germany), in the articles on delictual liability (in France and Chile), and in new article 1112 Cciv which, although requiring the observance of good faith, subjects liability to the presence of fault (in France).[165] At a theoretical level, the doctrines of *culpa in contrahendo* (in Germany) and precontractual liability (in France and Chile) 'do the job'[166] of good faith.

Nevertheless, one should not jump to the conclusion that good faith is completely irrelevant regarding precontractual liability for breaking off negotiations in the selected jurisdictions. First, it will always have the potential function, although in a somewhat indirect manner, of furthering the development of the doctrine. Secondly, it serves the function of providing additional validity to solutions that, although more directly based or entirely based on other legal provisions or on other doctrinal bases, can also be linked to the general good faith principle. Thirdly, in jurisdictions like the selected ones it is a commonplace to state that the objective standard of good faith gives rise to and defines the precontractual duties whose breach entails precontractual liability.[167] Currently, this would be its most relevant and active role.

Thus, it is necessary to pay special attention to this third role. In principle, for a lawyer from a civil law background, it does not give rise to any concern; on the contrary, because the courts and legal scholars feel comfortable with the language of good faith and because it is accepted that good faith is a general principle of law that applies to the precontractual stage, there is no need to question this affirmation. Yet, if a deeper analysis is made, it can be seen that, in practice, the terminology of breach of good faith duties does not materially influence the configuration of precontractual liability. The use of this language served or perhaps still serves the purpose of giving legitimacy to the doctrine of precontractual liability, but does not in practice define the establishment of this liability.

---

164 Requirements indicated by Storme (n. 108) p. 19.

165 Storme (n. 108) p. 19, albeit not referring specifically to the doctrine of precontractual liability.

166 Reinhard Zimmermann, *Roman Law, Contemporary Law, European Law: The Civilian Tradition Today* (OUP, 2001) p. 172.

167 e.g. Monsalve Caballero (n. 141) p. 47; Castronovo (n. 124) pp. 232, 234.

In Germany, it has been pointed out that the idea of a special relationship of mutual trust similar to a contractual relationship[168] has been used in a (failed) attempt to limit the field of application of good faith, in that only where this 'special connection' exists between two or more people does their conduct have to meet the standard of good faith, which is higher than the general standard that exists between strangers (the violation of which leads to tort liability).[169] Hence, good faith served the purpose of providing a legal basis that justified the imposition of a higher standard of conduct than that required in the non-contractual sphere to parties involved in a precontractual relationship governed by the contractual regime. This precontractual relationship gives rise to precontractual duties which could be said to emanate from good faith; but, after the 2001 reform, it is clear that their proper legal basis is in the legal provisions on *cic* liability. Therefore, *culpa in contrahendo* liability for broken negotiations can today be easily understood and implemented without resorting to good faith.

In France and Chile the conclusion is the same, although there are some differences with the analysis in German law. A difference between German and Chilean law is that the latter does not have an express legal provision establishing precontractual liability, and a difference between German and French and Chilean law is that in the latter two this liability is considered to be of a delictual nature or at least governed by the law of delict. The theoretical question which remains is whether the notion of 'breach of good faith duties' brings something different to what is essentially a delictual scenario. In other words, does good faith, when applied in a non-contractual sphere, give rise to duties that are different from the ones that can be considered to emanate from delict?

In theory, this should be the case. Good faith should impose on negotiating parties duties which are more stringent than the general duty of care that emanates from delict.[170] After all, they are not strangers; they are involved in negotiations which, although not binding, bring them close together. This is the view held by those (particularly in Chile) who argue that precontractual liability is, in effect, a special type of liability which belongs somewhere between delict and contract.[171] It is also the view held by those who believe that liability for breaking off negotiations is (or should be) of a contractual nature.[172] In this way, it seems that it is still relevant to phrase this liability in terms of breach of precontractual duties of good faith, as they would require a higher standard of conduct than the general duty not to harm others.

---

168 See Ch. 3, text to (n. 14) above.

169 Hesselink (n. 97) p. 635.

170 This seems to be the case in Dutch law where the stages of the negotiation process start from a delictual scenario progressing to a contract-like liability, see van Erp (n. 118) pp. 71–72.

171 See Ch. 5, text to (n. 36) above.

172 e.g. Castronovo (n. 124) p. 234.

However, as has been stated, in France and Chile the courts place particular emphasis in the fault element, with the notion of breach of good faith duties (or bad faith) becoming engulfed by it.[173] Therefore, although a terminology of breach of good faith duties (or bad faith) might be present, the courts in essence operate under the guidance of the legal provisions on delictual liability. Going even further, it is suggested that phrasing precontractual liability for breaking off negotiations in terms of breach of good faith duties is not strictly necessary in Chilean law (the same could be said of French law before the 2016 reform), as the fulfilment of the requirements of delictual liability is enough for precontractual liability to be imposed. If the language of breach of good faith duties is used it is basically to reaffirm the conclusion already reached on the basis of delict.

In the words of Kötz, 'good faith is mentioned only as an afterthought and only to embellish a judgment based on other grounds'.[174] While he is referring in general to some German cases, the statement can also be applied to the other selected jurisdictions regarding precontractual liability for breaking off negotiations.

IV. RELIANCE-BASED REMEDIES

That reliance is at the heart of precontractual liability for broken negotiations is further evidenced by the remedy generally available not only in the selected jurisdictions but also in certain harmonising instruments of private law: damages for the reliance interest. The protection that this liability provides is not aimed at forcing the negotiating parties to enter into a contract that one or both of them do not want, nor is it aimed at putting the claimant in a position as if the negotiated contract had been concluded; it is aimed at providing relief for the loss suffered by the claimant who relied on an expectation of the future conclusion of the negotiated contract induced by the defendant. This is the rule, but there are nuances and exceptions that must be explored.

1. PROTECTION OF THE RELIANCE INTEREST

It is necessary to make some terminological precisions. Regarding damages for breach of contract, a distinction is made between the reliance (or negative) interest and the expectation (or positive) interest. The protection of the reliance

---

173 See this Ch., text to (n. 158) and text following (n. 163) above.

174 Hein Kötz, 'Towards a European Civil Code: The Duty of Good Faith' in Peter Cane and Jane Stapleton (eds.), *The Law of Obligations: Essays in Celebration of John Fleming* (Clarendon Press, 1998) p. 250.

interest attempts to put the injured party into as good a position as he was in before the contract was made or in the position in which he would have been if the contract had never been made, whereas the protection of the expectation interest attempts to put the injured party into as good a position as he would have been if the contract had been performed.[175] This distinction does not necessarily correspond to that which differentiates between 'losses caused' (*damnum emergens*) and 'gains prevented' (*lucrum cessans*) because both the expectation interest and the reliance interest can, at least in theory, include losses caused and gains prevented.[176]

When the notions of expectation interest and reliance interest are applied in cases of precontractual liability, recovery of the former gives the claimant the financial equivalent of what he would have had if a valid contract had been entered into, including the profit he would have made, whereas recovery of the latter attempts to put the claimant back into the position he would have been in if no negotiations had taken place.[177] Therefore, reliance damages seek to compensate the injured party for the losses suffered by acting in reliance on the expectation of the future conclusion of the negotiated contract, and they generally include the expenses incurred during negotiations in view of the future conclusion of the contract (such as legal and travel expenses, cost of preparatory studies, plans, publicity) and may include the lost opportunity to conclude an alternative contract with a third party.[178] These heads of loss, however, present some particularities.

(a) *In the Selected Jurisdictions*

Precontractual liability for broken negotiations gives rise to a claim in contract (in Germany) or in delict (in France and Chile) for damages compensating the losses suffered by the claimant. In all of them it is true that '[a] claim for pre-contractual liability is essentially one for detrimental reliance. The claimant has invested time and money in the expectation of a contract which has failed to materialise'.[179]

In Germany, Jhering's notion of the 'negative contractual interest' formulated in the framework of his theory of *culpa in contrahendo*[180] today

175 Edwin Peel and G.H. Treitel, *The Law of Contract* (14th edn., Sweet & Maxwell, 2015) p. 7; L.L. Fuller and William R. Perdue, 'The Reliance Interest in Contract Damages: 1' (1936) 46 Yale LJ 52, p. 54.

176 Fuller and Perdue (n. 175) pp. 55–56.

177 *Ius Commune* (n. 133) p. 457.

178 *Ius Commune* (n. 133) p. 457.

179 Paula Giliker, *Pre-contractual Liability in English and French Law* (Kluwer Law International, 2002) p. 105; Paula Giliker, 'A Role for Tort in Pre-Contractual Negotiations? An Examination of English, French, and Canadian Law' (2003) 52 ICLQ 969, p. 970.

180 See Ch. 2, text to (n. 3) above.

persists as the 'reliance interest' (*Vertrauensschaden*), which is the interest generally protected in the wider theory of *culpa in contrahendo* developed after Jhering.[181] Hence, *cic* liability for breaking off negotiations generally translates into reliance damages,[182] which normally compensate expenses incurred in justified reliance on an expectation that the negotiated contract would definitely be concluded.[183] For expenses to be compensated, a causal connection between the aggrieved party's legitimate expectation and the expenditure incurred must exist,[184] but in cases of 'sham negotiations' the total reliance loss must be compensated.[185] Forgone opportunities may be recovered,[186] but proving that another contract would have been concluded and proving the content of such contract will likely present some difficulties.[187] In some cases where a person resigned from his employment in justified reliance on the success of negotiations for a new job, lost opportunities (the wages he would have received if he had not given up his current position) have been compensated.[188] Unlike some other *cic* liability groups of cases,[189] *culpa in contrahendo* liability for breaking off negotiations is not capped by the value of the expectation interest.[190]

In France, the general principles of delictual liability apply to precontractual liability. Consequently, according to the principle of *réparation intégrale*, the harm suffered and the damages awarded should correspond.[191] Therefore, losses suffered should be fully compensated but they must meet the general requirements of being direct and certain.[192] Unlike German law and common law jurisdictions, most courts and jurists do not distinguish between the expectation and the reliance interest in the award of damages.[193] Nevertheless, both in theory and in practice, the extent of the compensation awarded in cases of precontractual liability for broken negotiations corresponds to the protection

---

181 Markesinis, Unberath and Johnston (n. 4) pp. 93–95; Lorenz and Vogelsang, case 1, in Cartwright and Hesselink (n. 41) p. 36.

182 e.g. BGH 10 July 1970 (n. 88).

183 Lorenz and Vogelsang, case 1, in Cartwright and Hesselink (n. 41) p. 36; *Ius Commune* (n. 133) p. 470; e.g. BGH, 14 July 1967, LM §276 BGB (Fa) no. 23.

184 e.g. BGH 22 February 1989 (n. 67).

185 Lorenz and Vogelsang, case 1, in Cartwright and Hesselink (n. 41) p. 36.

186 Joachim Dietrich, 'Classifying Precontractual Liability: A Comparative Analysis' (2001) 21 Legal Studies 153, p. 178; Asúa (n. 65) pp. 71, 164.

187 Asúa (n. 65) p. 70 fn. 185.

188 e.g. BAG, 7 June 1963, NJW 1963, 1843, JZ 1964, 324; *Ius Commune* (n. 133) p. 470.

189 e.g. those in §§122, 179(2) BGB; see Ch. 3, text following (n. 66) above.

190 Hugh Beale and others, *Ius Commune Casebooks for the Common Law of Europe: Cases, Materials and Text on Contract Law* (2nd edn., Hart, 2010) p. 408.

191 Deshayes and Maître, case 1, in Cartwright and Hesselink (n. 41) p. 31.

192 Patrick Chauvel, 'Note on Cass com 7 January 1997 and 22 April 1997' D 1998 Jur 45, para. 20; Deshayes and Maître, case 1, in Cartwright and Hesselink (n. 41) p. 31.

193 Whittaker and Zimmermann (n. 122) p. 664 fn. 41.

of reliance.[194] The principle is to put the claimant into the position he would have been in if the negotiations had not taken place.[195] Damages for the harm suffered by the aggrieved party (which must be caused by the other party's fault) can include negotiation fees and expenses,[196] loss of opportunity, *préjudice moral* (non-economic harm), and a residual category of various types of harm.[197]

Regarding fees and expenses, a distinction is sometimes made between 'general costs' (those which are always incurred by negotiating with others in order to stay in business) and specific costs incurred in the negotiation, in order to affirm that the latter may be compensated while the former should not be.[198] Imprudently incurred expenses should be excluded[199] and compensation may be limited when the expenses incurred remain useful for the aggrieved party.[200] Regarding lost opportunities, a distinction is made between the loss of a chance to conclude a replacement contract with another party and the loss of the chance of concluding and benefiting from the contract under negotiation.[201] After *Manoukian*,[202] reaffirmed by the case law[203] and now also by article 1112(2) Cciv,[204] the loss of the chance of concluding and benefiting from the contract under negotiation cannot be compensated because there is no causation between the

194 Some speak of '*intérêt négatif*', e.g. Chauvel (n. 192) para. 21; Philippe Stoffel-Munck, 'Note on Cass com 26 November 2003' JCP éd E 2004, 738; Olivier Deshayes, 'Note on Cass civ 28 June 2006' JCP 2006 II 10130, p. 1511; Bertrand Fages, 'Note on Cass civ 7 January 2009' RTDciv 2009, 113.

195 Muriel Fabre-Magnan, *Droit des Obligations*, vol. I: Contrat et Engagement Unilatéral (4th edn., PUF, 2016) p. 271.

196 e.g. Cass com, 18 January 2011, no. 09-14617; Cass com, 13 October 2009, no. 08-16634; *Manoukian* case (n. 70).

197 Deshayes and Maître, case 1, in Cartwright and Hesselink (n. 41) pp. 29–31.

198 e.g. Joanna Schmidt, 'La Période Précontractuelle en Droit Français' (1990) 42 Revue Internationale de Droit Comparé 545, p. 550; Deshayes and Maître, case 1, in Cartwright and Hesselink (n. 41) p. 30 fn. 32.

199 Jacques Ghestin, *Traité de Droit Civil: La Formation du Contrat*, vol. I Le contrat – Le Consentement (4th edn., LGDJ, 2013) p. 552.

200 Philippe Stoffel-Munck, 'Thème 1: Les Pourparlers' (Séminaire en Droit des Contrats, Master 2 Droit Privé Général, Université Paris 1 Panthéon Sorbonne, 2011) p. 8.

201 Ghestin (n. 199) p. 554; Chauvel (n. 192) paras. 27–28; Deshayes and Maître, case 1, in Cartwright and Hesselink (n. 41) p. 30.

202 Cass com 26 November 2003 (n. 70).

203 See cases cited in Ch. 4, (n. 93) above.

204 According to Ministère de la Justice, *Rapport au Président de la République relatif à l'ordonnance n° 2016-131 du 10 février 2016 portant réforme du droit des contrats, du régime général et de la preuve des obligations* (Journal Officiel 2016) p. 9. In the original text of art. 1112(2), as introduced by *Ordonnance* no. 2016-131, compensation of the loss of benefits which were expected from the contract under negotiation was expressly excluded, but no mention was made of the loss of the chance to obtain the benefits which were expected from that contract (Ch. 4, n. 9). With the modification of the text of art. 1112(2) introduced by *Loi* no. 2018-287 (Ch. 4, n. 10) it is now expressly stated that the loss of the chance of benefiting from the contract under negotiation is also excluded from compensation. See text to (n. 245) below.

harm (lost chance to make profits from the contract under negotiation) and fault (circumstances which constitute fault in the exercise of the right to break off).[205] These decisions and new article 1112(2) Cciv, however, do not affect the loss of opportunity to conclude another contract with a third party, i.e. it is still possible to compensate the loss of the chance of concluding a replacement contract with another party,[206] as long as the aggrieved party proves the existence of an interested third party and the seriousness of the chance of concluding a contract with that party.[207] In determining the value of the lost chance the court will calculate the probability of success of the replacement contract,[208] and will apply a reduction percentage to the expected benefit of this contract.[209]

The actual amount of damages that will be awarded in a case of liability for broken negotiations is difficult to predict because a general feature of the quantification of damages in French law is that it is a matter of fact that belongs to the sovereign power of the *juges du fond*.[210] If contributory fault of the aggrieved party is established, its recovery may be reduced.[211]

In Chile, like in France, the general principles of delictual liability (including the principle of *reparación integral*)[212] apply to precontractual liability. The objective is to place the claimant in the position he would have been in if the illicit act had not been committed.[213] Therefore, only losses which meet

---

205 Stoffel-Munck (n. 194); John Cartwright, 'Cour de Cass, 26.11.2003 – "*Perte de Chance*" (Expectation Interest) and Liability of a Third Person in Case of Breaking Off Negotiations: English Case Note' (2005) 13 ERPL 455, p. 459. See Ch. 4, text to (n. 94) above.

206 e.g. Ruth Sefton-Green, 'Formation of Contract: Negotiation and the Process of Agreement' in John Cartwright and Simon Whittaker (eds.), *The Code Napoléon Rewritten: French Contract Law after the 2016 Reforms* (Hart Publishing, 2017) p. 60; Fabre-Magnan (n. 195) p. 271; Juliette Sénéchal, 'Contract Formation and Non-performance in French Law' in Reiner Schulze and Fryderyk Zoll (eds.), *The Law of Obligations in Europe, A New Wave of Codifications* (Sellier, 2013)) p. 353; François Terré, Philippe Simler and Yves Lequette, *Droit Civil: Les Obligations* (11th edn., Dalloz, 2013) p. 203; Ghestin (n. 199) p. 554; Olivier Deshayes, 'La Rupture des Pourparlers' (2008) 203 PA 4; Deshayes, 'Note on Cass civ 28 June 2006' (n. 194) p. 1511; Stoffel-Munck (n. 194); François Guy Trébulle, 'Note on Cass com 26 November 2003' Droit des Sociétés no. 3 2004 no. 37; Cartwright (n. 205) p. 460; Patrick Chauvel, 'Note on Cass com 7 April 1998' D 1999, 514, para. 18. This is recognised in the *Rapport au Président* (n. 204) p. 9, when referring to the precontractual liability to which art. 1112-1 can give rise. Also, Bruno Dondero, 'La Réforme du Droit des Contrats: Ordonnance n° 2016-131 du 10 Février 2016' (2016) 19 JCP éd E 1283 no. 26, para. 27.

207 Joanna Schmidt-Szalewski, 'Note on Cass com 7 April 1998' JCP éd E 1999, 579; e.g. CA Rennes, 29 April 1992, Bull Joly 1993 no. 132, note Daigre.

208 Giliker, *Pre-contractual Liability in English and French Law* (n. 179) p. 130; Schmidt-Szalewski, 'Note on Cass com 7 April 1998' (n. 207); Cartwright and Hesselink (n. 41) pp. 62–63.

209 Olivier Deshayes, 'Le Dommage Précontractuel' (2004) 2 RTDcom 187, para. 20.

210 Fabre-Magnan (n. 195) p. 271; Cartwright and Hesselink (n. 41) pp. 475–476; Schmidt (n. 198) p. 554.

211 Bell, Boyron and Whittaker (n. 8) p. 306 fn. 85; e.g. Cass com 15 October 2002 (n. 66).

212 See Ch. 5, text to (n. 31) above.

213 CS 29 December 2011, *Jiménez Mira con Armijo Cerda* (n. 66).

the general requirements of being direct and certain can be compensated.[214] A distinction between the expectation and the reliance interest is usually not made, but some legal scholars, following the German terminology, refer to *interés de confianza* (reliance interest) or *interés negativo* (negative interest) in order to explain the protection granted by precontractual liability, as opposed to the positive interest.[215] Sometimes the negative interest and the positive interest are, respectively, confused with the notions of *daño emergente* (losses caused) and *lucro cesante* (gains prevented),[216] and there are differences in the content that legal scholars give to *daño emergente* and *lucro cesante* in a precontractual setting.[217] However, both legal scholars and courts agree that compensation includes expenses and costs incurred, lost opportunities and *daño moral* (harm to non-pecuniary interests).[218] Regarding expenses, a distinction is sometimes made between 'provoked' and 'spontaneous' expenses in that only the former may be compensated.[219] Regarding lost opportunities, it seems that only the lost opportunity to enter into a replacement contract may be compensated.[220] There must be a causal relation between the losses suffered by the claimant and the *confianza* that has been created by the other party,[221] and it is said that the just measure of compensation must be found in this *confianza*.[222]

---

214 Barros Bourie, *Responsabilidad Extracontractual* (n. 105) pp. 236, 245.

215 See Ch. 5, text to (n. 116) above; e.g. Lilian San Martín, 'Responsabilidad Precontractual por Ruptura Injustificada de Negociaciones: *"Jiménez Mira, David Alejandro con Armijo Cerda, Antonio de los Ángeles" Corte Suprema, Rol 1872/2010*' (2013) 40 Revista Chilena de Derecho 317, p. 322; Hugo Rosende Álvarez, *Algunas Consideraciones sobre la Responsabilidad Precontractual* (Ediciones Universitarias de Valparaíso, 1979) p. 77.

216 The better view is that these notions should not be confused, Francisco Segura Riveiro, 'El Interés Indemnizable en las Hipótesis de Responsabilidad Precontractual' in Juan Andrés Varas Braun and others (eds.), *Estudios de Derecho Civil: Jornadas Nacionales de Derecho Civil 2005–2009*, vol. III (Abeledo Perrot, 2011) p. 111.

217 cf., San Martín (n. 215) p. 323; Rosario Celedón and Patricia Silberman, *Responsabilidad Precontractual por Ruptura de Negociaciones Contractuales* (Editorial Jurídica de Chile, 2010) pp. 139–140; Barrientos (n. 8) p. 65; Isabel Zuloaga Ríos, *Teoría de la Responsabilidad Precontractual. Aplicaciones en la Formación del Consentimiento de los Contratos* (3rd edn., Legal Publishing, 2008) pp. 167–168; Rosende Álvarez (n. 215) p. 77.

218 e.g. CS 12 April 2012, *Urrea Fuentes con Corpbanca* (n. 66); CS 29 December 2011, *Jiménez Mira con Armijo Cerda* (n. 66); Barros Bourie (n. 105) p. 1007; Iñigo de la Maza, 'El Retiro Unilateral como un Caso de Responsabilidad Precontractual' in Iñigo de la Maza (ed.), *Cuadernos de Análisis Jurídicos, Colección Derecho Privado III: Temas de Contratos* (Ediciones Universidad Diego Portales, 2006) p. 156; Segura (n. 216) pp. 112–114.

219 Rosende Álvarez (n. 215) pp. 67–68.

220 Barros Bourie (n. 105) p. 1007; CS 12 April 2012, *Urrea Fuentes con Corpbanca* (n. 66); CA Antofagasta, 12 January 2008, *Castillo Carvajal con Codelco Norte División Chuquicamata* (ended by settlement, CS 7 December 2009).

221 CS 29 December 2011, *Jiménez Mira con Armijo Cerda* (n. 66); de la Maza (n. 218) p. 157; Segura (n. 216) p. 112.

222 Iñigo de la Maza and Carlos Pizarro, *Responsabilidad Civil: Casos Prácticos* (5th edn., Abeledo Perrot, 2010) p. 52.

The quantification of damages is a matter of fact that cannot be reviewed by the Supreme Court.[223]

(b) *In Harmonising Instruments*

Although the efforts to harmonise European contract law currently seem to have come to a standstill or, at least, to have been considerably watered-down,[224] it is important to highlight that different harmonising instruments of contract law or of the law of obligations, both at a European and at an international level, and in accordance with the general trend in the selected jurisdictions, provide for the protection of the reliance interest in their treatment of liability for breaking off negotiations.

Among international instruments of harmonisation,[225] the 2016 UNIDROIT Principles of International Commercial Contracts (PICC)[226] state in article 2.1.15:

> (Negotiations in bad faith) (1) A party is free to negotiate and is not liable for failure to reach an agreement. (2) However, a party who negotiates or breaks off negotiations in bad faith is liable for the losses caused to the other party. (3) It is bad faith, in particular, for a party to enter into or continue negotiations when intending not to reach an agreement with the other party.

The Official Comments place special emphasis on the justified reliance of the other party on the successful outcome of the negotiations caused by the conduct of the party breaking off, in order to determine when a party may no longer be free to break off negotiations abruptly and without justification.[227] Where liability arises, it is limited to the compensation of the losses caused to the other

223 Arturo Alessandri Rodríguez, *De la Responsabilidad Extracontractual en el Derecho Civil Chileno (Título 35 del Libro IV del Código Civil)* (Editorial Jurídica de Chile, 2005) pp. 417–418.

224 The Proposal for a Regulation of the European Parliament and of the Council on a Common European Sales Law COM(2011) 635 (CESL) was withdrawn on 16 December 2014 by the EU Commission, and the legislative proposals that have been put forward are of a much narrower scope than the CESL: Proposal for a Directive of the European Parliament and of the Council on certain aspects concerning contracts for the supply of digital content COM(2015) 634 final, published on 9 December 2015, and Amended Proposal for a Directive of the European Parliament and of the Council on certain aspects concerning contracts for the online and other distance sales of goods COM(2017) 637 final, published on 31 October 2017.

225 The 1980 UN Convention on Contracts for the International Sale of Goods (CISG) does not have an art. like art. 2.1.15 PICC and it is arguable whether precontractual liability for breaking off negotiations falls outside the scope of the Convention.

226 Text of the Principles and Official Comments available at <http://www.unilex.info> accessed 2 May 2019.

227 Off. Cmt. 4 to art. 2.1.15, p. 62 (n. 226).

party and these include the expenses incurred in the negotiations and the lost opportunity to conclude another contract with a third person (the reliance or negative interest).[228] The aggrieved party may generally not recover the profit which would have resulted had the original contract been concluded (expectation or positive interest).[229] However, if the parties had expressly agreed on a duty to negotiate in good faith, all appropriate remedies for non-performance are available to them and these include the right to performance and other remedies reflecting the expectation interest[230] (presumably, expectation damages).[231]

Among the instruments of harmonisation of European[232] contract law or the law of obligations, prepared by different study groups, the Feasibility Study for a Future Instrument in European Contract Law of 3 May 2011 (FS), prepared by the Commission Expert Group on European Contract Law, stated:

> Article 27: Negotiations contrary to good faith and fair dealing (1) A person is free to negotiate and is not liable for failure to reach an agreement. (2) A person who is engaged in negotiations has a duty to negotiate in accordance with good faith and fair dealing and not to break off negotiations contrary to good faith and fair dealing. This duty may not be excluded or limited by contract. (3) A person who is in breach of the duty is liable for any loss caused to the other party by the breach. (4) It is contrary to good faith and fair dealing, in particular, for a person to enter into or continue negotiations with no real intention of reaching an agreement with the other party.

However, in a revised version of 19 August 2011 (which is the direct predecessor of the CESL) there is no article on liability for breaking off negotiations.[233]

The Draft Common Frame of Reference (DCFR)[234] states in article II.-3:301:

> Negotiations contrary to good faith and fair dealing (1) A person is free to negotiate and is not liable for failure to reach an agreement. (2) A person who is engaged in negotiations has a duty to negotiate in accordance with good faith and fair dealing and

---

228 Off. Cmt. 2 to art. 2.1.15, p. 60 (n. 226).
229 Off. Cmt. 2 to art. 2.1.15, p. 60 (n. 226).
230 Off. Cmt. 3 to art. 2.1.15, p. 61 (n. 226).
231 Zuloaga Ríos, 'Article 2.1.15' (n. 121).
232 In Latin America, an academic group has prepared a draft of Latin American Principles of Contract Law which contains an art. on precontractual liability: see Ch. 5 (n. 18) above.
233 Likewise, the CESL (n. 224) does not have a comparable provision, but it can be argued that precontractual liability may arise under it because art. 2(1) CESL imposes on the parties a duty to act in accordance with good faith and fair dealing (breach of which is sanctioned under art. 2(2) CESL) and this duty is considered also to apply to the precontractual stage, e.g. Hans Schulte-Nölke in Reiner Schulze (ed.), *Common European Sales Law (CESL): Commentary* (C.H. Beck, Hart, 2012) pp. 86–87, 90–91; Reiner Schulze and Fryderyk Zoll, *European Contract Law* (C.H. Beck, Hart, Nomos, 2016) p. 147.
234 Christian von Bar and Eric Clive (eds.), *Principles, Definitions and Model Rules of European Private Law: Draft Common Frame of Reference (DCFR) Full Edition*, vol. 1 (OUP, 2010).

> not to break off negotiations contrary to good faith and fair dealing. This duty may not be excluded or limited by contract. (3) A person who is in breach of the duty is liable for any loss caused to the other party by the breach. (4) It is contrary to good faith and fair dealing, in particular, for a person to enter into or continue negotiations with no real intention of reaching an agreement with the other party.

The heads of damages correspond to the reliance interest and include losses (expenses incurred, work done and loss on transactions made in reliance on the expected contract) and, in some cases, may include loss of opportunities.[235] The aggrieved party cannot claim to be put in the position as if the contract had been concluded and the remedy of specific performance is not available as it is considered that it might be impracticable to try to enforce specifically a duty to negotiate in good faith.[236]

The Acquis Principles (ACQP)[237] state in article 2:103:

> Negotiations contrary to good faith (1) A party is free to negotiate and is not liable for failing to reach an agreement. (2) However, a party who has conducted or discontinued negotiations contrary to good faith is liable for loss caused to the other party. (3) In particular, a party acts contrary to good faith if it enters into or continues negotiations with no real intention of reaching an agreement.

This article should be interpreted not only according to the requirements of good faith (art 2:101 ACQP) but also according to the legitimate expectations of the other party (art 2:102 ACQP).[238] Paragraph (2) establishes a liability for loss which arises especially where one party encourages the other to make irreversible investments in advance and go beyond the regular risks inherent in the business. The aggrieved party can claim compensation for all the expenses incurred or work done in reliance on the contract under negotiation (reliance damages) and, in some cases, even non-pecuniary damages may be compensated; but it cannot claim compensation for its loss of profit.[239]

The *Principes Contractuels Communs* (PCC), prepared by the *Société de Législation Comparée* and the *Association Henri Capitant des Amis de la Culture Juridique Française*, state in article 2:101:

> Duty to Negotiate in Good Faith and Fair Dealing (1) Parties are free to initiate, continue and break off pre-contractual negotiations, provided they act in accordance with the requirements of good faith and fair dealing. The failure of pre-contractual negotiations

235 DCFR (n. 234) art. II.-3:301 Comment H.

236 DCFR (n. 234) art. II.-3:301 Comments C and H.

237 Research Group on the Existing EC Private Law (Acquis Group), *Principles of the Existing EC Contract Law (Acquis Principles): Contract II General Provisions, Delivery of Goods, Package Travel and Payment Services* (Sellier, 2009).

238 ACQP (n. 237) art. 2:103 Commentary 2, p. 112.

239 ACQP (n. 237) art. 2:103 Commentary 3, p. 113.

> can only give rise to liability if it is the consequence of a fault or actions contrary to good faith and fair dealing of either party. (2) A party who enters into or pursues pre-contractual negotiations without the intention of concluding a contract, does not respect the requirement to negotiate in accordance with good faith and fair dealing. (3) A party who breaks off pre-contractual negotiations for no legitimate reason, while the other party could legitimately believe that a contract would be concluded, acts contrary to the requirements of good faith and fair dealing.[240]

Although this article does not expressly refer to the extent of liability for breaking off negotiations, it seems clear that the reliance element expressed in paragraph (3) protects the reliance interest.

The Principles of European Contract Law (PECL)[241] state in article 2:301:

> Negotiations Contrary to Good Faith (1) A party is free to negotiate and is not liable for failure to reach an agreement. (2) However, a party which has negotiated or broken off negotiations contrary to good faith and fair dealing is liable for the losses caused to the other party. (3) It is contrary to good faith and fair dealing, in particular, for a party to enter into or continue negotiations with no real intention of reaching an agreement with the other party.

The losses for which the party breaking off is liable include expenses incurred, work done, loss on transactions made in reliance of the expected contract, and may include loss of opportunities (reliance damages). The aggrieved party cannot claim to be put into the position in which he would have been if the contract had been concluded (expectation damages).[242]

Finally, the Academy of European Private Lawyers European Contract Code (AEPL Code)[243] states in article 6:

> Obligation of good faith 1. Each of the parties is free to undertake negotiations with a view to concluding a contract without being held at all responsible if said contract is not drawn up, unless his behaviour is contrary to good faith. 2. To enter into or continue negotiations with no real intention of concluding a contract is contrary to good faith. 3. If in the course of negotiations the parties have already considered the essentials of the contract whose conclusion is predictable, either party who breaks off negotiations without justifiable grounds, having created reasonable confidence in the other, is acting contrary to good faith. 4. If the situations considered in the above paragraphs occur,

---

240 English version in Bénédicte Fauvarque-Cosson and Denis Mazeaud (eds.), *European Contract Law, Materials for a Common Frame of Reference: Terminology, Guiding Principles, Model Rules* (Sellier, 2008) p. 575.

241 Ole Lando and Hugh Beale (eds.), *Principles of European Contract Law: Parts I and II Combined and Revised* (Kluwer Law International, 2000).

242 PECL (n. 241) art. 2:301 Comment G.

243 Text in Oliver Radley-Gardner and others, *Fundamental Texts on European Private Law* (Hart, 2003).

> the party who acted contrary to good faith shall be liable for the harm he has caused to the other party to the extent of the costs the latter had to incur while the contract was being negotiated. Loss of opportunities caused by the negotiations underway shall also be made good.

Paragraph 3 is particularly relevant because it uses the notion of 'reasonable confidence' as an element to trigger the liability of the party breaking off and then paragraph 4 lists the heads of damages protected by this liability, which correspond to the reliance interest.

2. GENERALLY NO PROTECTION OF THE EXPECTATION INTEREST

The expectation interest is usually not protected by precontractual liability for broken negotiations in the selected jurisdictions. There are, however, some particular scenarios, both in the selected jurisdictions and in other jurisdictions, where expectation damages or even specific performance of the contract are granted.

(a) *Expectation Damages*

Because negotiating parties are not under an obligation to enter into the negotiated contract, precontractual liability for broken negotiations does not give rise to expectation damages in the selected jurisdictions.[244] In France, new article 1112(2) Cciv expressly excludes the compensation of the loss of the benefits which were expected from the contract that was not concluded (i.e. expectation damages) and also the loss of the chance to obtain the expected benefits of this contract, as compensation of these losses would otherwise lead to indirectly giving effect to a contract that has not been concluded.[245]

In Germany, however, there are some *culpa in contrahendo* groups of cases where expectation damages have been awarded. Although these cases are not technically of 'broken negotiations' they are closely related to them. For instance, in the field of public bidding, the positive interest was compensated in a case where the claimant would have certainly been awarded the contract if

---

244 e.g. in Germany, BGH 6 February 1969, LM §276 BGB (Fa) no. 28; in France, Fabre-Magnan (n. 195) p. 271; Franck Violet, 'Note on CA Paris 10 March 2000' JCP 2001 II 10470; Chauvel (n. 192) para. 25; in Chile, CS 29 December 2011 (n. 66); Barros Bourie (n. 105) pp. 1007–1008; Segura (n. 216) p. 113.

245 *Rapport au Président* (n. 204) p. 9. See (n. 204) above.

the defendant had followed the correct tendering procedure.[246] Also, in a lack of formality case where the invalidity of the contract was harsh but not unbearable for the aggrieved party (the defendants), *cic* liability was imposed on the claimant, but with the peculiarity that the expectation interest was protected (monetary compensation that would enable the defendants to acquire a house of equivalent value).[247] This decision has been criticised because monetary compensation of the expectation interest is said to circumvent the form requirement, but it has also been pointed out that compensation of the reliance interest might have led to the same result if the reasoning is based on compensation of a lost opportunity: if the defendants had not relied on the contract with the claimant they would have probably bought another house which would have also risen in value.[248]

In other jurisdictions, both from the civil law and common law,[249] sometimes expectation damages are awarded in cases of broken negotiations. In Dutch law, the *Hoge Raad* has distinguished three stages in the negotiation process, with the particularity that in the third stage breaking off is in itself unlawful because the parties are truly no longer free to break off and, consequently, expectation damages may be awarded.[250] The elements which in Dutch law give rise to the third stage and to the protection of the expectation interest (justified reliance on an expectation of the future conclusion of the contract),[251] in the selected jurisdictions only give rise to the protection of the reliance interest.[252]

(b) Specific Performance

Precontractual liability for broken negotiations, in the selected jurisdictions, does not give rise to the remedy of specific performance, either in the form of an order to continue negotiations or in the form of an order to conclude the contract (or to consider the contract as concluded).[253] In Germany, however,

---

246 BGH, 25 November 1992, NJW 1993, 520 (*Oolitic Stones*), English translation in *Ius Commune* (n. 133) pp. 469–470.

247 BGH, 29 January 1965, NJW 1965, 812; for details of the case, see Ch. 3, text following (n. 229) above.

248 Faust and Wiese (n. 64) p. 125; Asúa (n. 65) pp. 72–73, 164–165.

249 For Australian law, see Ch. 7, text following (n. 404) below.

250 HR 18 June 1982 (*Plas v Valburg*), NJ 1983, 723, note C.J.H. Brunner, Ars Aequi 32 (1983) 758, note P. van Schilfgaarde; English translation in *Ius Commune* (n. 133) pp. 459–460. The *Plas v Valburg* doctrine has been limited by HR 14 June 1996 (*De Ruiterij v Ruiters*), NJ 1997, 481, note H.J. Snijders, and HR 12 August 2005 (*CBB v JPO*), NJ 2005, 467. Also, Martijn Hesselink, case 1, in Cartwright and Hesselink (n. 41) pp. 46–50.

251 *Plas v Valburg* (n. 250).

252 Hesselink, case 1, in Cartwright and Hesselink (n. 41) p. 48.

253 In Germany, e.g. BGH, 19 October 1960, LM §276 BGB (Fa) no. 11, NJW 61, 169; in France, e.g. Jourdain (n. 95) p. 131; Terré, Simler and Lequette (n. 206) p. 203; Philippe Malaurie, Laurent Aynès and Philippe Stoffel-Munck, *Droit des Obligations* (8th edn., LGDJ, 2016) p. 269; Fabre-Magnan (n. 195) p. 271; in Chile, e.g. Barrientos (n. 8) p. 111; Ch. 5, text to (n. 277) regarding CS 22 November 2001, *Luna con Bobadilla* case (n. 67).

in lack of formality cases (which technically belong to cases of *cic* for an invalid contract, but can be assimilated to cases of *cic* for broken negotiations) the remedy granted by the courts, applying the principle of *venire contra factum proprium*, is normally specific performance of the invalid contract.[254] It has already been noted that there is no distinct line of lack of formality cases in French law, and in Chilean law, in cases which could be labelled as such, the remedy granted has been reliance damages.[255]

In other jurisdictions,[256] specific performance is sometimes available. In Dutch law, breaking off in the third stage of negotiations[257] may lead to a court order to continue negotiations[258] and, according to some scholars, may even lead to a court order to actually conclude the contract.[259]

V. CONCLUSIONS

Expectation-based reliance is the true basis of precontractual liability for breaking off negotiations in the selected jurisdictions. It explains the essence of this liability, acting as its trigger and also as its measure. The protection of reliance is found not only in the remedies granted in the selected jurisdictions but also in those awarded in transnational or regional harmonising instruments. In the selected jurisdictions the objective standard of good faith can peacefully coexist with reliance and, furthermore, it can become merged with the trust dimension of reliance from which expectation-based reliance emanates. However, in these jurisdictions precontractual liability for broken negotiations is able to stand on its own and function without resorting to good faith.[260] While this finding does not lead to any substantial changes in the selected jurisdictions, it is of particular relevance for jurisdictions that do not embrace good faith in the precontractual stage, as will be seen in the next chapter.

---

254 e.g. BGH, 27 October 1967, BGHZ 48, 396; see Ch. 3, text to (n. 212) above.

255 See Ch. 4, text following (n. 349), and Ch. 5, text following (n. 299) above.

256 For Australian and English law, see Ch. 7, text to (nn. 409, 423) below, respectively.

257 See text to (n. 250) above.

258 e.g. Gerechtshof Amsterdam 7 May 1987 (*De Ziener*), NJ 1988, 430, English translation in *Ius Commune* (n. 133) pp. 467–468. Also Hesselink, case 1, in Cartwright and Hesselink (n. 41) p. 47.

259 van Schilfgaarde in note to *Plas v Valburg* (n. 250); *Ius Commune* (n. 133) p. 468.

260 Regarding new arts. 1104 and 1112 Cciv, see Ch. 4 s. II 3 above.

CHAPTER 7

POTENTIAL CONSEQUENCES OF THE RELIANCE APPROACH IN PRECONTRACTUAL LIABILITY FOR BREAKING OFF NEGOTIATIONS FOR ENGLISH LAW

Following on from the findings of the previous chapter, it is necessary to analyse the impact that the reliance approach could have in English law's treatment of liability for breaking off negotiations, particularly in the paradigm case. The chapter will first analyse the current position of English law regarding the treatment and solutions it provides for situations that in the selected jurisdictions would be considered as falling under the label of 'precontractual liability'. The focus is on whether its piecemeal solutions protect the paradigm case (section I). The chapter will then look at the notion of good faith in the common law world, particularly at English law's rejection of good faith during negotiations. It will argue that from this rejection it does not necessarily follow that the notion of precontractual liability should be also rejected (section II). The chapter will finally argue that the notion of reliance is already present in the piecemeal solutions currently available in English law, and that if the obstacle of good faith were to be removed and the emphasis shifted to the notion of reliance, the idea of liability for breaking off negotiations might face less opposition, exploring how such a liability in the paradigm case could be implemented (section III).

I. THE CURRENT POSITION OF ENGLISH LAW

Even though English law does not recognise precontractual liability as a general principle of liability,[1] it provides relief in certain factual situations that in the selected jurisdictions would fall under the general principle of precontractual

1 John Cartwright, *Contract Law: An Introduction to the English Law of Contract for the Civil Lawyer* (3rd edn., Hart, 2016) p. 74.

liability. These 'particular reason[s] for imposing liability'[2] can be referred to as 'piecemeal solutions'[3] that allow for the recovery of losses incurred or benefits unjustly received during the precontractual phase. However, it must be considered whether English law can achieve the same or similar results as the selected jurisdictions, albeit through different techniques and using a different language, in cases of precontractual liability.[4] It will be argued that in many cases it can but that in the paradigm case,[5] English law, as it currently stands, does not provide a remedy.

1. ESTOPPEL

English law recognises different forms of estoppel,[6] but only two types are relevant for determining whether they could provide a solution in cases of broken negotiations: promissory estoppel and proprietary estoppel.

The limitations that currently define promissory estoppel in English law do not allow it to provide relief in a case of broken negotiations.[7] The elements of promissory estoppel are: (i) a clear and unequivocal promise; (ii) the promisee has altered his position in reliance upon the promise (to his detriment); (iii) it is inequitable for the promisor to go back on his promise; (iv) the doctrine is limited to the variation of an existing contract in the absence of fresh consideration; (v) it cannot act as a cause of action; and (vi) its effect is generally suspensory not extinctive.[8]

The first limitation is requirement (iv). Promissory estoppel operates in the context of variations of existing contracts where no fresh consideration has been provided.[9] This is clearly not the case in situations of broken negotiations where, by definition, no contract has been concluded. The second limitation is found in requirement (v), often expressed in the well-known maxim that promissory estoppel can act as a shield but not as a sword.[10] The fact that

---

2 Cartwright (n. 1) p. 84.

3 Using the language of Bingham LJ in *Interfoto Picture Library Ltd v Stiletto Visual Programmes Ltd* [1989] QB 433 (CA).

4 John Cartwright, 'The English Law of Contract: Time for Review?' (2009) 17 ERPL 155, also published as John Cartwright, *The English Law of Contract: Time for Review?* (EM Meijers Instituut, 2009) p. 171.

5 Defined in Preface s. I above.

6 Ewan McKendrick, *Contract Law* (12th edn., Palgrave, 2017) pp. 97 ff.

7 John Cartwright, *Formation and Variation of Contracts* (2nd edn., Sweet & Maxwell, 2018) para. 2-12.

8 Ewan McKendrick, *Contract Law: Text, Cases, and Materials* (8th edn., OUP, 2018) pp. 219 ff.; Cartwright (n. 1) pp. 147 ff.; Jack Beatson, Andrew Burrows and John Cartwright, *Anson's Law of Contract* (30th edn., OUP, 2016) pp. 125 ff.

9 *Ajayi v RT Briscoe (Nigeria) Ltd* [1964] 1 WLR 1326 (PC) 1330; Cartwright (n. 7) para. 10-19.

10 *Combe v Combe* [1951] 2 KB 215 (CA) 224 (Birkett LJ).

promissory estoppel does not create a new cause of action, i.e. that it is not a source of obligations,[11] bars the typical effect of precontractual liability for broken negotiations which is to give rise to a claim of damages for the losses caused. This leads to a third limitation found in the effects of promissory estoppel (vi). It normally only produces a temporary effect of suspending the contractual rights of one party, even though it can sometimes have the effect of varying the contract permanently.[12] These effects are not applicable to situations of broken negotiations. A further limitation is found in requirement (i) because promissory estoppel is designed to prevent a party from going back on its promise, which consists of a representation of that party's intention not to enforce his full contractual rights against the other party.[13] In cases of broken negotiations, a promise (understood as a 'representation as to future conduct':[14] as to the intention to conclude in the future the negotiated contract) can be made, but it is not a requirement because a justified expectation of the future conclusion of the negotiated contract may arise or be encouraged by the general conduct of the party that later breaks off.[15]

Regarding proprietary estoppel, within the line of cases where the promisee relies to his detriment on the promise made by a landowner that he has or will be given an interest in land[16] (the 'promise-based' strand according to some authors)[17] it seems, at a first glance, that this type of estoppel could potentially provide a solution in a case of broken negotiations. It is reasonable to think that the elements of proprietary estoppel ((i) a representation or assurance made to the claimant relating to the acquisition of an interest in property, typically in land, (ii) reliance on the representation or assurance by the claimant, and (iii) detriment to the claimant in consequence of his (reasonable) reliance on the representation or assurance)[18] might be met in a case where a landowner was negotiating with a prospective buyer the sale of real estate (or other disposition of an interest in land) and where the landowner made a representation or assurance to the prospective buyer that the sale (or other disposition of an interest in land) would be concluded, and the prospective buyer relied on that

[11] *Combe v Combe* (n. 10); *Baird Textile Holdings Ltd v Marks & Spencer plc* [2001] EWCA Civ 274, [2002] 1 All ER (Comm) 737.

[12] *Central London Property Trust Ltd v High Trees House Ltd* [1947] KB 130 (KB); Cartwright (n. 7) paras. 10-30, 10-32; McKendrick (n. 8) p. 221.

[13] Cartwright (n. 7) para. 10-20; McKendrick (n. 8) p. 220.

[14] Cartwright (n. 1) p. 144.

[15] See Ch. 6 s. II 2 (a) above.

[16] McKendrick (n. 8) p. 225.

[17] e.g. Ben McFarlane, *The Law of Proprietary Estoppel* (OUP, 2014); Adam Shaw-Mellors, 'Proprietary Estoppel and the Enforcement of Promises: *Motivate Publishing FZ LLC v Hello Ltd* [2015] EWHC 1554 (Ch)' [2015] Conveyancer and Property Lawyer 529.

[18] *Thorner v Major* [2009] UKHL 18, [2009] 1 WLR 776 [29] (Lord Walker); McKendrick (n. 8) p. 225.

representation or assurance to his detriment, by incurring expenses or doing works on the property in view of the future conclusion of the contract, and where the landowner later broke off the negotiations.

Following the distinction made in the selected jurisdictions, it will be analysed whether proprietary estoppel can provide relief in two categories of cases. The first category corresponds to cases that have been termed as 'broken negotiations for the conclusion of a formal contract (for the sale of real estate)'.[19] The doctrine of proprietary estoppel, in theory, could be applied to such cases because in English law a contract for the sale or other disposition of an interest in land must fulfil certain formalities: it must be made in writing and must be signed by all the parties.[20] In practice, however, one particular case (*Cobbe v Yeoman's Row Management Ltd*)[21] presents some difficulties for concluding that proprietary estoppel could provide relief in such cases. While *Cobbe* could be considered as a 'lack of formality' case,[22] it seems more appropriate to classify it within the first category[23] because the negotiating parties had only reached an oral agreement in principle regarding the purchase of a property (that contained the agreed core terms but there still remained other terms to be agreed) and they both knew that this agreement was not a legally enforceable contract and that further negotiations would be required to conclude the formal contract.

In *Cobbe*, the House of Lords found that the elements of proprietary estoppel were not present and that no estoppel had arisen. It held that there was no expectation of a 'certain interest in land' but that the claimant's expectation was that further negotiations would take place and would lead to the conclusion of the formal contract;[24] his expectation was 'to get a contract'.[25] And even if he had an expectation of a 'certain interest in land', it was contingent on the grant of planning permission, on the course of further negotiations and on the conclusion of a formal written contract.[26] The uncertainty of the claimant's interest and the fact that the negotiations were 'subject to contract' (even if those words were not used because such a reservation is not needed in an oral agreement for the sale of land, which is by statute void)[27] were also obstacles for the claimant to be justified in relying on the oral agreement and on the defendant's conduct.[28] An additional obstacle seems to be the fact that the claimant was an 'experienced

---

19 For details in the selected jurisdictions, see Chs. 3, 4 and 5, ss. IV 1.

20 s. 2(1) Law of Property (Miscellaneous Provisions) Act 1989.

21 [2008] UKHL 55, [2008] 1 WLR 1752.

22 Category analysed in this Ch., text following (n. 36) below.

23 Supporting this view, Cartwright (n. 7) para. 5-28.

24 *Cobbe* (n. 21) [18], [20]–[21] (Lord Scott).

25 *Cobbe* (n. 21) [87] (Lord Walker).

26 *Cobbe* (n. 21) [21] (Lord Scott).

27 *Cobbe* (n. 21) [27] (Lord Scott).

28 Hugh Beale and others, *Ius Commune Casebooks for the Common Law of Europe: Cases, Materials and Text on Contract Law* (3rd edn., Hart, 2019) pp. 450–451.

property developer'[29] (which brings to mind the 'professional' quality of the parties taken into account in French law).[30]

The decision of the House of Lords in *Cobbe* makes it difficult to consider that proprietary estoppel could ever provide relief in a case of broken negotiations for the sale of real estate. It has been argued that this is due to the fact that the interest that the claimant will receive is frequently still subject to negotiation.[31] And, consequently, that proprietary estoppel could only provide relief in very limited cases where all the essential elements were agreed, where it is clear what property interest is to be granted to the claimant, and where the claimant thought that the defendant was fully committed (for example, if the negotiations were subject to contract and the defendant had waived this reservation, or if the defendant had made other representations such as that the documents of the negotiated contract had been signed).[32] An example where such requirements were met is *JT Developments Ltd v Quinn* (the proprietary interest was clear and there was no reservation).[33] In an earlier case (*Crabb v Arun District Council*),[34] where the acts of the defendants were so unequivocal that they justified the claimant's reliance,[35] proprietary estoppel was also able to provide relief. However, it seems that even in cases such as these, proprietary estoppel could today be refused if the court, following *Cobbe*, considered that the claimant's expectation was not 'of a certain interest in land' but 'to get a contract'. Additionally, these proprietary estoppel cases do not correspond to the paradigm case.

The second category corresponds to cases that have been termed as of 'lack of formality'.[36] Before *Cobbe*, proprietary estoppel could provide relief in such cases. In *Yaxley v Gotts*,[37] the Court of Appeal, relying on, among others, a report of the Law Commission entitled 'Formalities for Contracts for Sales etc. of Land' (Law Com. No. 164, 1987) which proposed section 2 of the Law of Property (Miscellaneous Provisions) Act 1989, considered that giving effect to an agreement which did not comply with this section through proprietary estoppel would not necessarily undermine the policy of the 1989 Act.[38] After *Cobbe*, however, there is some uncertainty as to whether proprietary estoppel can

29 *Cobbe* (n. 21) [27] (Lord Scott), [71], [91] (Lord Walker); see text to (n. 42) below.

30 See Ch. 4 s. III 1 above.

31 *Ius Commune* (n. 28) p. 451.

32 *Ius Commune* (n. 28) pp. 446, 451.

33 (1991) 62 P & CR 33 (CA).

34 [1976] Ch 179 (CA).

35 Lord Walker's comment on *Crabb* (n. 34) in *Cobbe* (n. 21) [79]; Ralph Gibson LJ's comments on *Crabb* (n. 34) in *JT Developments* (n. 33) 49.

36 For details in the selected jurisdictions, see Chs. 3, 4 and 5, ss. IV 2; e.g. case 11 in John Cartwright and Martijn Hesselink (eds.), *Precontractual Liability in European Private Law* (CUP, 2008) p. 311.

37 [2000] Ch 162 (CA).

38 *Yaxley* (n. 37) pp. 190–191 (Beldam LJ); Cartwright (n. 7) para. 5-28.

provide relief in these cases[39] because in *Cobbe*[40] the House of Lords 'cast doubt on whether the doctrine of proprietary estoppel should be allowed to avoid the formality requirements of section 2 of the 1989 Act'.[41] Following from *Cobbe* it might be concluded that this doctrine will not apply in cases of experienced commercial parties who knew the formality requirements and did not follow them[42] or in cases where the parties intended to make a formal contract but have not yet done so.[43]

Nevertheless, a more radical suggestion by Lord Scott (which did not take account of *Yaxley*[44] and which was an obiter dictum) that proprietary estoppel can never be used to 'render enforceable an agreement that statute has declared to be void'[45] has not generally been followed.[46] Furthermore, in *Cobbe* Lord Walker did not think it necessary or appropriate to consider the issue of the statutory formality.[47] It has also been argued that the rule of section 2 only regulates the requirements for a valid contract; therefore, it does not apply in cases where the claim is based on another doctrine that is capable of giving rise to rights such as proprietary estoppel.[48] This is consistent with the view taken by three of the judges in the Australian case of *Waltons Stores (Interstate) Ltd v Maher* who rejected the argument that an estoppel claim would be barred by section 54A of the Conveyancing Act 1919 (New South Wales) which imposed formality requirements on a contract for the sale or other disposition of land or of an interest in land.[49] However, even if it remains possible for proprietary estoppel to provide relief in lack of formality cases, this category does not correspond to the paradigm case.

39 *Ius Commune* (n. 28) p. 407.
40 *Cobbe* (n. 21) [29] (Lord Scott).
41 Cartwright (n. 1) p. 130.
42 *Cobbe* (n. 21) [27] (Lord Scott), [71], [91] (Lord Walker); Cartwright (n. 1) 130.
43 *Cobbe* (n. 21) [18] (Lord Scott); Cartwright (n. 1) p. 130.
44 *Yaxley* (n. 37).
45 *Cobbe* (n. 21) [29].
46 e.g. *Whittaker v Kinnear* [2011] EWHC 1479 (QB), [2011] 2 P & CR DG20 [28]–[30]; Cartwright (n. 7) para. 5-28; McFarlane (n. 17) p. 390.
47 *Cobbe* (n. 21) [93].
48 McFarlane (n. 17) pp. 355–356, 364–365, 374; Ben McFarlane, 'Proprietary Estoppel and Failed Contractual Negotiations' [2005] Conveyancer and Property Lawyer 501, pp. 512–513. Similarly, Lord Neuberger of Abbotsbury, 'The Stuffing of Minerva's Owl? Taxonomy and Taxidermy in Equity' [2009] CLJ 537, p. 546. In *Matchmove Ltd v Dowding* [2016] EWCA Civ 1233, the CA held that an oral agreement for the sale of land was enforceable under a constructive trust and that *Cobbe* did not prevent this (the trial judge had reasoned on the basis of both proprietary estoppel and constructive trust, but the appeal was based only on constructive trust).
49 (1988) 164 CLR 387 (HCA) 408 (Mason CJ and Wilson J), 433 (Brennan J); McFarlane (n. 17) p. 365.

2. TORT

English law does not have a general principle of tort liability (like German law and unlike French and Chilean law), but recognises a number of distinct torts.[50] A claim for damages in tort based on a party's 'precontractual fault' can only be brought by proof of an established tort.[51] The relevant ones for providing a solution in cases of broken negotiations are the tort of deceit and the tort of negligence, as both can operate in situations where one negotiating party made a false statement (a misrepresentation) on which the other relied and where no contract was concluded.[52]

The tort of deceit could provide a remedy in some cases of broken negotiations. This tort requires that (i) the defendant fraudulently (ii) made a false representation to the claimant (iii) with the intention that the latter act on it and (iv) he did act on it and suffered loss.[53] The claimant must establish fraud (i), i.e. that the defendant knew that his statement was false, or did not believe in its truth, or was reckless about its truth without caring whether it be true or false.[54] The false statement (ii) can be made orally, in writing or by conduct, and although the statement has to be of existing fact, a declaration of future intention may be treated as a representation of a present state of mind[55] and, in this way, a fraudulent misrepresentation of one's own intention is actionable in deceit.[56] The defendant must intend that the claimant act on the statement (iii)[57] and the claimant must act on the statement suffering loss (iv);[58] therefore, there must be a causal link between the claimant's reliance on the misrepresentation and the losses claimed.[59]

These requirements might be met in a case of 'sham negotiations'[60] where the negotiating party who later broke off fraudulently made a false statement to the other party during the negotiations about his intention to conclude the contract, intending for the other party to act upon such a statement, and which induced the other party to incur expenses or pass on other business opportunities.[61]

---

50 *Ius Commune* (n. 28) p. 134.

51 H.G. Beale (ed.) *Chitty on Contracts*, vol. I (33rd edn., Sweet & Maxwell/Thomson Reuters, 2018) para. 1-171.

52 Cartwright (n. 7) para. 2-14.

53 Cartwright, case 1, in Cartwright and Hesselink (n. 36) p. 24.

54 *Derry v Peek* (1889) 14 App Cas 337 (HL).

55 Simon Deakin, Angus Johnston and Basil Markesinis, *Markesinis and Deakin's Tort Law* (7th edn., OUP, 2013) pp. 466–467.

56 Cartwright (n. 1) p. 86; *Edgington v Fitzmaurice* (1885) 29 ChD 459 (CA).

57 *Peek v Gurney* (1873) LR 6 HL 377.

58 Deakin, Johnston and Markesinis (n. 55) p. 469.

59 Cartwright (n. 7) para. 2-15.

60 See Preface, text to (n. 7) above.

61 Cartwright, case 1, in Cartwright and Hesselink (n. 36) pp. 24–25; Cartwright (n. 7) para. 2-15. These heads of damages correspond to the reliance interest generally protected in the selected jurisdictions: see Ch. 6, text to (n. 179) above.

In *Cobbe*, although a claim in deceit was not made, Lord Scott considered whether it might have provided relief limited to consequential losses.[62] This tort, however, presents two particular obstacles to be a useful solution for cases of broken negotiations. First, fraud is very difficult to prove in English law.[63] Secondly, the factual scenario required for a tort of deceit to operate does not correspond to the paradigm case.

The tort of negligence could, in theory, provide a remedy in some cases of broken negotiations. This tort can cover different types of conduct and different types of harm.[64] The relevant category of negligence for the purposes of applying it in the precontractual context is liability for pure economic loss caused by a negligent misstatement.[65] Following the principle established by the House of Lords in *Hedley Byrne & Co Ltd v Heller & Partners Ltd*[66] a claimant may bring an action for pure economic loss if the defendant owed him a duty to take reasonable care in the provision of information or advice and failed to fulfil his duty of care causing loss to the claimant.[67] In order to determine when such a duty arises, Lord Reid referred to 'special relationships' between the claimant and the defendant

> where it is plain that the party seeking information or advice was trusting the other to exercise such a degree of care as the circumstances required, where it was reasonable for him to do that, and where the other gave the information or advice when he knew or ought to have known that the inquirer was relying on him.[68]

Lord Devlin held that the categories of special relationships which may give rise to a duty to take care include relationships which are 'equivalent to contract', meaning 'where there is an assumption of responsibility in circumstances in which, but for the absence of consideration, there would be a contract'.[69] The basis for the imposition of liability that has been drawn from this case is that of 'assumption of responsibility', i.e. the fact that the defendant had assumed responsibility towards the claimant.[70] In later cases it was made clear that it is not enough for it to be foreseeable that the claimant or someone else in the same position might rely on the information provided by the defendant.[71]

---

62 *Cobbe* (n. 21) [38].
63 McKendrick (n. 6) p. 251; Paula Giliker, *Pre-contractual Liability in English and French Law* (Kluwer Law International, 2002) p. 106.
64 Cartwright (n. 1) p. 39.
65 Deakin, Johnston and Markesinis (n. 55) pp. 143 ff.
66 [1964] AC 465 (HL).
67 Cartwright (n. 7) para. 2-16.
68 *Hedley Byrne* (n. 66) 486.
69 *Hedley Byrne* (n. 66) 528–529.
70 *Chitty* (n. 51) para. 1-220; *Ius Commune* (n. 28) p. 139.
71 *Ius Commune* (n. 28) p. 139.

Thus, in *Caparo Industries plc v Dickman*[72] a test of 'known reliance' was established.[73] Lord Oliver listed the key elements of the test for establishing the duty of care: that the defendant should have known the purposes for which his statement might be used; that the claimant was a person who he should have realised might use it for that purpose; and that the claimant would rely on it without taking independent advice.[74] Too much importance should not be placed on distinguishing between the tests of 'known reliance' and 'assumption of responsibility', as it has been pointed out that in cases that fall under the direct authority of *Caparo* both tests are two sides of the same coin: it is possible to describe the defendant's duty as based on the responsibility he has assumed towards the claimant by making a statement which he knows the claimant will probably rely on for a particular purpose.[75] Also in *Caparo*, Lord Bridge formulated the three-stage test to determine whether a duty of care is owed: foreseeability of damage, a relationship of proximity, and that it would be 'fair, just and reasonable' to impose a duty on one party for the benefit of the other.[76]

Hedley Byrne is a case where the 'contractual environment' of a claim in the tort of negligence, found in the 'special relationship' between the parties 'equivalent to contract', was considered a ground for the imposition of a duty of care, rather than a reason for rejecting one.[77] This 'special relationship' which gives rise to the duty of care evokes the special relationship that arises in German law by the mere opening of negotiations which also imposes duties of care.[78] In both legal systems it seems that the use of a 'special relationship' attempts to bring liability closer to contract, in that the existence of a contract or something similar to it justifies the existence of liability. However, there are important differences. First, in German law *culpa in contrahendo* liability is subject to the contractual regime,[79] while this specific head of liability in English law is tortious. Secondly, in English law the existence of a 'special relationship' as the central requirement for a duty of care to arise has sometimes been explained as summing up the idea that what matters is that the information or advice has been issued in a specific commercial or professional context.[80] Finally, German law establishes an abstract and general obligation between negotiating parties

---

72 [1990] 2 AC 605 (HL).

73 John Cartwright, *Misrepresentation, Mistake and Non-Disclosure* (4th edn., Sweet & Maxwell, 2016) p. 205.

74 *Caparo* (n. 72) 638; Cartwright (n. 73) p. 195.

75 Cartwright (n. 73) p. 205.

76 *Caparo* (n. 72) 617–618.

77 *Chitty* (n. 51) para. 1-216.

78 See Ch. 3, text to (n. 13) above.

79 See Ch. 3, text to (n. 3) above.

80 Deakin, Johnston and Markesinis (n. 55) p. 144.

from which more specific duties of care emanate,[81] whereas there is no authority in English cases for the imposition of a general duty of care in tort between negotiating parties.[82]

A duty of care can arise and the tort of negligence can apply in the context of negotiations where one party makes statements which are within his sphere of specialist knowledge or skill, and which reasonably induce the other party to trust him and to act on the basis of such statements,[83] and to enter into a contract (such as in *Esso Petroleum Co Ltd v Mardon*).[84] But the tort of negligence has only limited applicability in cases of broken negotiations (where no contract was entered into).[85] Such a case was *Box v Midland Bank Ltd*,[86] where the High Court awarded damages for the losses suffered by the claimant due to his reliance on the negligent misstatement of a bank manager who assured him that the consent of the head office to his application for a loan was a mere formality. Although some writers pointed to this case as an example of the expansion of the law of tort for negligent misrepresentations to promises made during negotiations where a final contract was not concluded,[87] others have pointed out that this case remains an isolated one.[88] Nevertheless, another example may be found in *Walford v Miles*,[89] a case of broken negotiations where no enforceable contract was entered into and which, ironically, seems to embody English law's rejection of precontractual liability.[90] In *Walford*, the House of Lords affirmed the decision of the Court of Appeal which upheld the judge's award of damages for 'negligent misrepresentation' for the costs incurred by the claimants (which included the costs of preparing a draft sale agreement).[91]

Despite this award in *Walford*, the general view is that tort liability for economic loss suffered by reliance on a statement which is shown to be wrong arises only within the confines of the *Hedley Byrne* principle and does not apply between parties negotiating for a prospective contract: they cannot have a right

---

81 See Ch. 3, text to (nn. 38, 41) above.
82 John Cartwright, 'Protecting Legitimate Expectations and Estoppel: English Law' in Bénédicte Fauvarque-Cosson (ed.), *La Confiance Légitime et L'Estoppel*, vol. 4 (Société de Législation Comparée, 2007) p. 330.
83 Cartwright (n. 1) p. 85.
84 [1976] QB 801 (CA).
85 Cartwright, case 3, in Cartwright and Hesselink (n. 36) p. 95; *Ius Commune* (n. 28) p. 443.
86 [1979] 2 Lloyd's Rep 391 (Com Ct), [1981] 1 Lloyd's Rep 434 (CA).
87 e.g. Nili Cohen, 'Pre-Contractual Duties: Two Freedoms and the Contract to Negotiate' in J. Beatson and Daniel Friedmann (eds.), *Good Faith and Fault in Contract Law* (Clarendon Press, 1995) p. 55.
88 Paula Giliker, 'A Role for Tort in Pre-Contractual Negotiations? An Examination of English, French, and Canadian Law' (2003) 52 ICLQ 969, p. 977.
89 [1992] 2 AC 128 (HL).
90 See this Ch. s. II 2 below.
91 (1991) 62 P & CR 410 (CA) 427–428 (Stocker LJ), 431–433 (Dillon LJ); see text to (n. 200) below.

of action in tort if during negotiations something is said on which they rely and a contract does not result.[92] Liability in negligence could be claimed by a person to whom inaccurate information was supplied, and who was thereby induced to refuse to conclude a contract and who suffered losses as a result of relying on the misrepresentation.[93] But this example does not correspond to the paradigm case.

Therefore, the tort of negligence, in its current state, does not protect the paradigm case. In fact, the tort of negligence for pure economic loss caused by a negligent misstatement differs from the paradigm case, in particular, and generally from broken negotiations cases in several ways. First, this tort only covers false or inaccurate information or advice cases, as the duty imposed is to take reasonable care in the provision of information or advice in favour of a person who relies on it for a foreseeable purpose,[94] and the scope of the duty has not been extended to a more general duty to respect the other negotiating party's interests.[95] This does not correspond to broken negotiations cases, where it is not necessary for liability to arise for one party to provide information or advice to the other, where liability can arise even if no false statements were made, and where statements are usually of intention,[96] which are not covered by the tort of negligence.[97] Secondly, a misrepresentation must have been believed by the claimant in order to give rise to a remedy,[98] whereas in cases of broken negotiations it is not required that the claimant believed that the contract would be concluded but rather that it was reasonable for him to expect that that would be the case.[99] Regarding broken negotiations, the issue is not about an induced mistake (as is the case in misrepresentations),[100] but about disappointed legitimate expectations.[101] Thirdly, unlike *Hedley Byrne* type cases, in situations of liability for broken negotiations it is not the case that there would be a contract but for the absence of consideration, as not all essential elements of the contract under negotiation might have been agreed.[102] Finally, the line of cases following *Hedley Byrne* do not correspond to the paradigm case, they rather correspond to German law cases of *culpa in contrahendo* liability of

---

92 Glidewell LJ in *Glen-Mor Fashions Ltd v Jaeger Company Shops Ltd* (CA, 20 November 1991), as cited by Deakin, Johnston and Markesinis (n. 55) p. 146.

93 Cartwright (n. 1) pp. 85–86.

94 Cartwright (n. 1) pp. 85–86.

95 Cartwright (n. 7) para. 2-11.

96 See Ch. 6 s. II 2 (a) above.

97 Cartwright (n. 7) para. 2-16 fn. 86.

98 Cartwright (n. 1) p. 176.

99 See Ch. 6 s. II 2 (b) above.

100 Cartwright (n. 1) p. 177.

101 See Ch. 6, text to (n. 61) above.

102 See Ch. 6, text to (n. 88), and this Ch., text to (n. 69) above.

the agent,[103] or to cases of liability of third parties for negligently providing false information.[104]

3. CONTRACT AND RESTITUTION

Some legal scholars emphasise that 'the courts have been able to place not insignificant limits on the ability of parties to withdraw from negotiations without incurring any liability for doing so' through the law of contract and the law of restitution.[105] These solutions, however, will be dealt with briefly as the factual scenarios that give rise to their application do not correspond to the paradigm case.

Regarding the law of contract, in some cases the courts have found that the negotiating parties have in fact concluded a contract,[106] although not the main negotiated contract but a subsidiary contract and that, consequently, they are contractually liable.[107] In *Blackpool and Fylde Aero Club Ltd v Blackpool Borough Council*,[108] the Court of Appeal upheld the claimant's claim for damages for breach of contract because, on the particular facts of the case, there was an implied contract to consider conforming tenders. Scholars seem to agree that the limited protection provided by tort in the precontractual period has led the courts to find solutions in the law of contract in deserving cases. Some categorically state that in the framing of liability for disappointed precontractual expectations the only and rare protection offered by English law is the device of a collateral contract, such as the one in *Blackpool*,[109] and others refer to 'an occasional temptation in the courts to resort to the law of contract to found a claim for damages' in situations of precontractual fault.[110]

During the negotiation of a contract, negotiating parties might enter into different forms of preliminary agreements in order to regulate some aspects of their negotiations.[111] Their enforceability varies in English law. If they are considered to be binding, liability for breach of contract will arise. One type of agreement which is contractually binding is a 'lock-out' agreement (not to enter into a contract with a third party or not to negotiate with third parties)

---

103 Basil Markesinis, Hannes Unberath and Angus Johnston, *The German Law of Contract: A Comparative Treatise* (2nd edn., Hart, 2006) p. 104.
104 Enrique Barros Bourie, *Tratado de Responsabilidad Extracontractual* (Editorial Jurídica de Chile, 2006) pp. 1030–1031.
105 McKendrick (n. 8) p. 6.
106 McKendrick (n. 8) p. 6.
107 Cartwright (n. 1) p. 86.
108 [1990] 1 WLR 1195 (CA).
109 Deakin, Johnston and Markesinis (n. 55) p. 146 fn. 274.
110 *Chitty* (n. 51) para. 1-171. Similarly, McKendrick (n. 8) pp. 6–7.
111 Cartwright (n. 1) p. 86.

as long as it is supported by consideration and the 'lock-out' is for a defined or definable period of time.[112] Other agreements that can also be contractually binding are those that regulate which negotiating party will bear the cost of precontractual work done or expenses incurred in case the negotiations should fail.[113] Preliminary agreements that 'lock-in' the negotiating parties, such as agreements to agree and agreements to negotiate (in good faith) are held to be unenforceable for lack of certainty.[114]

During the negotiations an agreement could be reached in principle or could expressly be made 'subject to contract'. The phrase 'subject to contract' (or similar) protects negotiating parties both from liability arising during the negotiations, as it means that each is free to withdraw at any time and that they know that pending the conclusion of a binding contract any cost incurred in preparation for such contract is at their own risk,[115] and also from being bound by contract until a later stage, because the agreement is subject to the preparation and signing of a formal contract.[116] In *Walford*,[117] the negotiations for the sale of a company and property were 'subject to contract' and this, to some extent, explains the result of the case.[118]

A contractual analysis is not applicable in the paradigm case because the negotiating parties have not reached a level of agreement that could allow a court to find that the contract under negotiation was in fact concluded, and they have not concluded any collateral or preliminary agreement.

The law of restitution can provide a solution in cases where a negotiating party has done precontractual work or incurred precontractual expenses in view of the contract under negotiation, at the request of the other party.[119] In some cases of failed negotiations the courts have found that the negotiating parties concluded a contract regarding the work done,[120] but in others they

---

112 Cartwright (n. 1) p. 88; *Ius Commune* (n. 28) p. 339. e.g. *Pitt v PHH Asset Management Ltd* [1994] 1 WLR 327 (CA). The lock-out agreement in *Walford* failed because it did not specify for how long it was to last, (n. 89) 139 (Lord Ackner).

113 Cartwright (n. 7) para. 2-23; Cartwright (n. 82) p. 331.

114 *Courtney & Fairbairn Ltd v Tolaini Brothers (Hotels) Ltd* [1975] 1 WLR 297 (CA); *Walford v Miles* (n. 89) 138; *Ius Commune* (n. 28) pp. 336, 440; Cartwright (n. 7) para. 2-06. For details, Edwin Peel, 'Agreements to Negotiate in Good Faith' in Andrew Burrows and Edwin Peel (eds.), *Contract Formation and Parties* (OUP, 2010); *Chitty* (n. 51) paras. 2-144 ff.

115 *Regalian Properties plc v London Docklands Development Corp* [1995] 1 WLR 212 (Ch) 231 (Rattee J).

116 Cartwright (n. 1) p. 79; *Ius Commune* (n. 28) p. 329.

117 *Walford v Miles* (n. 89).

118 *Chitty* (n. 51) para. 2-144. *Walford v Miles* (n. 89) is further analysed in this Ch. s. II 2 below.

119 Cartwright (n. 1) p. 92; e.g. case 3 in Reinhard Zimmermann and Simon Whittaker (eds.), *Good Faith in European Contract Law* (CUP, 2000) pp. 236 ff. Giliker (n. 63) p. xxiv, focuses on the specific scenario of services undertaken in anticipation of a contract.

120 e.g. *Brewer Street Investments Ltd v Barclays Woollen Co Ltd* [1954] 1 QB 428 (CA) (Somervell and Romer LJJ).

have provided a remedy in restitution on the basis that the defendant would otherwise be unjustly enriched at the claimant's expense.[121] For example, in *William Lacey (Hounslow) Ltd v Davis*[122] a claim for payment on a *quantum meruit* basis succeeded for the performance of precontractual services at the defendant's request. In *Cobbe*,[123] although the proprietary estoppel claim failed,[124] the House of Lords provided relief to the claimant by way of *quantum meruit* for his expenses and services in obtaining the planning permission. The amount of the *quantum meruit* represented the extent of the unjust enrichment for which the defendant company was held accountable.[125] In *British Steel Corp v Cleveland Bridge and Engineering Co Ltd*,[126] the claimant's claim for payment on a *quantum meruit* basis succeeded for the accelerated performance of obligations to be imposed by the supply contract under negotiation, at the defendant's request. In *Regalian*,[127] however, the claim in restitution failed not only because of the use of the words 'subject to contract'[128] but also because the costs which the claimants sought to recover had resulted in no benefit to the defendant and had not been incurred by way of accelerated performance of an anticipated contract at the defendant's request, but for the purpose of the claimants putting themselves in a position to obtain and perform the contract.[129]

These restitution cases do not correspond to the paradigm case, where no preliminary work in anticipation of the contract has been done, at the request of the defendant. In the paradigm case there is no enrichment of the defendant at the expense of the claimant and this is fatal for a restitutionary claim.[130] It has been pointed out that on the facts of *British Steel*[131] there does not seem to have been any conduct which would give rise to precontractual liability in a continental court and that it was simply a case of no contract having ever been concluded.[132] Indeed, it seems that *British Steel* is not really a case of precontractual liability for broken negotiations because the elements of this liability are lacking, particularly that it appears that there was no unjustified

121 Cartwright (n. 7) para. 2-27.
122 [1957] 1 WLR 932 (QB).
123 *Cobbe v Yeoman's Row Management Ltd* (n. 21).
124 See this Ch. s I. 1 above.
125 *Cobbe* (n. 21) [42] (Lord Scott).
126 [1984] 1 All ER 504 (QB).
127 *Regalian Properties plc v London Docklands Development Corp* (n. 115).
128 See text following (n. 114) above.
129 *Regalian Properties plc v London Docklands Development Corp* (n. 115) 216, 224, 225, 230 (Rattee J).
130 Ewan McKendrick, 'Work Done in Anticipation of a Contract Which Does Not Materialise' in W.R. Cornish and others (eds.), *Restitution, Past, Present and Future: Essays in Honour of Gareth Jones* (Hart Publishing, 1998) p. 172.
131 *British Steel Corp v Cleveland Bridge and Engineering Co Ltd* (n. 126).
132 *Ius Commune* (n. 28) p. 167.

breaking-off,[133] but simply that the parties failed to reach final agreement on the contract under negotiation. The same could perhaps be said about *Regalian*, where the negotiations broke down because the parties were unable to agree on the price and where there was truly no unilateral break-off.[134]

II. REMOVING THE OBSTACLE OF GOOD FAITH

This section is not meant to be a comprehensive exposition of the notion of good faith in common law jurisdictions and particularly in English law. Rather, it explains why a rejection of good faith in the precontractual period is seen as an obstacle to the acceptance of precontractual liability and argues that this should not be the case.

1. GOOD FAITH IN THE COMMON LAW WORLD

The acceptance of good faith in contract law in the common law world is not homogeneous. Some jurisdictions, such as the US and Australia, are situated on one side of the spectrum (the more liberal), while others, such as English law, are situated on the other side (the more conservative).

In the US, good faith in the performance and enforcement of contracts is recognised in the Restatement (Second) of Contracts ('§205. Duty of Good Faith and Fair Dealing. Every contract imposes upon each party a duty of good faith and fair dealing in its performance and its enforcement')[135] and in the Uniform Commercial Code (UCC) ('§1-304. Obligation of Good Faith. Every contract or duty within [the Uniform Commercial Code] imposes an obligation of good faith in its performance and enforcement').[136] 'Good faith' is defined in §1-201(b)(20) UCC as 'honesty in fact and the observance of reasonable commercial standards of fair dealing'.[137] This definition contains both a subjective and an objective element. These instruments, however, do not establish a good faith duty for the negotiation or the formation of a contract. Nevertheless, Comment (c) to §205 Restatement (Second) of Contracts recognises that bad faith in negotiations may be subject to sanctions[138] and, indeed, the courts have

---

133 See Ch. 6 s. I 3 (c) above.

134 *Regalian Properties plc v London Docklands Development Corp* (n. 115) 230 (Rattee J).

135 The American Law Institute, *Restatement of the Law Second: Contracts 2d*, vol. 2 (American Law Institute Publishers, 1981).

136 The American Law Institute and National Conference of Commissioners on Uniform State Laws, *Uniform Commercial Code* (2010–2011 edn., Thomson Reuters, 2010).

137 *Uniform Commercial Code* (n. 136).

138 *Restatement of the Law Second: Contracts 2d*, vol. 2 (n. 135) p. 100.

provided some remedies for bad faith conduct during negotiations.[139] Some legal scholars are favourable to a requirement of good faith in negotiations in some specific instances,[140] under the view that good faith should be understood as an 'excluder', with no general meaning of its own but excluding different forms of bad faith.[141]

In Australia there is considerable support from the courts and legal scholars for a requirement of good faith in contract law. It has been held that an agreement to negotiate in good faith may be enforceable and good faith in the performance of a contract has been seen in the general obligation to cooperate.[142] Some relief for improper conduct during the negotiations has been provided using the language of 'unconscionability'.[143] Although 'lack of good faith' and 'unconscionable conduct' are held to be different standards of behaviour (unconscionable conduct will show a lack of good faith but the converse is not necessarily true),[144] it is said that the language of unconscionability may not seem so very far removed from the principle of good faith known to civil law systems.[145]

Unlike the selected jurisdictions, the English law of contract does not recognise a general principle of good faith.[146] And, unlike the other common law jurisdictions previously referred to, English law has taken a much more restrictive approach towards accepting a requirement of good faith between contracting parties. It does not recognise a general duty to perform a contract in good faith, nor to exercise in good faith contractual rights, nor to renegotiate a contract in good faith, nor to negotiate a contract in good faith[147] (this will be the focus of the next sub-section).

English contract law has not always been so resistant towards good faith. In a 1766 case Lord Mansfield referred to good faith in the formation of contracts.[148] Although his view was later interpreted restrictively to apply only to duties of disclosure in contracts of insurance,[149] it should not be denied that

---

139 See text to (n. 395) below.

140 Robert Summers, 'The Conceptualisation of Good Faith in American Contract Law: A General Account' in Reinhard Zimmermann and Simon Whittaker (eds.), Good Faith in European Contract Law (CUP, 2000) pp. 121, 134, 136; Robert Summers, '"Good Faith" in General Contract Law and the Sales Provisions of the Uniform Commercial Code' (1968) 54 Virginia Law Review 195, pp. 220 ff., 223, 225, providing as an example *Hoffman v Red Owl Stores Inc*, 26 Wis2d 683, 133 NW2d 267 (1965).

141 Summers, '"Good Faith" in General Contract Law and the Sales Provisions of the Uniform Commercial Code' (n. 140) p. 196.

142 John W. Carter, *Contract Law in Australia* (6th edn., LexisNexis Butterworths, 2013) pp. 23, 31–32, 99–100.

143 e.g. *Waltons Stores (Interstate) Ltd v Maher* (n. 49).

144 Carter (n. 142) p. 29.

145 Cartwright (n. 1) p. 83.

146 *Chitty* (n. 51) para. 1-044.

147 Cartwright (n. 1) p. 64.

148 *Carter v Boehm* (1766) 3 Burr 1905, 1910.

149 Cartwright (n. 4) p. 159.

it reflected an element present in the sources of English commercial contract law.[150] The position of the modern law of contract seems to be that 'English law has, characteristically, committed itself to no such overriding principle [that in making and carrying out contracts parties should act in good faith] but has developed piecemeal solutions in response to demonstrated problems of unfairness'.[151]

In some types of contracts duties of good faith have been accepted both in their formation and performance.[152] At common law, parties to contracts of insurance owe each other duties of 'the utmost good faith' which impose on them extensive duties of disclosure, but this has been partly abrogated and amended by statute.[153] Contracts of partnership have been termed as 'contracts of good faith' meaning that negotiating parties owe each other duties of disclosure.[154] In contracts arising from fiduciary relations, duties are imposed on one party to act other than in its own interest and these duties are sometimes put in terms of good faith.[155] However, a good faith duty does not require one party to pursue the interests of the other at the expense of his own, like a fiduciary duty would require.[156] In contracts of employment it has been accepted that a term is to be implied to the effect that the '[employer] [will] not, without reasonable and proper cause, conduct itself in a manner likely to destroy or seriously damage the relationship of confidence and trust between employer and employee'[157] and the courts sometimes refer to this as an implied term requiring good faith and loyalty in both employer and employee.[158] This relationship of confidence and trust seems similar to the relationship of trust created by negotiations in German law, in that they both entail duties of good faith and loyalty that require parties to consider the interests of the other but not to submit to them at the expense of their own.[159]

In a relatively recent judgment at first instance Leggatt J argued that the traditional English hostility towards a doctrine of good faith in the performance

150 Simon Whittaker and Reinhard Zimmermann, 'Good Faith in European Contract Law: Surveying the Legal Landscape' in Reinhard Zimmermann and Simon Whittaker (eds.), *Good Faith in European Contract Law* (CUP, 2000) p. 42.

151 *Interfoto Picture Library Ltd v Stiletto Visual Programmes Ltd* (n. 3) 439 (Bingham LJ).

152 Cartwright (n. 1) p. 66.

153 Consumer Insurance (Disclosure and Representations) Act 2012 and Insurance Act 2015; *Chitty* (n. 51) paras. 1-049, 1-050.

154 *Chitty* (n. 51) para. 1-050.

155 *Chitty* (n. 51) para. 1-050.

156 Roger Brownsword, 'Two Concepts of Good Faith' (1994) 7 Journal of Contract Law 197, p. 210. In the context of employment contracts, *Lonmar Global Risks Limited v West* [2010] EWHC 2878 (QB) [152] (Hickinbottom J).

157 *Malik v Bank of Credit and Commerce International SA* [1998] AC 20 (HL) 33–34 (Lord Nicholls).

158 *Chitty* (n. 51) para 1-057.

159 See Ch. 3, text to (n. 12) above.

of contracts is misplaced and that a duty to perform a contract in good faith could be implied as a term in fact in any ordinary commercial contract based on the presumed intention of the parties.[160] In the context of the case, however, such a term was implied in a distribution agreement and it remains to be seen whether the courts will be willing to find that it can be implied in other types of contracts.[161] In more recent cases the courts have considered the proper approach to an express contractual term that requires the parties to act in good faith.[162] For instance, in a case before the Court of Appeal the interpretation of an express clause requiring the parties to cooperate with each other in good faith in a long-term contract to provide services was very much narrowed down.[163] In a very recent case, however, the High Court held that one of the parties to a contract with an express term requiring good faith, had failed to act in good faith towards the other party and had, therefore, breached this contractual clause.[164]

The notion of good faith entered into English law via EU legislation. A prominent example is the requirement of good faith in the test of unfair terms in consumer contracts under the Directive 93/13/EC on Unfair Terms in Consumer Contracts which was implemented into English law by the Unfair Terms in Consumer Contracts Regulations 1994 (SI 1994/3159), which were revoked and replaced by the UTCCR 1999 (SI 1999/2083), which, in turn, were revoked and replaced by the Consumer Rights Act 2015. The Act has kept the language of good faith in the fairness test (section 62(4) of Part 2). The courts did not experience particular difficulties in applying the objective criterion of good faith under the Regulations, recognising its European origin and not seeking to interpret it from a national perspective,[165] and it is likely that this will continue to be the case under the Act.

It seems that for English law the main difficulty for recognising and applying the concept of good faith lies in identifying its meaning.[166] There is no consensus as to its content.[167] The distinction between subjective and objective

160 *Yam Seng Pte Ltd v International Trade Corp Ltd* [2013] EWHC 111 (QB), [2013] 1 All ER (Comm) 1321, [131], [145], [153].

161 Cartwright (n. 1) p. 67; *Chitty* (n. 51) para. 1-058.

162 *Chitty* (n. 51) para. 1-053.

163 *Mid Essex Hospital Services NHS Trust v Compass Group UK & Ireland Ltd* [2013] EWCA Civ 200, [2013] BLR 265 [106] (Jackson LJ), [154] (Beatson LJ); *Chitty* (n. 51) para. 1-054.

164 *Health & Case Management Ltd v Physiotherapy Network Ltd* [2018] EWHC 869 (QB) [128]–[129] (Nicklin J); *Chitty* (n. 51) para. 1-054A.

165 McKendrick (n. 8) pp. 459, 483; e.g. *Director General of Fair Trading v First National Bank Plc* [2001] UKHL 52, [2002] 1 AC 481, [36] (Lord Steyn).

166 Spectrum of possible meanings in Ewan McKendrick, 'The Meaning of "Good Faith"' in Mads Andenas and others (eds.), *Liber Amicorum Guido Alpa: Private Law Beyond the National Systems* (British Institute of International and Comparative Law, 2007).

167 Roy Goode and Ewan McKendrick (ed.), *Goode on Commercial Law* (5th edn., Penguin Books, 2016) p. 103.

good faith, which is clear in the selected jurisdictions,[168] is not as clear in English law,[169] and the fact that subjective good faith appears to be the relevant one instead of the objective standard of good faith, has had drastic consequences in the precontractual period.[170] The courts have sometimes taken an incomplete and shifting view of what good faith means. In *Interfoto*, Bingham LJ defined good faith in terms that would be an acceptable approximation to its objective dimension for a civil lawyer:

> (...) does not simply mean that they should not deceive each other, a principle which any legal system must recognise; its effect is perhaps most aptly conveyed by such metaphorical colloquialisms as 'playing fair', 'coming clean' or 'putting one's cards face upwards on the table.' It is in essence a principle of fair and open dealing.[171]

But a crucial element of objective good faith was left out: that it is a standard of conduct. This aspect was recognised by Leggatt J in *Yam Seng*, where he stated that a key aspect of good faith is the observance of standards of commercial dealing and that the test of good faith is objective: although it is sensitive to the factual context, 'it depends not on either party's perception of whether particular conduct is improper but on whether in the particular context the conduct would be regarded as commercially unacceptable by reasonable and honest people'.[172] In *Mid Essex Hospital Services*, however, Jackson LJ understood good faith only as acting honestly,[173] which corresponds to English law's subjective understanding of 'good faith' as absence of dishonesty.[174] In *Petromec Inc v Petroleo Brasileiro SA Petrobas*,[175] Longmore LJ brought bad faith close to fraud,[176] whereas Leggatt J in *Yam Seng* recognised that not all bad faith conduct is dishonest.[177] In the selected jurisdictions it is clear that bad faith can be understood not only subjectively (as dishonesty) but also objectively (acting in breach of good faith).[178] Regarding the UTCCR, the House of Lords recognised that the requirement of good faith was an objective standard and in *First National Bank* equated it to a requirement of fair and open dealing.[179] Lord Bingham indicated that good faith 'looks to

---

168 See Ch. 6 s. III 1 above.

169 e.g. Roy Goode, *The Concept of 'Good Faith' in English Law* (Centro di studi e ricerche di diritto comparato e straniero, 1992) pp. 5–6.

170 See text following (n. 192) below regarding *Walford v Miles* (n. 89).

171 *Interfoto Picture Library Ltd v Stiletto Visual Programmes Ltd* (n. 3) 439.

172 *Yam Seng Pte Ltd v International Trade Corp Ltd* (n. 160) [138], [144].

173 *Mid Essex Hospital Services NHS Trust v Compass Group UK & Ireland Ltd* (n. 163) [112].

174 e.g. *Director General of Fair Trading v First National Bank Plc* [2000] 1 WLR 98 (ChD) 109 (Evans-Lombe J).

175 [2005] EWCA Civ 891, [2006] 1 Lloyd's Rep 121.

176 *Petromec Inc v Petroleo Brasileiro SA Petrobas* (n. 175) [119].

177 *Yam Seng Pte Ltd v International Trade Corp Ltd* (n. 160) [138].

178 See Ch. 6, text following (n. 121) above.

179 *Director General of Fair Trading v First National Bank Plc* (n. 165) [17] (Lord Bingham), [36] (Lord Steyn).

good standards of commercial morality and practice' and Lord Steyn stated that '[a]ny purely procedural or even predominantly procedural interpretation of the requirement of good faith must be rejected'.[180]

2. ENGLISH LAW'S REJECTION OF A GENERAL DUTY TO NEGOTIATE IN GOOD FAITH

Unlike the selected jurisdictions, English law does not recognise the notion of duties of good faith in the formation of contracts.[181] Consequently, the notion of a duty to negotiate a contract in good faith has been rejected. However, this book suggests that there is some confusion between two separate issues which should be clearly distinguished: 'the first issue' is whether an agreement to negotiate (in good faith) which obliges the parties to engage in negotiations and to pursue them or to continue them is enforceable, and 'the second issue' is whether the conduct of negotiating parties during the negotiations is regulated by duties (of good faith) even if no such agreement exists.[182] Only the second issue is relevant in relation to the paradigm case.

The leading case that is cited to reject a duty to negotiate in good faith is *Walford v Miles*.[183] It is suggested that this case only deals with the first issue, i.e. with an implied or express contractual obligation that imposes a positive duty to (continue to) negotiate in good faith.[184] Nevertheless, on the basis of this case it has been understood that negotiating parties do not owe each other any duties of good faith which arise by virtue of the negotiations themselves;[185] i.e. it has been extended to cover the second issue as well. In *Walford*, an implied duty to continue to negotiate in good faith was rejected and even an express agreement to negotiate in good faith was considered too uncertain to be enforceable.[186]

---

180 *Director General of Fair Trading v First National Bank Plc* (n. 165) [17] (Lord Bingham), [36] (Lord Steyn).

181 Cartwright (n. 1) p. 64; see Ch. 6, text to (n. 127) above.

182 A distinction along these lines seems to be recognised by, e.g., Johan Steyn, 'Contract Law: Fulfilling the Reasonable Expectations of Honest Men' (1997) 113 LQR 433, p. 439; Michael Furmston and G.J. Tolhurst, *Contract Formation: Law and Practice* (OUP, 2010) p. 370; J.W. Carter and M.P. Furmston, 'Good Faith and Fairness in the Negotiation of Contracts: Parts I and II' (1994) 8 Journal of Contract Law 1 and 93, pp. 3–4; Clara Asúa, 'Negotiating in Good Faith and the Agreement to Negotiate (with Reference to the Decision of the House of Lords in the Case of *Walford v Miles*' (1994) 2 ERPL 274, p. 281 fn. 19.

183 See (n. 89) above.

184 Matthias Storme, 'Walfords Chances Under Belgian Law' (1994) 2 ERPL 315, p. 321, seems to interpret the case in this way.

185 e.g. Cartwright (n. 1) p. 75.

186 *Walford v Miles* (n. 89) 138 (Lord Ackner); see text to (n. 114) above.

There are two strands in Lord Ackner's reasoning; one is that the very content of a duty to negotiate in good faith is uncertain and the other is that the adversarial nature of the relationship between negotiating parties is inconsistent with such a duty.[187] It is suggested that both arguments are unfounded. A duty to negotiate in good faith can work in practice despite the adversarial nature of the precontractual relationship. This is because objective good faith does not require a negotiating party to look after the interests of the other party or to subject its own interests to the interests of the other party (like a fiduciary duty would require);[188] each party is always entitled to pursue its own interests but in doing so it must take account of or have regard to the legitimate interests of the other party.[189] Furthermore, Lord Ackner envisaged only one possible model of negotiating: an antagonistic one, whereas, in practice, a spirit of cooperation is frequently present in commercial negotiations.[190] As to the uncertainty of its content, this is simply not the case. Leggatt J in *Yam Seng* recognised that '[t]here is nothing unduly vague or unworkable' about a duty of good faith.[191] In the selected jurisdictions the courts have identified specific duties emanating from the general principle of good faith and are able to identify when the standard of conduct imposed by objective good faith has been breached.[192]

The most problematic assumption made in *Walford* is that the notion of good faith involved is a subjective one. It seems that the problem originated with the incorrect argument put forward by the claimant that the test to determine whether there was a proper reason to end the negotiations was a subjective one.[193] Consequently, Lord Ackner questioned how a court could decide whether subjectively a proper reason existed.[194] The notion of good faith relevant here is an objective one, it is an objective standard of conduct and, as such, the courts in the selected jurisdictions have been able to identify which reasons for breaking off negotiations are reasonable or legitimate and which are not.[195]

---

187 *Walford v Miles* (n. 89) 138; Cartwright (n. 1) p. 78; McKendrick (n. 8) p. 483.

188 Brownsword (n. 156) p. 212; McKendrick (n. 166) p. 692; see text to (n. 156) above.

189 This is recognised by, e.g., Furmston and Tolhurst (n. 182) pp. 372–373; Carter and Furmston (n. 182) pp. 6–7; Hugh Beale, 'Commentary on "Good Faith and Fairness in Failed Contract Negotiations"' (1994) 8 Journal of Contract Law 120, p. 123; Brownsword (n. 156) p. 211; McKendrick (n. 166) p. 693.

190 Beale (n. 189) p. 122.

191 *Yam Seng Pte Ltd v International Trade Corp Ltd* (n. 160) [152]. Also, Steyn (n. 182) p. 439.

192 See Ch. 6, text to (nn. 127, 130) above.

193 *Walford v Miles* (n. 89) 136.

194 *Walford v Miles* (n. 89) 138.

195 See Ch. 6 s. I 3 (c) above. This is recognised by Cartwright (n. 7) para. 2-06 fn. 23.

Despite the criticism that *Walford* has received in England,[196] in other common law jurisdictions,[197] and in civil law jurisdictions,[198] the actual outcome of the case appears to be 'entirely appropriate on the facts'.[199] The claimants were awarded an amount in respect of their wasted expenses as damages for the defendants' misrepresentation that they would not go on negotiating with third parties (and not the much larger amount they were seeking as damages for breach of contract), even though the negotiations were subject to contract and the defendants may have had a good reason to break off.[200] It has been noted that the Walfords would have probably lost their case before a German or French court[201] (and also before a Chilean court). If a court in one of the selected jurisdictions were to consider that there was a good reason to break off, no liability would have been found, i.e. not even expenses would have been recovered as the only interest that is usually protected is the reliance interest.[202]

Regarding the first issue, *Walford* remains the authority for the rejection of an implied term to negotiate in good faith.[203] But it is not clear whether this is the case regarding an express term to negotiate in good faith. In *Petromec*, the Court of Appeal considered that Lord Ackner's observations in *Walford* were not binding on it to determine the validity of an express obligation to negotiate in good faith between commercial parties, contained in a complex concluded contract drafted by London solicitors.[204] Longmore LJ concluded that, although in the case the term was inapplicable as a matter of construction,[205] it would be 'a strong thing' to declare such a term unenforceable as this would 'defeat the

196 e.g. Steyn (n. 182) p. 439; Beatson, Burrows and Cartwright (n. 8) p. 69; Alistair Mills and Rebecca Loveridge, 'The Uncertain Future of *Walford v Miles*' [2011] LMCLQ 528; Cohen (n. 87) p. 52; Furmston and Tolhurst (n. 182) pp. 400–402; Carter and Furmston (n. 182) pp. 113–115; Beale (n. 189) p. 123; Brownsword (n. 156) pp. 204–205; Ewan McKendrick, 'Good Faith: A Matter of Principle?' in A.D.M. Forte (ed.), *Good Faith in Contract and Property Law* (Hart Publishing, 1999) pp. 51–52.

197 e.g. Ross Buckley, 'Walford v Miles: False Certainty About Uncertainty – An Australian Perspective' (1993) 6 Journal of Contract Law 58.

198 e.g. Sjef van Erp, 'Good Faith: A Concept "Unworkable in Practice"?' (1992) 1 Tilburg Foreign Law Review 215.

199 *Chitty* (n. 51) para. 2-144. Also, McKendrick (n. 8) p. 489.

200 *Ius Commune* (n. 28) pp. 338–339.

201 Hein Kötz, 'Towards a European Civil Code: The Duty of Good Faith' in Peter Cane and Jane Stapleton (eds.), *The Law of Obligations: Essays in Celebration of John Fleming* (Clarendon Press, 1998) pp. 253–254.

202 See Ch. 6, text to (n. 179) above.

203 *Yam Seng* only opened up the possibility of implying a term to perform in good faith; see text to (n. 160) above.

204 *Petromec Inc v Petroleo Brasileiro SA Petrobas* (n. 175) [121] (Longmore LJ); *Chitty* (n. 51) para. 1-052.

205 *Petromec Inc v Petroleo Brasileiro SA Petrobas* (n. 175) [112]–[113].

reasonable expectations of honest men'.[206] Regarding the second issue, *Walford* also remains the authority for the rejection of good faith duties governing the conduct of negotiating parties (although the facts of *Walford* should restrict it only to the first issue).[207] Apart from the reasons given in *Walford* to reject a duty to negotiate in good faith,[208] reasons relating to the differences in the business and legal culture between England and the continental countries,[209] and to the different types of cases litigated before the courts[210] have also been mentioned. As the second issue is the relevant one in the paradigm case, this will be the focus of what follows.

Much has been written[211] and several arguments have been given for and against the recognition of a doctrine of good faith or a general duty of good faith in English contract law,[212] and three views have been identified: a negative one against adopting a general principle of good faith, a neutral one which inclines towards scepticism, and a positive one which supports the recognition of a general doctrine of good faith.[213] Within the neutral view there are two versions: the indifference thesis which considers that it makes no difference whether English law operates with a general doctrine or with piecemeal solutions, and the equivalence thesis which states that there is a strict equivalence between a general doctrine and the piecemeal solutions.[214] Because the object here is to argue neither for nor against the recognition of a doctrine of good faith in English contract law, it suffices to point out that the neutral view, in both versions, is inaccurate and this is proven by English law's attitude towards liability for broken negotiations.

The piecemeal solutions available in English law are not equivalent to the solutions that good faith has provided in the selected jurisdictions to deal

206 *Petromec Inc v Petroleo Brasileiro SA Petrobas* (n. 175) [121], citing Steyn (n. 182).

207 See text to (n. 184) above.

208 See text to (n. 187) above.

209 Sjef van Erp, 'A European "Culpa in Contrahendo" Doctrine? Towards a Model of Contract as a Legal Relationship and Situation-Specific Duties to Inform' in Santiago Espiau and Antoni Vaquer Aloy (eds.), *Bases de un Derecho Contractual Europeo* (Tirant Lo Blanch, 2003) p. 73.

210 Kötz (n. 201) p. 256.

211 Favouring the adoption of a general requirement of good faith, e.g. Brownsword (n. 156) p. 208; regarding Australian law, H.K. Lücke, 'Good Faith and Contractual Performance' in P.D. Finn (ed.), *Essays on Contract* (Law Book Company Limited, 1987). Against, e.g. Lord Ackner in *Walford* (n. 89); regarding Canadian law, Michael G. Bridge, 'Does Anglo-Canadian Contract Law Need a Doctrine of Good Faith?' (1984) 9 Canadian Business Law Journal 385.

212 Arguments in, e.g. Roger Brownsword, *Contract Law: Themes for the Twenty-First Century* (2nd edn., OUP, 2006) ch. 6; Cartwright (n. 1) pp. 64–66, 75–79; *Yam Seng* (n. 160) [123], [146]–[152]; McKendrick (n. 196).

213 Brownsword (n. 212) pp. 114 ff.; analysed in McKendrick (n. 8) pp. 490–498.

214 Brownsword (n. 212) pp. 120–121.

with these cases of precontractual liability, because the same results cannot always be reached. It has been shown that English law provides no relief in the paradigm case.[215] Therefore, it is not indifferent whether, in this area, English law operates with its limited piecemeal solutions or with a general doctrine of good faith as, in all likelihood, if a general doctrine had been accepted relief would have been given or at least would be possible in the paradigm case. It is common to find statements that the differences between English law and other legal systems regarding the treatment of good faith are more of legal form than of substance, and that conclusions that are reached in other legal systems through good faith can be reached in other ways by English law,[216] but this is not entirely accurate as the lack of relief in the paradigm case shows. The difference, regarding duties of good faith during negotiations, seems to be not only of form but also of substance.[217] Therefore, while it might be true that there is no need for a doctrine of good faith if there are other doctrines that 'do the job',[218] the question is what happens when there are no such other doctrines.

A possible answer is that English law should recognise a general doctrine of good faith and that the breach of good faith duties during negotiations may give rise to liability,[219] or that the absolute rejection of a duty to negotiate in good faith should be reconsidered.[220] Although it has been stated that '[i]t seems likely that, sooner or later, English contract law will come to accept the existence of a doctrine of good faith',[221] it is also likely that this recognition will be limited to the performance of a contract. Another possible answer is to say that nothing should be done; English law rejects good faith in the negotiation stage, only provides relief in particular established categories, and cases that fall outside their scope, like the paradigm case, are simply not valued as deserving protection.[222] But another possibility, which will be analysed next, is that the acceptance or refusal to provide relief in situations of precontractual liability is not necessarily connected to accepting or rejecting good faith in the precontractual stage.

---

215 See this Ch. s. I above.

216 e.g. McKendrick (n. 8) p. 482.

217 Kötz (n. 201) p. 257; Cartwright (n. 1) p. 65.

218 Simon Whittaker and Reinhard Zimmermann, 'Coming to Terms with Good Faith' in Reinhard Zimmermann and Simon Whittaker (eds.), *Good Faith in European Contract Law* (CUP, 2000) p. 684.

219 e.g. McKendrick (n. 8) p. 7; Roy Goode, 'The Codification of Commercial Law' (1988) 14 Monash University Law Review 135, p. 151.

220 Steyn (n. 182) pp. 438–439.

221 McKendrick (n. 8) p. 498.

222 Cartwright (n. 1) pp. 53, 54 fn. 8.

3. THE REJECTION OF A GENERAL DUTY TO NEGOTIATE IN GOOD FAITH DOES NOT HAVE TO IMPLY THE REJECTION OF PRECONTRACTUAL LIABILTY FOR BREAKING OFF NEGOTIATIONS

Precontractual liability, as a notion but not as a general theory,[223] has recently been acknowledged by English legal scholars and it is generally conceived as being necessarily or at least partly connected with the notion of good faith.[224] It is considered that a general principle of precontractual liability cannot be accepted because a general principle of good faith is rejected.[225] When it is stated that English law recognises a very limited scope of duties between negotiating parties[226] and this is connected to the argument that '[t]he existence and scope of pre-contractual duties depends on what stance a legal system takes towards the general principle of good faith',[227] the inference seems to be that the absence of a general duty of good faith in English law[228] means the absence of specific precontractual duties of good faith, and this would be fatal to provide relief in situations of precontractual liability which do not fit into the particular liabilities recognised by English law. Indeed it is argued that even though there is no general duty to negotiate in good faith, there are 'plenty of other ways of dealing with particular problems of unacceptable conduct occurring in the course of negotiations'[229] where English law provides relief.[230] And the explanation of cases that do not give rise to liability (like the paradigm case) lies in the rejection

223 John Cartwright, 'Negotiation and Renegotiation: An English Perspective' in John Cartwright, Stefan Vogenauer and Simon Whittaker (eds.), *Reforming the French Law of Obligations: Comparative Reflections on the Avant-projet de réforme du droit des obligations et de la prescription ('the Avant-projet Catala')* (Hart Publishing, 2009) p. 52.

224 e.g., Furmston and Tolhurst (n. 182) p. 381; Stathis Banakas, 'Liability for Contractual Negotiations in English Law: Looking for the Litmus Test' (2009) 1 InDret 1; *Chitty* (n. 51) paras. 1-166 ff. and 2-201 ff.: 'pre-contractual liability' is used in cases where a contract was entered into and, since its 32nd edn. (2015), another section deals with 'liability when negotiations do not produce a contract'.

225 *Chitty* (n. 51) para. 1-171; Roy M. Goode, 'England' in ICC (ed.), *Formation of Contracts and Precontractual Liability* (ICC Publishing, 1990) p. 59.

226 Cartwright (n. 4) p. 174.

227 Ingeborg Schwenzer, Pascal Hachem and Christopher Kee, *Global Sales and Contract Law* (OUP, 2012) p. 278.

228 See text to (n. 146) above.

229 CA judgment in *Cobbe v Yeoman's Row Management Ltd* [2006] EWCA Civ 1139, [2006] 1 WLR 2964 [4] (Mummery LJ). Similarly, Cohen (n. 87) pp. 31–32; *Chitty* (n. 51) para. 2-202; Alexander Loke, 'Insights from Comparing the Contract Laws of Asia on Formation and Third Party Beneficiaries' in Mindy Chen-Wishart, Alexander Loke and Stefan Vogenauer (eds.), *Formation and Third Party Beneficiaries* (OUP, 2018) p. 533.

230 For details on the current solutions that English law provides, see this Ch. s. I above.

of a general duty to negotiate in good faith, which is said to reflect the values of English contract law.[231]

English law's approach towards precontractual liability has led some scholars (both from the civil law and from the common law) to view some of English law's piecemeal solutions as ultimately based on good faith or in accordance with good faith.[232] And where these particular liabilities are not viewed as emanating from good faith it is still possible to draw parallels between them. For instance, in *Cobbe*, regarding proprietary estoppel, Lord Walker stated that it is

> a flexible doctrine which the court can use, in appropriate circumstances, to prevent injustice caused by the vagaries and inconstancy of human nature. But it is not a sort of joker or wild card to be used whenever the court disapproves of the conduct of a litigant who seems to have the law on his side. Flexible though it is, the doctrine must be formulated and applied in a disciplined and principled way.[233]

The same could be said of good faith in the selected jurisdictions.[234] It should be noted that the role that proprietary estoppel plays (or could play) in providing relief in lack of formality cases in English law is played by good faith in German law.[235]

It has been argued that the concept of good faith should not keep common law and civil law lawyers divided.[236] It has also been pointed out that where similar cases will not be decided in the same way in continental jurisdictions and in England, the explanation of the different result 'must surely lie elsewhere than in the presence (…) and the absence (…) of a broad good faith standard'.[237] Furthermore, it has been suggested that English law has no implicit objection to precontractual liability and that this is supported by the relief provided by its piecemeal solutions.[238] Collins, starting from a narrow and subjective notion of good faith, has argued that the sources of precontractual obligations in English law can be conceived as deriving from a general principle which is better described as a duty to negotiate with care rather than as a principle to bargain in good faith.[239] He concedes, however, that if good faith is objectively

231 Cartwright (n. 4) pp. 156, 174.

232 e.g. Ana Quiñones Escámez, 'Buena Fe y Lealtad Contractual' in Sixto Sánchez Lorenzo (ed.), *Derecho Contractual Comparado: Una Perspectiva Europea y Transnacional* (Thomson Reuters, 2009) pp. 370–371; McKendrick (n. 8) pp. 6–7.

233 *Cobbe v Yeoman's Row Management Ltd* (n. 21) [46].

234 See Ch. 6, text to (n. 117) above.

235 See this Ch., text following (n. 36); and Ch. 3, text to (n. 199) above.

236 Martijn W. Hesselink, 'The Concept of Good Faith' in Arthur S. Hartkamp and others (eds.), *Towards a European Civil Code* (4th edn., Kluwer Law International, 2011) p. 648.

237 Kötz (n. 201) p. 250.

238 Giliker (n. 88) p. 972.

239 Hugh Collins, *The Law of Contract* (4th edn., LexisNexis, 2003) p. 181.

understood as a standard of conduct (as it is in the selected jurisdictions) it might be equivalent to a duty to negotiate with care.[240]

It is necessary to go a step further. The better view is that in cases of broken negotiations, precontractual liability is based on a notion other than good faith (even objectively understood) and that the development of this liability in English law (if it were desired) would not require a change in its approach towards good faith, but a change of focus to another notion which is well known to it.

III. CHANGING THE FOCUS TO RELIANCE AND A POSSIBILITY FOR DEVELOPMENT

It has been shown that in the selected jurisdictions good faith (or the breach of this objective standard) is not the true basis of precontractual liability because it is reliance that lies at its heart.[241] The proposal is that in order to explain the solutions that English law provides in situations of precontractual liability and in order to consider a possible development of the law to grant relief in the paradigm case, it is not necessary to resort to the notion of good faith at all. There is no need to explain the imposition of this liability in terms of breach of good faith duties because the basis of this liability, particularly in the paradigm case, is the notion of reliance which is much more familiar to English law.

It might be argued that the courts are reluctant to overturn long-standing principles of the common law,[242] but at least two counter-arguments are possible. First, it could be argued that there is no common law principle that refuses liability for broken negotiations. *Walford*[243] should not be seen as an obstacle because this case centred around a positive duty to negotiate and this is not what breaking off negotiations cases are about; they are not concerned with whether negotiating parties are obliged to continue to negotiate and what the content of this obligation is (unless there is a preliminary agreement that imposes such an obligation). In the paradigm case, *Walford* should be distinguished. The paradigm case has nothing to do with agreements to continue to negotiate (in good faith), whereas it is possible to argue that the authority of *Walford* should be restricted to the rejection of an implied (or even an express) duty to continue to negotiate in good faith emanating from an agreement.[244] Secondly, if the first counter-argument is rejected, it could still be argued that the common law

---

240 Collins (n. 239) p. 219.
241 See Ch. 6 s. V above.
242 Cartwright (n. 1) p. 143.
243 *Walford v Miles* (n. 89).
244 See text to (nn. 184, 207) above.

principle that refuses liability for broken negotiations has been based on the rejection of good faith during negotiations. If the basis of this liability is shifted from the notion of good faith to the notion of reliance, the obstacle of good faith is removed and the way is clear for the recognition of precontractual liability for broken negotiations, not as a general principle of liability but as a possible liability in deserving cases.

This section will first highlight the fact that in English law, while a general principle of good faith is not recognised, both dimensions of reliance exist, although not as a matter of general principle but only in specific justified instances.[245] It will be shown that the current piecemeal solutions all involve to some extent the notion of reliance. The difference from the selected jurisdictions is that in English law the expectation dimension of reliance does not emanate from the trust dimension of reliance, which in the selected jurisdictions is equivalent to the principle of good faith.[246] This section will then address the most difficult obstacle for the acceptance of liability in the paradigm case in English law: on what basis to found the claim for damages? It will be seen that unless there is a development in the current law, there is no basis on which to found such a claim.

1. THE EXISTING RELIANCE

Both legal scholars from a common law and a civil law background have pointed out that the notion of (reasonable) reliance recognised in the common law tradition is similar if not equivalent to the notion of reliance (embodied in the notions of *Vertrauen*,[247] *confiance/croyance légitime*[248] and *confianza legítima*)[249] present in the selected jurisdictions. These notions are also seen as equivalent or similar to the notion of reasonable expectations found in the common law tradition.[250]

Some have pointed out the closeness between objective good faith (in the civil law) and the reasonable expectations of the parties (in the common law)[251]

245 This is recognised in Cartwright (n. 223) p. 55.
246 See Ch. 6 s. III 2 above.
247 Markesinis, Unberath and Johnston (n. 103) pp. 104–105; Basil S. Markesinis and Hannes Unberath, *The German Law of Torts: A Comparative Treatise* (4th edn., Hart Publishing, 2002) p. 58.
248 Hélène Aubry, *L'influence du Droit Communautaire sur le Droit Français des Contrats* (PUAM, 2002) pp. 253, 255 fn. 889, 256; Deshayes and Maître, case 7, in Cartwright and Hesselink (n. 36) p. 202 fn. 19.
249 Enrique Barros Bourie, *Tratado de Responsabilidad Extracontractual* (Editorial Jurídica de Chile, 2006) p. 1009.
250 e.g. Aubry (n. 248) pp. 253, 255 fn. 889, 256.
251 e.g. Steyn (n. 182) p. 439; Brownsword, *Contract Law* (n. 212) p. 127.

in the formation and in the performance of contracts.[252] But in cases of precontractual liability for broken negotiations it is possible to focus solely on the related notions of reliance and expectations. Although it is clear that English law has not elevated reliance to a general principle of the law of contract, it is also clear that in the formation of contracts there are manifestations of the protection of one party's reasonable reliance on the other.[253] The piecemeal solutions currently available for situations of precontractual liability[254] are a good example of this.

(a) *Reliance in General*

In some of the piecemeal solutions the notion of reliance is essential (as in promissory and proprietary estoppel) or at least very relevant for defining them (as in the torts of deceit and negligence).

The principle of *venire contra factum proprium*, which protects legitimate expectations and which is sometimes argued to be the basis of precontractual liability in the selected jurisdictions,[255] finds an expression in the notion of estoppel.[256] The protection of legitimate expectations is not a doctrine of English private law but is a doctrine under development in public law and it has been pointed out that there are close similarities (although also some significant differences) between the public law doctrine of legitimate expectations and the private law doctrine of estoppel.[257] In both there is a clear and unambiguous promise, undertaking or representation by one party which creates in the other an expectation or belief, and the latter is allowed to hold the former to his representation because he has relied on it.[258]

The core principle of estoppel is reliance.[259] In promissory estoppel it is the promisee's reliance on the promisor's promise not to enforce his strict legal rights, i.e. the fact that the promisee has done something that he might not have done due to the promisor's promise.[260] In proprietary estoppel it is the claimant's reliance on a representation or assurance by the landowner relating to the acquisition of an interest in property:[261] the landowner has created or encouraged

---

252 e.g. Whittaker and Zimmermann (n. 218) pp. 676–677.

253 Cartwright (n. 1) p. 68; Bertrand de Coninck, 'Le Droit Commun de la Rupture des Négociations Précontractuelles' in Marcel Fontaine (ed.), *Le Processus de Formation du Contrat: Contributions Comparatives et Interdisciplinaires à L'Harmonisation du Droit Européen* (Bruylant LGDJ, 2002) p. 34.

254 See this Ch. s. I above.

255 See Ch. 3 s. III 2, Ch. 4 s. II 1 (e), and Ch. 5 s. II 1 (c) above.

256 *Ius Commune* (n. 28) p. 366.

257 Cartwright (n. 82) p. 327.

258 Cartwright (n. 82) p. 327.

259 Cartwright (n. 1) pp. 143, 149.

260 See requirement (ii) in text to (n. 8) above.

261 See requirement (ii) in text to (n. 18) above.

an expectation that the claimant has or would have an interest in land and the latter has expended money on the property in reliance on that expectation, with the knowledge of the landowner.[262] In broken negotiations the reliance element is different in that one negotiating party trusted the other ('trust-based reliance') and expected the future conclusion of the negotiated contract ('expectation-based reliance'), but it is the same in that that negotiating party did something which it would not have done (for instance, incurred expenses) if it had not been for the expectation generated by the other negotiating party who later broke off.[263] Detrimental reliance is not evident in all cases of promissory estoppel,[264] is required in cases of proprietary estoppel,[265] and is also present in claims of precontractual liability for broken negotiations.[266] There is a shared similarity in that in all it is inequitable or unconscionable for one party to do something: in promissory estoppel for the promisor to go back on his promise,[267] in proprietary estoppel the conduct of the representor must be unconscionable,[268] and in broken negotiations for a negotiator to break off after it had induced expectation-based reliance in the other party.[269] 'Unconscionability' or 'unfairness' in estoppel (like good faith and reliance in broken negotiations)[270] is used as an 'objective value judgment on *behaviour* (regardless of the state of mind of the individual in question)',[271] amounting to a moral judgement of the conduct of the promisor.[272]

The torts of deceit and negligence both have the effect of protecting the reliance of one negotiating party on a representation made by the other.[273] In deceit the claimant must have relied on the misrepresentation, i.e. the misrepresentation must have induced him to act and incur losses.[274] In negligence the notion of reliance is prominent in the test for establishing a duty of care.[275] It is also very relevant in providing the causal link between the defendant's statement and the claimant's loss.[276] In *Caparo*, Lord Oliver emphasised that what unites liability for negligent statements[277] is that the damage 'lies always in the reliance by

262 e.g. *JT Developments Ltd v Quinn* (n. 33).
263 See Ch. 6, text to (n. 71) above.
264 McKendrick (n. 8) pp. 220, 226.
265 See requirement (iii) in text to (n. 18) above; Andrew Robertson, 'Estoppels and Rights-Creating Events: Beyond Wrongs and Promises' in Jason W. Neyers, Richard Bronaugh and Stephen G.A. Pitel (eds.), *Exploring Contract Law* (Hart Publishing, 2009) pp. 220–221.
266 See Ch. 6, text to (n. 179) above.
267 See requirement (iii) in text to (n. 8) above; McKendrick (n. 8) p. 221.
268 *Cobbe* (n. 21) [92] (Lord Walker); Cartwright (n. 82) p. 326.
269 See Ch. 6 s. II 1 (b) above.
270 See Ch. 6 s. II 1 (a) and Ch. 6 s. III 1 above.
271 *Cobbe* (n. 21) [92] (Lord Walker).
272 Collins (n. 239) p. 84.
273 Cartwright (n. 82) p. 330.
274 See text to (nn. 58, 59) above.
275 See text to (n. 75) above.
276 *Chitty* (n. 51) para. 1-176.
277 Cartwright (n. 73) p. 193 fn. 81.

somebody upon the accuracy of that which the word communicates and the loss or damage consequential upon that person having adopted a course of action upon the faith of it'.[278] Under both torts the remedy provided is damages for the losses suffered in reliance on the fraudulent or negligent statement, but they are calculated on the basis of a test of directness in the case of deceit and on the basis of a test of foreseeability in the case of negligence.[279] This remedy corresponds to the reliance interest generally protected in the selected jurisdictions.[280]

(b) *Trust-Based Reliance*

Even though trust-based reliance does not exist as a general principle in English law (that could be equivalent to the principle of good faith in the selected jurisdictions), a trust element is present in some of its piecemeal solutions.

In some of the proprietary estoppel cases analysed above[281] reference was made to the 'close relationship'[282] or 'relationship of trust'[283] between negotiating parties and to the fact that the promisee trusted the promisor.[284] English case law on proprietary estoppel, like German lack of formality cases, 'gives great weight' to reliance on the conduct of the other party.[285] In some of the tort of negligence cases analysed above,[286] it was highlighted that one party reasonably trusted or relied on the other to exercise a degree of care as the circumstances required,[287] and it has been pointed out that this duty of care only arises where the relative positions of the parties are such that the claimant is entitled to rely and does rely on what the other party says.[288] In the context of *Hedley Byrne* liability, when a claimant reasonably relies on a statement it not only means that he uses it but also that he is entitled to trust in it.[289] Regarding precontractual agreements, *Walford*[290] has been criticised for the failure of the courts to act as

278 *Caparo Industries plc v Dickman* (n. 72) 635.
279 Deakin, Johnston and Markesinis (n. 55) pp. 254–255, 469; Cartwright (n. 7) para. 2-16.
280 See Ch. 6 s. IV 1 (a).
281 In this Ch. s. I 1.
282 *Yaxley v Gotts* (n. 37) 169 (Walker LJ).
283 *Cobbe v Yeoman's Row Management Ltd* (n. 21) [89] (Lord Walker).
284 *Yaxley v Gotts* (n. 37) 169 (Walker LJ).
285 Markesinis, Unberath and Johnston (n. 103) p. 86.
286 In this Ch. s. I 2.
287 e.g. *Hedley Byrne* (n. 66), see text to (n. 68) above; *Esso Petroleum* (n. 84), see text to (n. 83) above.
288 Cartwright (n. 1) p. 85.
289 John Cartwright, 'Liability in Negligence: New Directions or Old?' (1997) 13 ConstLJ 157, p. 159. The reasonableness of the claimant's reliance was key in a recent case of professional negligence: *Steel v NRAM Ltd (formerly NRAM Plc)* [2018] UKSC 13, commented by Emily Gordon, 'Out With the Old, In With the Older? *Hedley Byrne* Reliance Takes Centre Stage' (2018) 77 Cambridge Law Journal 251, p. 254.
290 *Walford v Miles* (n. 89).

guarantors of the trust element in contracting,[291] and for hindering rather than facilitating giving effect to the reasonable expectations of business people.[292] In *Yam Seng*, it was recognised that the expectation of honesty which underlies almost all contractual relationships is essential to commerce, which depends critically on trust, and that in this case there was a relationship dependent on the mutual trust of two individuals.[293]

This reasoning could be extended to precontractual relationships. McFarlane, who proposes a three-stage model of the precontractual relationship, recognises that in the second stage (where some form of agreement in principle has been reached) the liability that may arise supports the inherent trust in negotiations by preventing one party from abusing the other's trust.[294] Other common law legal scholars, although focusing on US law, have argued that trust is an important factor even in arm's length negotiations, that interpersonal trust is one of the 'fundamental psychological conditions for the successful coordination of complex commercial transactions', and that there is a need for mechanisms that deter people from abusing such trust by engaging in opportunistic conduct.[295]

(c) *Expectation-Based Reliance*

It has been argued that in common law jurisdictions all cases imposing precontractual liability have common elements which are present irrespective of whether the courts have used contract, restitution, estoppel or tort.[296] These elements are: (a) a belief (at least on the part of the claimant) that a contract exists, or an expectation of a future contract; (b) the claimant has relied detrimentally on that belief or expectation; and (c) the defendant's conduct is such that (i) an obligation to bear the risk of an incomplete agreement has been or will be assumed by the defendant, or (ii) the risk of an incomplete agreement is imposed upon the defendant.[297] These elements do not differ

---

291 Jo Shaw, 'Pre-contractual Negotiations in English Law: *Walford v Miles* and its Aftermath' (1994) 2 ERPL 269, p. 272.

292 Beatson, Burrows and Cartwright (n. 8) p. 69.

293 *Yam Seng Pte Ltd v International Trade Corp Ltd* (n. 160) [135], [171].

294 Ben McFarlane, 'The Protection of Pre-Contractual Reliance: A Way Forward?' (2010) 10 OUCLJ 95, pp. 97, 101–102.

295 G. Richard Shell, 'Opportunism and Trust in the Negotiation of Commercial Contracts: Toward a New Cause of Action' (1991) 44 Vanderbilt Law Review 221, pp. 225, 252 fn. 138, 265. Also, Juliet P. Kostritsky, 'Bargaining with Uncertainty, Moral Hazard, and Sunk Costs: A Default Rule for Precontractual Negotiations' (1993) 44 Hastings Law Journal 621, pp. 650 fn. 98, 680–681.

296 Joachim Dietrich, 'Classifying Precontractual Liability: A Comparative Analysis' (2001) 21 Legal Studies 153, p. 164.

297 Dietrich (n. 296) pp. 165–170.

significantly from the requirements for establishing a successful claim for precontractual liability for broken negotiations in civil law jurisdictions.[298] Indeed, they embody the expectation-dimension of reliance identified in the selected jurisdictions.[299]

This dimension of reliance is present and is protected in some of English law's piecemeal solutions. Most noticeably in the type of restitution cases analysed above.[300] McKendrick refers to the expectation of both parties that a contract would be concluded and the fact that such an expectation has not been fulfilled as the basis for intervention.[301] In *William Lacey*, the claimant was led to believe that he would receive the contract because he was told that his tender was the lowest and that he could expect to obtain the contract;[302] consequently, his reliance on a contract yet to be concluded was protected.[303] In *British Steel* '[b]oth parties confidently expected a formal contract to eventuate'[304] and acted on that basis. And in *Cobbe* the defendant encouraged the claimant's expectation that the negotiations for the formal contract would be successful.[305] In a case where a contractual solution was provided, reference was made to the 'confident assumptions of commercial parties',[306] notion which can be related to expectation-based reliance.

In the proprietary estoppel cases analysed above[307] it is clear that one party encouraged an expectation in the other and the latter relied on it. For a claim in proprietary estoppel to be successful the expectation must be to obtain a 'right'[308] or a 'certain interest in land',[309] whereas in broken negotiations cases the expectation is that the negotiated contract will be concluded. Such was the expectation in *Cobbe*[310] and this is one of the reasons why the proprietary estoppel claim failed. However, proprietary estoppel cases and broken negotiations cases converge in that hopes are not enough,[311] a subjective belief is not enough;[312] what is required is a reasonable or legitimate expectation.[313] In the analysis

---

298 Dietrich (n. 296) pp. 179–180.
299 See Ch. 6 s. II 1 (a) above.
300 See this Ch. s. 1 3.
301 McKendrick (n. 130) p. 181.
302 *William Lacey (Hounslow) Ltd v Davis* (n. 122) 934, 939 (Barry J).
303 Gareth Jones, 'Claims Arising Out of Anticipated Contracts Which Do Not Materialize' (1980) 18 UWOLRev 447, p. 456.
304 *British Steel Corp v Cleveland Bridge and Engineering Co Ltd* (n. 126) 511 (Robert Goff J).
305 *Cobbe v Yeoman's Row Management Ltd* (n. 21) [18] (Lord Scott).
306 *Blackpool and Fylde Aero Club Ltd v Blackpool Borough Council* (n. 108) 1201 (Bingham LJ).
307 In this Ch. s. I 1.
308 *Crabb v Arun District Council* (n. 34) 186 (Lord Denning MR), 196 (Scarman LJ).
309 *Cobbe v Yeoman's Row Management Ltd* (n. 21) [20] (Lord Scott).
310 See text to (nn. 24, 25) above.
311 *Cobbe v Yeoman's Row Management Ltd* (n. 21) [66] (Lord Walker); *A-G of Hong Kong v Humphreys Estate (Queen's Gardens) Ltd* [1987] AC 114 (PC) 124.
312 *JT Developments Ltd v Quinn* (n. 33) 50 (Ralph Gibson LJ).
313 *Crabb v Arun District Council* (n. 34) 197 (Scarman LJ); see Ch. 6 s. II 2 (b) above.

of the concept of reliance within estoppel in general, Collins has indicated that detrimental reliance must be reasonable in all circumstances and this 'reasonableness' is defined by excluding situations where reliance is unreasonable.[314]

Although the language of 'legitimate expectations' is not commonly used in the private law of contract, the protection of an expectation created by one party and relied on by the other underlies, albeit not as a general principle, English law's piecemeal solutions for cases of precontractual liability.[315] The legitimacy of an expectation created by a promise means that the promisee has been led to believe, on reasonable grounds, that he can rely on the expectation.[316] This is the meaning relevant in cases of broken negotiations. A narrower meaning, according to which an expectation is made legitimate by the fact that the promisee has provided consideration,[317] is not applicable to these cases because they do not look towards the enforcement of a promise but only to the protection of detrimental reliance.[318]

It has been suggested that a defendant has created a 'legitimate expectation of contract' when, having regard to the relationship between the parties, he has conducted himself in a way which he should have foreseen would lead the claimant to reasonably act to his detriment, such as making a promise to enter into a contract in the future, to request the performance of services, or any act or omission that would foreseeably induce the claimant to reasonably believe that a binding contract would be entered into.[319]

2. HOW TO DEVELOP THE LAW

The solutions currently on offer in English law for imposing liability for disappointed precontractual expectations are 'rarely, if ever, available'[320] and no relief is provided in the paradigm case.[321] It has been stated that 'it is inconceivable that either the legislative or the judiciary would consider the introduction of such a principle [*culpa in contrahendo* or *responsabilité*

314 Collins (n. 239) pp. 75, 81–83.
315 Cartwright (n. 82) pp. 321, 328–329, 332.
316 Cartwright (n. 82) pp. 335.
317 Cartwright (n. 82) p. 335.
318 See the details of reliance-based remedies in Ch. 6 s. IV.
319 Geoffrey F. Cauchi, 'The Protection of the Reliance Interest and Anticipated Contracts Which Fail to Materialize' (1981) 19 UWOLRev 237, p. 268, analysing Canadian, American and English law cases.
320 Deakin, Johnston and Markesinis (n. 55) p. 146 fn. 274.
321 See this Ch. s. I above.

précontractuelle] to English law',[322] but other English scholars have stressed the need for review of this area of the law,[323] have even recommended the recognition of precontractual liability,[324] or at least have expressed a favourable view towards it.[325] The aim of this book is not to try to convince English lawyers that a change of view is necessary. The aim of this work is to explore how English law could grant relief in the paradigm case if it were ever desired. The rejection of good faith in the negotiation stage should not bar the possibility of providing protection in deserving cases of broken negotiations.[326] The issue is through which means relief might be provided. Considering that the protection of reliance on legitimate expectations is at the heart of these cases[327] and that some of English law's piecemeal solutions recognise and protect this expectation-based reliance,[328] English law should not have difficulties in providing adequate protection to the paradigm case. Therefore, it is necessary to explore which piecemeal solution[329] could be developed in order to provide relief in such a case.

(a) Contract and Restitution

Because a contractual solution is not possible in the paradigm case,[330] the development of a contractual approach will not be analysed here, but it suffices to say that currently English law provides protection in cases of broken negotiations where a collateral contract was found to be concluded.[331] The possibility of obtaining relief is more uncertain in cases where a preliminary agreement was concluded because its enforceability depends on what type of agreement the courts consider it to be.[332]

Likewise, a restitutionary solution is not possible in the paradigm case.[333] However, English law provides relief in cases where negotiations eventually failed and work was done in anticipation of the contract or expenses were incurred, at the request of the other negotiating party.[334] In these cases some

322 D.K. Allen, 'England' in Ewoud H. Hondius (ed.), *Precontractual Liability: Reports to the XIIIth Congress International Academy of Comparative Law, Montreal, Canada, 18–24 August 1990* (Kluwer Law, 1991) p. 143.
323 Cartwright (n. 4) p. 170.
324 Collins (n. 239) p. 178.
325 Beale (n. 189) pp. 121, 123.
326 See this Ch. s. II 3 above.
327 See Ch. 6 s. II 1 (b) above.
328 See this Ch. s. III 1 (c) above.
329 See this Ch. s. I above.
330 See this Ch. s. I 3 above.
331 See text to (n. 107) above.
332 See this Ch., text following (n. 111) above.
333 See this Ch., text following (n. 129) above.
334 See this Ch., text to (n. 119) above.

legal scholars defend the restitutionary analysis over other possible grounds of liability such as estoppel or tort,[335] while others argue in favour of other grounds such as contract.[336] Some have challenged the restitutionary analysis due to the existing difficulties in English law particularly in determining whether there is enrichment and whether it is unjust.[337] Regarding enrichment, in some cases the courts have not required an objective benefit to have been conferred on the defendant by the claimant's work, but have concluded that the fact that the work was done at the defendant's request, in circumstances where the work was not intended to be done gratuitously, was sufficient to establish that he was enriched or had obtained a benefit for which he must pay.[338] It has been pointed out that such a claim looks more like an implied contractual claim than a restitutionary claim.[339]

A prominent legal scholar on the law of restitution recognised that, in exceptional cases, it is attractive to protect a negotiating party's legitimate expectation based on a reasonable belief (derived from the other party's conduct) that a contract will eventually be concluded, even though the other party has not obtained a benefit.[340] He argued, however, that the preferable approach to explain the imposition of liability might be through the extension of proprietary estoppel because it avoids the analysis of the meanings of 'benefit' or 'fault'.[341] Similarly, another author has argued that promissory estoppel, as developed in Australia, is the better explanation because it focuses on the unconscionable conduct of the defendant (the true basis of liability) and provides more remedial flexibility.[342]

In any case, the law of restitution requires the conferment of a benefit on the defendant for a claim to succeed (even if the enrichment is only found in the fact that the defendant requested the work)[343] and, consequently, a restitutionary claim is for the benefit gained by the defendant at the

---

335 e.g. McKendrick (n. 130) pp. 189–190; James Edelman, 'Liability in Unjust Enrichment where a Contract Fails to Materialize' in Andrew Burrows and Edwin Peel (eds.), *Contract Formation and Parties* (OUP, 2010).

336 e.g. Steve Hedley, 'Work Done in Anticipation of a Contract Which Does Not Materialise: A Response' in W.R. Cornish and others (eds.), *Restitution, Past, Present and Future: Essays in Honour of Gareth Jones* (Hart Publishing, 1998) pp. 195, 198; Dietrich (n. 296) p. 164.

337 e.g. Hedley, 'Work Done in Anticipation of a Contract Which Does Not Materialise: A Response' (n. 336) p. 197; Steve Hedley, 'Restitution: Contract's Twin?' in Francis D. Rose (ed.), *Failure of Contracts: Contractual, Restitutionary and Proprietary Consequences* (Hart Publishing, 1997) pp. 267, 270–271; Giliker (n. 63) pp. 88–92, 164; Giliker (n. 88) pp. 972–973; Dietrich (n. 296) p. 163.

338 McKendrick (n. 130) p. 175; Cartwright (n. 7) para. 2-27.

339 Cartwright (n. 7) para. 2-27 fn. 180.

340 Jones (n. 303) p. 453. Also, Cauchi (n. 319) p. 251.

341 Jones (n. 303) pp. 454, 457.

342 John Carter, 'Contract, Restitution and Promissory Estoppel' (1989) 12 UNSWLJ 30, p. 45.

343 See text to (n. 338) above.

claimant's expense.[344] It is not aimed at protecting detrimental reliance, which is the interest protected in precontractual liability for broken negotiations.[345] Therefore, although in restitution cases expectation-based reliance is present, it is unlikely that restitution might be the way forward for protecting the paradigm case.

(b) Tort

Tort law offers limited protection in cases of precontractual liability.[346] Because the paradigm case does not correspond to the factual scenario required for the tort of deceit to operate,[347] the focus of this sub-section is on whether it is possible to develop the tort of negligence in order to provide relief in the paradigm case.

Establishing liability in negligence in cases of broken negotiations is very difficult because the courts are reluctant to award damages in tort in cases where the loss is purely financial.[348] Thus, proposing the extension of this tort to cover the paradigm case appears to be an arduous task. While it has been pointed out that there is little support for recovery in tort,[349] it has also been noted that because the nature of the claim is one of detrimental reliance, it seems to fall more naturally within the law of tort than within the law of contract,[350] and it has been argued that the duty of care during negotiations fits into the broader scheme of the law of tort.[351] During the period of expansion of the tort of negligence that took place after *Hedley Byrne*,[352] some legal scholars argued that it would not be unreasonable for the law of tort to protect the legitimate reliance interest of negotiating parties[353] and some cases appeared to reaffirm this suggestion.[354]

Nevertheless, the dominant view remains that *Hedley Byrne* did not give rise to a general duty of care in relation to economic losses, that normally there is no duty of care under *Hedley Byrne* between business parties negotiating at

---

344 Jones (n. 303) p. 457.

345 See Ch. 6 s. IV 1; Dietrich (n. 296) p. 161 fn. 42. Kelvin Koh, 'A Principled Response to Pre-contractual Remuneration' (2012) 28 ConstLJ 277, pp. 278–279, 294, proposes a model where promissory estoppel should be invoked in cases of detrimental reliance and restitution in cases of wrongful transfer of value.

346 See this Ch. s. I 2 above.

347 See this Ch., text following (n. 63) above.

348 *Ius Commune* (n. 28) p. 440; Giliker (n. 63) p. 105.

349 Giliker (n. 63) p. 96 fn. 184; Giliker (n. 88) pp. 978, 991; Furmston and Tolhurst (n. 182) pp. 384, 404.

350 Giliker (n. 88) pp. 970, 973.

351 Collins (n. 239) p. 182; see text to (n. 239) above.

352 *Hedley Byrne & Co Ltd v Heller & Partners Ltd* (n. 66); Deakin, Johnston and Markesinis (n. 55) p. 110.

353 Cauchi (n. 319) p. 271.

354 e.g. *Esso Petroleum Co Ltd v Mardon* (n. 84); *Box v Midland* (n. 86).

arm's length,[355] that there is no general common law duty of care owed between negotiating parties during negotiations for a contract,[356] and that such a general duty (or even more particularised duties of care) are not likely to be developed due to the courts' reluctance to impose mutual duties on negotiating parties.[357] This reluctance seems to stem from the courts' view of the nature of negotiations[358] which, in turn, involves the rejection of a duty to negotiate in good faith.[359] Hence, McKendrick has argued that if a duty to negotiate in good faith were recognised, then a sudden and unexplained withdrawal from negotiations might give rise to liability in tort for breach of this duty; but that in the absence of such a duty there can be no general liability in tort.[360]

Several requirements would have to be met for the tort of negligence to be able to provide relief in the paradigm case: (i) the existence of a duty of care; (ii) breach of such duty; (iii) breaking off by one party; (iv) with absence of a justified reason; (v) reliance of the other party; and (vi) economic loss of the other party. Requirements (iii)–(vi) should not be problematic as their rationale (analysed in the selected jurisdictions)[361] could be applicable in English law. Requirements (i) and (ii), however, present some difficulties.

In order to impose liability in negligence it is necessary to determine whether the defendant owed to the claimant a duty to take reasonable care and whether this duty has been breached.[362] The first requirement is for the law to acknowledge a 'duty situation' but the courts have the power to create new 'duty situations'.[363] The courts have been able to use the tort of negligence to provide relief in novel claims for compensation because '[t]he conceptual structure of negligence is highly flexible and capable of general application'.[364] In *Donoghue v Stevenson*, Lord Macmillan stated that 'the categories of negligence are never closed'[365] and in the same case Lord Atkin formulated the 'neighbour principle'[366] in order to explain how a new category of duty could be found.[367] Lord Devlin later developed this principle in *Hedley Byrne* as the 'principle

355 Deakin, Johnston and Markesinis (n. 55) pp. 110, 146.
356 Cartwright (n. 73) pp. 621–622 fn. 200.
357 Cartwright (n. 82) p. 330; Cartwright, case 6, in Cartwright and Hesselink (n. 36) p. 168; Cartwright and Hesselink (n. 36) p. 466.
358 Cartwright and Hesselink (n. 36) p. 466.
359 *Walford v Miles* (n. 89).
360 McKendrick (n. 130) p. 190.
361 See Ch. 6 ss. I 3 (c), II, IV.
362 Cartwright (n. 1) pp. 39, 181; Robert Stevens, 'Restitution: Contract's Twin? – A Comment' in Francis D. Rose (ed.), *Failure of Contracts: Contractual, Restitutionary and Proprietary Consequences* (Hart Publishing, 1997) p. 276.
363 Deakin, Johnston and Markesinis (n. 55) pp. 102, 109.
364 Deakin, Johnston and Markesinis (n. 55) p. 99.
365 [1932] AC 562 (HL Sc) 619.
366 *Donoghue v Stevenson* (n. 365) 580.
367 Cartwright (n. 1) p. 42; *Ius Commune* (n. 28) p. 136.

of proximity'.[368] In each case, the formulation of these principles allowed the courts to extend the application of negligence to new categories of cases.[369]

Therefore, it is suggested that the courts could, if a case like the paradigm case came before them, recognise a mutual duty of care between negotiating parties which would be breached where one party induced in the other a reasonable or legitimate expectation that the negotiated contract would be concluded and then broke off the negotiations without a justified reason, and the other party suffered economic loss as a result of his reliance on this induced expectation. Furthermore, this duty and its breach could be framed without resorting to a duty to negotiate in good faith.[370] Because the rationale of tort liability for negligent misstatements (*Hedley Byrne* type of cases) does not correspond to the rationale of liability for broken negotiations,[371] it would be preferable for the courts to develop a new category of duty within the tort of negligence, rather than stretching the scope of *Hedley Byrne* in order to cover the paradigm case. In *Customs and Excise Commissioners v Barclays Bank plc*,[372] the House of Lords discussed the methodology for extending the scope of duties of care in the tort of negligence and it seems that the preferred method is by analogy with existing categories of liability.[373]

Breaking off negotiations is not a tort[374] and the suggestion (if the law were to be developed) is not that any breaking-off would constitute a tort but that only in deserving cases, where all the requirements of liability are met,[375] breaking off negotiations could give rise to liability in negligence. This solution would bring English law closer to the French (and Chilean) delictual approach to cases of precontractual liability.[376] In fact, English tort of negligence cases and the paradigm case share several elements: there is a close relationship ('a pre-tort relationship of some kind')[377] between the negotiating parties that justifies the imposition of a duty of care,[378] the applicable standard in order to determine

368 *Hedley Byrne & Co Ltd v Heller & Partners Ltd* (n. 66) 515, 524–525, 530–531; Paul Mitchell, 'Hedley Byrne & Co Ltd v Heller & Partners Ltd (1963)' in Charles Mitchell and Paul Mitchell (eds.), *Landmark Cases in the Law of Tort* (Hart Publishing, 2010) p. 176.

369 Cartwright (n. 1) pp. 42–43.

370 See this Ch. s. III above.

371 See this Ch. s. I 2 above.

372 [2006] UKHL 28, [2007] 1 AC 181.

373 Deakin, Johnston and Markesinis (n. 55) p. 115.

374 Cartwright (n. 7) para. 2-11.

375 See text following (n. 360) above.

376 See Ch. 4, text to (n. 15), and Ch. 5, text to (n. 23) above.

377 Deakin, Johnston and Markesinis (n. 55) p. 113; cf. Ch. 6 s. I 3 (a) above.

378 e.g. *Donoghue v Stevenson* (n. 365); *Hedley Byrne & Co Ltd v Heller & Partners Ltd* (n. 66); *Esso Petroleum Co Ltd v Mardon* (n. 84) 827–828 (Ormrod LJ); *Ius Commune* (n. 28) p. 137; Carlo Castronovo, 'Precontractual Liability' in José Lebre de Freitas and others (eds.), *Estudos em Homenagem ao Professor Doutor Carlos Ferreira de Almeida*, vol. II (Almedina, 2011) pp. 226–227; cf. Ch. 6 s. I 3 (b) above.

whether this duty has been breached is that of the reasonable man,[379] it is foreseeable that the other negotiating party might suffer loss due to the conduct of the party who later breaks off,[380] and there is reasonable reliance on the part of the claimant.[381]

However, the greatest obstacle appears to be that it is unlikely that the courts would find an assumption of responsibility between equal negotiating parties[382] (as is the case in the paradigm case) and, consequently, no duty of care that might be breached could arise. It seems that the reluctance of the courts to develop a duty of care in the tort of negligence rests on the underlying principle that because the relationship between negotiating parties is inherently adversarial, courts should not develop implied duties that would alter that balance of risk.[383] Nevertheless, even in *Walford*, where both parties were 'men of business',[384] the courts were able to provide relief to the claimants via the tort of negligence[385] (although the language used by the Lords Justices evokes deceit).[386]

Therefore, the possibility to extend the tort of negligence to cover the paradigm case must not be rejected offhand. Considering that there have been periods where the courts have been more open to expand negligence,[387] that the aim of precontractual liability of protecting detrimental reliance falls squarely into the realm of tort,[388] and that the history of the law of negligence 'exhibits a sturdy refusal to be confined by arbitrary forms and rules where justice indicates otherwise',[389] it is not unthinkable that if an appropriate case came before the courts they might be willing to provide relief via the development of the tort of negligence. *Yam Seng* might prove useful to this effect, as the argument made by Leggatt J in giving content to the objective standard of good faith[390] is transferable to the tort of negligence in order to give content to a duty to take reasonable care in negotiating.

---

379 e.g. *Donoghue v Stevenson* (n. 365) 619 (Lord Macmillan); *Hedley Byrne & Co Ltd v Heller & Partners Ltd* (n. 66) 486 (Lord Reid); cf. Ch. 6, text to (nn. 54, 130) above.

380 *Hedley Byrne & Co Ltd v Heller & Partners Ltd* (n. 66); cf. Ch. 4, text to (n. 131), and Ch. 5, text to (n. 153) above.

381 See text to (n. 287) above; CA judgment in *Walford v Miles* (n. 91) 432 (Dillon LJ); cf. Ch. 6 s. II 2 (b) above.

382 See text to (n. 70) above; Giliker (n. 88) p. 976.

383 Cartwright (n. 223) p. 58.

384 [1990] 1 EGLR 212 (QB) 215.

385 See text to (n. 91) above.

386 *Walford v Miles* (n. 91).

387 See text to (n. 352) above. Consider also, *Henderson v Merrett Syndicates Ltd* [1995] 2 AC 145 (HL), where the House of Lords extended the *Hedley Byrne* principle to cover cases of economic loss brought about by the negligent performance of services.

388 See text to (nn. 350, 351) above.

389 *Norsk Pacific Steamship Co v Canadian National Railway Co* [1992] 1 SCR 1021 (Supreme Court of Canada) 1146 (McLachlin J).

390 See text to (n. 172) above.

(c) Estoppel

In their current form, neither promissory nor proprietary estoppel can provide relief in the paradigm case.[391] However, a development of estoppel, following the course taken by other common law jurisdictions, would appear to be a viable option for English law to provide relief in the paradigm case. While estoppel (particularly proprietary estoppel) has more of an expectation flavour in English law[392] than in Australia or the US, in all of these common law jurisdictions equitable estoppel is founded upon reliance[393] and the remedy granted is often reliance damages.

Both the US and Australia have adopted promissory estoppel in a broader form than English law[394] and this explains why they are able to use it to provide relief in cases of broken negotiations while English law cannot.[395] In the US, *Hoffman v Red Owl*[396] remains the pivotal case in this area, where the Supreme Court of Wisconsin adopted the doctrine of promissory estoppel as stated in §90 of the Restatement (First) of Contracts.[397] It ruled that the promise which gives rise to the cause of action does not need to meet the requirements of a complete offer, and endorsed the view that where damages are awarded they should be only such as are necessary to prevent injustice and that their amount may be determined by the claimant's expenditure or change of position in reliance. It approved the items of damages which protected the claimant's reliance interest (actual losses and expenses) and confirmed that the claimant could not recover for loss of future profits because this is not a breach of contract action.[398] Although compensation for lost opportunities was not pleaded, it is possible to argue that they should be a component of reliance damages.[399]

In Australia, the leading case is *Waltons Stores*,[400] where the High Court of Australia adopted a broad doctrine of equitable estoppel (which may act as a

---

391 For details, see this Ch. s. I 1 above.

392 See text to (n. 423) below.

393 van Erp (n. 209) p. 70; Cartwright (n. 1) p. 154.

394 Cartwright (n. 4) p. 164.

395 Schwenzer, Hachem and Kee (n. 227) p. 275; see text to (n. 7) above.

396 *Hoffman v Red Owl Stores Inc* (n. 140).

397 Now replaced by §90 Restatement (Second) of Contracts: 'Promise Reasonably Inducing Action or Forbearance. (1) A promise which the promisor should reasonably expect to induce action or forbearance on the part of the promisee or a third person and which does induce such action or forbearance is binding if injustice can be avoided only by enforcement of the promise. The remedy granted for breach may be limited as justice requires', The American Law Institute, *Restatement of the Law Second: Contracts 2d*, vol. 1 (American Law Institute Publishers, 1981).

398 Illustration 10 to §90 Restatement (Second) of Contracts (n. 397) p. 245; Summers, '"Good Faith" in General Contract Law and the Sales Provisions of the Uniform Commercial Code' (n. 140) p. 224.

399 E. Allan Farnsworth, *Farnsworth on Contracts*, vol. 1 (3rd edn., Aspen, 2004) pp. 390–391.

400 *Waltons Stores (Interstate) Ltd v Maher* (n. 49).

cause of action and does not require a pre-existing legal relationship) capable of applying to precontractual negotiations.[401] According to the line of reasoning of Mason CJ, Wilson J and Brennan J, the company was estopped from retreating from its implied promise to complete the contract, as it was unconscionable for it to stand by in silence, knowing that the claimants were relying to their detriment on an expectation that a binding contract would come into existence; inaction which constituted clear encouragement or inducement to the claimants to continue to act on the basis of such an expectation.[402] Brennan J emphasised that the object of this equity is not to compel the estopped party to fulfil the other party's expectation but to avoid the detriment which, if the expectation goes unfulfilled, the relying party will suffer.[403]

Despite this stated object, the remedy granted was damages in lieu of specific performance, thus protecting the expectation interest.[404] The dichotomy between the stated object and the relief given has been criticised by legal scholars who argue that there should be a correspondence between them resulting in the protection of the reliance interest.[405] Nevertheless, the dichotomy may be understood if it is considered that *Waltons Stores* is really a lack of formality case (because the terms of the negotiated contract had been agreed and only fulfilment of the formality requirement was pending)[406] where detrimental reliance can only be adequately compensated by enforcement of the expectation.[407] The court held that the company was estopped from denying that it was bound (although no binding contract for a lease had come into existence) and that it should be treated 'as though it had executed and delivered the original deed'.[408] Therefore, the remedy would have been specific performance except for the fact that it was held in the lower courts to be no longer appropriate.[409]

Some legal scholars have advocated for a clearer or more developed law of estoppel in English law. Nolan has argued that because the doctrines of promissory and proprietary estoppel remain underdeveloped in English law, this has resulted in an inadequate legal response to the problem of detrimental reliance on non-contractual statements of intention, concluding that it is

---

401 Giliker (n. 63) pp. 154–155; Furmston and Tolhurst (n. 182) p. 387; Cartwright, case 8, in Cartwright and Hesselink (n. 36) p. 236.

402 *Waltons Stores (Interstate) Ltd v Maher* (n. 49) pp. 407–408 (Mason CJ and Wilson J), 410, 430 (Brennan J). The test for liability in *Waltons* is similar to the one applied in continental jurisdictions, *Ius Commune* (n. 28) p. 464.

403 *Waltons Stores (Interstate) Ltd v Maher* (n. 49) pp. 423, 433.

404 Donal Nolan, 'Following in their Footsteps: Equitable Estoppel in Australia and the United States' (2000) 11 KCLJ 202, p. 210; *Ius Commune* (n. 28) p. 456.

405 e.g. Giliker (n. 63) pp. 158–159.

406 *Waltons Stores (Interstate) Ltd v Maher* (n. 49) 397 (Mason CJ and Wilson J).

407 Nolan (n. 404) p. 212.

408 *Waltons Stores (Interstate) Ltd v Maher* (n. 49) 430 (Brennan J).

409 *Waltons Stores (Interstate) Ltd v Maher* (n. 49) (Gaudron J); Furmston and Tolhurst (n. 182) p. 388.

possible and, perhaps, probable that English law will follow the path taken by American and Australian law towards a more fully developed doctrine of equitable estoppel.[410] McFarlane has criticised the limitation of proprietary estoppel to cases concerning the acquisition of rights in land, which prevent its general use as a means to protect precontractual reliance, and has proposed the extension of the reliance principle underlying some proprietary estoppel cases.[411] In a recent case it was considered that proprietary estoppel may be available regarding the renewal of a licence of intellectual property rights (although it was not on the facts of the case)[412] and this has been viewed as supporting an extension of the promise-based strand of proprietary estoppel beyond land.[413] McFarlane and Robertson, commenting on *Cobbe v Yeoman's Row Management Ltd*, have indicated that it would be unfortunate if proprietary estoppel (which they consider as the doctrine best equipped to protect reliance) were prevented from fulfilling that role in the future.[414]

The idea of developing a general principle to unify the different types of estoppels and overcome their differences has been discussed in English case law and academic literature but has faced a generally negative response.[415] However, the justification for the rule that promissory estoppel cannot create a cause of action while proprietary estoppel can, has been challenged.[416] The question has been raised whether English courts should follow *Waltons Stores*, where it was rejected that allowing promissory estoppel to give rise to a cause of action would undermine the doctrine of consideration.[417] Giliker has suggested that the strongest argument for providing a ground for recovery in precontractual liability cases is the development of a broad doctrine of equitable estoppel, capable of compensating detrimental reliance. She argues that the foundations already exist in English law cases where the conduct of one negotiating party encouraged the other to believe that he was no longer acting at his own risk, and that '[i]t would take merely one further step for the English courts to follow the lead of the Australian courts and recognise estoppel as a more satisfactory response to the question of pre-contractual negotiations and risk'.[418] The estoppel approach, in precontractual liability cases traditionally dealt with through the

410 Nolan (n. 404) p. 222.
411 McFarlane (n. 294) pp. 117–118, 120, 122; see text to (n. 421) below.
412 *Motivate Publishing FZ LLC v Hello Ltd* [2015] EWHC 1554 (Ch), 2015 WL 3479918 [61], [73] (Birss J).
413 Shaw-Mellors (n. 17) p. 536.
414 Ben McFarlane and Andrew Robertson, 'The Death of Proprietary Estoppel' [2008] LMCLQ 449, p. 460.
415 McKendrick (n. 8) pp. 225–227; Cartwright (n. 7) para. 10-49.
416 e.g. Nolan (n. 404) p. 207; McKendrick (n. 8) pp. 223, 227, 240; Collins (n. 239) p. 87; Giliker (n. 63) p. 151.
417 *Waltons Stores (Interstate) Ltd v Maher* (n. 49) 427 (Brennan J).
418 Giliker (n. 63) pp. 138, 96, 103, 151.

law of restitution, is also supported by Jones[419] and Carter.[420] McFarlane has argued that English law recognises a promissory principle that may provide non-contractual protection to precontractual reliance in cases where one negotiating party reasonably relied on a precontractual promise made by the other party, but that this principle is mainly implemented through proprietary estoppel which, unfortunately and unjustifiably, prevents it from applying more broadly.[421]

In proprietary estoppel cases the remedy awarded is 'the minimum equity to do justice'[422] but it normally tends towards the protection of the expectation interest by granting the representee the promised interest in land.[423] In *Crabb*, it was held that equity should be satisfied by granting the claimant a right of access and a right of way without any payment by the claimant,[424] and in *Humphreys Estate* Lord Templeman considered that there was no difficulty in the court devising an order for specific performance if the agreement in principle had become binding by estoppel[425] (which it had not). Sometimes the remedy will protect the representee's reliance (reimbursement of expenditure incurred) rather than his expectation, particularly where the value of the expectation is disproportionate to the value of the detriment incurred.[426] Furthermore, some argue that proprietary estoppel is aimed at protecting detrimental reliance, and that the award of expectation-based relief can be reconciled with this view because in some cases there is no other way to protect against detriment than by the enforcement of the promise.[427]

An additional argument in favour of explaining cases of precontractual liability as based on estoppel is the 'unconscionability' or 'unfairness' that underlies both doctrines.[428] Emphasis on unconscionability would bring estoppel closer to the law of wrongs.[429] In *Waltons Stores*, Brennan J noted that equitable estoppel complements the tortious remedies and enhances the remedies available to a party who has relied on what another has induced him to believe.[430] And in the US, legal scholars have noted that the decision in *Red Owl*, which allowed

419 See text to (n. 341) above.
420 See text to (n. 342) above.
421 McFarlane (n. 294) pp. 95, 98, 105, 116, 122.
422 *Crabb v Arun District Council* (n. 34) 198.
423 McKendrick (n. 8) p. 244; Cartwright (n. 1) p. 154 fn. 121; *Ius Commune* (n. 28) p. 468.
424 *Crabb v Arun District Council* (n. 34).
425 *A-G of Hong Kong v Humphreys Estate (Queen's Gardens) Ltd* (n. 311) 120.
426 *Jennings v Rice* [2002] EWCA Civ 159, [2003] 1 P & CR 8 [21], [50]; Cartwright (n. 7) para. 10-07 fn. 41; McFarlane (n. 17) p. 445; Robertson (n. 265) p. 222.
427 Robertson (n. 265) pp. 223–224; McFarlane (n. 17) pp. 431, 438, 442–443.
428 See text to (nn. 267–269) above.
429 Different views as to the nature of estoppel in McKendrick (n. 8) pp. 240 ff.
430 *Waltons Stores (Interstate) Ltd v Maher* (n. 49) 427.

recovery based on reliance,[431] might have been fitted into tort.[432] It is also possible to draw a comparison between the application of a broad notion of estoppel that protects detrimental reliance and the use of delict in precontractual liability cases in French law.[433] In Australia, in order to provide a basis for the doctrine of equitable estoppel that emerged after *Waltons Stores*,[434] Spence has defined a duty to ensure the reliability of induced assumptions, which gives rise to a primary obligation to prevent harm and to a secondary obligation to compensate the relying party for the harm suffered, stressing that it is the inducement of reliance, rather than merely inducing an assumption, that brings about this duty.[435] It has been noted that this duty should be qualified in that the assumption must be reasonable in the particular context.[436]

This broad conception of estoppel corresponds with precontractual liability's aim to protect detrimental reliance in cases of broken negotiations in the selected jurisdictions (and in different harmonising instruments).[437] Therefore, it appears that as long as a cause of action emanating from estoppel in cases of broken negotiations is confined to the protection of detrimental reliance, there should be no concern of undermining contract law and the way would be cleared for the acceptance of a broader notion of estoppel.[438] As such, developing promissory estoppel or eliminating the differences between it and proprietary estoppel could be a viable option for providing relief in broken negotiations cases, especially in the paradigm case, in English law.

It has been pointed out that it is not out of the question that the Supreme Court might be persuaded to allow promissory estoppel to create a new cause of action,[439] or even that it is only a matter of time;[440] yet, there is no clear indication that English courts are prepared to take promissory estoppel in the direction that the Australian or US courts have.[441] The Court of Appeal has stated that if the law regarding estoppel is to be developed or corrected, this must be done by the Supreme Court.[442] After *Cobbe*,[443] which rejected the Court of Appeal's

---

431 *Hoffman v Red Owl Stores Inc* (n. 140); see text to (n. 398) above.

432 E. Allan Farnsworth, *Contracts* (4th edn., Aspen, 2004) p. 197; Summers, '"Good Faith" in General Contract Law and the Sales Provisions of the Uniform Commercial Code' (n. 140) p. 258.

433 Giliker (n. 63) pp. 135, 157.

434 *Waltons Stores (Interstate) Ltd v Maher* (n. 49).

435 Michael Spence, *Protecting Reliance: The Emergent Doctrine of Equitable Estoppel* (Hart Publishing, 1999) pp. 1–2.

436 Koh (n. 345) p. 280.

437 For details on reliance-based remedies, see Ch. 6 s. IV 1 above.

438 Giliker (n. 63) p. 156.

439 Cartwright (n. 1) p. 83.

440 Collins (n. 239) p. 88.

441 Cartwright, case 8, in Cartwright and Hesselink (n. 36) p. 237.

442 *Baird Textile Holdings Ltd v Marks & Spencer plc* (n. 11) [55] (Judge LJ).

443 *Cobbe v Yeoman's Row Management Ltd* (n. 21).

decision to grant relief via proprietary estoppel where one negotiating party had disappointed the expectation that he had given rise to in the other party about the future conclusion of a contract of sale of property,[444] it is doubtful whether the Supreme Court will be willing to develop a doctrine of estoppel, beyond cases of negotiations for the sale of land, to impose liability where such an expectation has been raised and then disappointed by the unconscionable conduct of the defendant, causing detrimental reliance to the claimant.[445] Additionally, some legal scholars disagree with the view that estoppel is the preferable explanation of precontractual liability cases. Dietrich, for instance, argues that the principles underlying the imposition of liability via estoppel are derivative from principles of contract and tort.[446] Giliker counter-argues that the factors[447] which Dietrich finds present in a 'grey area' between contract and tort can alternatively be explained in terms of estoppel, which would have the advantage of providing a single doctrine capable of explaining the case law.[448]

Even if the appropriate case came before the Supreme Court, and it decided to allow promissory estoppel to create a new cause of action, or to merge promissory and proprietary estoppel into a single doctrine of equitable estoppel, or to remove proprietary estoppel's limitation to cases concerning the acquisition of interests in land, other characteristics of these doctrines would still need to be modified in order for them to be able to provide relief in cases of broken negotiations. First, promissory estoppel is designed to grant relief in situations where a 'promise' was made and this notion appears to have a more technical and restricted meaning[449] than in the selected jurisdictions. In the latter, the claimant's expectation of the future conclusion of the negotiated contract emanates from the defendant's 'conduct', a wide notion which includes explicit or implicit promises or behaviour;[450] in general, saying or doing something but also refraining from saying or doing something that should have been said or done, which created or encouraged in the other party an expectation as to the future conclusion of the contract.[451] Perhaps shifting the focus from the finding of a promise or undertaking to the more general notion of the conduct of the defendant (like in proprietary estoppel cases)[452] would be required. However, McFarlane requires an agreement in principle and a promise that such an

444 CA judgment in *Cobbe v Yeoman's Row Management Ltd* (n. 229) [7] (Mummery LJ).
445 Cartwright and Hesselink (n. 36) pp. 464, 468; *Ius Commune* (n. 28) pp. 456–457.
446 Dietrich (n. 296) p. 156 fn. 17.
447 See text to (n. 297) above.
448 Giliker (n. 63) p. 96 fn. 183.
449 See text to (n. 13) above.
450 van Erp (n. 209) p. 70.
451 See Ch. 6 s. II 2 (a) above.
452 e.g. *Crabb v Arun District Council* (n. 34) 189, 198; *Cobbe v Yeoman's Row Management Ltd* (n. 21) [16].

agreement will be honoured for liability to arise under an extended principle of proprietary estoppel.[453] These elements are not required in broken negotiations cases in the selected jurisdictions.[454] Because McFarlane categorises as promised-based[455] the proprietary estoppel cases analysed above,[456] he concludes that, in the absence of a promise, the inducement or encouragement of an expectation cannot support a proprietary estoppel claim.[457] Robertson differs, arguing that proprietary estoppel is based on an induced assumption and not on a promise (the essence of which is a commitment).[458]

Secondly, the reasoning behind promissory and proprietary estoppel does not correspond to the reasoning of precontractual liability: promissory estoppel is about making promises binding in the absence of consideration or, at least, about preventing a person from acting inconsistently with his promise,[459] and proprietary estoppel is about enforcing representations relating to the acquisition of an interest in property,[460] whereas precontractual liability is about compensating losses caused by unjustly disappointing a legitimate expectation, not about forcing a person to conclude a contract.[461] Restricting the remedy to the protection of the reliance interest might take care of this concern, although, in practice, sometimes the expectation interest is protected.[462] Thirdly, legal scholars who advocate for promissory or equitable estoppel to provide a new cause of action in the context of precontractual liability, or for the extension of the principle underlying proprietary estoppel, only refer to cases where services were performed or work was undertaken in anticipation of a contract that does not materialise,[463] which do not correspond to the paradigm case.

In sum, it remains doubtful whether the courts will be willing to develop either promissory estoppel or promise-based proprietary estoppel in a way that would allow them to provide relief in the paradigm case, but it is not inconceivable that they might decide to do so if the appropriate case came before them, and it is kept firmly in mind that the aim is to protect detrimental reliance.

---

453 McFarlane (n. 294) pp. 105, 121; *The Law of Proprietary Estoppel* (n. 17) pp. 71, 73, 88; 'Proprietary Estoppel and Failed Contractual Negotiations' (n. 48) p. 503.

454 See Ch. 6, text to (n. 88) above.

455 See text to (n. 17) above.

456 See this Ch. s. I 1 above.

457 McFarlane (n. 17) pp. 47 ff., 53.

458 Robertson (n. 265) pp. 211, 213.

459 See text following (n. 7) above.

460 See text to (n. 18) above.

461 For details of reliance-based remedies, see Ch. 6 s. IV above.

462 In Australia, see text to (n. 404) above; in England, see text to (n. 423) above.

463 e.g. Giliker (n. 63); Spence (n. 435) pp. 87 ff.; McFarlane (n. 294) p. 120; McFarlane (n. 17) p. 89.

(d) A New Liability Rule

Some American legal scholars have proposed the construction of a new liability rule to deal with situations of precontractual liability. One author has suggested a new cause of action denominated 'opportunistic breach of the bargaining relationship', which excludes normal negotiation costs from the category of compensable precontractual investments.[464] Thus, it would not be useful in the paradigm case because it would not lead to the compensation of the type of losses that are generally compensated in this case.[465] Another author has proposed a new legal default rule that would enforce an implicit commitment of the promisor that he will notify the promisee of changes in his willingness to negotiate or will assume some liability for the promisee's reliance.[466] This liability rule would also not be useful in the paradigm case because it is designed to only compensate sunk costs requested by the promisor.[467] Finally, another legal scholar has proposed a new cause of action in contract for losses that result from reliance on negligent misrepresentations during negotiations, posing as an example *Red Owl* type cases,[468] but recognising that this solution would require significant changes in the law of contract.[469]

Given the difficulties in developing from known grounds of liability a solution to protect the paradigm case,[470] it seems unlikely that (should there be a desire to provide such protection by English law) the chosen tool would be an entirely new cause of action that cannot be classified as falling into one of the existing piecemeal solutions. Nevertheless, the creation of an entirely new cause of action would have the benefit of being free from the requirements of the existing piecemeal solutions that currently block the grant of relief in the paradigm case.

IV. CONCLUSIONS

In English law the paradigm case does not give rise to liability. Focusing on good faith as the basis of liability arising during negotiations bars the vision of a notion that is already present in the solutions currently provided by English law in situations of precontractual liability: 'reliance' in both its dimensions.

464 Shell (n. 295) pp. 276–278.
465 See Ch. 6 s. IV 1 above.
466 Kostritsky (n. 295) pp. 630, 672, 681.
467 Kostritsky (n. 295) p. 682 fn. 254.
468 Mark Gergen, 'Liability for Mistake in Contract Formation' (1990) 64 Southern California Law Review 1, pp. 27, 38–39.
469 Gergen (n. 468) p. 38.
470 See this sub-s. letters (a), (b), (c) above.

Rethinking this liability in terms of reliance rather than good faith could help to shed light on the fact that the reasoning behind the solutions provided by English law is not too different from the reasoning behind the solutions provided by other common law jurisdictions (US and Australia) and by civil law jurisdictions (particularly the selected jurisdictions). Therefore, if change in this area were desired, inspiration could be drawn from the reliance approach to precontractual liability for breaking off negotiations. It remains to be seen whether English courts will be willing to develop this area of the law and, if so, through which means they will do so. The tort of negligence and estoppel (provided that the remedy is confined to reliance damages) seem to be the strongest candidates. Between the two, it is suggested that liability in the paradigm case fits better into the reasoning of negligence (breach of a duty of care) than into the reasoning of estoppel (going back on one's word).

BIBLIOGRAPHY

Abeliuk Manasevich R., *Contrato de Promesa, de Opción y Otros Acuerdos Previos* (3rd edn., Abeledo Perrot, 2012)

——, *Las Obligaciones* vol. II (6th edn., Legal Publishing, 2014)

Alessandri A., Somarriva M. and Vodanovic A., *Tratado de Derecho Civil: Partes Preliminar y General*, vol. I (7th edn., Editorial Jurídica de Chile, 2005)

——, *Tratado de Derecho Civil: Partes Preliminar y General*, vol. II (7th edn., Editorial Jurídica de Chile, 2005)

——, *Tratado de las Obligaciones*, vol. 2 (2nd edn., Editorial Jurídica de Chile, 2004)

Alessandri Rodríguez A., *De la Responsabilidad Extracontractual en el Derecho Civil Chileno (Título 35 del Libro IV del Código Civil)* (Editorial Jurídica de Chile, 2005)

——, *De los Contratos* (reprint 1993, 1st edn., Editorial Jurídica de Chile, 2004)

Allen D., 'England' in Hondius E.H. (ed.), *Precontractual Liability: Reports to the XIIIth Congress International Academy of Comparative Law, Montreal, Canada, 18–24 August 1990* (Kluwer Law, 1991)

Arroyo Amayuelas E., 'A Spanish Perspective on the General Theory of Contract' in Cartwright J. and Whittaker S. (eds.), *The Code Napoléon Rewritten: French Contract Law after the 2016 Reforms* (Hart Publishing, 2017)

Asúa C., 'Negotiating in Good Faith and the Agreement to Negotiate (with Reference to the Decision of the House of Lords in the Case of *Walford v Miles*' (1994) 2 ERPL 274

Asúa González C., *La Culpa in Contrahendo: Tratamiento en el Derecho Alemán y Presencia en Otros Ordenamientos* (Universidad del País Vasco, 1989)

—— and Hualde Sánchez J.J., 'Codificación de la *Culpa in Contrahendo* en el Derecho Alemán' in Cabanillas Sánchez A. and others (eds.), *Estudios Jurídicos en Homenaje al Profesor Luis Díez-Picazo*, vol. II (Thomson Civitas, 2003)

Aubry H., *L'influence du Droit Communautaire sur le Droit Français des Contrats* (PUAM, 2002)

Banakas S., 'Liability for Contractual Negotiations in English Law: Looking for the Litmus Test' (2009) 1 InDret 1

Barcia Lehmann R., 'La Influencia del *Code Civil* y del Derecho Alemán en el Sistema Patrimonial Chileno: Sistema de Derechos Reales y Personales' in Varas Braun J.A. and others (eds.), *Estudios de Derecho Civil: Jornadas Nacionales de Derecho Civil 2005–2009*, vol. I (Abeledo Perrot Legal Publishing Chile, 2011)

Barrientos M., 'Culpa *In Contrahendo* en Mutuo Hipotecario' (2012) 39 Revista Chilena de Derecho 829

——, 'Nuevos Deberes Precontractuales de Información en los Certificados de Cobertura Provisorio, Definitivo y la Propuesta del Contrato de Seguro' (2015) 22 Revista de Derecho 65

Barrientos Zamorano M., *Daños y Deberes en las Tratativas Preliminares de un Contrato* (2nd edn., Legal Publishing, 2010)

——, 'Los Tratos Preliminares en la Relación Precontractual' (2008) 14 Revista de Derecho de la Empresa 9
Barros Bourie E., 'Límites de los Derechos Subjetivos Privados. Introducción a la Doctrina del Abuso de Derecho' (1999) 7 Revista Derecho y Humanidades 11
——, *Tratado de Responsabilidad Extracontractual* (Editorial Jurídica de Chile, 2006)
Barros E., 'Derecho y Moral: Consideraciones A Propósito de la Teoría de los Delitos Económicos' (1983) 10 Estudios Públicos 1
Beale H., 'Commentary on "Good Faith and Fairness in Failed Contract Negotiations"' (1994) 8 Journal of Contract Law 120
—— and others, *Ius Commune Casebooks for the Common Law of Europe: Cases, Materials and Text on Contract Law* (3rd edn., Hart, 2019)
—— and others, *Ius Commune Casebooks for the Common Law of Europe: Cases, Materials and Text on Contract Law* (2nd edn., Hart, 2010)
—— and others, *Ius Commune Casebooks for the Common Law of Europe: Cases, Materials and Text on Contract Law* (Hart, 2002)
Beale H.G. (ed.), *Chitty on Contracts*, vol. I (33rd edn., Sweet & Maxwell/Thomson Reuters, 2018)
Beatson J., Burrows A. and Cartwright J., *Anson's Law of Contract* (30th edn., OUP, 2016)
Bell J., Boyron S. and Whittaker S., *Principles of French Law* (2nd edn., OUP, 2008)
Boetsch Gillet C., *La Buena Fe Contractual* (Ediciones Universidad Católica de Chile, 2015)
Borghetti J.-S., '*The Definition of* la faute *in the* Avant-projet de réforme' in Cartwright J., Vogenauer S. and Whittaker S. (eds.), *Reforming the French Law of Obligations: Comparative Reflections on the Avant-projet de réforme du droit des obligations et de la prescription ('the Avant-projet Catala')* (Hart Publishing, 2009)
Bridge M.G., 'Does Anglo-Canadian Contract Law Need a Doctrine of Good Faith?' (1984) 9 Canadian Business Law Journal 385
Brownsword R., *Contract Law: Themes for the Twenty-First Century* (2nd edn., OUP, 2006)
——, 'Two Concepts of Good Faith' (1994) 7 Journal of Contract Law 197
Buckley R., 'Walford v Miles: False Certainty About Uncertainty – An Australian Perspective' (1993) 6 Journal of Contract Law 58
Bussani M. and Mattei U., 'The Common Core Approach to European Private Law' (1997–1998) 3 ColumJEurL 339
Canaris C.-W., 'Ansprüche wegen "positiver Vertragsverletzung" und "Schutzwirkung für Dritte" bei nichtigen Verträgen' [1965] JZ 475
——, *Die Vertrauenshaftung im deutschen Privatrecht* (1971)
Cañas O'Rian R., 'De la Culpa Civil' (Licenciado en la Facultad de Leyes thesis, Universidad de Chile, 1904)
Carter J., 'Contract, Restitution and Promissory Estoppel' (1989) 12 UNSWLJ 30
—— and Furmston M., 'Good Faith and Fairness in the Negotiation of Contracts: Parts I and II' (1994) 8 Journal of Contract Law 1 and 93
Carter J.W., *Contract Law in Australia* (6th edn., LexisNexis Butterworths, 2013)
Cartwright J., '"Commercial" Contracts: Do They Exist in English Law?' in Carvajal L. and Toso Á. (eds.), *Estudios de Derecho Comercial: Octavas Jornadas Chilenas de Derecho Comercial* (Thomson Reuters, 2018)

——, *Contract Law: An Introduction to the English Law of Contract for the Civil Lawyer* (3rd edn., Hart, 2016)
——, 'Cour de Cass, 26.11.2003 – "*Perte de Chance*" (Expectation Interest) and Liability of a Third Person in Case of Breaking Off Negotiations: English Case Note' (2005) 13 ERPL 455
——, *The English Law of Contract: Time for Review?* (EM Meijers Instituut, 2009)
——, 'The English Law of Contract: Time for Review?' (2009) 17 ERPL 155
——, *Formation and Variation of Contracts* (2nd edn., Sweet & Maxwell, 2018)
——, 'Liability in Negligence: New Directions or Old?' (1997) 13 ConstLJ 157
——, *Misrepresentation, Mistake and Non-Disclosure* (4th edn., Sweet & Maxwell, 2016)
——, 'Negotiation and Renegotiation: An English Perspective' in Cartwright J., Vogenauer S. and Whittaker S. (eds.), *Reforming the French Law of Obligations: Comparative Reflections on the Avant-projet de réforme du droit des obligations et de la prescription ('the Avant-projet Catala')* (Hart Publishing, 2009)
——, 'Protecting Legitimate Expectations and Estoppel: English Law' in Fauvarque-Cosson B. (ed.), *La Confiance Légitime et L'Estoppel*, vol. 4 (Société de Législation Comparée, 2007)
——, Fauvarque-Cosson B. and Whittaker S., 'Appendix' in Cartwright J. and Whittaker S. (eds.), *The Code Napoléon Rewritten: French Contract Law after the 2016 Reforms* (Hart Publishing, 2017)
—— and Hesselink M. (eds.), *Precontractual Liability in European Private Law* (CUP, 2008)
——, Vogenauer S. and Whittaker S. (eds.), *Reforming the French Law of Obligations: Comparative Reflections on the Avant-projet de réforme du droit des obligations et de la prescription ('the Avant-projet Catala')* (Hart Publishing, 2009)
Carvajal P.-I., 'Prólogo' in Barrientos Zamorano M., *Daños y Deberes en las Tratativas Preliminares de un Contrato* (2nd edn., Legal Publishing, 2010)
Castronovo C., 'Precontractual Liability' in Lebre de Freitas J. and others (eds.), *Estudos em Homenagem ao Professor Doutor Carlos Ferreira de Almeida*, vol. II (Almedina, 2011)
Cauchi G.F., 'The Protection of the Reliance Interest and Anticipated Contracts Which Fail to Materialize' (1981) 19 UWOLRev 237
Celedón R. and Silberman P., *Responsabilidad Precontractual por Ruptura de Negociaciones Contractuales* (Editorial Jurídica de Chile, 2010)
Chabas F., *Discursos y Conferencias sobre Responsabilidad Civil* (Publicaciones Programa de Doctorado en Derecho, Facultad de Derecho, Universidad de Chile, 2014)
Chauvel P., 'Note on Cass com 7 April 1998' D 1999, 514
——, 'Note on Cass com 7 January 1997 and 22 April 1997' D 1998 Jur 45
Claro Solar L., *Explicaciones de Derecho Civil Chileno y Comparado*, vol. XI De las Obligaciones II (Editorial Jurídica de Chile, 1992)
——, *Explicaciones de Derecho Civil Chileno y Comparado*, vol. XI De las Obligaciones II (Imprenta Nascimento, 1937)
Code de Commerce, 111th ed., 2016, Dalloz
Cohen N., 'Pre-Contractual Duties: Two Freedoms and the Contract to Negotiate' in Beatson J. and Friedmann D. (eds.), *Good Faith and Fault in Contract Law* (Clarendon Press, 1995)
Collins H., *The Law of Contract* (4th edn., LexisNexis, 2003)
Colombo S., 'The Implications of Good Faith in Culpa in Contrahendo' (JSD thesis, Yale Law School, 1990)

Corral H., *Lecciones de Responsabilidad Civil Extracontractual* (2nd edn., Legal Publishing, 2013)
Cour de cassation, *Rapport Annuel 2006* (La Documentation Française, 2006)
Dagorne-Labbé Y., 'Note on Cass com 11 July 2000' PA 2001 no 57 p 19
Danis-Fatôme A., *Apparence et Contrat* (LGDJ, 2004)
Darbellay J., *Théorie Générale de L'Illicéité en Droit Civil et en Droit Pénal* (Éditions Universitaires, 1955)
de Ángel Yagüez R., *Tratado de Responsabilidad Civil* (1993)
de Coninck B., 'Le Droit Commun de la Rupture des Négociations Précontractuelles' in Fontaine M. (ed.), *Le Processus de Formation du Contrat: Contributions Comparatives et Interdisciplinaires à L'Harmonisation du Droit Européen* (Bruylant LGDJ, 2002)
de la Maza I., 'El Retiro Unilateral como un Caso de Responsabilidad Precontractual' in de la Maza I. (ed.), *Cuadernos de Análisis Jurídicos, Colección Derecho Privado III: Temas de Contratos* (Ediciones Universidad Diego Portales, 2006)
—— and Pizarro C., *Responsabilidad Civil: Casos Prácticos* (5th edn., Abeledo Perrot, 2010)
de Meulenaere O., 'De la culpa in contrahendo ou des dommages-intérêts dans les conventions nulles ou imparfaites' (1893) II Oeuvres choisies 1
Deakin S., Johnston A. and Markesinis B., *Markesinis and Deakin's Tort Law* (7th edn., OUP, 2013)
Dejean de la Bâtie N., 'Responsabilité Délictuelle' in Ponsard A. and Fadlallah I. (eds.), *Aubry et Rau: Droit Civil Français*, vol. VI-2 (8th edn., Librairies Techniques, 1989)
Deshayes O., 'La Rupture des Pourparlers' (2008) 203 PA 4
——, 'Le Dommage Précontractuel' (2004) 2 RTDcom 187
——, 'Note on Cass civ 28 June 2006' JCP 2006 II 10130
——, 'Note on Cass com 18 September 2012 and Cass civ 19 September 2012' Revue des Contrats 2013 no 1 p 98
Dietrich J., 'Classifying Precontractual Liability: A Comparative Analysis' (2001) 21 Legal Studies 153
Domínguez Águila R., 'Comentarios de Jurisprudencia 1' (2005) 217–218 Revista de Derecho Universidad de Concepción 305
——, 'La Influencia de la Doctrina Francesa en el Derecho Chileno' in Pizarro Wilson C. and Tapia Rodríguez M. (eds.), *Cuadernos de Análisis Jurídicos, Colección Derecho Privado II: De la Codificación a la Descodificación* (Ediciones Universidad Diego Portales, 2005)
——, *Teoría General del Negocio Jurídico* (2nd edn., Editorial Jurídica de Chile, 2013)
Domínguez Benavente R., Domínguez Águila R. and Domínguez Hidalgo C., 'Comentarios de Jurisprudencia 1' (1996) 199 Revista de Derecho Universidad de Concepción 179
——, Domínguez Águila R. and Domínguez Hidalgo C., 'Comentarios de Jurisprudencia 3' (1998) 204 Revista de Derecho Universidad de Concepción 187
——, 'Comentarios de Jurisprudencia 4' (1996) 200 Revista de Derecho Universidad de Concepción 192
Dondero B., 'La Réforme du Droit des Contrats: Ordonnance n° 2016-131 du 10 Février 2016' (2016) 19 JCP éd E 1283
Ducci C., *Derecho Civil: Parte General* (4th edn., Editorial Jurídica de Chile, 2005)
Durry G., 'Note on Cass civ 3 October 1972 and Cass civ 12 April 1976' RTDciv 1977, 127
——, 'Note on Cass com 20 March 1972' RTDciv 1972, 779

Ebke W.F., 'Federal Republic of Germany' in ICC (ed.), *Formation of Contracts and Precontractual Liability* (ICC Publishing, 1990)

—— and Steinhauer B.M., 'The Doctrine of Good Faith in German Contract Law' in Beatson J. and Friedmann D. (eds.), *Good Faith and Fault in Contract Law* (Clarendon Press, 1995)

Edelman J., 'Liability in Unjust Enrichment where a Contract Fails to Materialize' in Burrows A. and Peel E. (eds.), *Contract Formation and Parties* (OUP, 2010)

Eiler S., *De la Formación del Consentimiento en los Contratos* (Editorial Nascimento, 1935)

Engel C. and Schmelzer A., 'Committing the English and the Continental Way: An Experiment' (2017) Preprints of the Max Planck Institute for Research on Collective Goods <https://ssrn.com/abstract=3024525> accessed 18 April 2019

Eyzaguirre C. and Rodríguez J., 'Expansión y Límites de la Buena Fe Objetiva – A Propósito del "Proyecto de Principios Latinoamericanos de Derecho de los Contratos"' (2013) 21 Revista Chilena de Derecho Privado 137

Fabre-Magnan M., *Droit des Obligations*, vol. I: *Contrat et Engagement Unilatéral* (4th edn., PUF, 2016)

Facco J.H., '*Good Faith* en el Ejercicio de Poderes Contractuales Discrecionales (¿Un Punto de Contacto entre *Common Law* y *Civil Law*?)' (2012) 22 Revista de Derecho Privado 149

Fages B., 'Existe-t-il un *Vertrauensschutz* en Droit Français des Contrats?' in Fauvarque-Cosson B. and Jung P. (eds.), *La Confiance: 11èmes Journées Bilatérales Franco-allemandes, Paris, 22 et 23 Novembre 2012* (Société de Législation Comparée, 2013)

——, 'Note on Cass civ 7 January 2009' RTDciv 2009, 113

Faggella G., 'Dei Periodi Precontrattuali e della loro Vera ed Esatta Costruzione Scientifica' in *Studi Giuridici in Onore di Carlo Fadda*, vol. III (1906)

Farnsworth E.A., *Contracts* (4th edn., Aspen, 2004)

——, 'Duties of Good Faith and Fair Dealing under the UNIDROIT Principles, Relevant International Conventions, and National Laws' (1995) 3 Tulane Journal of International and Comparative Law 47

——, *Farnsworth on Contracts*, vol. 1 (3rd edn., Aspen, 2004)

——, 'Precontractual Liability and Preliminary Agreements: Fair Dealing and Failed Negotiations' (1987) 87 ColumLRev 217

Faust F. and Wiese V., 'Protecting Legitimate Expectations The German Perspective' in Fauvarque-Cosson B. (ed.), *La Confiance Légitime et L'Estoppel*, vol. 4 (Societé de Législation Comparée, 2007)

Fauvarque-Cosson B., 'Negotiation and Renegotiation: A French Perspective' in Cartwright J., Vogenauer S. and Whittaker S. (eds.), *Reforming the French Law of Obligations, Comparative Reflections on the Avant-projet de réforme du droit des obligations et de la prescription ('the Avant-projet Catala')* (Hart Publishing, 2009)

—— and Mazeaud D. (eds.), *European Contract Law, Materials for a Common Frame of Reference: Terminology, Guiding Principles, Model Rules* (Sellier, 2008)

Feldmann C. and Löwisch M., '§311' in Mansel H-P (ed.), *J von Staudingers Kommentar zum Bürgerlichen Gesetzbuch*, vol. Buch 2: Recht der Schuldverhältnisse (Sellier, 2012)

Flume W., *Allgemeiner Teil des Bürgerlichen Rechts II* (4th edn., 1992)

Foster N. and Sule S., *German Legal System and Laws* (4th edn., OUP, 2010)

Fuentes de la Sotta A., 'La Responsabilidad por el Hecho de Otro en Materia Contractual' (Licenciado en Ciencias Jurídicas thesis, Universidad de Chile, 1938)
Fueyo Laneri F., *Instituciones de Derecho Civil Moderno* (Editorial Jurídica de Chile, 1990)
Fuller L., *The Morality of Law* (Rev. edn., Yale University Press, 1969)
Fuller L.L. and Perdue W.R., 'The Reliance Interest in Contract Damages: 1' (1936) 46 Yale LJ 52
Furmston M. and Tolhurst G., *Contract Formation: Law and Practice* (OUP, 2010)
García Rubio M.P. and Otero Crespo M., 'La Responsabilidad Precontractual en el Derecho Contractual Europeo' (2010) 2 InDret Revista para el Análisis del Derecho 1
Garofalo A.M., 'Il ruolo dell'affidamento nella responsabilità precontrattuale' (2018) 11 Teoria e Storia del Diritto Privato <http://www.teoriaestoriadeldirittoprivato.com/media/rivista/2018/contributi/2018_Contributi_Garofalo.pdf> accessed 31 January 2019
Gergen M., 'Liability for Mistake in Contract Formation' (1990) 64 Southern California Law Review 1
Ghestin J., *Traité de Droit Civil: La Formation du Contrat*, vol. I Le contrat – Le Consentement (4th edn., LGDJ, 2013)
Giliker P., *Pre-contractual Liability in English and French Law* (Kluwer Law International, 2002)
——, 'A Role for Tort in Pre-Contractual Negotiations? An Examination of English, French, and Canadian Law' (2003) 52 ICLQ 969
Gómez Balmaceda R. and Rosende Álvarez H., 'Comentario Crítico' in Fundación Fernando Fueyo Laneri (ed.), *Estudios sobre Reformas al Código Civil y Código de Comercio: Título Preliminar, Teoría de la Imprevisión, Contratos Preparatorios* (Editorial Jurídica de Chile, 2000)
Goode R., 'The Codification of Commercial Law' (1988) 14 Monash University Law Review 135
——, *The Concept of 'Good Faith' in English Law* (Centro di studi e ricerche di diritto comparato e straniero, 1992)
——, Kronke H. and McKendrick E. (eds.), *Transnational Commercial Law: Texts, Cases and Materials* (2nd edn., OUP, 2015)
—— and McKendrick E. (ed.), *Goode on Commercial Law* (5th edn., Penguin Books, 2016)
Goode R.M., 'England' in ICC (ed.), *Formation of Contracts and Precontractual Liability* (ICC Publishing, 1990)
Gordley J. and von Mehren A., *An Introduction to the Comparative Study of Private Law: Readings, Cases, Materials* (CUP, 2006)
Gordon E., 'Out With the Old, In With the Older? *Hedley Byrne* Reliance Takes Centre Stage' (2018) 77 Cambridge Law Journal 251
Gutteridge H.C., *Comparative Law: An Introduction to the Comparative Method of Legal Study & Research* (2nd edn., Cambridge University Press, 1949)
Guzmán Brito A., *Andrés Bello Codificador: Historia de la Fijación y Codificación del Derecho Civil en Chile* vol. I (Ediciones de la Universidad de Chile, 1982)
Häcker B., '*La Troisième Jeunesse du Code Civil*: A German Lawyer Looks at the Reform of French Contract Law' in Cartwright J. and Whittaker S. (eds.), *The Code Napoléon Rewritten: French Contract Law after the 2016 Reforms* (Hart Publishing, 2017)

Hedley S., 'Restitution: Contract's Twin?' in Rose F.D. (ed.), *Failure of Contracts: Contractual, Restitutionary and Proprietary Consequences* (Hart Publishing, 1997)

——, 'Work Done in Anticipation of a Contract Which Does Not Materialise: A Response' in Cornish W.R. and others (eds.), *Restitution, Past, Present and Future: Essays in Honour of Gareth Jones* (Hart Publishing, 1998)

Herresthal C., '10 Years after the Reform of the Law of Obligations in Germany – The Position of the Law of Obligations in German Law' in Schulze R. and Zoll F. (eds.), *The Law of Obligations in Europe: A New Wave of Codifications* (Sellier, 2013)

Hertel C., '§125' in *Staudinger Kommentar zum BGB* (2004)

Hesselink M.W., 'The Concept of Good Faith' in Hartkamp A.S. and others (eds.), *Towards a European Civil Code* (4th edn., Kluwer Law International, 2011)

Holman, Fenwick, Willan, 'Global Trends in International Trade and the Laws that Underpin Them: Identifying and Analysing the Key Trends and the Legal Issues that Need to be Resolved to Support the Further Development of International Trade' (2015) <http://www.hfw.com/HFW-Global-trends-in-international-trade-February-2015> accessed 31 January 2019

Hondius E.H., 'General Report' in Hondius E.H. (ed.), *Precontractual Liability: Reports to the XIIIth Congress International Academy of Comparative Law, Montreal, Canada, 18–24 August 1990* (Kluwer Law, 1991)

Houtcieff D., *Le Principe de Cohérence en Matière Contractuelle*, vol. 2 (PUAM, 2001)

Huber P., 'Contract Formation and Non-Performance in German Law' in Schulze R. and Zoll F. (eds.), *The Law of Obligations in Europe: A New Wave of Codifications* (Sellier, 2013)

Jaluzot B., *La Bonne Foi dans les Contrats: Étude Comparative des Droit Français, Allemand et Japonais* (Dalloz, 2001)

Jones G., 'Claims Arising Out of Anticipated Contracts Which Do Not Materialize' (1980) 18 UWOLRev 447

Jourdain P., 'Rapport Français' in Association Henri Capitant (ed.), *La Bonne Foi: (Journées Louisianaises) Tome XLIII 1992* (Litec, 1994)

Jung P., 'La Protection de la Confiance en Droit Allemand des Contrats' in Fauvarque-Cosson B. and Jung P. (eds.), *La Confiance: 11èmes Journées Bilatérales Franco-allemandes, Paris, 22 et 23 Novembre 2012* (Société de Législation Comparée, 2013)

Kessler F. and Fine E., 'Culpa in Contrahendo, Bargaining in Good Faith, and Freedom of Contract: A Comparative Study' (1964) 77 HarvLRev 401

Kleinheisterkamp J., 'Latin America, Influence of European Private Law' in Basedow J. and others (eds.), *The Max Planck Encyclopedia of European Private Law*, vol. II (OUP, 2012)

Koh K., 'A Principled Response to Pre-contractual Remuneration' (2012) 28 ConstLJ 277

Kostritsky J.P., 'Bargaining with Uncertainty, Moral Hazard, and Sunk Costs: A Default Rule for Precontractual Negotiations' (1993) 44 Hastings Law Journal 621

Kötz H., *European Contract Law* (Gill Mertens and Tony Weir tr., 2nd edn., OUP, 2017)

——, 'Legal Families' in Basedow J. and others (eds.), *The Max Planck Encyclopedia of European Private Law*, vol. II (OUP, 2012)

——, 'Towards a European Civil Code: The Duty of Good Faith' in Cane P. and Stapleton J. (eds.), *The Law of Obligations: Essays in Celebration of John Fleming* (Clarendon Press, 1998)

Lando O. and Beale H. (eds.), *Principles of European Contract Law: Parts I and II Combined and Revised* (Kluwer Law International, 2000)

Larenz K., 'Bemerkungen zur Haftung für "culpa in contrahendo"' in *Festschrift für Ballerstedt* (1975)

——, *Lehrbuch des Schuldrechts*, vol. I Allgemeiner Teil (13th edn., 1982)

—— and Wolf M., *Allgemeiner Teil des Bürgerlichen Rechts* (9th edn., 2004)

——, *Allgemeiner Teil des Bürgerlichen Rechts* (8th edn., 1997)

Larraín Ríos H., *Lecciones de Derecho Civil* (Editorial Jurídica de Chile, 1994)

Le Coq J.-F., 'The Stakes and Objectives of the Reforms of Contract Law, General Regime and Proof of Obligations' (2017) 6 IBLJ 515

Lecourt A., 'Note on CA Agen 21 August 2002' JCP 2003 II 10162

Legrand P., 'Pre-contractual Disclosure and Information: English and French Law Compared' (1986) 6 Oxford Journal of Legal Studies 322

León Hurtado A., *La Voluntad y la Capacidad en los Actos Jurídicos* (4th edn., Editorial Jurídica de Chile, 1991)

Leveneur L., 'Présentation Générale de la Réforme du Droit des Contrats, du Régime Général et de la Preuve des Obligations' (2016) 5 CCC

Lévy E., *La Vision Socialiste du Droit* (Marcel Giard, 1926)

——, *Les Fondements du Droit* (Librairie Félix Alcan, 1933)

Loke A., 'Insights from Comparing the Contract Laws of Asia on Formation and Third Party Beneficiaries' in Chen-Wishart M., Loke A. and Vogenauer S. (eds.), *Formation and Third Party Beneficiaries* (OUP, 2018)

López Santa María J. and Elorriaga De Bonis F., *Los Contratos: Parte General* (6th edn., Legal Publishing Chile, 2017)

Lord Neuberger of Abbotsbury, 'The Stuffing of Minerva's Owl? Taxonomy and Taxidermy in Equity' [2009] CLJ 537

Lorenz W., 'Germany' in Hondius E.H. (ed.), *Precontractual Liability: Reports to the XIIIth Congress International Academy of Comparative Law, Montreal, Canada, 18-24 August 1990* (Kluwer Law, 1991)

Lücke H., 'Good Faith and Contractual Performance' in Finn P. (ed.), *Essays on Contract* (Law Book Company Limited, 1987)

Mackaay E., 'Good Faith in Civil Law Systems: A Legal-Economic Analysis' (2012) 18 Revista Chilena de Derecho Privado 149

——, 'Good Faith in Civil Law Systems: A Legal-Economic Analysis' (2011) 74 Cirano-Scientific Series 1

Mainguy D., 'Contract Negotiation and Formation' (2017) 6 International Business Law Journal 563

Malaurie P., Aynès L. and Stoffel-Munck P., *Droit des Obligations* (8th edn., LGDJ, 2016)

Mankowski P. and Müller M., 'Formation' in Leible S. and Lehmann M. (eds.), *European Contract Law and German Law* (Kluwer Law International, 2014)

Manzanares A., 'La Responsabilidad Precontractual en la Hipótesis de Ruptura Injustificada de las Negociaciones Preliminares' (1984) 37 Anuario de Derecho Civil 687

Marín Narros, H., *Estudio de los Principales Acuerdos Precontractuales con Modelos en Inglés y en Español* (Bosch Editor, 2012).

Markesinis B., Lorenz W. and Dannemann G., *The German Law of Obligations, Volume I The Law of Contracts and Restitution: A Comparative Introduction* (Clarendon Press, 1997)

——, Unberath H. and Johnston A., *The German Law of Contract: A Comparative Treatise* (2nd edn., Hart, 2006)
Markesinis B.S. and Unberath H., *The German Law of Torts: A Comparative Treatise* (4th edn., Hart Publishing, 2002)
Mazeaud D., 'La Confiance Légitime et L'Estoppel: Rapport Français' in Fauvarque-Cosson B (ed.), *La Confiance Légitime et L'Estoppel*, vol. 4 (Societé de Législation Comparée, 2007)
Mazeaud H., Mazeaud L. and Tunc A., *Traité Théorique et Pratique de la Responsabilité Civile Délictuelle et Contractuelle*, vol. I (6th edn., Éditions Montchrestien, 1965)
McFarlane B., *The Law of Proprietary Estoppel* (OUP, 2014)
——, 'Proprietary Estoppel and Failed Contractual Negotiations' [2005] Conveyancer and Property Lawyer 501
——, 'The Protection of Pre-Contractual Reliance: A Way Forward?' (2010) 10 OUCLJ 95
—— and Robertson A., 'The Death of Proprietary Estoppel' [2008] LMCLQ 449
McKendrick E., *Contract Law* (12th edn., Palgrave, 2017)
——, *Contract Law: Text, Cases, and Materials* (8th edn., OUP, 2018)
——, 'Good Faith: A Matter of Principle?' in Forte A. (ed.), *Good Faith in Contract and Property Law* (Hart Publishing, 1999)
——, 'The Meaning of "Good Faith"' in Andenas M. and others (eds.), *Liber Amicorum Guido Alpa: Private Law Beyond the National Systems* (British Institute of International and Comparative Law, 2007)
——, 'Work Done in Anticipation of a Contract Which Does Not Materialise' in Cornish W.R. and others (eds.), *Restitution, Past, Present and Future: Essays in Honour of Gareth Jones* (Hart Publishing, 1998)
Medicus D., 'Verschulden bei Vertragsverhandlungen' in Bundesminister der Justiz (ed.), *Gutachten und Vorschläge zur Überarbeitung des Schuldrechts I* (Haymanns, 1981)
Mestre J., RTDciv 1989, 739
——, RTDciv 1988, 340
——, 'Note on CA Paris 13 December 1984' RTDciv 1986, 97
——, 'Note on Cass com 22 April 1997' RTDciv 1997, 651
Mills A. and Loveridge R., 'The Uncertain Future of *Walford v Miles*' [2011] LMCLQ 528
Ministère de la Justice, *Rapport au Président de la République relatif à l'ordonnance n° 2016-131 du 10 février 2016 portant réforme du droit des contrats, du régime général et de la preuve des obligations* (Journal Officiel, 2016)
Mitchell P., 'Hedley Byrne & Co Ltd v Heller & Partners Ltd (1963)' in Mitchell C. and Mitchell P. (eds.), *Landmark Cases in the Law of Tort* (Hart Publishing, 2010)
Momberg R. and Vogenauer S. (eds.), *The Future of Contract Law in Latin America: The Principles of Latin American Contract Law* (Hart Publishing, 2017)
—— and Vogenauer S., 'The Principles of Latin American Contract Law: Text, Translation, and Introduction' (2018) 23 Uniform Law Review 144
Monsalve Caballero V., 'El Comportamiento del Contratante como Determinante para la Calificación de la Ruptura Injustificada de las Negociaciones: Visión desde el Derecho Europeo' (2009) 119 Vniversitas 251
——, 'La Buena Fe como Fundamento de los Deberes Precontractuales de Conducta: Una Doctrina Europea en Construcción' (2008) 30 Revista de Derecho 30

——, 'La Ruptura Injustificada de los Tratos Preliminares' (Doctoral Thesis, Universidad de Salamanca, 2008)
Mordechai Rabello A., 'The Theory Concerning Culpa in Contrahendo Precontractual Liability: From Roman Law to the German Legal System – A Hundred Years After the Death of Jhering' in Mordechai Rabello A. (ed.), *European Legal Traditions and Israel* (Harry and Michael Sacher Institute for Legislative Research and Comparative Law, Hebrew University of Jerusalem, 1994)
Moura Vicente D., *Da Responsabilidade Pré-Contratual em Direito Internacional Privado* (Almedina, 2001)
Muir-Watt H., 'Les Pourparlers: De la Confiance Trompée à la Relation de Confiance' in Rémy-Corlay P. and Fenouillet D. (eds.), *Les Concepts Contractuels Français à L'heure des Principes du Droit Européen des Contrats* (Dalloz, 2003)
Nicholas B., *The French Law of Contract* (2nd edn., Clarendon, 1992)
——, 'The Pre-contractual Obligation to Disclose Information: English Report' in Donald Harris and Denis Tallon (eds.), *Contract Law Today: Anglo-French Comparisons* (Oxford University Press, 1989)
Nirk R., 'Culpa in Contrahendo – Eine geglückte richterliche Rechtsfortbildung – Quo Vadis?' in Hefermehl (ed.), *Festschrift Philipp Möhring* (1975)
Nolan D., 'Following in their Footsteps: Equitable Estoppel in Australia and the United States' (2000) 11 KCLJ 202
Peel E., 'Agreements to Negotiate in Good Faith' in Burrows A. and Peel E. (eds.), *Contract Formation and Parties* (OUP, 2010)
—— and Treitel G., *The Law of Contract* (14th edn., Sweet & Maxwell, 2015)
Peñailillo Arévalo D., *Obligaciones: Teoría General y Clasificaciones, La Resolución por Incumplimiento* (Editorial Jurídica de Chile, 2003)
Planiol M., *Traité Élémentaire de Droit Civil*, vol. II (3rd edn., LGDJ, 1949)
Prado Puga A., 'Sobre la Responsabilidad Civil Precontractual' (2015) 32 Revista Actualidad Jurídica 167
Puech M., *L'Illicéité dans la Responsabilité Civile Extracontractuelle* (LGDJ, 1973)
Puelma Accorsi Á., 'Ponencia Principal' in Fundación Fernando Fueyo Laneri (ed.), *Estudios sobre Reformas al Código Civil y Código de Comercio: Título Preliminar, Teoría de la Imprevisión, Contratos Preparatorios* (Editorial Jurídica de Chile, 2000)
Quiñones Escámez A., 'Buena Fe y Lealtad Contractual' in Sánchez Lorenzo S. (ed.), *Derecho Contractual Comparado: Una Perspectiva Europea y Transnacional* (Thomson Reuters, 2009)
Radley-Gardner O. and others, *Fundamental Texts on European Private Law* (Hart, 2003)
Ramos R., *De la Responsabilidad Extracontractual* (4th edn., Legal Publishing, 2008)
Research Group on the Existing EC Private Law (Acquis Group), *Principles of the Existing EC Contract Law (Acquis Principles): Contract II General Provisions, Delivery of Goods, Package Travel and Payment Services* (Sellier, 2009)
Risueño M., *De las Obligaciones Precontractuales* (Soc. Imp. y Lito. Universo, 1933)
Robertson A., 'Estoppels and Rights-Creating Events: Beyond Wrongs and Promises' in Neyers J.W., Bronaugh R. and Pitel S.G.A. (eds.), *Exploring Contract Law* (Hart Publishing, 2009)
Rodríguez Grez P., *Nuevas Tendencias de la Responsabilidad* (Abeledo Perrot, 2011)
Rosende Álvarez H., *Algunas Consideraciones sobre la Responsabilidad Precontractual* (Ediciones Universitarias de Valparaíso, 1979)

Rosende H., 'La Responsabilidad Precontractual en la Formación del Consentimiento en los Contratos Reales y Solemnes' in Fundación Fueyo (ed.), *Instituciones Modernas de Derecho Civil: Homenaje al Profesor Fernando Fueyo Laneri* (Editorial Jurídica ConoSur, 1996)
Rosher P., 'French Contract Law Reform' (2016) 17 Business Law International 59
Rossel M., 'La Indemnización de Perjuicios en la Formación del Consentimiento y en el Contrato de Transporte Terrestre' (Licenciado en Ciencias Jurídicas y Sociales thesis, Universidad de Chile, 1966)
Rowan S., 'The New French Law of Contract' (2017) 66 ICLQ 805
Saavedra F.J., 'El Principio General de la Buena Fe' in Fundación Fueyo (ed.), *Instituciones Modernas de Derecho Civil: Homenaje al Profesor Fernando Fueyo Laneri* (Editorial Jurídica ConoSur, 1996)
Saavedra Galleguillos F.J., *Teoría del Consentimiento* (Editorial Jurídica ConoSur, 1994)
Saintourens B., 'Note on Cass com 11 July 2000' Bull Joly 2000 no 288
Saleilles R., 'De la Responsabilidad Precontractual a propósito de un Estudio sobre la Materia' (1908) V Revista de Derecho y Jurisprudencia 127
——, 'De la Responsabilité Précontractuelle à propos d'une Étude Nouvelle sur la Matière' (1907) 6 RTDCiv 697
Salgado Ramírez C., 'Breve Introducción a la Responsabilidad Precontractual en la Teoría de Rudolf von Jhering' in González de Cancino E., Cortés Moncayo É. and Navia Arroyo F. (eds.), *Estudios de Derecho Civil en Memoria de Fernando Hinestrosa*, vol. I (Universidad Externado de Colombia, 2014)
San Martín L., 'Responsabilidad Precontractual por Ruptura Injustificada de Negociaciones: *"Jiménez Mira, David Alejandro con Armijo Cerda, Antonio de los Ángeles" Corte Suprema, Rol 1872/2010*' (2013) 40 Revista Chilena de Derecho 317
Schmidt J., 'L'Évolution de la Responsabilité Précontractuelle en Droit Français' in Weick G. (ed.), *Entwicklung des Deliktsrechts in rechtsvergleichender Sicht* (Metzner, 1987)
——, 'La Période Précontractuelle en Droit Français' (1990) 42 Revue Internationale de Droit Comparé 545
——, 'La Sanction de la Faute Précontractuelle' (1974) 72 RTDciv 46
——, *Négociation et Conclusion de Contrats* (Dalloz, 1982)
Schmidt J.P., 'Sentencias famosas: Alemania. Sobre el caso de los "rollos de linóleo"' (2013) 24 Revista de Derecho Privado Universidad Externado de Colombia 329
Schmidt-Szalewski J., 'France' in ICC (ed.), *Formation of Contracts and Precontractual Liability* (ICC Publishing, 1990)
——, 'France' in Hondius E.H. (ed.), *Precontractual Liability: Reports to the XIIIth Congress International Academy of Comparative Law, Montreal, Canada, 18–24 August 1990* (Kluwer Law, 1991)
——, 'Note on Cass com 7 April 1998' JCP éd E 1999, 579
Schmidt Hott C. and Doyharçabal Casse S., 'Chile' in Alterini A.A. and López Cabana R. (eds.), *Enciclopedia de la Responsabilidad Civil*, vol. II (Abeledo Perrot, 1998)
Schulze R. (ed.) *Common European Sales Law (CESL): Commentary* (CH Beck, Hart, 2012)
—— and Zoll F., *European Contract Law* (CHBECK, Hart, Nomos, 2016)
Schwenzer I., Hachem P. and Kee C., *Global Sales and Contract Law* (OUP, 2012)
Sefton-Green R., 'Formation of Contract: Negotiation and the Process of Agreement' in Cartwright J. and Whittaker S. (eds.), *The Code Napoléon Rewritten: French Contract Law after the 2016 Reforms* (Hart Publishing, 2017)

Segura Riveiro F., 'El Interés Indemnizable en las Hipótesis de Responsabilidad Precontractual' in Varas Braun J.A. and others (eds.), *Estudios de Derecho Civil: Jornadas Nacionales de Derecho Civil 2005–2009*, vol. III (Abeledo Perrot, 2011)

Sénéchal J., 'Contract Formation and Non-performance in French Law' in Schulze R. and Zoll F. (eds.), *The Law of Obligations in Europe, A New Wave of Codifications* (Sellier, 2013)

Shaw J., 'Pre-contractual Negotiations in English Law: *Walford v Miles* and its Aftermath' (1994) 2 ERPL 269

Shaw-Mellors A., 'Proprietary Estoppel and the Enforcement of Promises: *Motivate Publishing FZ LLC v Hello Ltd* [2015] EWHC 1554 (Ch)' [2015] Conveyancer and Property Lawyer 529

Shell G.R., 'Opportunism and Trust in the Negotiation of Commercial Contracts: Toward a New Cause of Action' (1991) 44 Vanderbilt Law Review 221

Sirena P., 'The New Design of the French Law of Contract and Obligations: An Italian View' in Cartwright J. and Whittaker S. (eds.), *The Code Napoléon Rewritten: French Contract Law after the 2016 Reforms* (Hart Publishing, 2017)

Smits J. and Calomme C., 'The Reform of the French Law of Obligations' (2016) 23 Maastricht Journal 1040

Spence M., *Protecting Reliance: The Emergent Doctrine of Equitable Estoppel* (Hart Publishing, 1999)

Stevens R., 'Restitution: Contract's Twin? – A Comment' in Rose F.D. (ed.), *Failure of Contracts: Contractual, Restitutionary and Proprietary Consequences* (Hart Publishing, 1997)

Steyn J., 'Contract Law: Fulfilling the Reasonable Expectations of Honest Men' (1997) 113 LQR 433

Stoffel-Munck P., *L'Abus dans le Contrat: Essai d'une Théorie* (LGDJ, 2000)

——, 'Note on Cass com 26 November 2003' JCP éd E 2004, 738

——, 'Thème 1: Les Pourparlers' (Séminaire en Droit des Contrats, Master 2 Droit Privé Général, Université Paris 1 Panthéon Sorbonne, 2011)

Stoll H., 'Tatbestände und Funktionen der Haftung für Culpa in Contrahendo' in Ficker (ed.), *Festschrift Ernst von Caemmerer* (1978)

Storme M., 'Walfords Chances Under Belgian Law' (1994) 2 ERPL 315

Storme M.E., 'Good Faith and Contents of Contracts in European Private Law' in Espiau Espiau S. and Vaquer Aloy A. (eds.), *Bases de un Derecho Contractual Europeo* (Tirant Lo Blanch, 2003)

Strong S.I., Fach Gómez K. and Carballo Piñeiro L., *Comparative Law for Spanish-English Speaking Lawyers: Legal Cultures, Legal Terms and Legal Practices* (Edward Elgar Publishing, 2016)

Summers R., 'The Conceptualisation of Good Faith in American Contract Law: A General Account' in Zimmermann R. and Whittaker S. (eds.), *Good Faith in European Contract Law* (CUP, 2000)

——, '"Good Faith" in General Contract Law and the Sales Provisions of the Uniform Commercial Code' (1968) 54 Virginia Law Review 195

Tapia Rodríguez M., *Código Civil 1855–2005: Evolución y Perspectivas* (Editorial Jurídica de Chile, 2005)

Tapia Suárez O., 'De la Responsabilidad Civil en General y de la Responsabilidad Delictual entre los Contratantes' (Licenciado en Ciencias Jurídicas thesis, Universidad de Concepción, 1941)

Tegethoff M., '*Culpa in Contrahendo* in German and Dutch Law – a Comparison of Precontractual Liability' (1998) 5 Maastricht Journal of European and Comparative Law 341

Terré F. (ed.) *Pour une Réforme du Droit de la Responsabilité Civile* (Dalloz, 2011)

—— (ed.) *Pour une Réforme du Droit des Contrats* (Dalloz, 2009)

——, Simler P. and Lequette Y., *Droit Civil: Les Obligations* (11th edn., Dalloz, 2013)

The American Law Institute, *Restatement of the Law Second: Contracts 2d*, vol. 2 (American Law Institute Publishers, 1981)

——, *Restatement of the Law Second: Contracts 2d*, vol. 1 (American Law Institute Publishers, 1981)

—— and National Conference of Commissioners on Uniform State Laws, *Uniform Commercial Code* (2010–2011 edn., Thomson Reuters, 2010)

Trébulle F.G., 'Note on Cass com 26 November 2003' Droit des Sociétés no 3 2004 no. 37

van Erp S., 'A European "Culpa in Contrahendo" Doctrine? Towards a Model of Contract as a Legal Relationship and Situation-Specific Duties to Inform' in Espiau Espiau S. and Vaquer Aloy A. (eds.), *Bases de un Derecho Contractual Europeo* (Tirant Lo Blanch, 2003)

——, 'Good Faith: A Concept "Unworkable in Practice"?' (1992) 1 Tilburg Foreign Law Review 215

Varela R., *Derecho Comercial: Obligaciones y Contratos*, vol. III (Editorial Universitaria S.A., 1966)

Vergara Varas P.P., 'La Responsabilidad Precontractual: Un Necesario Desvarío para Enfrentar la Cultura del Litigio' in Fábrega Vega H. (ed.), *Estudios Jurídicos en Homenaje a los Profesores Fernando Fueyo Laneri, Avelino León Hurtado, Francisco Merino Scheihing, Fernando Mujica Bezanilla, Hugo Rosende Subiabre* (Ediciones Universidad del Desarrollo, 2007)

Viney G. and Jourdain P., *Traité de Droit Civil: Les Conditions de la Responsabilité* (4th edn., LGDJ, 2013)

Violet F., 'Note on CA Paris 10 March 2000' JCP 2001 II 10470

Vivanco Luengo P., 'Aspectos Relevantes de la Responsabilidad Precontractual por Ruptura Injustificada de Negociaciones Precontractuales' (2008) 17 Revista de Derecho 139

Vodanovic A., *Manual de Derecho Civil: Parte Preliminar y General*, vol. II (4th edn., LexisNexis, 2006)

Vogenauer S., '"General Principles" of Contract Law in Transnational Instruments' in Gullifer L. and Vogenuaer S. (eds.), *English and European Perspectives on Contract and Commercial Law: Essays in Honour of Hugh Beale* (Hart Publishing, 2014)

——, 'The Avant-projet de réforme: An Overview' in Cartwright J., Vogenauer S. and Whittaker S. (eds.), *Reforming the French Law of Obligations, Comparative Reflections on the Avant-projet de réforme du droit des obligations et de la prescription ('the Avant-projet Catala')* (Hart Publishing, 2009)

von Bar C. and Clive E. (eds.), *Principles, Definitions and Model Rules of European Private Law: Draft Common Frame of Reference (DCFR) Full Edition*, vol. 1 (OUP, 2010)

von Hein J., 'Culpa in Contrahendo' in Basedow J. and others (eds.), *The Max Planck Encyclopedia of European Private Law*, vol. I (OUP, 2012)

von Jhering R., *Culpa in contrahendo ou Indemnização em Contratos Nulos ou Não Chegados à Perfeição* (Mota Pinto P. tr., Almedina, 2008)

——, 'Culpa in contrahendo, oder Schadensersatz bei nichtigen oder nicht zur Perfection gelangten Verträgen' (1861) 4 Jahrbücher für die Dogmatik des heutigen römischen und deutschen Privatrechts 1
von Mehren A., *The Civil Law System: Cases and Materials for the Comparative Study of Law* (Prentice-Hall, 1957)
——, 'Formal Requirements' in *International Encyclopedia of Comparative Law*, vol. VII (JCB Mohr (Paul Siebeck) and Martinus Nijhoff Publishers, 1998)
——, 'The Formation of Contracts' in *International Encyclopedia of Comparative Law*, vol. VII (JCB Mohr (Paul Siebeck) and Martinus Nijhoff Publishers, 1992)
—— and Gordley J., *The Civil Law System: An Introduction to the Comparative Study of Law* (2nd edn., Little, Brown and Company, 1977)
Whittaker S. and Zimmermann R., 'Coming to Terms with Good Faith' in Zimmermann R. and Whittaker S. (eds.), *Good Faith in European Contract Law* (CUP, 2000)
——, 'Good Faith in European Contract Law: Surveying the Legal Landscape' in Zimmermann R. and Whittaker S. (eds.), *Good Faith in European Contract Law* (CUP, 2000)
Youngs R., *Sourcebook on German Law* (2nd edn., Cavendish, 2002)
Zimmermann R., *The New German Law of Obligations: Historical and Comparative Perspectives* (OUP, 2005)
——, *Roman Law, Contemporary Law, European Law: The Civilian Tradition Today* (OUP, 2001)
Zimmermann R. and Whittaker S. (eds.), *Good Faith in European Contract Law* (CUP, 2000)
Zuloaga Ríos I., 'Article 2.1.15' in Vogenauer S. (ed.), *Commentary on the UNIDROIT Principles of International Commercial Contracts (PICC)* (2nd edn., OUP, 2015)
——, *Teoría de la Responsabilidad Precontractual. Aplicaciones en la Formación del Consentimiento de los Contratos* (3rd edn., Legal Publishing, 2008)
Zumbansen P., 'The Law of Contracts' in Reimann M. and Zekoll J. (eds.), *Introduction to German Law* (2nd edn., Kluwer Law International, 2005)
Zweigert K. and Kötz H., *Introduction to Comparative Law* (Weir T. tr., 3rd rev. edn., Clarendon Press, 1998)

INDEX

ABOUT THE AUTHOR

Isabel Zuloaga (DPhil, MJur University of Oxford) is Assistant Professor of Commercial Law at the Pontificia Universidad Católica de Chile (UC). Before joining the UC Law Faculty in 2017, she taught Civil Law at Adolfo Ibáñez University, in Santiago and Viña del Mar, Chile, and practiced law in the fields of Mergers and Acquisitions and Corporate Finance. She is interested in Civil and Commercial Law and Comparative Private Law, particularly Contract Law. Her recent research focusses on precontractual liability, the formation of contracts, preliminary agreements and the harmonisation of private law.

www.ingramcontent.com/pod-product-compliance
Ingram Content Group UK Ltd.
Pitfield, Milton Keynes, MK11 3LW, UK
UKHW051847100926
8556IPUK00005B/495

9 781780 686509